Farm and Nation

in Modern Japan

Farm and Nation in Modern Japan

Agrarian Nationalism, 1870-1940

THOMAS R. H. HAVENS

PRINCETON UNIVERSITY PRESS

LCC: 73-16774
ISBN: 0-691-03101-0

Library of Congress Cataloging in Publication data
will be found on the last printed page of this book

Publication of this book has been aided by a grant
from The Andrew W. Mellon Foundation

This book has been composed in Linotype Janson

Printed in the United States of America
by Princeton University Press
Princeton, New Jersey

Preface

Yoi mura   Good villages
Yoi hito   Good people
Yoi rekishi   Good history

Itō Chūbei, frontispiece executed May 1962 for
Toyosatosonshi (History of Toyosato Village),
Shigaken, Toyosatomura, 1963

ALMOST anyone who has lived in Japan or read its recent history eventually develops ideas about what makes that nation distinctive. Some persons regard her twentieth-century experience as a minor variation of a pattern common to all industrializing peoples. Others insist that indigenous cultural traditions have strongly affected Japan's recent past, making comparisons with other societies risky. This book discusses what one aspect of Japanese civilization, village agriculture, has meant to some of her leading thinkers during the past century, and how farming related to perceptions of history and national uniqueness in Japan from the Meiji restoration of 1868 to World War II.

The modified Hepburn system used in the 1954 edition of *Kenkyusha's New Japanese-English Dictionary* has served as the authority for romanizing Japanese terms throughout this book. Macrons have been used to indicate long vowels in all words save the most familiar proper nouns. The Wade-Giles system has been followed for Chinese terms and the McCune-Reischauer system for Korean ones. Japanese names are given in the customary Japanese manner, with the family name preceding the personal one, except for cases of Western language publications in which Japanese authors or editors have chosen to place their personal names first. All dates have been converted to the Gregorian calendar.

v

I am grateful to the editors of the *Japan Christian Quarterly* for permission to reprint in Chapter II portions of my article, "Religion and Agriculture in Nineteenth-century Japan: Ninomiya Sontoku and the Hōtoku Movement," *Japan Christian Quarterly*, xxxviii, 2, Spring 1972, 98-105, and to the editors of *Monumenta Nipponica* for permission to reprint in Chapter XII a compressed version of my article, "Katō Kanji (1884-1965) and the Spirit of Agriculture in Modern Japan," *Monumenta Nipponica*, xxv, 3-4, Autumn 1970, 249-266.

Funds from the National Endowment for the Humanities, the Leopold Schepp Foundation, and Connecticut College supported various stages of the research for this study, and a Fulbright research fellowship aided the final phase of preparing the manuscript. I am grateful to each of these sources for generous assistance.

I am indebted to the directors and staffs of the following libraries for help with the materials used in this study: National Diet Library, Tokyo; Harvard-Yenching Library; Gest Oriental Library, Princeton University; East Asiatic Library, University of California, Berkeley, especially Eiji Yutani; Connecticut College Library, especially Helen Aitner; Waseda University Library; and the collection of the Shakai Kagaku Kenkyūjo (Institute of Social Sciences), Waseda University, especially Katsumura Shigeru.

I am particularly grateful to Kawahara Hiroshi for friendly counsel about my research and generous hospitality during 1972-1973 when I was a visiting fellow at Waseda University. I am also indebted to these colleagues in Japan for help with my research: Denda Isao, Hashikawa Bunzō, Kazue Kyōichi, Matsuzawa Tetsunari, Ōkubo Toshiaki, Takizawa Makoto, Tsukuba Hisaharu, and Tsunazawa Mitsuaki.

For general advice about my work, I am grateful to Delmer M. Brown, Ronald P. Dore, Marius B. Jansen, Katherine M. Maxim, Fred G. Notehelfer, Kenneth B. Pyle, Irwin Scheiner, Kent C. Smith, Valdo H. Viglielmo, and

Ann Waswo. I am especially indebted to Penelope Brown, for stimulating comments on the text, particularly on Japanese nationalism; to Miles Fletcher, for helpful suggestions about the latter half of the book; to Christopher E. Lewis, for invaluable comments about Meiji and Taishō local history; and to Carol Gluck and my wife Betsy F. Havens for thorough readings of the entire manuscript. Rhea Lavigne, Joan McLaughlin, Katherine Snyder, and Leslie Tervo kindly assisted with materials. R. Miriam Brokaw, Joanna Hitchcock, and the staff of Princeton University Press provided their customary expert editorial care. I alone bear responsibility for errors of fact, translation, or interpretation.

July 1973

Contents

Tables

Farm and Nation

in Modern Japan

Chapter 1

Agrarian Thought and Japanese Modernization

EACH May the emperor of Japan wades into a paddy on the grounds of the imperial palace in central Tokyo to perform a symbolic planting of young rice shoots. Each September or early October he harvests the rice in his shirt sleeves under a warm late summer sun. The new rice is taken as an offering to the Ise Grand Shrine in Mie Prefecture, where until 1945 Amaterasu Ōmikami was worshiped as the great ancestress of the Japanese imperial line. Although much of the mythology associated with the state shrine system evaporated after World War II, many Japanese continue to believe that a visit, if not a pilgrimage, to Ise should be undertaken by every citizen at least once in his life.[1] The annual ceremonial offering by the emperor doubtless reinforces this conviction. After the ritual is completed, the rice is used to make sake that is dedicated to the imperial ancestors on Labor Thanksgiving Day, November 23. In these traditional ceremonies, the emperor expresses gratitude to farmers for producing the nation's staple crop.

Farming has historically been so closely tied to Japanese thought and belief that its importance has usually been taken

[1] See D. C. Holtom, *The National Faith of Japan* (London: Kegan Paul, 1938), pp. 133-137, for a description of the place of the Ise shrine in prewar Shinto. See also Miyamoto Tsuneichi, *Ise sangū* [Pilgrimage to Ise] (Tokyo: Shakai Shisōsha, 1972).

3

for granted and only rarely acknowledged. So long as agriculture provided the main source of gainful employment and national wealth, Japanese political practices and social patterns were closely articulated with farming, which remained the economic cornerstone of the nation until at least the start of the twentieth century. Most premodern political and social thinkers in Japan, both official and nonofficial, assumed that agricultural production was vital for a happy and prosperous country. Likewise, the dominant religion, Shinto, perpetuated the beliefs and rituals of a distinctly rural society. Many Shinto prayers and ceremonies were fitted to the cycle of the seasons. The ancient sacred festivals, still celebrated today, were associated with the new year, planting, rainy season (and attendant purification ceremonies to exorcise illness), harvest, and other aspects of agricultural fertility.[2] Yet it is doubtful whether many premodern adherents of the Shinto deities paid conscious heed to the specifically agricultural implications of their faith, since farming already helped define the scope of most thought and belief in the cultural ecumene of old Japan.

Even when industry eclipsed farming during the past century as Japan's most productive occupation, agriculture remained indispensable for overall economic growth by feeding the nation, supplying laborers for the cities, and earning surpluses that were used to import industrial technology from abroad. Nevertheless, its position as the economic foundation of the country gradually eroded, and farming correspondingly lost some of its importance in shaping the general cultural matrix of Japanese thought, but it retains a residual influence as the background for a good deal of contemporary philosophic, social, economic, and political writing. By now perhaps only 15 percent of the Japanese labor force is engaged in the primary occupations of farming, fishing, and forestry, but this figure understates

[2] See U. A. Casal, *The Five Sacred Festivals of Ancient Japan: Their Symbolism and Historical Development* (Tokyo: Sophia University Press, 1967).

4

the true impact of rural life on Japanese society. A large proportion of today's city residents were born and reared on farms, and many others are affected by the rural village as a repository of traditional Japanese civilization.[3] In short, the rise of industrial Japan has reduced agriculture, once preeminent in shaping indigenous culture, merely to one of many components in Japanese thought. But the growth of metropolitan life cannot blot out the continuing impact of the countryside, whether as bastion of support for the present Liberal Democratic Party or as romantic ideal for utopians disenchanted with city living.

The slow diminution of farming in the popular consciousness during the past century coincided with the rise of Japan as a modern state. Nationalism was probably the most vital element in the successful program of modernization initiated during the Meiji era (1868-1912). Wealth and power (*fukoku kyōhei*) were the main aims of national strengthening in the decades following the Meiji restoration in 1868. Modernizing nationalists pursued these objectives by encouraging industry, urbanization, and centralized government—objectives that ran counter to the agrarian, rural, decentralized character of premodern Japan. The ruling Meiji oligarchy, whose commitment to nationalism is beyond dispute, systematically introduced Western values and patterns of thought as a part of its campaign to build a modern, enlightened populace. Such new ideas naturally competed, and sometimes sharply contended, with that large bulk of traditional Japanese thinking that assumed the predominance of agricultural society. Japan's experience in this respect was hardly unique. Modernization routinely involves the expansion of a national industrial economy, a unified state, and an integrated society. Such trends usually diminish the impact of farming on national life, both quantitatively as chief employer and qualitatively as a force molding indigenous thought and value.

[3] See Richard K. Beardsley, John W. Hall, and Robert E. Ward, *Village Japan* (Chicago: University of Chicago Press, 1959), p. xiv.

Nevertheless it would be a mistake to assume that agriculture has been incompatible with an awareness of nationality in modern Japan. Since 1868 certain nation-centered ideologies have helped to specify more clearly the place of farming in public thought: immanent traditional assumptions have turned into explicit modern statements. No longer a universalistic influence shaping the national consciousness, agriculture in the twentieth century has been specifically highlighted as one of a number of main influences affecting Japanese thinking. Japanese nationalists have clarified and trimmed, but few if any have tried to destroy, the imprint of the farm on the country's collective self-image.

To be sure, early modernizers such as Fukuzawa Yukichi (1834-1901) vigorously attacked the "evil customs and absurd practices" of the overwhelmingly feudal (hence agrarian) Tokugawa period (1603-1868).[4] Nevertheless, right from the start the Meiji oligarchs trumpeted the virtues of farming, and farm policy was a central, and often frustrating, concern of the entire Meiji era. Rather soon after the vogue of liberal Western ideas in the 1870s had run its course, political and social writers began to search Japan's past for ways to disclose the secret of her national distinctiveness. A number of them found that agriculture provided the answer.

[4] Fukuzawa Yukichi, *Gakumon no susume* (Tokyo, 1872), translated as *An Encouragement of Learning* by David A. Dilworth and Umeyo Hirano (Tokyo: Sophia University Press, 1969); Fukuzawa Yukichi, *Fukuō jiden* (Tokyo, 1899), translated as *The Autobiography of Fukuzawa Yukichi* by Eiichi Kiyooka, new translation (Tokyo: Hokuseido Press, 1960). Two excellent studies of Fukuzawa are Carmen Blacker, *The Japanese Enlightenment: A Study of the Writings of Fukuzawa Yukichi* (Cambridge: Cambridge University Press, 1964), and Albert M. Craig, "Fukuzawa Yukichi: The Philosophical Foundations of Meiji Nationalism," *Political Development in Modern Japan*, ed. Robert E. Ward (Princeton: Princeton University Press, 1968), pp. 99-148.

6

Agrarianism in Modern Japan

Agrarianism, the penchant for extolling the economic and social merits of farm production and rural life, is a recurring theme in the history of most countries undergoing the transition from a village-based farming economy to urbanization and industrialization. Since 1868 agrarianism in Japan has taken its principal form as Nōhonshugi, literally "agriculture-as-the-essence-ism." Its proponents, known as Nōhonshugisha, were diverse critics and theorists who used farming as the basis for their visions of an ideal Japanese social and political order. During the height of their activity, from the 1890s through the 1930s, these agrarian ideologues included radicals and reactionaries, officials and farmers, soldiers and civilians, utopians and pragmatists, city dwellers and rural residents. Although much else divided them, these writers were linked by a common exposure to the modernization process, a mutual concern for the nation's future, and a shared conviction that agriculture was crucial for creating a stable, harmonious Japan. Nōhonshugisha were not philosophers but men thinking about their state and society in predominantly agricultural terms. Some were tillers of the soil, but many had little practical experience in the field or paddy. These agrarianists, as I shall call them, were thus distinct from the vast majority of farmers, agronomists, rural technicians, and others employed in the countryside who had little interest in social theory or public policy. The agrarianists differed from other intellectuals chiefly in the importance they placed on farming as the mainstay of Japanese civilization.

Nōhonshugi is a catchall for a wide spectrum of farm-related ideas expounded by these agrarian ideologues.[5] In a

[5] For a general discussion of Nōhonshugi, see Mori Hiroshi, *Kome to Nihon bunka* [Rice and Japanese Culture] (Tokyo: Hyōgensha, 1972); Adachi Ikitsune, "Nōhonshugi no saikentō" [A Reappraisal of Theories on Agrarianism], *Shisō* [Thought], No. 423, September 1959, pp. 56-68; Nakamura Yūjirō, *Kindai Nihon ni okeru seido to*

7

sense, all people agree that agriculture is pivotal because it provides their sustenance, but this alone does not make them adherents of Nōhonshugi. Nor is it sufficient to equate Japanese agrarianism with physiocratic economics, Shinto animism, or Confucian reverence for peasant farming, important as each may have been as a precondition. Nōhonshugi may be described as a loose bundle of farm-centered social and political ideas that emerged in response to the enigmas and tensions created by Japanese modernization after 1868. The principal Nōhonshugi beliefs included a faith in agricultural economics, an affirmation of rural communalism, and a conviction that farming was indispensable to those qualities that made the nation unique. Before modernization and the rising awareness of nationality that accompanied it, there was much agrarian thought but not yet Nōhonshugi as a set of prescriptions for correcting imbalances in a rapidly changing society. Not until a national policy of industrialization was implemented after 1868 did agrarianism arise as a conscious, if ill-defined, ideology that variously upheld farming on social, economic, political, and spiritual grounds. Only when people began to question seriously whether agriculture should continue to

---

shisō [Thought and Institutions in Modern Japan] (Tokyo: Miraisha, 1967), pp. 271-292; Okutani Matsuji, "Nihon ni okeru nōhonshugi shisō no nagare" [Trends in Agrarian Thought in Japan], *Shisō*, No. 407, May 1958, pp. 1-15; Sakurai Takeo, "Shōwa no nōhonshugi" [Agrarianism in the Shōwa Period], *Shisō*, No. 407, May 1958, pp. 42-54; Takeuchi Tetsuo, "Nōhonshugi bunseki e no zenteiteki shomondai—shu to shite bunseki shikaku ni tsuite" [Preliminary Problems in Analyzing Agrarianism—With Emphasis on Analytical Viewpoints], *Shimane Nōka Daigaku kenkyū hōkoku* [Shimane Agricultural University Research Reports], No. 9, A-3, March 1961, pp. 53-59; Tsukuba Hisaharu, "Nihon nōhonshugi josetsu" [Introduction to Japanese Agrarianism], *Shisō no kagaku* [Science of Thought], No. 18, June 1960, pp. 4-12; Tsunazawa Mitsuaki, *Nihon no nōhonshugi* [Japanese Agrarianism] (Tokyo: Kinokuniya Shoten, 1971); Tsunazawa Mitsuaki, *Nōhonshugi no kenkyū* [Studies on Agrarianism] (Nagoya: Fūbaisha, 1968).

8

be the most economically productive and ethically approved occupation did its diverse partisans, for diverse reasons, begin to defend it.

At the risk of oversimplification, Nōhonshugi from 1868 to 1945 will be separated in the chapters that follow into two types, bureaucratic and popular, the latter somewhat overshadowing the former after World War I. The bureaucratic type was a body of forceful rhetoric and sporadic national programs designed to conserve and extend the agricultural productivity that was essential for Japan's new industrial expansion. Some bureaucrats sponsored agriculture as a part of the state's industrialization programs; others sought to protect it against the malevolent impact of those programs. Such figures as Shinagawa Yajirō (1843-1900) and Hirata Tōsuke (1849-1925), both leading Meiji bureaucrats, and the scholar Yokoi Tokiyoshi (1860-1927) wrote in a tradition that exalted frugality, duty, hard work, and the village economy as the backbone of the nation. Bureaucratic Nōhonshugi had a great appeal to the ordinary small landowner, not because he cared one whit for the industrialization which his taxes supported, but because he feared the growing trend toward farm commercialism and land consolidation. He was comforted to have major public officials defend the small farm in an age of onrushing capitalism. This form of agrarianism represented a firm intrabureaucratic response, and at some points a direct reaction, to the state's development program.

Popular Nōhonshugi likewise arose in the early twentieth century as a result of modernization. When the urban economy began to displace farming as the most productive sector as a result of the industrial buildup during the Sino-Japanese and Russo-Japanese wars and World War I, it was no longer sufficient to continue official farm policies that tried to preserve agriculture "as it was." The broad landlord classes now felt themselves attacked not only by capitalism from above but also by tenants and low prices from below. The rice riots of 1918 and the intensifying tenancy disputes of the teens and twenties, products of steady urbanization and overall economic instability, seemed to symbolize both the frustration and the potential power of the cultivators.[6] The result was that popular Nōhonshugi turned to outright anti-capitalism and sought to retrieve for agriculture—both as an economic activity and as a state of mind—its former position of superiority in national life. Agrarian ideologues now began to gloss over the conflicts between tenants and landlords, trying to rally the entire rural population against urban society and industry. Okada On, a leader of the Imperial Agricultural Association (Teikoku Nōkai), minimized the tenant conflicts in 1929: "Most landlords are small landholders with two to five hectares and do not wield the net. They have been chased into the same huge net with the tenant farmers by industrial and commercial capitalism and are wrenched just as much as the tenants. The conflict between sardines and mackerel caught in the same net is like the tenant struggle in our countryside."[7] While such bombast did not succeed in wishing away antagonisms in the villages, it did manage to spread Nōhonshugi ideas far beyond the landowning classes. The defensive agrarianism of the Taishō (1912-1926) and early Shōwa (1926-) eras appealed to the economic and social self-interest of landholders and cultivators alike and no longer signified an ideology promoted primarily from above.

As the plight of the countryside grew steadily more serious, especially after the great crash of 1929, popular Nōhonshugi took on antiestablishment overtones that held a strong attraction for the young military officers involved in the May 15 incident of 1932 and other political upheavals.

[6] See William W. Lockwood, *The Economic Development of Japan: Growth and Structural Change, 1868-1938* (Princeton: Princeton University Press, 1954), pp. 55-64, on economic conditions after World War I, and Ronald P. Dore, *Land Reform in Japan* (London: Oxford University Press, 1959), pp. 71-91, for a summary of rural unrest.

[7] Okada On, *Nōgyō keiei to nōsei* [Agricultural Administration and Policy] (Tokyo: Ryūginsha, 1929), p. 10.

Such ideologues as Gondō Seikyō (1868-1937) and Tachibana Kōzaburō (1893-) were closely identified with Nōhonshugi in its most active phase in the 1930s. With them the popularization of agrarianism in the countryside was completed. They forcefully denounced centralized government, industrial capitalism, foreign culture, and the national bureaucrats who a scant generation earlier had been the main advocates of Nōhonshugi. Gondō and Tachibana inspired occasional efforts for radical political change, but each sought a national rededication to the romantic communalism of Japan's premodern village society, and neither accepted the powerful centralized state that accompanied Japanese militarism in the late 1930s and early 1940s.

Bureaucratic agrarianism, although quiescent during and after World War I, reappeared in several forms when the rural economy floundered in the late 1920s. The leading agricultural official Ishiguro Tadaatsu (1884-1960) and other career civil servants pressed plans within the government for rural relief. The army talked from time to time about the farmers' predicament, although few concrete measures were adopted until after 1937, when military control of the state was secure (and then probably for reasons of domestic harmony in a time of national mobilization, rather than because of devotion to Nōhonshugi ideals). The ethics textbooks used in the national school system after November 1936 conferred official recognition on agrarianism as a major source of civic virtue.[8] Most notable, perhaps, was the confluence of bureaucratic and popular Nōhonshugi in the state-supported schemes for overseas colonization led by the private schoolmaster Katō Kanji (1884-1965). Agrarian ideologues, both official and popular, had championed expansionism for many decades. Now Katō's programs for Manchurian emigration in the 1930s represented the renewed cooperation of public and private Nōhonshugi as Japan mobilized for total war.

[8] See Robert K. Hall, *Shūshin: The Ethics of a Defeated Nation* (New York: Columbia University Teachers College, 1949).

Agrarianism and the Modernization of Japan

One of the great accomplishments of the Meiji leadership was earning the esteem of the Western powers, who had forcibly disrupted Japan's diplomatic isolation in 1853 and required her to accept discriminatory trade treaties. Japan's portentious victory over Russia in 1904-1905 was emblematic of the respect in which the country wash held by the end of the Meiji era. This stunning conquest, which stirred anticolonial sentiments throughout Asia, confirmed the new international status Japan had won at the turn of the century when the major Western nations accepted her demands and permitted the unequal treaties to lapse. From this point forward, foreign observers almost always regarded Japanese modernization as a success story, as indeed it was in many respects. From E. Herbert Norman's pioneering study of the Tokugawa to Meiji transition, published in 1940, to the six volume *Studies in the Modernization of Japan*,[9] which appeared during 1965-1971, non-Japanese specialists of determinist, "value-free," and other historical outlooks almost unanimously accounted Japanese *aggiornamento* as a positive accomplishment. Although a good deal less sanguine about the benefits of modernization, most Japanese scholars concurred that their country had indeed become a modern society by almost any objective index.

In such a climate of appraisal, it would be easy to ignore

[9] E. Herbert Norman, *Japan's Emergence as a Modern State* (New York: Institute of Pacific Relations, 1940); *Studies in the Modernization of Japan*, published by Princeton University Press: *Changing Japanese Attitudes toward Modernization*, ed. Marius B. Jansen, 1965; *The State and Economic Enterprise in Japan*, ed. William W. Lockwood, 1965; *Aspects of Social Change in Modern Japan*, ed. Ronald P. Dore, 1967; *Political Development in Modern Japan*, ed. Robert E. Ward, 1968; *Tradition and Modernization in Japanese Culture*, ed. Donald H. Shively, 1971; *Dilemmas of Growth in Prewar Japan*, ed. James W. Morley, 1971. In Japan, recent writings by scholars such as Kano Masanao, Kinbara Samon, and especially Irokawa Daikichi have probed local history and societal trends not well treated in earlier overviews of modernization.

the frustrations and disruptions that accompanied modernization in Japan. Recent writers have begun to recognize more fully the shadowy aspects of Japanese development. A token of the new uncertainty is the final volume of *Studies in the Modernization of Japan*, which editor James W. Morley aptly titled *Dilemmas of Growth in Prewar Japan*. As research extends beyond leaders and elites to society as a whole, crosscurrents and riptides become evident. Whether they will cause scholars to confirm or revise their present evaluation of Japanese modernization cannot yet be known, but one likely result will be a better understanding of the relative merits of modern life compared with the condition of Japanese society before the mid-nineteenth century. It would be just as foolish, of course, to condemn Japanese modernization out of hand as it would be to accept Fukuzawa's blanket renunciation of the feudal era. But to allow the worth of Japanese development to go unquestioned would be to mix fact and value by perpetuating the assumption that modernization was good simply because it happened.

Nationalism has been tightly linked with modernization in Japan and by now may have become the main organizing theme in studies of her recent past. A review of Nōhonshugi ideas is useful in evaluating the impact of both of these historical forces. A look at Japanese agrarianism offers a convenient focus for examining attitudes skeptical of the merits of modernization, held by public officials and private citizens alike, and it yields fresh reasons for doubting how uniformly the advantages of development extended to Japanese society at large. A study of Nōhonshugi also presents an opportunity to consider the ways in which farm thought helped to shape modern Japanese nationalism both as it was reflected in theoretical writings and as it was expressed in concrete political behavior.

My hope is to guide the reader through the profusion of Nōhonshugi ideas from the Meiji restoration to World War II by discussing the major writings and speeches of

13

leading agrarian ideologues. In the strictest sense, these men represent no one but themselves. Taken together, however, they signify the variegated range of farm-oriented thinking about modern Japanese civilization that was enshrouded by the mantle of Nōhonshugi. Guided in part by the judgment of Japanese colleagues,[10] I have chosen writers who appear to have been the most cogent spokesmen for agrarianism, from its beginnings in the Meiji bureaucracy to its final nationalist phase in the 1930s.

It is important for anyone who takes up the history of their ideas to recognize that the intellectual historian is only one of many observers of Japan's recent past. Felix Gilbert has written that "intellectual history cannot claim to be the true or only history; modern intellectual history arose after a belief in the control of events by ideas had collapsed. . . . it is no longer possible to see ideas as determining events or floating freely above them."[11] Hence the need to look also at the lives of these agrarianists and the main economic and political currents that affected the intellectual choices they made. The precise consequences of their thinking are almost impossible to measure, although I shall suggest some conclusions when it seems prudent to do so. Throughout I shall emphasize meaning and significance rather than impact or influence, in order to try to explain the place of farm and nation in the recent history of a country whose emperor even today sows seed, reaps grain, prays for fertility, and ceremonially exalts agriculture.

[10] I am especially grateful to Hashikawa Bunzō, Kawahara Hiroshi, and Tsukuba Hisaharu.

[11] Felix Gilbert, "Intellectual History: Its Aims and Methods," *Historical Study Today*, ed. Felix Gilbert and Stephen R. Graubard (New York: W. W. Norton & Co., Inc., 1972), pp. 148, 155.

Chapter II

Early Modern Farm Ideology and the Growth of Japanese Agriculture, 1870-1895

THE steep mountain slopes, narrow valleys, and sharp seaside cliffs that dominate Japan's fifteen-hundred-mile-long volcanic archipelago scarcely create an ideal locale for one of the world's most productive agricultural economies. Only 15 percent of the total land area is available for farming, and much of it is deficient in natural fertility and irrigation. On the other hand, most of the country is blessed with a mild climate, abundant and well-distributed rainfall, and a long growing season, permitting double cropping in many areas. Throughout much of the country, the lowlands and gentler slopes are reserved for rice paddies, irrigated for many centuries by a network of dikes and canals that draw on short, swift streams. Except in the northeast, winter wheat, barley, and other cool-season crops fare well on drained paddy fields during the relatively dry, gentle winters. Vegetables and fruits grow in great numbers, with the steeper hills often given over to orchards or the ubiquitous bamboo. Only in the northeast are sizeable lands devoted to pasture, although most farms include small barnyard animals and fowl.

Lush and beautiful though the countryside is, ever since antiquity human ingenuity and hard labor have been more responsible than Japan's modest environmental assets for the economic well-being of society. The wet rice agriculture practiced in Japan at least since the time of Christ requires intensive care, especially at the time of transplanting seedlings and at the harvest. Such methods demand a high labor to land ratio, and together with the terrain they account for the small size of the typical Japanese farm, both historically and today. Although oxen and other draft animals have always been widely used, the scale of farming has inhibited mechanization as a substitute for human labor, even in the twentieth century when farm machinery could be efficiently produced in Japan.[1]

The family has long been the basic unit of rural labor; clusters of households have been grouped into communities known as *buraku*. These settlements of a few dozen or, at most, a few hundred persons have served as the building-blocks of rural society, just as their slightly larger administrative counterparts, the *mura* or villages, have been the smallest legal and political entities for nearly a century. (When modern bureaucratic agrarianists referred to farm villages, or *nōson*, they usually meant the *mura* imposed by the central state in 1888-1890. Popular Nōhonshugisha, however, ordinarily used farm villages to mean the traditional *buraku*.)

The Tokugawa Background for Modern Farm Thought

When the armies of Tokugawa Ieyasu (1542-1616) ended a century of feudal warfare with their decisive victories at Sekigahara (1600) and Osaka (1615), Japan entered a long period of peace and rural prosperity. The Tokugawa era, extending from 1603 to the Meiji restoration in 1868, is also called the Edo period, because Ieyasu and his successors built their permanent capital in the city of Edo (now Tokyo) in the heart of the country's richest farmland, the Kantō plain. There they instituted a unique form of mature

---

[1] For a description of the Tokugawa land system, see Thomas C. Smith, *The Agrarian Origins of Modern Japan* (Stanford: Stanford University Press, 1959), pp. 1-11.

feudal rule, known as the *bakuhan* system, in which the military government of the Tokugawa family (*bakufu*) acted as overlord, beneath which some two hundred and fifty fiefs (*han*) exercised regional hegemony.

Although this form of government was a striking innovation, the shift of political power from Kyoto to Edo also reaffirmed a number of historical practices and traditions that affected the development of people's thinking about agriculture. First of all, wealth in land once again became the economic foundation for rule. The Tokugawa family controlled about one-fifth of the productive land area in Japan, sufficient to meet most *bakufu* expenses, whereas Ieyasu's earlier rivals in the Kansai (Kyoto-Osaka-Kobe) area had depended considerably on trade for their income. Second, power returned to the east, a stronghold of traditional, farm-oriented Shinto beliefs when compared with western Japan, where Buddhist and Christian influences were strong. Third, the political capital was once more situated in a region with distinctly hierarchical social patterns, whereas the Kansai district by this time was somewhat more egalitarian. Finally and most importantly, the move to Edo in time came to signify a switch in economic policy from promoting international trade, which had flourished in the sixteenth century, to encouraging diplomatic isolation, containing commerce, and fostering agricultural production.

These trends did not, of course, comprise a frozen monolith throughout the long centuries of Tokugawa rule, and indeed great economic growth occurred.[2] But to a remarkable degree the favorable attitude of the *bakufu* toward agriculture remained the prevailing official view of eco-

[2] Furushima Toshio, *Nihon nōgakushi* [History of Japanese Agriculture] (Tokyo: Nihon Hyōronsha, 1946), I, is a standard source for Tokugawa agricultural history. For a survey of the Edo period merchant economy, see Charles D. Sheldon, *The Rise of the Merchant Class in Tokugawa Japan, 1600-1868* (Locust Valley, N.Y.: J. J. Augustin, Inc., 1958).

nomics until Commodore Matthew C. Perry's squadron reached Uraga Bay in 1853, exposing Japan to the liberal economic orbit of the nineteenth-century West. Since the Edo period was truly "the womb and hothouse"[3] of both forms of modern Japanese agrarianism, bureaucratic and popular, it will be useful to sketch the range of farm-centered thought, both official and nonofficial, during this late feudal era.

"Agriculture is the root, trade and industry the branches."[4] This arid but time-honored maxim had been a canon of state economic policy for many centuries in Japan. To this the Tokugawa *bakufu* added a great outpouring of rhetoric to justify its profarming policies. One reason for the Tokugawa fondness of agriculture was that many *bakufu* advisers were adherents of the orthodox Shushi (Chu Hsi) school of Confucianism, and as a result most of them regarded as axiomatic the *Ta hsüeh* idea, "Let the producers be many and the consumers be few. Let there be activity in the production and economy in the expenditure. Then the wealth will always be sufficient."[5] Because Confucian counsel was kept in Edo, it was natural that the static Shushi view of national wealth should prevail.

Second, it is easy to imagine that an abundantly landed regime, eager to maximize its own revenues while depriving its rivals of potential sources of new wealth, would uphold farming even to the point of urging the cultivator to be "the docile instrument of a feudal policy."[6] Some Neo-Confucian fundamentalists even spoke of relocating the warrior class

[3] Sakurai Takeo, "Nōhonshugi—sono rekishi, riron, jiban" [Agrarianism—Its History, Theory, and Foundation], *Rekishi kagaku* [Science of History], IV, 3, March 1935, p. 119.

[4] *Nō wa moto nari, shōkō wa sue nari.*

[5] *Ta hsüeh* [Great Learning], ch. 10, 19, quoted in John W. Hall, *Tanuma Okitsugu (1719-1788): Forerunner of Modern Japan* (Cambridge, Mass.: Harvard University Press, 1955), p. 157.

[6] E. Herbert Norman, *Andō Shōeki and the Anatomy of Japanese Feudalism, Transactions of the Asiatic Society of Japan*, series 3, II (Tokyo, 1949), 276.

(samurai) on the land, to offset the attractions of life in the castle towns. Yet when times were bad in the countryside, Edo officials wasted little time before pinning the blame on the sloth and indolence of the farmers; surely, they reasoned, the cultivators were at fault for failing to live up to the ideals of rural life. Government agricultural pronouncements routinely began with such phrases as "peasants are stupid people" or "since peasants are people who lack sense or forethought."[7] However unrealistic and disdainful these ideas may have been in an economy that was slowly but irrepressibly maturing, most Tokugawa officials accepted placid Confucian views that glorified farming and resisted commercialization,[8] whether out of intellectual conviction or the instinct for survival.

A third consideration is that the state extolled agriculture out of a concern for social stability. To put an end to decades of turbulent and sometimes violent social change, the *bakufu* classified the public into four broad groups: samurai, farmers, artisans, and merchants (*shi-nō-kō-shō*). Although the stated model was the fourfold Confucian stratification of Chinese society, the Tokugawa rulers' real aim seems to have been merely to set off the warrior class as a distinct elite, since it was upon the samurai that the *bakufu*'s own political power was based. Ambivalent though the Tokugawa family may have been about enforcing class lines among commoners, its intellectuals in residence spent a great deal of time urging each member of society to lead a style of life appropriate to his status. As Ogyū Sorai (1666–1728), the scholar of Chinese classics and *bakufu* adviser, wrote in 1728: "To prize the root and suppress the branches was the rule of the ancient sages. The root is agriculture. The branches are commerce and industry. Clearly throughout history agriculture declines when commerce and industry rise. Samurai and farmers have permanently fixed occupations and depend entirely on the land for their

---

[7] Ibid.   [8] See Hall, pp. 60-61.

survival. This is a proper basis for government."[9] Sorai's leading disciple, the great Sinophile Dazai Shundai (1680-1747), expressed most clearly the Confucian moral opprobrium of commerce and dim view of peasant proclivities:

Agriculture is the foundation of all other productivity. All classes are fed by the farmer. When artisans and merchants increase, they merely stimulate the luxury of the people because they produce useless commodities. As the labour of the farmer, however, is essentially disagreeable, farmers are generally anxious to get out of their kind of work. This must be strictly forbidden by law, else the production of the necessities of life will fall below the amount required.[10]

Notable throughout such writings of the mid and late Edo period is not merely the call for freezing class lines in a feudal political system based on farming but also the implicit acknowledgment that the fate of the warrior was tied to the peasantry, since farmers paid the taxes that underwrote samurai salaries. As the quip went, *nō* (farming) meant *nō* (tax payment). When Sorai pointed out that the warrior and cultivator were each bound to "the land for their survival," without the right to change occupations, he conceded that to a great degree the elite class was helpless to forestall the slow erosion of its privileged position caused by the growth of commerce. The farmer, in practice, could flee to the city, whereas the samurai was legally and ethically obliged to eschew any other calling. Until very late in the era, remarkably few warriors, other than masterless samurai (*rōnin*), yielded to the temptation.

An added reason for promoting agriculture was that it was the economic basis for a sound army. The state accepted

[9] Ogyū Sorai, *Seidan* (Political Discourses), 1728, quoted in Sakurai, p. 121.

[10] Dazai Shundai, quoted in Garrett Droppers, "Some Economic Theories of Old Japan," *Transactions of the Asiatic Society of Japan*, series 1, xxiv, 1896, vii.

the autarkic premise that self-sufficiency was vital to the Tokugawa family's own military strength, but since samurai were set apart by virtue of their monopoly on arms-bearing, the government officially rejected the ancient idea of the farmer-soldier (*nōhei*).[11] Most *bakufu* administrators saw the economic value of farming to government defense policy, but few connected it to a clear conception of nation, before the end of the Edo period. Instead, their orientation was toward protecting the state against its internal enemies.

In short, the Edo regime lionized farming, perhaps in word more than in deed, for diverse reasons: to implement the economic views of the Confucian ideology it patronized, to maximize its own revenues, to deprive potential rivals of commercial wealth, to stabilize Japanese society, and to assure its own defense. It is tempting to view *bakufu* agrarianism as the exploitative hypocrisy of a state founded on a "serf-like 'poor peasant economy,'"[12] but it seems more appropriate to say that the government's support of farming drew at least as much strength from moral and political conviction as it did from desperation, scorn, or envy about socioeconomic developments beyond its control. Although a sound merchant economy was emerging by the late Tokugawa period, the official outlook on farming throughout the era remained truly conservative, trying to retain a time-honored system that still worked quite well. It was only with the rise of industrial Japan in the late nineteenth century that the state, under new political leadership, endorsed any really backward-looking farm policies, in an effort to restore a prior condition of Japanese farming.

[11] On *nōhei*, see Kumazawa Banzan, *Daigaku wakumon* [Questions on the Great Learning], ch. 12, quoted in *Sources of Japanese Tradition*, comp. Ryusaku Tsunoda, ed. William T. deBary (New York: Columbia University Press, 1958), pp. 391-392. See also Norman, pp. 11-12, 277.

[12] Sakurai, p. 122. Tsukuba Hisaharu, "Nihon nōhonshugi josetsu" [Introduction to Japanese Agrarianism], *Shisō no kagaku* [Science of Thought], No. 18, June 1960, pp. 6-7, recognizes the multiple motives of the Tokugawa family in supporting farming.

Farm thought in the Edo period was not confined to the abstract intellectualizing of court Confucianists, who, as Sansom put it, thought highly of agriculture but not of agriculturalists. Agrarianism also had an important existence as a body of optimistic natural philosophy that was deeply rooted in the countryside long before Confucian blandishments about the virtues of cultivation began to pour out from Edo. In the broadest sense, agrarian fundamentalism—a positive view of society based on small village farming— was a formless concept linked to Japan's climate (*fūdo*), natural setting, distinctive forms of social organization, and indigenous deities.[13] Agriculture connoted not merely the fact but also the consciousness of living close to nature. Most Japanese have long regarded their climate as agreeable and their land as fertile, sometimes to the point of treating nature as a benevolent force to be trusted rather than a fearsome phenomenon to be respected.[14] Such an idealistic, optimistic outlook laid a basis for village solidarity in premodern Japan, insofar as the common worship of local gods was connected with fertility in the agricultural cycle.

These assumptions provided the Tokugawa leaders with a deep reservoir of general proagriculture sentiment, but in several respects Confucian agrarianism conflicted with the natural philosophy of the countryside. The latter emphasized family ties, whereas *bakufu* Confucianism attempted to direct loyalties to feudal overlords. The folk outlook on farm-

[13] See Takeuchi Tetsuo, "Nōhonshugi bunseki e no zenteiteki shomondai—shu to shite bunseki shikaku ni tsuite" [Preliminary Problems in Analyzing Agrarianism—With Emphasis on Analytical Viewpoints], *Shimane Nōka Daigaku kenkyū hōkoku* [Shimane Agricultural University Research Reports], No. 9, A-3, March 1961, pp. 54-56. For a modern outlook on *fūdo*, see Watsuji Tetsurō, *Fūdo* (Tokyo: Iwanami Shoten, 1935), translated as *A Climate—A Philosophical Study* by Geoffrey Bownas (Tokyo: Japanese National Commission for UNESCO, 1961). Also see Iinuma Jirō, *Nihon nōgyō gijutsushi* [History of Japanese Agricultural Technology] (Tokyo: Miraisha, 1971).

[14] On this point, see Tsukuba, pp. 4-7.

ing also differed from the state position in its stress on the oneness of gods and man (*shinjin gōitsu*).[15] What is more, the corporate consciousness of villagers pointed up communal harmony and discouraged the strict class divisions enunciated by the state. Finally, the pre-Confucian ideal of the unity of politics and religious ceremony (*saisei itchi*) was founded on the village as the primary locale of corporate Shinto ritual and basic unit of self-government. While the *bakufu* in practice exercised little control over farm villages, nevertheless Confucian canons of centralized rule ran counter to the longstanding custom of village autonomy. Still it would be unwise to exaggerate the divergence between state and popular attitudes. In many respects Tokugawa pronouncements about farming had a wide appeal precisely because this inchoate corpus of rural beliefs was so widely diffused throughout Japanese society.

More tangible was a second stream of nonofficial farm thought in the Edo period, the practical teachings of men who promoted agricultural improvements, aptly labeled "technologists" by Thomas C. Smith.[16] As persons concerned with increasing the material prosperity of the countryside, the technologists were not preoccupied with overall questions of politics or society, and thus they were only indirect forebears of the modern Nōhonshugisha. Nonetheless such men as Miyazaki Yasusada (Antei; 1623-1697), Ōkura Nagatsune (1768-1844), Andō Shōeki (late seventeenth to mid-eighteenth centuries), and Satō Nobuhiro (1769-1850) did a great deal to reify popular thinking about farming, and their refrain served as a distinct counterpoint to the official ideology. They believed that education and technical improvements, not Confucian frugality and diligence, grew more grain.[17] Hence they differed not just

[15] Takeuchi, p. 54.

[16] Thomas C. Smith, "Ōkura Nagatsune and the Technologists," *Personality in Japanese History*, ed. Albert M. Craig and Donald H. Shively (Berkeley: University of California Press, 1970), p. 127.

[17] See Miyazaki Yasusada, *Nōgyō zensho* [Farmer's Compendium]

from the orthodox *bakufu* position but also from the amor-
phous agrarian naturalism, which shared their belief in the
capacity of humans to improve themselves but emphasized
simple gathering of the bounty of nature rather than progressive technology.

Satō was especially noteworthy because he was drawn to
the thought of the advocate of National Learning Hirata
Atsutane (1776-1843) late in his career and began to couple
technical progress in farming with Shinto natural philosophy. Satō believed that remote gods had patronized agricultural productivity, and ever since it was an imperative of
nature "for rulers to employ every means in their power for
the sake of agriculture . . . [this] is the way to carry out the
divine will of creation and to assist in the cultivation of
nature."[18] Satō's economic centralism distinguished him
sharply from both the self-sufficient village communalism
of his own times and the economic localism of most subsequent popular Nōhonshugi partisans, but his preliminary
attempts to yoke farms and deities in the early nineteenth
century within a reasonably coherent conception of nation
foreshadowed the Shinto-inspired agrarian nationalism of
more outspoken farm ideologues in the twentieth century.

The treatises of technologists and utopians, together with
the hazy rural natural philosophy grounded in Shinto beliefs, suggest that the range and diversity of agrarian thought
in the Edo period soared far beyond the Confucian inter-
dictions and exhortations of the *bakufu*. These writers and
schools of thought by no means exhaust the ideological

---

quoted in Katayama Seiichi, "Meiji zenki nōgyō shidōsha no nōgyō
kyōikukan" [The Farm Education Outlooks of Early Meiji Farm
Leaders], *Nihon Daigaku Seishin Bunka Kenkyūjo-Kyōiku Seido
Kenkyūjo kiyō* [Bulletin of the Nihon University Cultural Research
Institute and Educational System Research Institute], IV, June 1967,
207. See also Norman, *passim*.

[18] Satō Nobuhiro, "Yōzō kaikuron" [Creation and Cultivation],
Keizai taiten [Compendium of Economics], XVIII, quoted in *Sources
of Japanese Tradition*, p. 574.

options which existed during the intellectually rich Tokugawa period, but they clearly indicate the continuing prominence of agricultural considerations during Japan's late feudal era.

Popular agrarianism in the Edo period peaked with the practical and moral teachings of Ninomiya Sontoku (Kinjirō; 1787-1856). Ninomiya and his colleagues shared a commitment to practical improvements in Japanese farming, but from their private positions outside the state they also reasserted the importance of moral exhortation and agreed that the cultivators should raise production and pay their taxes. Ninomiya acted as a reformer within the feudal hierarchy and mounted no direct challenge to the economic basis of Tokugawa rule. So noteworthy was his success as a technologist that the state finally put him in an official post; so remarkable were his ethical maxims that Ninomiya was ultimately lionized as a paragon of virtue in the national ethics textbooks in the 1930s.[19] The Hōtoku (Repaying Virtue) movement founded by his followers was both a magnet and an organ of popular agrarianism after the Meiji restoration. The Ninomiya tradition became a central thread binding multiple strands of agrarian thought, both official and nonofficial, moral and practical, feudal and modern, as Japan gradually shifted from a rural economy to industrial capitalism.

Ninomiya's central teaching was *hōtoku*, the idea that the benefits received from heaven, man, and earth should be repaid. If people collectively repaid their blessings, he believed, a peaceful and prosperous country (*fukoku anmin*) would be created and a "true society" would result—one in which all persons would be ennobled. The means of achieving *hōtoku*, he taught, consisted of sincerity (*shisei*), dili-

---

[19] See Robert K. Hall, *Shūshin: The Ethics of a Defeated Nation* (New York: Columbia University Teachers College, 1949), p. 204f. Even today in many Japanese schoolyards can be found statues of Ninomiya, absorbed in a book held in one hand, with a bundle of faggots slung over his shoulder grasped in the other.

gence (*kinrō*), thrift (*bundo*), and yielding to others (*suijō*).[20] All but the last had been prominent virtues in Tokugawa Confucian ethics, but Ninomiya combined them in a novel fashion, transforming these seemingly pious qualities into a practical code with powerful impact.

Although the concepts of *bundo* and *suijō* assumed a static economy, Robert N. Bellah has correctly asserted that Ninomiya's doctrines subsequently played a social role not unlike that of Christianity in the rise of European capitalism. Although Bellah has probably overemphasized the degree to which economic recovery and spiritual salvation were fused in Hōtoku thought,[21] it is easy to imagine that the new urban work force, bringing such values as hard work and thrift from the farms, proved immensely helpful in the industrialization program of the Meiji state after 1868.

But Ninomiya's teachings themselves stressed self-improvement within the stable social and administrative structure of Tokugawa Japan. By exhorting the individual to act in concert with his neighbors for the common good, Ninomiya directed attention away from reliance on the initiative of the state, which had heretofore been primarily responsible for economic relief. Yet if he prodded men into resisting the ravages of nature, Ninomiya proposed no measures to relieve the heavy tax burdens borne by the farm villages. In no sense was he a rural leveler;[22] the direction of his dogmas was upward, toward individual self-improvement within a communal village society dominated by the political overlordship of the *bakuhan* system. Although Nino-

[20] For a study of Ninomiya's ethics and a detailed bibliography, see Thomas R. H. Havens, "Religion and Agriculture in Nineteenth-century Japan: Ninomiya Sontoku and the Hōtoku Movement," *Japan Christian Quarterly*, xxxviii, 2, Spring 1972, 98-105.

[21] Robert N. Bellah, *Tokugawa Religion: The Values of Pre-Industrial Japan* (Glencoe, Ill.: The Free Press, 1957), p. 128.

[22] Robert C. Armstrong, *Just Before the Dawn: The Life and Work of Ninomiya Sontoku* (New York: Macmillan, 1912), p. 255.

miya encouraged a degree of rural industrialization, he forcefully asserted that agriculture was the most important calling: "The masses of the people are the foundation of a State and of all occupations agriculture is the basic one. . . . It must be highly valued and strongly encouraged. If the root is adequately nourished, there is no doubt that the branches will flourish."[23]

As a consequence, Ninomiya's thought, like that of various court Neo-Confucianists, rural technologists, and partisans of village natural philosophy before him, as yet represented no fundamental challenge to the ideological consensus underpinning the Japanese polity and society. Instead, his teachings confirmed two centuries later the static policy implications of moving the political capital to Edo back in 1603: the primacy of wealth in land rather than trade, of Shinto beliefs and gods, of social hierarchy and knowing one's station, and of encouraging farm production. Ninomiya both affirmed and conserved the central importance of intensive wet rice agriculture and the *buraku* communities in which its practitioners have lived, close to nature, since earliest times.

The Setting for Agricultural Development, 1870-1895

The wealth of the country is dependent on the quantity of goods produced. . . . The people's industries have not had sufficient encouragement from the government as they have just begun to develop. Skill and knowledge

[23] *Ninomiya Sontoku: His Life and "Evening Talks,"* ed. Ishiguro Tadaatsu (Tokyo: Kenkyūsha, 1955), pp. 243-245. This book is primarily a translation, by Yamagata Isō, of *Ninomiyaō yawa* [Ninomiya's Evening Talks], written down from memory between 1884 and 1888 by Fukuzumi Masae (1824-1892), one of Ninomiya's ablest followers, in *Fukuzumi Masae senshū* [Selected Works of Fukuzumi Masae], *Ninomiya Sontoku zenshū* [Complete Works of Ninomiya Sontoku] (Shizuoka: Ninomiya Sontoku Igyō Sen'yōkai, 1931), XXXVI, 666-853. See also Nakamura Yūjirō, *Kindai Nihon ni okeru seido to shisō* [Thought and Institutions in Modern Japan] (Tokyo: Miraisha, 1967), pp. 294-296.

must be given to the people and complete regulations established. The government and officials must all exert every effort to encourage industry and to increase production.[24]

With these words Minister of Home Affairs Ōkubo Toshimichi (1830-1878) inaugurated the modern era of Japanese economic growth in 1873. Ōkubo was a leading figure in the small oligarchy of samurai from western Japan who had overthrown the Tokugawa *bakufu* in a nearly bloodless coup and "restored" the teenaged Meiji emperor to political authority in January 1868, closing out Japan's eight-hundred-year history of feudal rule.

The insurgents seemed to agree that language is the dress of thought: their choice of the term "restoration" (*ishin*) to characterize their action was deliberate. They consciously portrayed the Meiji restoration as a metaphor for the ancient Japanese ideal, honored above all in the farm villages, of the unity of politics and religious ceremony. By theoretically reuniting the sacred functions of the emperor, deriving from his ceremonial position as chief priest of Shinto, with his renewed temporal duties as political sovereign, the Meiji oligarchs used the venerable imperial institution as a focus of new public loyalties emerging in response to decades of diplomatic pressure from abroad and political incompetence at home. In practice, Ōkubo and his associates had simply replaced the Tokugawa family as thurifers of the imperial regalia, using the throne to legitimize decisions taken among themselves, without the emperor's personal discretion. Yet this note of functional continuity from Tokugawa to Meiji is offset by the remarkable innovations that were made in the 1870s, in law, administration, education, military affairs, the economy, and virtually every other sector of national life. So broad and permanent were the changes that many per-

---

[24] Okubo Toshimichi, 1873, quoted in Hugh Borton, *Japan's Modern Century*, 2nd ed. (New York: Ronald Press, 1970), p. 129.

sons have come to regard Meiji less as a restoration than a revolution.[25]

When Ōkubo Toshimichi spoke of working "to encourage industry and to increase production," he set the tone not just for the Meiji government's economic policies but also, in the long run, for the performance of the country's entire economy. Under active state guidance that continues in altered forms even today, the Japanese economy sailed steadily toward the national goal of enriching the country and strengthening the army (*fukoku kyōhei*). As in many modernizing countries, economic policy became a trustworthy tool of national integration and political development, so that Japan could compete successfully in a world of rich and powerful states. From this it is evident that within less than twenty-five years official attitudes toward economics had been greatly transformed by the chain of events, both internal and external, that propelled Japan into the modern era.

Ōkubo and the other Meiji oligarchs knew that industrialization was the main path to national wealth, but they also understood that an overwhelmingly agricultural economy, with 80 percent of the labor force employed in farming, could not be converted to industrialism overnight. Like state planners everywhere, they realized that farm production set the limits for industrial growth, by feeding the expanding urban population, creating capital for investment, providing raw materials for manufacturing, and, ideally, supplying a surplus for export, thereby earning foreign exchange with which the state could import capital equipment to launch new enterprises. Thus the Japanese leaders fashioned policies that, paradoxically, exploited and nurtured

[25] See, e.g., Thomas C. Smith, "Japan's Aristocratic Revolution," *Yale Review*, L, 3, Spring 1961, 370-383; Marius B. Jansen, "The Meiji State: 1868-1912," *Modern East Asia: Essays in Interpretation*, ed. James B. Crowley (New York: Harcourt, Brace & World, 1970), pp. 102-108.

29

agriculture at the same time: to make farming pay for industrialization, it must pay to be engaged in farming.

Although my chief concern is with attitudes toward farming, it is important to outline the economic context within which agrarian thinking, both official and popular, took place during the years from the Meiji restoration to the Sino-Japanese War of 1894-1895. There can be no shred of doubt that, with government encouragement, farm output grew almost without interruption from the 1870s right up to the rural depression of the 1920s. Table 1 sug-

TABLE 1

AGRICULTURAL OUTPUT, 1878-1937
(Five-Year Averages)

Year	Agricultural Output, Constant Million Yen	General Agricultural Production Index
1878-1882	904	100
1883-1887	1,032	114
1888-1892	1,196	132
1893-1897	1,308	145
1898-1902	1,558	172
1903-1907	1,628	180
1908-1912	1,875	207
1913-1917	1,966	217
1918-1922	2,189	242
1923-1927	2,057	228
1928-1932	2,287	253
1933-1937	2,534	280

SOURCE: *Agriculture and Economic Growth: Japan's Experience*, ed. Kazushi Ohkawa, Bruce F. Johnston, and Hiromitsu Kaneda (Princeton and Tokyo: Princeton University Press and University of Tokyo Press, 1970), p. 38.

gests that general agricultural production more than doubled between 1880 and 1915. Especially noteworthy is the fact that this great increase occurred despite an almost constant average farm size (about 1.0 hectares) and rural labor force

(15.5 million in 1878, 14.5 million in 1912).[26] Although population growth in the countryside was relatively high during this period, the urban economy expanded fast enough to absorb unneeded rural workers without notable labor shortages or excesses in either sector until the 1920s. At the same time, agricultural growth was strong enough to allow even more spectacular increases in industrial output, especially in the years following the Sino-Japanese and Russo-Japanese wars.[27] Japan in these years was an unusual example of an industrializing country that raised its agricultural productivity within a system of small-scale farming, without major reductions in rural population or the dislocations of village life that might have accompanied mass migrations to the cities.

Despite the modern determinist contention that Japan's economic development before World War I took place atop a traditional agricultural base characterized by "feudal

[26] *Agricultural Development in Modern Japan*, ed. Takekazu Ogura, 2nd ed. (Tokyo: Fuji Publishing Co., 1968), pp. 618-619 (hereafter cited as Ogura). For detailed statistics on Japanese economic growth, see *Chōki keizai tōkei, suikei to bunseki* (English title: *Estimates of Long-Term Economic Statistics of Japan Since 1868*), ed. Ohkawa Kazushi, Shinohara Miyohei, and Umemura Mataji, 13 vols. (Tokyo: Tōyō Keizai Shinbunsha, 1966–), esp. vols. 9 and 13.

[27] For data and analysis of industrial growth, see William W. Lockwood, *The Economic Development of Japan: Growth and Structural Change 1868-1938* (Princeton: Princeton University Press, 1954), pp. 18-37. See also Henry Rosovsky, *Capital Formation in Japan, 1868-1940* (Glencoe, Ill.: The Free Press, 1961); James I. Nakamura, *Agricultural Production and the Economic Development of Japan, 1873-1922* (Princeton: Princeton University Press, 1966); *Agriculture and Economic Growth: Japan's Experience*, ed. Kazushi Ohkawa, Bruce F. Johnston, and Hiromitsu Kaneda (Princeton: Princeton University Press, and Tokyo: University of Tokyo Press, 1970); *Economic Growth: The Japanese Experience Since the Meiji Era*, ed. Lawrence Klein and Kazushi Ohkawa (Homewood, Ill.: Richard D. Irwin, Inc., 1968). The problem of using reliable statistics is treated in Henry Rosovsky, "Rumbles in the Ricefields: Professor Nakamura vs. the Official Statistics," *Journal of Asian Studies*, XXVII, 2, February 1968, 347-360.

production relations,"[28] a number of technological and institutional innovations affected rural life during the period 1870-1895. On the one hand, the national government carried out Ōkubo's injunction that "skill and knowledge must be given to the people" by energetically promoting new farming techniques, especially during the 1870s. Land improvement schemes, better irrigation and drainage, more rational soil use, improved seeds, more fertilizers, and the like had an important long term impact on farm output.[29] On the other hand, the state enacted major revisions in the tax and landholding systems in 1873, further discrediting the notion of an unchanging rural Japan.

Briefly put, the land tax law of 1873 granted legal land ownership by deed to the customary possessors who had previously occupied it in their own names under feudal regulations. Henceforth land could be freely bought and sold. Government surveys accompanying the new law "discovered" so many previously unregistered lands that the recorded tax base was increased by 48 percent.[30] Taxes were fixed at 3 percent cash payment per annum, based on land price, which was approximately the same level as when payments were made in kind during the Edo period. Estimates of the real burden vary, but it seems to have been little heavier in the Meiji era than earlier in the century.[31] The effect of the new tax law was to recognize legally a large landlord class (many of them petty owner-cultivators), a sizeable group of part owners, part tenants, and a smaller class of tenants, roughly in the proportion of 45 : 35 : 20.[32]

[28] Sakurai, p. 122. [29] See Ogura, p. 624.
[30] Ronald P. Dore, Land Reform in Japan (London: Oxford University Press, 1959), pp. 14-17.
[31] Ibid.; Ogura, p. 108. An additional local tax of up to one percent was also permitted. On land taxes, see also Smith, Agrarian Origins, pp. 100-101, 159f.
[32] See Dore, p. 17. The figures are estimates for 1868. It is almost impossible to distinguish mathematically among large, medium, and small landlords at any time between 1873 and World War II, nor did the later agrarianists who spoke optimistically of the small and

From the perspective of state planners, the new tax system had certain evident merits. It permitted year-to-year budgeting, since tax obligations were fixed regardless of output. It created a nationwide mechanism for accumulating revenue for the expenses of governing and for industrial subsidies. It brought previously untaxed lands under the law, spreading tax obligations more equitably and reducing potential unrest. The new scheme benefited large landlords the most and tenants the least, because rents continued to be paid in kind (about half the crop, as in the Edo period). Since population pressure on the land remained relatively strong throughout the Meiji era, rents also stayed high. By contrast, landlords' tax obligations were somewhat lower than previously (because of a broader tax base), and they were fixed at definite cash levels.

In a generally inflationary age, both tenant and landlord could obtain favorable prices for the crops they marketed directly or indirectly, but the value of the tenant's rent also rose. On the other hand, the landlord's taxes rose much more slowly, and then under the impact of local levies.[33] To the landlord it was generally advantageous to rent surplus lands to tenants, not only because of the prevailing high rates that renting commanded but also because it was expensive to hire

---

medium landlords as ideal social types attempt to define them in terms of precise landholdings. In general a large landlord was one who could live entirely on rents from tenants. Usually at least ten hectares of good paddy or the equivalent in upland fields was needed for this purpose. Lands in the single-crop regions of the northeast were, of course, less productive than those in the multiple crop areas further south. A small landlord might own one or two hectares, a part of which he rented to tenants whereas a *jisakunō*, or owner-farmer, usually held one half to one hectare and worked it by himself. The medium landlord, who rented part of his land and worked the rest, might own something like five hectares. As large landlords drifted off to the cities and became absentee owners, the small and medium landholder, and later the owner-farmer, was regarded as the backbone of village society by Nōhonshugisha. I am grateful to Ann Waswo, in private correspondence, for advice on this point.

[33] Ogura, p. 18.

the field hands that intensive rice growing demanded, should the landlord try to cultivate the land himself.

The drift toward tenancy accelerated in the 1880s as a result of stiff deflationary measures taken by the oligarchy in 1881 under the new Minister of Finance, Matsukata Masayoshi (1835-1924). Rice prices quickly fell to 4.8 yen per koku, half their level in 1880. After a number of relatively fat years, this sudden pinch effectively doubled the proportion of a landlord's income given over to taxes.[34] Many small landowners were consequently forced into debt to pay taxes, and a large number of owner-farmers, perhaps as many as five hundred thousand families, lapsed into tenant status.[35] Tables 2 and 3 display the classifications of farm

TABLE 2

FARM FAMILIES CLASSIFIED BY LAND STATUS

Year	Owner-Farmer %	Part Owner-Farmer, Part Tenant %	Tenant Farmer %
1868	ca. 45.0	ca. 35.0	ca. 20.0
1883-1884	37.4	42.9	19.7
1888	33.3	45.1	21.6
1899	35.4	38.4	26.2
1902	33.9	38.0	28.1
1907	33.7	37.7	28.6
1912	32.5	39.8	27.7

SOURCE: Ronald P. Dore, *Land Reform in Japan* (London: Oxford University Press, 1959), p. 17; *Agricultural Development in Modern Japan*, ed. Takekazu Ogura, 2nd ed. (Tokyo: Fuji Publishing Co., 1968), p. 18.

families and the proportion of land in tenancy from the restoration to World War I. The land thus defaulted fell into the hands of large landlords and, more and more, city

[34] Ann Waswo, "Landlords and Social Change in Prewar Japan," Ph.D. dissertation in history, Stanford University, 1969, p. 54.

[35] Ogura, p. 654.

merchant speculators. By World War I, the percentage of land in tenancy had stabilized at about 45 percent, where it remained until the U.S. occupation land reform of 1946. Likewise the number of tenant families grew steadily as a result of the Matsukata deflation, reaching a peak early in the twentieth century. The effects of these changes in the 1880s were long lasting: a concentration of landownership in fewer hands, absentee landlordism by the 1890s, diminished face-to-face relationships between owners and tenants, a debt spiral that made it difficult to escape tenant status, and a gradual weakening of community ties and customary contacts, as control over landed wealth was no longer entirely in the hands of village residents.

TABLE 3

PROPORTION OF LAND AREA CULTIVATED
BY TENANT FARMERS TO TOTAL CULTIVATED LAND

Year	Proportion %
1868	ca. 30.0
1883-1884	36.8
1887	39.3
1892	40.0
1903	44.5
1908	45.4
1913	45.5

SOURCE: Ronald P. Dore, *Land Reform in Japan* (London: Oxford University Press, 1959), p. 17; *Agricultural Development in Modern Japan*, ed. Takekazu Ogura, 2nd ed. (Tokyo: Fuji Publishing Co., 1968), p. 18.

While overall agricultural production climbed quite steadily from the Meiji restoration to World War I, the Sino-Japanese War of 1894-1895 is a good bench mark for gauging the effects of the land tax and the landholding system it fostered. In 1888-1892, despite two decades of stimulating industrialization, the government still derived 85.6 percent of its tax revenues from the land tax. Twenty years and two wars later, the land tax accounted for only 42.9 percent of total state tax income, despite a doubling of the absolute value of the land tax from 38 million yen to 79 million yen.[36] Farming clearly was crucial for the solvency of the government until the mid-1890s, but thereafter new taxes on new revenue sources sprouted rapidly as industrialization spread. This created an uneasy situation in which landowners' real tax obligations to government at all levels were growing heavier, whereas the state depended on farming less completely than in the early Meiji period. No small part of the rural unrest that emerged after 1900 can be attributed to these changing relationships between taxpayers and the state.

Farm Policy in the Early Meiji Period

When the Meiji government decided to lift both industrial and agricultural production in the 1870s, it decisively set aside the Tokugawa canon that farming should be preserved as the unchanging economic foundation of society. The goal of government agricultural policy in the early Meiji years was distinctly modern and clearly nationalist: farm output must be increased to create a rich country and strong people. In practice, agricultural exports (mainly tea, silk, and silkworm eggs) accounted for 70 to 80 percent of total exports in the early Meiji period.[37] No longer was farming officially to be regarded as a virtue in itself; instead it must be articulated with a larger economic policy that would bring Japan wealth, power, and international respect.

The means to be employed were both modern and traditionalistic. On the one hand, the state quickly introduced

[36] Ibid., p. 22.
[37] Ibid., p. 153. On Ōkubo's attitude toward agriculture and national strengthening, see Denda Isao, *Kindai Nihon nōsei shisō no kenkyū* [Studies on Modern Japanese Agricultural Administration Thought] (Tokyo, Miraisha, 1969), p. 61.

technical improvements and agricultural education, and some leading statesmen advocated the commercialization of agriculture on a large scale. On the other hand, the government echoed the Tokugawa encouragements to thrift and diligence, especially in the 1880s, although it did so for modernizing, not conserving, purposes.

The first official agency for farm policy was the Kannōkyoku (Office for Encouraging Agriculture), created within the Minbushō, or Ministry of Public Affairs, in 1870. After many changes, this unit reemerged as the new Ministry of Agriculture and Commerce (Nōshōmushō) in 1880. The agency's policies were shaped in part by the report of the Iwakura mission to America and Europe in 1872-1873, which concluded that (1) agricultural development varied among Western countries, but all were more advanced than Japan; (2) agricultural growth required education and experimentation; and (3) agricultural science and techniques were best spread through schools and colleges, such as those founded under the 1862 Morrill Land Grant Act in the United States.[38] With farmers no longer legally bound to their occupations, the government maintained, it was critically important that a new class of progressive cultivators take the lead in raising output.

As a consequence, beginning in 1877 the government set up agricultural experiment stations throughout Japan to demonstrate Western techniques, products, and machinery. As was true for many other government programs in the 1870s, foreign advisers were hired to accelerate farm improvements. The state also opened a series of agricultural schools. These various efforts required many years to take full effect, and their part in enhancing productivity must be weighed against the many other factors which spurred output. These activities reveal the government's conviction, as Matsukata put it in 1879, that "the development of agriculture must not rely merely on practical experience. First

[38] Katayama, pp. 164-165, 209-210.

you must have science and only then will you begin to have success."[39] Strapped by other heavy budget commitments, the Meiji state invested relatively little in rural technical education and public works[40] in the years before the Sino-Japanese War, but Matsukata's words were a firm denial of the Tokugawa belief that farmers were too stupid to need any education and show that the Meiji oligarchs hardly intended to preserve Japanese farming in its premodern condition.

Most emblematic of the early Meiji view that agriculture should serve national economic policy was the enthusiasm of some government leaders for large-scale commercial farming. Well aware that land consolidation and big farms had caused great spurts of productivity in Western countries, men such as Ōkubo, Matsukata, Itō Hirobumi (1841-1909), and later Inoue Kaoru (1836-1915) called for mechanization and extensive farming wherever possible. Although their attempts to implement ranch farming met with some success in Hokkaido and Iwate prefectures,[41] the deck was stacked against large-scale agriculture: rice was the richest crop in most areas of Japan and required vast amounts of labor, the rural population was too large to be thrown off the land as ranching demanded, and there was a scarcity of capital and machinery for large-scale operations. Perhaps

[39] Matsukata Masayoshi, "Nōshō hensan no gishi" [The Meaning of Compiling Farm Books], 1879, quoted in Katayama, p. 186.

[40] Lockwood, p. 247, suggests that 10 percent of tax revenues, a low figure, went to these activities, with half supplied by local governments. On the experiment stations, see Sakurai Takeo, *Nihon nōhonshugi* [Japanese Agrarianism] (Tokyo: Hakuyōsha, 1935), pp. 151-153; Niwa Kunio, "The Reform of the Land Tax and the Government Programme for the Encouragement of Industry," *The Developing Economics*, IV, 4, December 1966, 470-471; Ogura, pp. 3-15, 152, 320-322.

[41] Ogura, p. 152. On large-scale farming, see Denda, p. 72; Sakurai, "Nōhonshugi—sono rekishi, riron, jiban," pp. 123-126; Sakurai, *Nihon nōhonshugi*, pp. 14-15, 80-82, 147-151; Ogura, pp. 150-153; Ogura Takekazu, *Agrarian Problems and Agricultural Policy in Japan* (Tokyo: Institute of Asian Economic Affairs, 1967), pp. 11-12.

the most salutary result of the government's extensive farming doctrine was to bring more lands under cultivation, especially in northern Japan.[42] The fact remains that renting lands out to tenants was more profitable for large landowners than ranch-scale operations, and after Ōkubo's assassination in 1878 the state placed less hope in large farming.

During the same period the bureaucracy also unveiled a program to promote agricultural development within the existing small-scale structure of Japanese farming by creating a system of itinerant veteran farmers (later replaced by trained agronomists) to spread new techniques throughout the countryside.[43] The government also sponsored the Dai Nihon Nōkai (Agricultural Society of Japan), formed in 1881. A quasi-official organization based on local farm discussion groups which had arisen in the mid-1870s, the Dai Nihon Nōkai emphasized experience equally with science. Its announced purpose was to "exchange agricultural knowledge and experience and especially to plan the reform and improvement of agriculture."[44] Under chief secretary Shinagawa Yajirō (1843-1900), then an official in the new Ministry of Agriculture and Commerce and later a cabinet minister under several premiers, the Dai Nihon Nōkai held discussions all over the country to promote production

[42] Ogura, *Agrarian Problems*, p. 11.

[43] See Takeuchi Tetsuo, "Nōhonshugi to nōson chūsansō" [Agrarianism and the Farm Village Middle Class], *Shimane Nōka Daigaku kenkyū hōkoku* [Shimane Agricultural University Research Reports], No. 8, A, March 1960, p. 229. On veteran farmers, see Ogura, pp. 15-16, 157-158, 299-301; Shūjirō Sawada, "Innovation in Japanese Agriculture," *The State and Economic Enterprise in Japan*, ed. William W. Lockwood (Princeton: Princeton University Press, 1965), p. 340; John R. McEwan, "The Confucian Ideology and the Modernization of Japan," *The Modernization of Japan*, ed. Tōbata Seiichi (Tokyo: Institute of Asian Economic Affairs, 1966), I, 237.

[44] Denda, p. 76. On the Dai Nihon Nōkai, see Sawada, p. 340; Okutani Matsuji, *Shinagawa Yajirō den* [Biography of Shinagawa Yajirō] (Tokyo: Kōyō Shoin, 1940), p. 169; McEwan, p. 238; Ogura, p. 302; Morita Shirō, *The Development of Agricultural Cooperative Associations in Japan* (Tokyo: Japan FAO Association, 1960), p. 16.

39

through the cooperation of the "conscientious" landlords who dominated village society.

Moral uplift also had a place in the Meiji scheme of fostering farm development, but the assumptions and purposes underlying the oligarchs' exhortations to farmers were substantially different from those prevalent among Tokugawa Confucianists. Hard work and frugality had specific monetary advantages to the new leaders, who believed in economic growth, whereas in the premodern view these qualities were ethically desirable for their own sakes in a static agrarian economy. Thus the Meiji emperor could tell the guests at the opening of the Komaba Agricultural School in January 1878, "We think that agriculture is the foundation of the country," but his words had lost the Confucian freight of a century before. Now, the emperor continued, "let production continue to increase, and let the people continue to prosper. We must practice the study" of agriculture.[45] Science and progress, not eternal economic stasis, were moral in their own right.

The Confucianist educator Nishimura Shigeki (1828-1902), an influential Meiji bureaucrat, stressed that the countries of Europe were thriving because their people were frugal and diligent.[46] Such notes were struck repeatedly in the 1880s, especially when the government exported rice to improve its trade balance after the collapse of 1881, all the while urging the farmers to restrict consumption. An edict from the Nōshōmushō in 1885 urged that labor and thrift were the means to escape the poverty imposed by urbanization.[47] As one observer put it, "the export of rice in this period was, so to speak, a 'hunger export.' "[48] However

[45] Meiji emperor, January 24, 1878, quoted in Katayama, p. 209.

[46] Donald H. Shively, "Nishimura Shigeki: A Confucian View of Modernization," Changing Japanese Attitudes Toward Modernization, ed. Marius B. Jansen (Princeton: Princeton University Press, 1965), p. 208.

[47] Fukutake Tadashi, Nihon no nōson shakai [Japanese Rural Society] (Tokyo: Tokyo Daigaku Shuppankai, 1953), pp. 180-181.

[48] Ogura, p. 183.

pious and self-serving these exhortations, the theme of sacrifice for the sake of modernization runs throughout, and the emphasis is no longer on the glorification of self-denial for its own sake.

By the mid-1880s, the state had switched most of its attention to working within the small-scale farm system, and it had begun to accommodate its earlier interest in technical education to the realities of a rural society dominated by landlords. Increasingly it had to cope with practical problems hindering farm growth. In 1884, for example, the Nōshōmushō was obliged to upgrade the quality of market rice through rigid inspection programs, since much rice was rotting and sake production was affected.[49] These changes seemed to constitute appropriate adjustments to a decade's experience with promoting output—especially in light of the farm depression of the 1880s—but in no sense did they indicate a policy swing away from stimulating agricultural production as a part of the overall quest for wealth and power. Despite tactical shifts, the Meiji oligarchs remained firmly wedded to their modernizing outlook on farming.

Popular Farm Thought and the Nineteenth-Century Hōtoku Movement

The new government was quite secure enough to set farm policy as it saw fit during the 1870s and 1880s without fears of a serious challenge to its own power from the countryside. At the same time the cooperation, or at least acquiescence, of farmers large and small was highly desirable if agriculture was to play the modernizing role cast for it by Ōkubo. Part of the impetus for rural improvements in the early Meiji period came from the farm villages themselves, where after the land revision of 1873 "conscientious farmers" (*tokunō*) and other progressive landlords pressed both technical improvement and moral uplift upon the cultivators, in order to grow bigger crops and increase the landlords'

[49] Waswo, pp. 47-66; Ogura, pp. 163-165.

41

own incomes.[50] Most progressive landlords realized full well that the state's motive for advocating technical education in the 1870s and 1880s was primarily to increase tax revenues by means of expanded farm production, although this had the side effect of feathering landowners' nests as well. But, since their own interests coincided with those of the government, *tokunō* generally took the lead in land improvement in their own districts. In the earlier Meiji period, these progressive farmers usually supported the state's technological innovations, but by the 1890s many of them began to demand that the government do more for the landholding classes, both technologically and fiscally. One especially prominent organization of conscientious farmers was the Meiji period Hōtokusha (Repaying Virtue Society), several of whose leaders became persuasive exponents of popular farm thought in the 1870s and 1880s.

Taken together, the Hōtoku societies founded by Ninomiya Sontoku's pupils in the late Tokugawa period formed a sizeable farm-improvement movement in the Meiji era, under the leadership of landlords who were at once innovative and didactic.[51] These organizations by no means encapsulated the full range of opinion found within the very diverse landowning class. To some progressive local leaders, the echoes of feudal moralism rendered the Hōtoku societies too anachronistic to deserve their loyalty. To more traditional farmers, the Hōtoku interest in self-improvement and technical change was too great a departure to warrant allegiance. But the movement merits attention, first because of its appeal to precisely that village leadership class which became the object of official patronage after 1900, and second because, of all the popular agrarian ideologies in modern Japan, Hōtoku teachings eventually came to enjoy the greatest favor within the government.

Although Ninomiya Sontoku preached the virtues of sincerity, diligence, thrift, and yielding to others throughout

---

[50] Waswo, pp. 40-45; Dore, pp. 44-50.
[51] See Dore, pp. 44-53.

the first half of the nineteenth century, his impact on the Hōtoku movement was more inspirational than organizational.[52] The earliest Hōtokusha were apparently started in Tōtōmi in the 1840s by Agoin Gidō (1789-1863) and Okada Saheiji (1812-1878),[53] both of whom applied Ninomiya's principles to farm management and shopkeeping with great profit. These small predominantly landlord organizations were most notably credit societies. The man most responsible for spreading Hōtoku thought was Tomita Takayoshi (1814-1890), a scholar and technologist who helped to establish Hōtoku societies in present-day Fukushima, Kanagawa, and Shizuoka prefectures in the 1850s.[54] Tomita wrote *Hōtokuron* (Theory of Repaying Virtue) in 1850, explaining that the purpose of the movement was to make the country thrive and build a "true society" by "making sincerity the foundation, emphasizing diligence, making one's lot in life the substance, and practicing self-restraint

[52] Kiyoshi Ogata, *The Co-operative Movement in Japan* (London: P. S. King & Son, Ltd., 1923), p. 26.

[53] Emori Itsuo, "Meijiki no Hōtokusha undō no shiteki shakaiteki haikei" [Historical and Social Background of the Meiji Period Hōtokusha Movement], *Hōritsu ronsō* [Collection of Legal Theories], Meiji University, part 1, XL, 1, October 1966, pp. 86-87. See Haraguchi Kiyoshi, "Hōtokusha no hitobito" [Hōtokusha Members], *Nihon jinbutsushi taikei* [Outline History of Talented Persons in Japan], ed. Konishi Shirō (Tokyo: Asakura Shoten, 1960), V, 255-264; Naramoto Tatsuya, *Ninomiya Sontoku* (Tokyo: Iwanami Shoten, 1959), pp. 162-169; Ogata, pp. 39-40; Saitō Osamu, "Hōtokusha undō no kuronorojii—19 seiki kōhan ni okeru keizaiteki henka e no nōmin no taiō" [Chronology of the Hōtokusha Movement—The Response of Farmers to Economic Changes in the Latter Half of the Nineteenth Century], *Mita Gakkai zasshi* [Journal of the Mita Gakkai], LXIV, 8, August 1971, 227-228.

[54] For Tomita see Koide Kōzō, *Kyōdo o okoshita senjin no omokage* [Memories of Forebears who Revived Their Home Towns] (Tokyo: Nihon Jichi Kensetsu Honbu, 1958), pp. 140-166; Naramoto, pp. 155-160; Emori, part 1, pp. 95-98; Hirose Yutaka and Hirose Toshiko, *Ninomiya Sontoku no kōtei Tomita Takayoshi* [Tomita Takayoshi, Ninomiya Sontoku's Senior Disciple] (Tokyo: Nihon Kōshikai, 1953), pp. 226-244.

and aiding others."[55] Both this work and *Hōtokuki* (Record of Repaying Virtue), which Tomita wrote right after Ninomiya's death in 1856, were realistic guides based on experience, not sophisticated bodies of theory, and their impact was understandably less intellectual than practical.

With the overthrow of the *bakuhan* system in 1868 and the consequent tax and landholding reforms, the Hōtoku movement grew somewhat discredited, insofar as it was tied to the feudal land relations and stratified social system of the Tokugawa era. The spirit of the new age, typified by the "civilization and enlightenment" (*bunmei kaika*) outlook of the Meiji Six Society, flowed directly against the notion of accepting one's inherited social position. However helpful the Hōtoku stress on self-help and free credit may have been to certain late Tokugawa villages, its premodern overtones would plainly require modification if the movement was to remain dynamic in the 1870s. This task of adaptation fell to another of Ninomiya's disciples, the National Learning advocate Fukuzumi Masae (1824-1892).[56]

Fukuzumi organized the Meiji period's first Hōtokusha in 1874 and defined its goals in these terms:

> The purpose of the Hōtokusha is to help the poor and to aid them to unite in helping one another, first by opening their hearts and developing goodness of character among them, and secondly by assisting them to open up wild lands, improve irrigation and roads, repair bridges and river banks, and, in general, doing all that is of benefit to the poor. It begins by helping the poorest and encouraging and rewarding the good.[57]

[55] Tomita Takayoshi, *Hōtokuron* [Theory of Repaying Virtue], 1850, quoted in Hirose, p. 228.

[56] For Fukuzumi see Haraguchi, pp. 264-272; Nakamura, *Kindai Nihon ni okeru seido to shisō*, p. 297; Yoshimoto Tadasu, *A Peasant Sage of Japan: The Life and Work of Ninomiya Sontoku* (London: Longmans, 1912), pp. 227-228; Emori, part 1, pp. 90-109.

[57] Fukuzumi Masae, as recorded by Yoshimoto Tadasu, quoted in *Sources of Japanese Tradition*, p. 586.

44

Here Fukuzumi expressed the twin themes that brought so many progressive landlords into the Hōtoku movement: character-building and practical improvements. These remained the primary emphases of the Hōtoku societies until they were taken over by the state early in the twentieth century.

There was more to Meiji Hōtoku thought, however, than ethics and technology (which after all had been staples since Ninomiya's time). Fukuzumi offered a reinterpretation of the Hōtoku tradition in *Fukoku shōkei* (Shortcut to Enriching the Country), written during 1873-1874. For Ninomiya's teachings to remain valid, he believed, men must understand that the way of nature meant the way of the Shinto gods (*kami*). He claimed that farm growth was not inconsistent with the new economic policies of the Meiji era:

> Making every effort to protect against poor crops, starvation, and epidemic, to assist the very poor, and to reverse declines, we place priority on encouraging both agriculture and industry to flourish, thus increasing production, causing wealth to accumulate, enriching the country, making all the people prosperous, carrying out the divine will of creation, and supporting the evolution of nature.[58]

It was now the "divine will of creation" that both agriculture and industry prosper—quite a departure from the farm-centered teachings of Ninomiya within a static, feudal understanding of economics. Yet both saint and disciple served the state to which each was loyal. Just as Ninomiya's doctrines appeared after 1868 to be conservative and tied to the feudal political culture of his era,[59] so Fukuzumi's en-

[58] Fukuzumi Masae, *Fukoku shōkei* [Shortcut to Enriching the Country], 1873-1874, quoted in Haraguchi, p. 268.

[59] On this point see Ogata, pp. 29-31; Denda, pp. 108-109; Hirose, p. 226; Okutani Matsuji, *Ninomiya Sontoku to Hōtokusha undō* [Ninomiya Sontoku and the Hōtokusha Movement] (Tokyo: Kōyō Shoin, 1936), p. 201; Haraguchi, p. 272.

thusiasm for linking agricultural improvement to the way of the gods and the development plans of the Meiji oligarchy seemed flawed by his ingenuous attachment to the religious and economic motifs of the new age.

Fukuzumi's only peer as a Hōtokusha organizer in the early Meiji period was the progressive landlord Okada Ryōichirō (1839-1915), who was less concerned than he with Shinto and correspondingly more interested in economic growth.[60] Most striking was Okada's belief that rural industrial development must parallel agricultural growth. One of his motives for entrepreneurship through the Hōtokusha was to provide employment for village residents and to stimulate productive activity that would improve rural conditions. More important seems to have been his assumption that national economic development depended on farming, by exporting rice, tea, and silk. More open to the rise of manufacturing than other Hōtoku leaders, Okada nevertheless insisted that industry be scattered throughout the countryside,[61] underlining his belief that the rural areas must be the foundation of national prosperity. Okada's outlook seems to have been affected by a utilitarian conviction that the simultaneous development of agriculture and industry would benefit the most persons (he is known to have read works by Jeremy Bentham and J. S. Mill).[62]

As a progressive rural entrepreneur in sericulture and food processing, Okada helped to update Hōtoku teachings by accommodating, to a degree, the drive for industrial growth of the Meiji period. At the same time he criticized the state for policies that favored manufacturing over farming, and he was a strong opponent of centralized industrialization induced from above. His ideas formed a type of producer class philosophy: within the limits of the landlord system and his belief in the primacy of agriculture, he was a

[60] For Okada see Denda, pp. 88-114; Haraguchi, pp. 272-282; Naramoto, pp. 170-175; Nakamura, *Kindai Nihon ni okeru seido to shisō*, p. 297.

[61] See Denda, pp. 107-108.   [62] Ibid., pp. 109-110.

great innovator, both in spreading credit, technology, and job opportunities and in encouraging individual initiative as a part of overall national economic growth.

By Okada's time, Hōtoku thought had clearly come very far from Ninomiya's outlook in the late feudal period. But Okada's seemingly progressive position was tenable only so long as farming dominated the economy. By the 1890s, as industrialism spread, the limitations of Okada's producer class assumptions became apparent, and the Hōtoku movement took on an increasingly conservative hue. Indeed, by the mid-1880s Okada had lost touch with local farming and devoted most of his time to administering national Hōtoku activities. In 1890 he moved to Tokyo, where he sat in the lower house of the Diet and contented himself with his sugar enterprises.

The fortunes of the Hōtoku movement in the first half of the Meiji period depended to a great extent on the practical leadership of Fukuzumi and Okada, but local economic conditions also had a bearing on the formation of new societies. To be sure, both Fukuzumi's focus on Shinto and Okada's concern for entrepreneurship were signs of a specific national consciousness not evident in Ninomiya's teachings a few decades earlier. This new consciousness helped them attune their movement to the new ideological requirements of the Meiji period and explains in part why Hōtoku societies continued to attract members. Yet the large number of new Hōtokusha formed in the mid-1880s showed a direct relationship to the economic miseries of the Matsukata deflation.[63] In the face of dropping farm prices and total rural debts of 200,000,000 yen, many peasants turned to rioting, most notably in the Chichibu uprising of November 1884.[64] Landowners, meanwhile, found the favorable Hōto-

[63] Of the 103 societies founded between 1874 and 1889, 64 were begun during the three years 1884 to 1886. Emori, part 1, p. 117.

[64] See Mikiso Hane, *Japan: A Historical Survey* (New York: Charles Scribner's Sons, 1972), pp. 304-306; Irwin Scheiner, "The Mindful Peasant: Sketches for a Study of Rebellion," *Journal of*

kusha credit arrangements to be one of the few avenues of escape from debt, especially in the rock bottom years 1884 and 1885. It seems likely that specific local problems of credit, debt, and taxes, rather than a theoretical commitment to the doctrines of Fukuzumi and Okada, prompted most landlords to join the Hōtokusha.[65] No doubt some progressive farmers shared their enthusiasm for national growth, but on the whole the movement's vicissitudes probably turned on immediate problems facing landowners in their day-to-day operations.

By the 1890s the Hōtoku organizations were approaching the limits of their effectiveness in promoting rural growth. The capital they mustered for village rehabilitation was modest in relation to the need, and small owner-farmers continued to slide into tenancy. More generally, Fukuzumi's echoes of Shinto mythology had an odd ring to many persons educated in the new school system or otherwise affected by the cosmopolitan influences of *bunmei kaika* in the earlier Meiji period. Even Okada's progressive Hōtoku doctrines appeared to many observers to be anachronistic, formalistic, and too cautious in tempo for the economic expansion and aggressive speculation of the 1890s.[66] Nevertheless the Hōtoku movement remained powerful in many regions through the end of the century and provided considerable backing for government farm proposals in the 1890s.

Just as the Hōtokusha played an important institutional part in the transition from an agrarian to a capitalist economy, they also contributed to a changing awareness of the economic significance of agriculture in many landlords'

Asian Studies, xxxii, 4, August 1973. At the University of California, Berkeley, Stephen Vlastos is preparing a study of the Fukushima peasant movement in mid-Meiji.

[65] See Saitō, p. 234; Okutani, Ninomiya Sontoku, pp. 262-274; Emori, part 1, pp. 98-99.

[66] Haraguchi, p. 272; Sakurai, *Nihon nōhonshugi*, p. 211; Nakamura, *Kindai Nihon ni okeru seido to shisō*, pp. 297-298.

minds during the period 1870-1895. Having restyled Ninomiya's premodern teachings to suit the fashion of a new
age, Hōtoku thought in the Meiji era stretched the farm-
first tradition but never burst it. Because agriculture remained its central pillar, the Hōtoku outlook gradually
turned into a special-interest ideology with the rise of industrial Japan. By the early twentieth century the Hōtoku
approach was so tamed that it received support and encouragement from the same central government whose
policies Okada had vigorously attacked a generation earlier.
When it became apparent that traditional farm-centered
ideologies such as Hōtokushugi could not remain vital in an
age of onrushing capitalism, the ground was cleared for true
Nōhonshugi—a body of ideas designed to counteract industrialism and reconstruct Japanese society by regaining
the virtues of an agricultural era now irretrievably past.

Early Meiji Farm Policies and Japanese Agrarianism

Both the official attitudes and policies toward farming and
the thought of conscientious farmers during the 1870s
and 1880s unquestionably played a critical part in the
nation's economic growth and permanently redirected the
course of agricultural development in Japan. Just as Fukuzumi and Okada recast Hōtoku ideas to fit their times, so too
the state farming programs and pronouncements differed
both in substance and in sentiment from the agricultural
outlook of the Tokugawa government. To some specialists,
this difference is sufficient to mark out the first half of the
Meiji period as the initial phase of the official proforming
ideology known as bureaucratic Nōhonshugi. Sakurai
Takeo, a provocative observer, regards Nōhonshugi as primarily a political doctrine created by the Meiji oligarchy to
preserve the farm villages on which their own power was
based.[67] Whereas the Tokugawa *bakufu* had revered agri-

[67] Sakurai, *Nihon nōhonshugi*, p. 81. See also Sakurai, "Nōhonshugi
—sono rekishi, riron, jiban," pp. 119-120; Sakurai Takeo, "Shōwa
no nōhonshugi" [Agrarianism in the Shōwa Period], *Shisō* [Thought],

culture "for its own sake" (jūnōshugi), Sakurai has written, Nōhonshugi now emerged as "a reflection of the contradiction between the development of bourgeois elements and feudal production relations (i.e., petty serf economics)."[68]

Okutani Matsuji, another modern scholar, has echoed Sakurai's view: "The formation of Nōhonshugi thought is premised on a crisis in the original feudal system, that is, the development of the commercial economy to a fixed stage, corresponding to the absolutist stage in politics"[69] (in the early Meiji period). Okutani acknowledges that an agricultural revolution had not yet taken place in Japan at this time, so that the oligarchy protected its rural base by resorting to premodern farm ideas. Also characteristic of early Meiji state agrarianism, Okutani maintains, was its strong support of the emperor system,[70] a carry-over from premodern society. Despite these wrinkles peculiar to Japan, Okutani concludes that official Nōhonshugi in the early Meiji period closely resembled the physiocratic economics of eighteenth-century France. He cites François Quesnay (1694-1774), Anne Robert Jacques Turgot (1727-1781), and Jean-Charles Léonard Simon de Sismondi (1773-1842) as critics of capitalism who upheld farming in an age of industrialization.[71] Like Japanese agrarian thinkers in both Tokugawa and Meiji times, they regarded agricultural labor alone as productive and saw it as the foundation of all other enterprise.

Although Sakurai and Okutani have properly noted that Nōhonshugi developed as a response to the growth of trade

---

No. 407, May 1958, pp. 42-54; Tsunazawa Mitsuaki, Nōhonshugi no kenkyū [Studies on Agrarianism] (Nagoya: Fūbaisha, 1968), pp. 10-12; Nakamura, Kindai Nihon ni okeru seido to shisō, pp. 278-281; Adachi Ikitsune, "Nōhonshugi no saikentō" [A Reappraisal of Theories on Agrarianism], Shisō, No. 423, September 1959, p. 57.

[68] Sakurai, "Nōhonshugi—sono rekishi, riron, jiban," p. 122.

[69] Okutani Matsuji, "Nihon ni okeru nōhonshugi shisō no nagare" [Trends in Agrarian Thought in Japan], Shisō, No. 407, May 1958, p. 3. See also Tsunazawa, pp. 17-19; Nakamura, Kindai Nihon ni okeru seido to shisō, pp. 281-285; Adachi, p. 52f.

[70] Okutani, "Nagare," p. 3.   [71] Ibid., pp. 1-2.

and industry, each appears to be premature in timing insofar as bureaucratic agrarianism is concerned. As diligent as the state may have been in stimulating industrial enterprises in the 1870s and 1880s, it is beyond dispute that the economy was still predominantly rural before the Sino-Japanese War, with insufficient capitalism for agrarian ideologies to react against. However elusive a concept Nōhonshugi may be, few of its primary attributes appear to have been present in the agricultural thinking of the early Meiji state. No important bureaucrats as yet trumpeted the merits of village communalism; little was heard of the subsequent theme that farming was at the heart of Japan's national essence. Indeed, the weight placed on Nōhonshugi as a political doctrine should not be permitted to obscure its equally important place in popular thought. It was not just an ideology of the establishment; in time its main stream became essentially antiestablishment. Most importantly, state agricultural thought stressed farm policy as a key element in Japan's overall program of modernization; true Nōhonshugi advocates, whether bureaucrats or private citizens, made farming a foil to the complications produced by that program.

What is more, to say that the oligarchs tried to preserve the farm village in its premodern condition in order to maintain their own political power is to overlook the growth-oriented objectives and progressive technical-educational programs of state farm policy after the restoration. Farm life was no doubt nearly as dull and burdensome in the late nineteenth century as it had been a hundred years earlier, but it seems unwarranted to portray Japanese agriculture by the mid-Meiji period as unchanged since antiquity.[72]

When Okutani identifies agrarianist thought with the "absolutist" politics of the earlier Meiji period, he appears to regard it as a response to political feudalism rather than to economic modernism. Indeed, by tying Nōhonshugi ideas to the physiocratic doctrines of prerevolutionary France, Oku-

[72] See Adachi, p. 58.

tani has virtually conceded that the so-called bureaucratic agrarianism of the period 1868-1890 was grounded in a preindustrial farm economy which merely wanted preservation, not yet restoration. Moreover, his emphasis on the connection between farming and the imperial institution seems to slight the nationalist objectives of the Meiji bureaucrats. As in all major state policies after 1868, service to the emperor was urged upon the cultivators not just to reinforce old bonds which had been neglected in the feudal era but primarily to pursue the new goals of wealth and power, symbolically sanctioned by the Meiji emperor.

One might well ask whether it is proper to equate physiocratic economics with Japanese farm thought in either the Tokugawa or Meiji eras. The French physiocrats believed that land was the only source of wealth, a proposition congenial to Neo-Confucian economics. Quesnay is rumored to have put it tersely: "Poor peasants, poor kingdom; poor kingdom, poor sovereign."[73] Physiocrats opposed the mercantilistic view that money was the essence of wealth and should be accumulated by each nation by minimizing imports. Instead, they believed in free trade, an unrestricted flow of capital, and reduced taxes.[74] To this end, Turgot advocated a single tax or *impôt unique*, on the net product of the land—the income of the landowning class.[75]

Free trade was almost unknown in Japanese agricultural discourses, either before the restoration or after. The prevailing view of the Edo period was that of the Neo-Confucianist Arai Hakuseki (1657-1725), who feared that foreign trade would harm the state. Even in the mid-nineteenth

[73] Léon Say, *Turgot*, trans. Melville B. Anderson (Chicago: A. C. McClurg & Co., 1888), p. 47.

[74] "Physiocratic School," *Encyclopedia Britannica* (Chicago, 1959), XVII, 885-886; Douglas Dakin, *Turgot and the Ancien Régime in France* (London: Methuen & Co., 1939), p. 295.

[75] See Mario Einaudi, *The Physiocratic Doctrine of Judicial Control* (Cambridge, Mass.: Harvard University Press, 1938), p. 11; Dakin, p. 296; Henry Higgs, *The Physiocrats* (London: Macmillan, 1897), pp. 11-13.

century, exclusionists in Japan clamored in a most unphysio-
cratic manner that the country was importing useless wool-
ens in exchange for the substance of wealth: gold, silver, and
copper.[76] Kanda Takahira (1830-1898), a Meiji modernizer
and otherwise no exclusionist, also took these precious
metals, not land, to be the real source of wealth. In the
Meiji era the state's near-mercantilist development policies
obviously transcended physiocratic economic philosophy,
and much later, in the twentieth century, those who advocated the return to a society based on village farming also
looked on international trade with suspicion. The French
physiocrats' interest in lower taxes likewise struck no responsive chords among government officials in Japan, before
or after 1868, although the same cannot, of course, be said
of the taxpayers themselves. Both the French physiocrats
and the popular agrarian ideologues in Japan arose during
hard times on the farms, and both resisted exorbitant taxes
imposed from above, which in the case of France were as
high as 82 percent of net produce.[77]

The physiocratic conception of politics was grounded on
a natural order in which few disputes arose so long as men
obeyed the rules of nature.[78] In this respect there was a
resemblance both with the Confucian idea of man and nature in the universe and with the communal natural philosophy of the Japanese countryside, with its Shinto overtones.
To insure that equal conditions and uniform rules prevailed,
the physiocrats favored a single despot whose prerogative
would be strictly limited to identifying the true natural law
in cases of conflict. This outlook was theoretically congenial with the Confucian notion of rule by virtue and
nonaction, although the Tokugawa state rarely conformed
to this ideal. Clearly the activism of the Meiji state exceeded

[76] William G. Beasley, "Introduction," *Select Documents on Japanese Foreign Policy, 1853-1868*, ed. William G. Beasley (London:
Oxford University Press, 1955), p. 9.

[77] Higgs, p. 10.

[78] See "Physiocratic School," p. 885; Einaudi, pp. 10-28.

by far the limited despotism envisioned by Quesnay and Turgot. The real parallel seems to arise in the village self-rule scheme of Gondō Seikyō (1868-1937) in the 1920s, since Gondō accepted the emperor but distrusted almost all other authorities above the village level.

Important exceptions to this overall pattern of dissimilarity between Japanese and French agrarianism can be culled from the vast body of economic thought bequeathed by the Tokugawa era. Dazai Shundai shared with the physiocrats not only the notion that all wealth came from the soil but also the idea that taxation should be based on the net product of the land.[79] Andō Shōeki sought a citizen-state of independent farmers who lived within the laws of nature under a limited political authority.[80] Still, it must be granted that the analogy between Japanese farm thought and French physiocratic economics is only partial. Not only did the two societies inherit different cultural traditions and confront different economic problems, but also the diversity of Japanese agrarianism makes it difficult to establish a precise correspondence with physiocratic ideas. As a rule, Japanese farm ideologues (with the exception of Ōkubo and others in the early Meiji period) favored small-scale agriculture, whereas Turgot and the other physiocrats held that large farms were the key to progress.[81]

In this respect Thomas Jefferson's vision of a nation of small farmers may come closer to the ideal sought by Japan's agrarian ideologues after the middle of the Meiji era. The physiocrats cared little more for the individual peasant's welfare than did the lofty Tokugawa Confucianists; they saw agriculture as a source of wealth, whereas to Jefferson it was a wellspring of human qualities that were requisite for self-rule. He wrote John Jay in 1785: "Cultivators of the earth are the most valuable citizens. They are the most vigorous, the most independent, the most virtuous, and

---

[79] Droppers, pp. xi-xii. [80] Norman, pp. 299-303.
[81] Say, p. 51.

they are tied to their country, and wedded to its liberty and interests by the most lasting bonds. . . . I consider the class of artificers as the panders of vice, and the instruments by which the liberties of a country are generally overturned."[82] Yet while Jefferson stressed liberty and citizenship, his Japanese counterparts usually emphasized subjecthood, communalism, and men's obligations to others within the self-ruling village.

Two conclusions seem to emerge. First, the evidence for similarity between French physiocratic thinking and Japanese agrarianism is conflicting, sometimes contradictory. Second, the official view of agriculture during the earlier Meiji period was neither especially physiocratic nor very harmonious with the thought of those subsequent agrarian ideologues known as Nōhonshugisha. It is to the growth of their ideas that I shall now turn.

[82] Thomas Jefferson to John Jay, August 23, 1785, quoted in A. Whitney Griswold, *Farming and Democracy* (New York: Harcourt Brace, 1948), p. 31.

Chapter III

Bureaucratic Agrarianism in the 1890s

THE surprising victory over the forces of the Ch'ing Empire in 1894-1895, a bold accomplishment in its own right, was also a sign that times in Japan had changed greatly, both in substance and in mood, since the 1868 restoration. Together with the creation of parliamentary government in 1889, the abolition of the unequal treaties with the European powers in 1899, and the victory over Russia in 1904-1905, Japan's triumph in the Sino-Japanese War was a giant step forward in the national effort to pull level with the West. The war coincided with a rising sentiment of nationalism in the 1890s, as a "new generation"[1] of administrators, writers, businessmen, educators, journalists, and politicians expressed a fresh sense of national self-confidence in contrast with the cultural self-abasement of the 1870s.

Partly as a result of the war, the 1890s was also a decade of great economic change and expansion. Both imports and exports doubled, and a number of large-scale industries became established, a trend encouraged by the government for

[1] Kenneth B. Pyle's phrase, in *The New Generation in Meiji Japan* (Stanford: Stanford University Press, 1969). See also Donald Keene, "The Sino-Japanese War of 1894-95 and Its Cultural Effects in Japan," *Tradition and Modernization in Japanese Culture*, ed. Donald H. Shively (Princeton: Princeton University Press, 1971), pp. 121-175, on postwar nationalism.

56

political and military reasons.[2] The Sino-Japanese War
affected agriculture profoundly, although indirectly, by ac-
celerating industrialization and thus redefining the relative
importance of farming and the urban sector. This fact,
together with long-term forces such as inflation, the spread
of technical education, peasant unrest, the concentration of
landownership in fewer hands, and the failure of the government's large-scale farming program, helps to account for the
major shifts in state agricultural policy which had occurred
by 1900. By that date the government had taken a number
of steps to fortify small-scale farming in the aftermath of
rural depression and tenant unrest in the 1880s, culminating
in the agricultural association law (Nōkaihō) of 1899 and
the producers' cooperative law (Sangyō Kumiaihō) of 1900.
At this point it is possible to identify the first concrete effects
of Nōhonshugi ideas on government farm policy.

The changing perceptions of rural needs that underlay
these measures can be traced primarily to new outlooks
within the Ministry of Agriculture and Commerce (Nōshōmushō) and other bureaucratic agencies, especially the views
of such officials as Ishikawa Rikinosuke (1845-1915), Maeda
Masana (1850-1921), Shinagawa Yajirō (1843-1900), and
Hirata Tōsuke (1849-1925). Each supported small-scale
farming and thought that the state should bolster the village
landowning classes, not only as a way of increasing production but also as a means of forestalling rural decay provoked
by industrialization. Their efforts, fortified from below by
support from landlord-dominated organizations such as the
Hōtokusha, brought about important changes in state attitudes and policies toward farming by the end of the century.

Ishikawa and Maeda: Landlord-Officials and the Protection of Small-Scale Farming

Two groups of government officials in the 1890s deserve
credit for the gradual reorientation of state approaches to

[2] Mikiso Hane, *Japan: A Historical Survey* (New York: Charles
Scribner's Sons, 1972), p. 332.

farming. One consisted of senior, cabinet-rank career bureaucrats and members of the Genrōin (Council of Elders), such as Shinagawa Yajirō, Hirata Tōsuke, and Tani Kanjō (1837-1911). The other was a loose group of officials at various rungs of local and national government who were also progressive landlords. The senior bureaucrats were naturally more instrumental in seeing new laws through the Diet, while landlord-officials like Ishikawa Rikinosuke and Maeda Masana were especially effective in sensitizing Japanese politicians and administrators to the concerns of progressive but discomfited village landholders, such as those who joined the Hōtoku movement.

Although their careers were often dissimilar, both Ishikawa and Maeda spent years in public service and also devoted a great deal of time to private farming. Each represented that segment of the village leadership, the *tokunō*, which was open to technical innovation and educational change and accepted the need for national economic growth —provided farming was not slighted in the process. In the long run, this conscientious farming outlook foundered because it could not elude the stubborn fact that a country trying to industrialize with limited resources almost inevitably places a low priority on protecting agriculture. Still, men like Ishikawa and Maeda, in their dual capacities as farmers and officials, represented a powerful interest to the national government in the 1890s. As a bridge between *tokunō* attitudes and the bureaucratic agrarianism of Shinagawa, Hirata, and Tani, they spoke for the larger landowners who still worked at least a part of their lands directly, persons who were adversely affected by the deflationary policies of the 1880s and the gradual advance of capitalism a decade later.

Ishikawa came to his interest in enhancing small-scale farming directly from the soil.[3] Born in 1845 to a farm fam-

[3] For Ishikawa see Takehana Yūkichi, *Akita no hitobito* [Persons from Akita] (Akitaken: Kōhō Kyōkai, 1964), pp. 6-25; Koide Kōzō, *Kyōdo o okoshita senjin no omokage* [Memories of Fore-

58

ily on the outskirts of Akita, he devoted seven years to reviving the Ishikawa family lands before accepting a post in the prefectural industrial development section in 1873. He left office in 1885 and set about rehabilitating his own *buraku*, Yamada, which had been jolted by depression. He drafted a seven-year village development plan which was successfully completed in about five years. At Maeda Masana's urging, he later became an itinerant lecturer on modern farm technology and traveled as far as Kyushu.

Ishikawa is best known for a method of village self-help which he called *tekisanchō*, or appropriate production investigation. Each village, he believed, should conduct careful land surveys, take stock of its natural and human resources, and determine the most appropriate crops to grow and products to emphasize. Equally important, he argued, was character building: "The main point of *tekisanchō* is not simply to check the soil qualities of fields and paddies. Rather the most important thing is to create talented men. If we do not nurture talented men, it will not matter how much profit or economy we have. These talented men must have honorable feelings toward mother nature."[4] These words carry obvious premodern Confucian overtones, especially in their emphasis on *jinzai*, or talented persons, and they also note farmers' obligations to nature. But Ishikawa agreed with Hōtoku leaders such as Fukuzumi and Okada that economic growth and increased production were important not just for the village but also for the whole country. The paradoxical nature of Ishikawa's traditionalistic yet progressive farm outlook may have enhanced its appeal to

---

bears Who Revived Their Home Towns] (Tokyo: Nihon Jichi Kensetsu Honbu, 1958), pp. 1-22; Kodama Shōtarō, *Ijin Ishikawaō no jigyō to genkō* [Words and Deeds of the Illustrious Ishikawa] (Tokyo: Heibonsha, 1929), pp. 177-188, 370-414, 474-488; Kawakami Tomizō, *Ishikawa Rikinosuke* (Akitaken, Shōwamachi: Ishikawaō Iseki Hozonkai, 1964), pp. 130-144.

[4] Ishikawa Rikinosuke, "Tekisanchō yōryō" [Outline of Appropriate Production Regulation], 1896, quoted in Kodama, p. 383.

both conscientious farmers eager for technical improvements and didactic landlords who could not accept the more pious moralizing of the Hōtoku school. Yet most significant was his role, as a person with wide government contacts, in pleading for farm development policies which placed local landowners' interests uppermost.

More progressive and more influential than Ishikawa in supporting small-scale farming was the landlord-official Maeda Masana.[5] After studying in France for six years, Maeda returned to Japan in early 1877 to take a post in the Ministry of Finance, dealing with foreign trade, and in 1879 was assigned to investigate farm conditions for the ministry. When the Ministry of Agriculture and Commerce was formed in November 1880, Maeda was given a concurrent appointment in it as well. His duties took him on inspection tours all over Japan in the early 1880s, exhorting farmers to produce more crops and handicrafts for export while simultaneously witnessing the depressing effects of Matsukata's deflationary measures.

The result of his travels throughout the countryside was a policy paper prepared for the Nōshōmushō in late 1884,

[5] For Maeda see *Kōgyō ikenta—Maeda Masana kankei shiryō* ["Advice on Promoting Enterprise" *et al.*—Materials Relating to Maeda Masana], ed. Andō Yoshio and Yamamoto Hirobumi (Tokyo: Kōseikan, 1971); Soda Osamu, *Maeda Masana* (Tokyo: Yoshikawa Kōbunkan, 1973); Chō Yukio, "Nashonarizumu to 'sangyō' undō—Maeda Masana no shisō to katsudō" [Nationalism and the "Production" Movement—The Career and Thought of Maeda Masana], *Kindai Nihon keizai shisōshi* [History of Modern Japanese Economic Thought], ed. Chō Yukio and Sumiya Kazuhiko (Tokyo: Yūhikaku, 1969), I, 85-113; Kajinishi Mitsuhaya, "Maeda Masana," *Nihon jinbutsushi taikei* [Outline History of Talented Persons in Japan], ed. Konishi Shirō (Tokyo: Asakura Shoten, 1960), V, 284-311; Okutani Matsuji, "Nihon ni okeru nōhonshugi shisō no nagare" [Trends in Agrarian Thought in Japan], *Shisō* [Thought], No. 407, May 1958, p. 5; Denda Isao, *Kindai Nihon keizai shisō no kenkyū—Nihon no kindaika to chihō keizai* [Studies on Modern Japanese Economic Thought—Japanese Modernization and Rural Economics] (Tokyo: Miraisha, 1962), pp. 114-123.

entitled "Kōgyō iken" (Advice on Promoting Enterprise). This document, which formed the basis for state farm policies in the late 1880s, upheld the Meiji goals of industrialization and national wealth but called for greater attention to farming. Maeda believed that a shortage of capital blocked growth ("capital does not match enterprise"),[6] and he pressed for more government loans, reduced interest rates and transport charges, agricultural societies in the villages, new farm technology, and more experiment centers. Coupled with aid from the state, he said, should be greater forbearance and diligence by farmers.[7]

Maeda hoped to reorganize Japanese agriculture as the basis for national industrial growth by creating greater investment capital through overseas trade. Like Okada Ryōichirō and Ishikawa Rikinosuke, he thought village prosperity was vital for a thriving national economy. Maeda's policies in 1884, however, included fewer moral injunctions to peasants than Ishikawa or the Hōtoku movement. Much of what he proposed in "Kōgyō iken" became state farm policy in the late 1880s and early 1890s (especially the spread of technical information and formation of agricultural associations), even though Maeda left office after a government reshuffle in 1885 and did not return for four years.

After reentering public life as a Nōshōmushō department head and member of the Council of Elders, he published

---

[6] Maeda Masana, "Kōgyō iken" [Advice on Promoting Enterprise], 1884, quoted in Thomas C. Smith, *Political Change and Industrial Development in Japan: Government Enterprise, 1868-1880* (Stanford: Stanford University Press, 1955), p. 37. This work is reprinted in *Meiji zenki zaisei keizai shiryō shūsei* [Collected Materials on Early Meiji Finances and Economics], xviii, 1931. On Maeda's policies, see Denda, pp. 97-99, 117-123; Chō, pp. 99-113; *Agricultural Development in Modern Japan*, ed. Takekazu Ogura, 2nd ed. (Tokyo: Fuji Publishing Co., 1968), pp. 156-157 (hereafter cited as Ogura); Denda Isaō, *Kindai Nihon nōsei shisō no kenkyū* [Studies on Modern Japanese Agricultural Administration Thought] (Tokyo: Miraisha, 1969), pp. 74-75.

[7] Denda, *Nōsei*, p. 137.

Shoken (Findings) in 1892, setting forth new prescriptions for Japanese agriculture. Here Maeda distinguished between the "characteristic industries of Japan," the rural ones which should be encouraged, and the newly risen "mechanized industries,"[8] which should be minimized. Although he attacked "parasitic" urban interests which threatened the rural basis of society, Maeda was equally critical of village stand patters who refused to try the new technology: "When we consider why Japanese agriculture does not advance, we find that it is clearly due solely to the fact that agriculturalists adhere determinedly to barbarous practices and are devoid of any ideas of a scientific kind."[9] He concluded with a list of proposals for raising farm output and called on the government to intervene on behalf of the rural producer classes, to redress the favoritism heretofore shown to urban industries.

Maeda left office in October 1893 and devoted the rest of his life to farm organizations in his capacity as a large landowner. His goal was still to increase exports and thereby augment the national wealth, but he no longer relied on the state to get the job done quickly. He not only served as chief secretary of the quasi-official Dai Nihon Nōkai after April 1894 but also formed rural associations that helped to stimulate the producers' cooperative law of 1900.[10] Because he attacked mechanization, thought that village landowners could best lead economic progress, and encouraged farmers in Confucianistic terms, Maeda is often ranked as a conservative defender of landlords' interests[11] who used his official

[8] Maeda Masana, *Shoken* [Findings], 1892, quoted in Okutani, "Nagare," p. 5.

[9] Maeda Masana, *Shoken* [Findings], 1892, quoted in John R. McEwan, "The Confucian Ideology and the Modernization of Japan," *The Modernization of Japan*, ed. Tōbata Seiichi (Tokyo: Institute of Asian Economic Affairs, 1966), I, 240.

[10] Chō, p. 93.

[11] See Adachi Ikitsune, "Nōhonshugi no saikentō" [A Reappraisal of Theories on Agrarianism], *Shisō*, No. 423, September 1959, pp. 56-57, 60-61; McEwan, p. 238.

posts to shore up agriculture in an age of industrialization. Paradoxically, he had a clearer vision of national economic needs and a more open attitude toward technical change than most of the conscientious farmers of his era. Maeda worked closely with the Hōtokusha in the 1890s to muster support for farm bills in the Diet, but his thought was much more technocratically oriented than Fukuzumi's, Okada's, or even Ishikawa's. Maeda approached farm betterment through statistics, surveys, resource studies, and the other scientific trappings of formal agricultural administration (*nōsei*).

Consistently a nationalist in long-range objective, Maeda trusted central government as a friend of the farms far more than most agrarian thinkers in his era.[12] His shift to private rural organizing in the 1890s was more a result of state inaction than a rejection of centralized power, even though he ended up working closely with men such as Ishikawa and Okada in building local landowners' organizations and credit societies. To the extent that he thought agriculture should serve the growth programs of the central state, Maeda stood apart from both the Hōtoku movement and the later champions of a farm-first policy. But to the degree that he wanted productivity to originate in the countryside, and insofar as he chided the government for favoring urban-centered manufacturing, Maeda was one of the earliest partisans of Nōhonshugi.

Shinagawa, Hirata, and the Credit Association Bill of 1891

The pump priming, procurement, and overall stimulus of the Sino-Japanese War were the most visible economic activities of the Meiji regime in the 1890s. But the decade was also one of busy state efforts in agricultural affairs. With the exception of the occupation era after World War II, no other period in Japanese history has produced so many

---

[12] On this point see Denda, *Keizai shisō*, p. 114; Chō, p. 111.

laws, edicts, and regulations affecting farming, nor has any other decade been characterized by such ardent debate within the government over agricultural policy.

In the confusing stream of legislative proposals dealing with farming in the 1890s, certain measures favored large landlords and others appealed to smaller owner-cultivators, as befitted the shifting nature of the landowning classes. In general the state's farm policies aimed at revitalizing the rural economy, after the crises of the 1880s, to serve as a continuing foundation for national industrial expansion. Among the most important laws were the credit association bill of 1891, the national agricultural experiment station legislation of 1893, rural banking acts in 1896 and 1897, the farmland replotment law of 1899, the agricultural association law in the same year, and the producers' cooperative law of 1900. Government policy, as reflected in this legislation, had now become firmly rooted in the small-farm system. From these programs emerged a new theme that deserves attention: the first conscious justifications by high administrators for protecting smaller landowners against both industrialism and the commercialization of large landlords. Shinagawa Yajirō (1843-1900) and Hirata Tōsuke (1849-1925) were two powerful bureaucrats who promoted the interests of small farmers in the last decade of the nineteenth century.

Shinagawa and Hirata are best known, insofar as farm policy is concerned, for their support of the 1891 credit association bill and the producers' cooperative law in 1900, but both had been strong adherents of small farming even when the state was promoting large-scale agriculture in the early Meiji era. Shinagawa was born in 1843 to a Chōshū warrior family in the castle town of Hagi and at the age of fifteen became a student of the outspoken exclusionist Yoshida Shōin (1830-1859).[13] After the 1868 restoration he

[13] For Shinagawa see Okutani Matsuji, *Shinagawa Yajirō den* [Biography of Shinagawa Yajirō] (Tokyo: Kōyō Shoin, 1940); Denda, *Nōsei*, pp. 81-89; Sakurai Takeo, *Nihon nōhonshugi* [Japanese Agrarianism] (Tokyo: Hakuyōsha, 1935), pp. 203-204; Roger F.

was sent to Europe by the new government and served as a consular official in Germany from 1874 to 1876, later returning as ambassador in 1886-1887. He subsequently married the niece of the great statesman Yamagata Aritomo (1838-1922) and became something of an *éminence grise* in party politics in the 1890s, maneuvering unsuccessfully in 1892 to rig Diet elections in favor of government candidates.[14]

After coming back to Japan in 1876, Shinagawa held a series of offices in the Ministry of Internal Affairs (Naimushō) and, after 1880, in the new Ministry of Agriculture and Commerce. He soon vigorously opposed the prevailing proindustry outlook of the state, writing in 1884:

Agriculture is the foundation of the family and the foundation of the country. First came the fields, then families and villages, and then the country began. . . . Thus agriculture must be called the basis of all occupations and the foundation of the state. Japan originally used agriculture to establish a state, and all such things as public taxes and families' food and clothing came from the land. All sorts of institutions were also based on farming. This may be called a true agriculture based country.[15]

Shinagawa opposed commercialized farming and the state's drive to export rural crops because they exploited the small farmer. Instead, he encouraged a spirit of self-reliance and frugality for farmers, and when he became minister of internal affairs in 1891 he pressed for a national system of credit associations to help destitute small farmers regain prosperity.

Hackett, *Yamagata Aritomo in the Rise of Modern Japan, 1838-1922* (Cambridge, Mass.: Harvard University Press, 1971), passim.

[14] For accounts of this episode, see Hackett, pp. 150-152; George Akita, *Foundations of Constitutional Government in Modern Japan, 1868-1900* (Cambridge, Mass.: Harvard University Press, 1967), pp. 97-100.

[15] Shinagawa Yajirō, 1884, quoted in Denda, *Nōsei*, pp. 87-88.

Unlike Shinagawa, Hirata Tōsuke was not a clansman of the leading Meiji oligarchs, but he rose to even greater heights to become, with Kiyoura Keigo (1850-1942), one of Yamagata's two closest political associates after 1890.[16] Born in 1849 as the son of a samurai in Yonezawa fief in modern Yamagata Prefecture, Hirata joined the Iwakura mission after the restoration and stayed on to study in Germany, where he became friends with the young diplomat Shinagawa. After returning to Japan he took a post in the Ministry of Finance and became related by marriage to both Yamagata and Shinagawa. In 1890 he became a member of the house of peers (Kizokuin) and joined the privy council. As a Yamagata protégé, he was appointed minister of agriculture and commerce in the first Katsura cabinet (1901), later served in the Imperial Household Ministry, and topped off his career in 1922 when he was designated lord keeper of the privy seal.

Like Shinagawa, Hirata had been deeply impressed by the credit cooperative movement during his stay in Germany, and in 1891, with his appointment to head the legal bureau (Hōseikyoku), came the opportunity to work toward creating credit associations in Japan. With Shinagawa's advice and encouragement, Hirata drafted a credit association bill (Shin'yō Kumiai Hōan) and presented it to the second Diet in 1891. His model was the German industrial and economic organization law of 1889, reflecting the thought of Franz Hermann Schulze-Delitzsch (1808-1883), a cooperative leader who stressed self-help, local autonomy, and frugality.[17] Hirata's draft provided for credit units under the general supervision of the Ministry of Internal Affairs,

---

[16] For Hirata see Hackett, passim; Katō Fusakura, *Hakushaku Hirata Tōsuke den* [Biography of Count Hirata Tōsuke] (Tokyo: Hiratahaku Denki Hensan Jimusho, 1927), pp. 95-193; Tsunazawa Mitsuaki, *Kindai Nihon no dochaku shisō—nōhonshugi kenkyū* [Modern Japanese Home Town Thought—Studies on Agrarianism] (Nagoya: Fūbaisha, 1969), pp. 16-28; Denda, *Nōsei*, pp. 138-143.

[17] Okutani, *Shinagawa*, p. 266; Tsunazawa, pp. 20-21.

not the Ministry of Finance, conforming with the revised local self-rule regulations put into effect by the Naimushō in 1888-1890. In this way he hoped to make the village, town, or city a virtually autonomous basis of organization for the credit societies, in line with Schulze-Delitzsch's precepts.

The basic purpose of the bill was to establish rural credit associations that would make more money available to the "backbone owner-cultivators" (*chūken jisakunō*) throughout Japan, now that the world market economy had entered the countryside. When the bill reached the Diet on November 28, 1891, Shinagawa argued its merits in a speech to the Kizokuin, first reviewing Japan's economic progress since 1868 and then citing the adverse effects of capitalism on the farm villages: "The tendency of the so-called poor people to weaken is exceedingly deplorable. According to a survey in 1884-1885, debts secured by land reached 200,300,000 yen. What is more, when we look at the number of land sales recorded in 1887, 78 percent of them did not exceed twenty-five yen."[18] This meant, of course, not only that the aggregate rural debt was gigantic but also that the number of debtors was very high, since most land transactions (many of them foreclosures) involved very small plots.

"Small farmers, merchants, and craftsmen," Shinagawa continued, "truly occupy an essential position in national production, and I believe they constitute the foundation of the nation. However, as you know, these essential people who are small- and medium-sized producers are tending to

[18] Shinagawa Yajirō, 1891 Kizokuin speech, quoted in Tsunazawa, p. 17. The entire speech is reprinted in Okutani, *Shinagawa*, pp. 267-272. Tsunazawa estimates that the depression caused a 41 percent drop in the number of landholders who paid taxes of five yen or more between 1881 and 1895. Since five yen was the minimum property qualification for voting for representatives in the Diet, fewer persons were qualified in 1895 (1,079,447) than might have voted in 1881 (1,809,610) if elections had been held in that year. See Tsunazawa, p. 15.

lose their productive capacity. It is a terrible situation."[19] It was therefore urgent, he concluded, to shield the little man from the growing concentration of economic power in fewer hands:

> The government earlier resolutely enacted a new system of local self-rule, . . . but if it does not create ways to protect the output of smaller producers, I believe that the main point of providing a self-rule system will have been discarded. What then about the expansion of national authority and the development of national power? By providing credit facilities for the smaller producers, the credit association bill which the government has introduced here will make it possible for them to use capital at low interest and at the same time will encourage a spirit of industry and self-help. Thus its object is to nurture local efficiency.[20]

Hirata defended the bill in similar terms, reflecting his determination to protect the small village landowner as the cornerstone of national development:

> Thus living is very difficult for smaller producers, who comprise the great majority of the national population. The nation's productive power is bound to waste away. If we do not establish facilities for making credit available to the people who use cash—the smaller producers who are now so agitated—if we do not develop their productive powers and find a way to deal with the free competition economy, we will live to regret it someday. The facilities we need are precisely credit associations.[21]

[19] Shinagawa Yajirō, 1891 Kizokuin speech, quoted in Sakurai Takeo, "Nōhonshugi—sono rekishi, riron, jiban" [Agrarianism—Its History, Theory, and Foundation], Rekishi kagaku [Science of History], IV, 3, March 1935, 127.

[20] Shinagawa Yajirō, 1891 Kizokuin speech, quoted in Tsunazawa, p. 17.

[21] Hirata Tōsuke, "Shin'yō kumiairon" [On Credit Associations], 1891, quoted in Tsunazawa, p. 16.

Shinagawa and Hirata agreed that economic progress for Japan rested securely on small landholding. They accepted the inevitability of commercialization but wanted to counter its competitive advantages by making the lifeblood of capitalism—money—much more widely available to the small producers. But "industry and self-help," as Shinagawa noted, were also important; neither of these bureaucrats saw any contradiction in blending premodern and capitalist elements to aid small farming. Here was an undeniably new emphasis in official agricultural thought in Japan: the specific acknowledgement, at the highest level of the national administration, that farming must be fortified against the spread of a commercial economy if it was to continue to contribute to overall national development.

Also new to Nōhonshugi was Shinagawa's interest in self-rule. He had even less faith than Maeda Masana in the central government's capacity to manage economic development, inasmuch as state planning since the 1870s had done little for small-scale agriculture. Shinagawa certainly was no anarchist. He believed in national strength, and to some extent he had accepted the self-rule system instituted in 1888-1890 only because of popular pressures from the Jiyū Minken (Freedom and Popular Rights) movement.[22] But he also sought a society based on strong village units, imbued with the communalism (*kyōdōtai*) of premodern times. He repeatedly urged that "people's production" be the cornerstone of Meiji economic expansion, and he consistently maintained that smaller producers, organized in self-ruling units, should be "the basis of the state."[23] Credit associations, he hoped, would become the economic underpinning of the new self-rule system.

Hirata and Shinagawa, the first major exemplars of bureaucratic Nōhonshugi, affirmed a faith in the virtues of farm production and producer alike, sought to shore up farming—especially small farming—against commercializa-

[22] Tsunazawa, p. 18.   [23] Denda, *Nōsei*, p. 87.

tion, supported a high degree of local political autonomy, and favored the social solidarity of the village community. Merely by popularizing agrarianist thought in high places, they played a big part in spreading Nōhonshugi views. Clearly the German credit system influenced their proposal, but to what degree did their ideas resemble the doctrines of the Hōtoku movement and other agrarian thinkers in the early Meiji period?

In presenting the credit bill to the Diet, Shinagawa himself acknowledged the link with the Hōtokusha: "There are many precedents for organizing credit associations," he said—the medieval cooperatives (*kō*, *mujin*, or *tanomoshi*), the five-family neighborhood associations (*goningumi*), and the Hōtokusha.[24] For some years Shinagawa had been close to Fukuzumi Masae and Okada Ryōichirō, and he had been instrumental in having the government publish Tomita Takayoshi's *Hōtokuki* in 1883. Shinagawa also had a hand in arranging posthumous honors for Ninomiya Sontoku in 1891. Hirata is said to have approached Fukuzumi and Okada for advice before drafting the credit bill in 1891,[25] the beginning of even greater government cooperation with the Hōtokusha in the 1890s. Both Shinagawa and Hirata, in other words, were plainly familiar with Hōtoku thought when they launched their credit association movement.

The Shin'yō Kumiai and Hōtokusha resembled each other in that they both spoke of the traditional rural virtues

[24] Shinagawa Yajirō, 1891 Kizokuin speech, quoted in Sakurai, *Nihon nōhonshugi*, p. 210. See also Kiyoshi Ogata, *The Co-operative Movement in Japan* (London: P. S. King & Son, Ltd., 1923), p. 2; Galen M. Fisher, "The Cooperative Movement in Japan," *Pacific Affairs*, XI, 4, December 1938, 478.

[25] Emori Itsuo, "Meijiki no Hōtokusha undō no shiteki shakaiteki haikei" [Historical and Social Background of the Meiji Period Hōtokusha Movement], *Hōritsu ronsō* [Collection of Legal Theories], Meiji University, part 1, XL, 1, October 1966, 116; Naramoto Tatsuya, *Ninomiya Sontoku* (Tokyo: Iwanami Shoten, 1959), p. 162; Sakurai, *Nihon nōhonshugi*, p. 207; Emori, part 2, XL, 2-3, November 1966, 47-49; Tsunazawa, p. 19.

of thrift and hard work. Each valued the premodern family and *buraku* systems, and each was concerned with lending money to increase farm output on a village-by-village basis. However, the typical Hōtokusha depended on rich landlords for deposits and tried to embrace all farmers, from tenants to large landholders, within its membership. The credit associations, by contrast, relied on government funds (albeit locally administered) and to some degree were designed to offset the economic power of large property owners, many of whom were now living in cities. But the real difference between Shinagawa and Hirata on the one hand and Okada, Fukuzumi, and even Ishikawa Rikinosuke on the other was a matter of timing and tempo in Japanese modernization. Meiji Hōtoku thought represented a progressive mix of ethical and practical instructions for betterment within the matrix of a predominantly agricultural society. The credit association movement, arising twenty years later when industry was beginning to challenge agriculture in importance, was obliged to cope with a degree of commercialism unforeseen by Okada and Fukuzumi in the 1870s. As a result, the Shin'yō Kumiai hoped to revive and restore not just the economic well-being but also the social and political position of the small farmer—something the early Meiji Hōtoku movement had still taken pretty much for granted.

Hirata attacked the Hōtokusha for their quaint conservatism in the milieu of the 1890s, criticizing in particular the idea of fulfilling one's station in life as too feudal.[26] He nevertheless conceded that the Hōtokusha were good organizational paradigms for the credit societies. It seems appropriate to describe the credit associations as modern organizations designed to deal with new problems of economic growth unimagined by Okada, Fukuzumi, and Ishikawa, no matter how much these men favored national

[26] Emori, part 2, pp. 52-53. On the Hōtokusha connection with the Shin'yō Kumiai, see also Tsunazawa, pp. 19-20; Emori, part 2, pp. 52-64; Okutani, "Nagare," p. 5; Ogata, pp. 45-46.

economic growth. Shinagawa and Hirata were at once more progressive and more traditionalistic than the Hōtoku leaders. They spoke less often of the updated feudal farm virtues than had their predecessors, and on the whole they stressed rational planning to spread the flow of capital to farmers. Yet they were also the first important agrarian ideologues within the government to talk seriously of restoring local self-rule and village communalism, since only in the 1890s was it apparent that these were growing extinct.

Owner-Cultivators and the Producers' Cooperative Law of 1900

The credit association bill of 1891 failed to become law because the second Diet was dissolved before action could be taken.[27] It is difficult to estimate, except *ex silentio*, whether any significant opposition to the measure existed. We may infer a lack of broad enthusiasm from the fact that the proposal was not revived until it had been transformed into the producers' cooperative bill six years later. In the interim Hirata and Shinagawa bent great efforts to found private, self-financing credit associations, often with the cooperation of the Hōtoku movement. Beginning with two societies in Shizuoka in 1892, credit associations multiplied until at least ninety-five of them had been created by the turn of the century.[28] Economic strains produced by the Sino-Japanese War no doubt encouraged the rise of credit societies after 1895, just as they provoked rice riots and demands for rent reductions among tenants in some sections of the country.[29]

Although the Diet failed to enact the credit bill, a great deal of important farm legislation was passed in the 1890s, much of it catering to large landlords. For example, the

[27] Okutani, *Shinagawa*, pp. 275-276; Tsunazawa, p. 21; Ogura, p. 251.

[28] Okutani, *Shinagawa*, p. 319. Denda, *Nōsei*, p. 89, gives the figure of 171 associations.

[29] See Okutani, "Nagare," p. 6.

revised civil code (Minpō) put into effect in 1898 acknowledged the Hōtokusha as legal organizations, and it also
conferred recognition on many customary landlord rights
without doing the same for tenants.[30] The state tried to
encourage land improvements through tax exemptions, especially in the farmland replotment law of 1899. This act
was intended to improve crop yields now that Japan had
become a net importer of rice after the Sino-Japanese War,
but it primarily benefited large landowners[31] and did nothing
to correct the conditions which Shinagawa and Hirata had
attacked. The government also promoted new rice inspection plans that offered incentives mainly to landlords.[32]
When the Diet finally voted credit for rural improvements,
it did so first by passing the Hypothec Bank of Japan and
Agricultural and Industrial Bank laws of 1897. Unlike the
credit association proposal of 1891, these laws created central
banks, controlled by national and prefectural officials, which
because of stiff security requirements in real property made
loans, in effect, only to large landlords.[33]

Most emblematic of the large landowner bias of state
agricultural policy during these years was the agricultural
association law (Nōkaihō) of 1899. Local farm discussion
societies had existed for many years, and since 1881 they
had been placed under the umbrella of the quasi-official Dai
Nihon Nōkai. The state found the local agricultural associations inadequate for implementing the new farm technology
it favored, while local leaders regarded the Nōkai as ineffective channels for representing their interests to the government. The 1899 law tried to remedy both deficiencies. It
required every local and prefectural political unit to have an
agricultural society, supported by public funds. The state

[30] Ogata, pp. 54-55; Ogura, p. 126.
[31] Ogura, pp. 240-242.
[32] Ann Waswo, "Landlords and Social Change in Prewar Japan,"
Ph.D. dissertation in history, Stanford University, 1969, pp. 65-66;
Ogura, pp. 163-164.
[33] Ogura, pp. 20-21, 263-264.

regarded this as a great step forward, since official organizations now existed everywhere to carry out its technical programs. At the same time, large landlords were pleased by the law's provision that only they must join the associations (for other farmers membership was optional). This gave large landholders de facto domination of the Nōkai.[34] At the apex sat the Imperial Agricultural Association, or Teikoku Nōkai, founded in 1910 as the successor to the Dai Nihon Nōkai. By 1917 there were 557 county and 48 urban agricultural associations throughout the country, beneath which 11,573 local units acted as agricultural extension societies for the state and as sounding boards for the interests of landlords.[35]

Such government activity on behalf of large landlords reflected the changing fortunes of the big property-owning class after the Sino-Japanese War. Large landlords were pressing the government (through the Nōkai, for example) for support in collecting rents, since many obstreperous tenants were refusing to pay in the late 1890s. What is more, the land tax had been raised in 1899, and would be raised again in 1904 and 1905, creating pressures for subsidies to landholders by way of partial compensation. Thirdly, more and more landlords left the land for the comforts and profitable investment opportunities of the cities as rents commanded by tenancy rose, and fewer progressive farmers of the sort typified by Ishikawa and Maeda were left behind to take an interest in agricultural innovation, forcing the state to fill the void.[36] As a consequence, the government

---

[34] Ibid., pp. 248-249, 303-304; Denda, *Nōsei*, p. 133.

[35] Ogata, p. 97; Ogura, p. 248.

[36] See Ogura Takekazu, *Agrarian Problems and Agricultural Policy in Japan* (Tokyo: Institute of Asian Economic Affairs, 1967), p. 12. Ann Waswo identifies 1900 as the point after which it grew less profitable to work one's own land than to rent to tenants. Rising rice prices after 1890 heightened the incentive to lease lands to tenants who paid rents in kind, which could be marketed at great profit to the landlord. By 1908, 67.9 percent of landowners holding five hectares or more did not cultivate their property. Large landlords

found itself, against its will, functionally replacing that large landowning class which its legislation was trying to entice to stay on as the pilot of the rural economy. The net effect of the acts which favored large landlords was to improve life for those among them who chose to remain on the land and to create a modern rural economy that was now firmly grounded on commercialized agriculture dominated by large landholders.

This state of affairs was very far from the ideal of local autonomy and village leadership in Japanese economic growth advocated by Shinagawa, Hirata, and the Hōtoku school. Not only were they opposed to such sustained intervention from above, but they were also dissatisfied with the bias toward large landlords and commercialized agriculture. Clearly the state's basic policy was still that of the early Meiji years, to use farming to pay for industrialization, whatever the costs to smaller producers. Despite the new legislative activism, however, state agricultural administrators could not sociologically replace the departed large landowners and former progressive farmers. In time the loss of face-to-face contacts between landlords and tenants helped to redefine land, labor, and property relationships— sometimes violently, as in the tenant unrest of the 1920s.

A more immediate result was a modest but growing tendency for the government to pay heed to another village social stratum: that large group of owner-cultivators, or *jisakunō*, whom Shinagawa and Hirata called the "backbone village leadership class." As larger landlords abandoned the soil and owner-farmers gradually became dominant in village society, counterprogressive forces came into play. Large landowners had usually been the most innovative

---

clearly invested much more heavily in industry after the Russo-Japanese War of 1904-1905. Another incentive to absentee ownership was the wish to escape the house tax (*kosūwari*) levied in the villages, since it took an especially deep bite after 1900. See Waswo, pp. 81-104.

cultivators during the two decades when the government pressed for Western-style technical improvements. Now that petty owner-cultivators took on a more substantial role in rural life, it was understandable that their old social and economic habits, carefully guarded by generations of industrious, self-respecting small property owners, should return to prominence. Although large landlords continued to be the main beneficiaries of national farm policy during the later Meiji period, their somewhat diminished influence in village life meant that Hirata and Shinagawa attracted increasing support for their small-farming ideas within the government by the end of the century. When the Diet finally voted to create producers' cooperatives in 1900, the government found itself committed to supporting small landowners—a policy that persisted until World War II.

One instance of dissent within the Meiji leadership against programs favoring big landowners occurred when General Tani Kanjō used Nōhonshugi ideas to lament the demise of small owner-farmers and assail the state's large farming outlook in an 1898 Diet speech, in which he adduced military reasons for supporting small-scale farming: "Often in modern military societies there is talk of self-sufficiency in ordnance, seeking to produce in one's own country large steel plate that cannot yet really be produced anywhere except in France, England, and Germany. . . . even more than self-sufficiency in ordnance, we need self-sufficiency in foodstuffs."[37] To this autarkic argument he added that owner-farmer families were a good source of soldiers in wartime and that they were an excellent foil to the dangerous socialist movement which had recently taken root in

[37] Tani Kanjō, December 1898 Kizokuin speech, *Tani Kanjō ikō* [Remaining Works of Tani Kanjō], II, 220, quoted in Sakurai, "Nōhonshugi—sono rekishi, riron, jiban," p. 127. See also Ogura, pp. 156, 323; Ronald P. Dore, *Land Reform in Japan* (London: Oxford University Press, 1959), pp. 57-60; Sakurai, *Nihon nōhonshugi*, pp. 159-163; Sakurai Takeo, *Nihon nōgyō no saihensei* [The Reorganization of Japanese Agriculture] (Tokyo: Chūō Kōronsha, 1940), pp. 14-15.

Japan.[38] Tani admitted that his ideas came from Napoleon's vision of independent soldier-farmers (they also resembled Kumazawa Banzan's view in the seventeenth century). Tani described his ideal small owner-farmer in these words: "What I most hope for are independent farmers. I mean families with one to two hectares who cultivate their own lands, who will not freeze even when it is cold, who will escape death even in poor crop years, and who in good years can live together in happy family harmony."[39] He acknowledged that the Meiji government could not provide the same level of support for farming as it had for industry and trade, but he warned that, if the number of independent farmers was permitted to decline, "the foundation of the state would be endangered."[40]

Tani lashed out in frustration not only against state favoritism to industry but also against depression, debt, and despair, forces that had both enriched the large property owners and hounded many owner-cultivators into tenancy. No doubt his paean of independent proprietors was also partly politically motivated, since the government was eager to curry favor with *jisakunō* in light of demands from opposition parties in the Diet for lower land taxes and reductions in farm debt.[41] However little Tani had to offer by way of firm economic solutions, his was a major voice on

[38] Katherine M. Maxim, "Agrarian Response to Industrialization: Populism and Nohon-shugi," B.A. thesis in history, Connecticut College, 1970, pp. 41-42; Sakurai, *Nihon nōhonshugi*, p. 83; Sakurai, "Nōhonshugi—sono rekishi, riron, jiban," pp. 126-127. See also Dore, p. 62.

[39] Tani Kanjō, *Chiso zōhiron* [On Whether to Increase Land Taxes], ed. Nihon Shinbunsha, 1898, p. 25, quoted in Sakurai, *Nihon nōgyō no saihensei*, p. 29.

[40] Quoted in Sakurai, "Nōhonshugi—sono rekishi, riron, jiban," p. 126.

[41] Kokura Kuraichi, "Nōsei oyobi Nōkai" [Agricultural Administration and the Agricultural Associations], *Nihon nōgyō hattatsushi* [History of the Development of Japanese Agriculture], ed. Nōgyō Hattatsushi Chōsakai (Tokyo: Chūō Kōronsha, 1955), v, 310.

behalf of owner-farmers, citing fresh reasons of national defense that soon became firmly glued to the core of Nō-honshugi beliefs.

Although little could be done legislatively to halt the decline of *jisakunō* in the 1890s, the bureaucratic proponents of aid to small farmers earned an important victory in 1900 when the producers' cooperative law was passed. Whereas the agricultural association law of 1899 established governmental organizations to promote technical growth and tighten agricultural administration with the aid of large landholders, the producers' cooperative act was directly concerned with economic activity, especially interest rates and loans, for smaller cultivators. Support for extending credit to *jisakunō* through cooperatives was especially strong in the Naimushō and Nōshōmushō.[42] When the latter introduced a producers' cooperative bill in 1897, Minister Enomoto Takeaki (1836-1908) stressed financial reasons for adopting it:

> Since production is the basis of the national economy, its rise and fall obviously bears a direct relationship to the ebb and flow of our national fortunes. This is evident when we look at industrial society in Japan today. With the exception of a certain portion of industry, this [bill] relates to the productivity of almost all producers. Generally these persons are poor in resources, and thus it is impossible for them to plan for the reform and development of their individual enterprises. This is a very lamentable fact about the national economy.[43]

Mere exhortations to diligence, frugality, and careful regulation of farm expenses, Enomoto stated, were insufficient to stabilize rural finances. Aid from the great banks must be enlisted, he said, even though "at present most banks limit their help to meeting the monetary convenience of indus-

[42] Denda, *Nōsei*, p. 133; Tsunazawa, p. 23.
[43] Enomoto Takeaki, 1897 Diet speech, quoted in Tsunazawa, p. 22.

trial society." He blasted the Hypothec and Agricultural and Industrial Banks because "their benefits are limited to the great capitalists and regrettably do not extend to smaller producers."[44] Thus the Nōshōmushō presented the bill "so that the government will establish credit associations for the smaller producers; so that we can create four types of associations, cooperative buying, selling, producing, and consuming; so that we can have mutual liaison among all these types of associations; and so that we can reform and develop each of these individual enterprises."[45]

The government's case for producers' cooperatives was founded on basic economic issues. Neither Enomoto nor the backers of the bill when it was finally voted in 1900 revived Shinagawa's earlier arguments about "firming up the local self-rule system," nor did they explicitly admit their interest in strengthening the backbone village leadership class. Despite the careful attention to bread-and-butter reasoning by its conservative bureaucratic backers, the bill was promptly attacked as a socialistic obstacle to true economic development.[46] Its critics were right in stating that cooperative movements usually involve a theoretical contradiction with unfettered capitalist competition. In promoting cooperatives as a means of strengthening the rural tax base needed for continued industrial expansion, the government was potentially limiting the chances for capitalism to penetrate the domestic rural market. In practice, however, rural cooperatives rarely have a substantial braking effect on commercialization, although they often improve conditions for individual farmers. This proved to be the case in Japan, where the worst economic and social fears of the cooperatives' opponents did not materialize.

The most active and influential supporter of the creation of cooperatives was Hirata Tōsuke, who wrote the producers' cooperative law (Sangyō Kumiaihō) of 1900. Hirata

[44] Ibid., pp. 22-23.   [45] Ibid., p. 23.
[46] Tsunazawa, p. 74.

was a mercantilist who greatly feared that Japan's position as a rice importer after 1895 would threaten her in times of war.[47] He believed that the country must regain self-sufficiency in agriculture in order to become a truly strong state and that credit must be extended to hard-pressed *jisakunō* to achieve this. Shortly before the Diet vote on the Sangyō Kumiaihō in February 1900, Hirata denounced private profit and stressed that the cooperative movement would enhance the common profit of society.[48] Many years later he recalled the virtues of cooperation: "The basis of the cooperative is trust. Without trust there is no cooperative. Trust is born of the concept of responsibility, which means not cheating one's self. . . . Spiritual cooperation and unity plus material cooperation and help are the inner meaning of cooperatives."[49] Such ideas accorded well with the Japanese heritage of village communalism and helped to dispel fears that the Sangyō Kumiai would be a radical departure for rural Japan.

After much debate and certain technical changes, the Nōshōmushō's proposal was finally enacted on February 22, 1900, just four days before the death of one of its greatest supporters, Shinagawa Yajirō. It provided for both producers' and consumers' cooperatives, as well as for short-term credit facilities with limited government financing. A major aim of the law was to reduce the power of middlemen, merchants, and moneylenders who had profited greatly from the small-landowning system in recent years.[50] This act differed from the 1891 credit association bill in that it was

[47] Hirata Tōsuke, "Nōhonshugi to kōgyō no hatten" [Agrarianism and the Development of Industry], 1897? *Nōgyō sekai* [World of Agriculture], III, 7, quoted in Denda, *Nōsei*, pp. 143-144.
[48] Katō, p. 186.
[49] Hirata Tōsuke, March 1921, quoted ibid., p. 187.
[50] Ogura, pp. 251-265; Ogura, *Agricultural Problems*, p. 15; Denda, *Nōsei*, p. 138. See also Fisher, p. 480; Ogata, pp. 88-89; Tadao Wikawa, "Our Co-operative Movement," *Contemporary Japan*, I, 3, December 1932, 434.

modeled on the Rochdale and F. W. Raiffeisen examples in Britain and Germany, rather than on the Schulze-Delitzsch cooperatives. This meant that it created credit societies separate from cooperative buying and selling, set limits of liability not present in the 1891 proposal, and offered new tax exemptions to the cooperative associations.[51] Six procedural amendments were added to the law between 1900 and 1926, expanding the functions of the Sangyō Kumiai.

Apart from its technical advantages over the 1891 bill, this law evidently received support in the Diet because economic trends after the Sino-Japanese War had created concern for the plight of the *jisakunō*. As tenancy rose and the numbers of owner-farmers and part owner, part tenants fell (see Tables 2 and 3), the logic of Shinagawa's, Hirata's, Tani's, and Enomoto's various arguments apparently became more persuasive. Yet it would be foolish to regard the new law as a boon to all cultivators. For one thing, its passage was yoked to that of the repressive police peace law (Chian Keisatsuhō) of 1900, which was soon used to clamp down on tenant unrest as well as labor union activity. For another, the short-term loans now offered by Sangyō Kumiai were available only to small landowners whose personal credit ratings were high, and not as a rule to poor tenants or part owner, part tenant cultivators who wished to purchase the full lands they worked.[52] Finally, in many cases larger landlords, as chief depositors in the new credit societies, came to dominate them in much the same way as they controlled the Hōtokusha and the agricultural associations.[53] Nevertheless the new law made it possible for a credit line to extend downward, beyond the largest landholders, to the broad group of small proprietors who worked their own

[51] Tsunazawa, pp. 24-25; Ogura, p. 251; Fisher, p. 480.

[52] See Denda, *Nōsei*, p. 138; Tsunazawa, p. 24.

[53] Denda, *Nōsei*, p. 138; Ogura, p. 265; Morita Shirō, *The Development of Agricultural Cooperative Associations in Japan* (Tokyo: Japan FAO Organization, 1960), p. 7.

lands and formed the elite of village society in the early twentieth century. The law thus suited the advocates of ever greater capitalist expansion because it provided ways to boost farm output, and it also pleased the partisans of Nōhonshugi by aiding the backbone small producer.

Unlike the agricultural associations founded at the same time, the producers' cooperatives were only indirectly answerable to the government, even in funding. In their credit functions and high level of local autonomy, they more closely resembled the Hōtokusha of the early Meiji period. Indeed, Hirata Tōsuke pressed the similarity in 1907 when he wrote:

> We can expect to attain true cooperation and unity by supporting both capitalists and landlords, both workers and tenants. The tides of fortune continually seek to implement [Ninomiya's] teachings. The promotion of production cannot succeed without the full cooperation and conformity of each individual. This is why in achieving a sound producers' association we must base it on this sort of spirit.[54]

In reality there was little of this emphasis in the cooperatives. Whereas the Hōtoku units were concerned with moral uplift, technology, education, and charity as well as credit, the producers' cooperatives were almost exclusively focused on money matters. The cooperatives, moreover, were creatures of the Meiji state, not privately organized in the rural districts, and they drew inspiration from foreign movements as well as from the native precedents cited by Shinagawa in 1891.[55] Still, however modern, centrally instituted, and

[54] Hirata Tōsuke, "Sangyō Kumiai to Hōtokushugi" [Producers' Cooperatives and Hōtoku Thought], Shimin [These People], II, 4, part 3, 1907, reprinted in Hōtoku no shinzui [The Essence of Hōtoku], ed. Tomeoka Kōsuke (Tokyo: Keiseisha Shoten, 1908), p. 104.

[55] Ogata, pp. 47-48, 84-87; Morita, pp. 16-17. Okutani Matsuji, Ninomiya Sontoku to Hōtokusha undō [Ninomiya Sontoku and the Hōtokusha Movement] (Tokyo: Kōyō Shoin, 1936), pp. 327-331,

economically oriented they may have been, the new Sangyō Kumiai catered to the same rural landholding classes as the Hōtokusha, although on a nationwide basis far exceeding the reach of the Hōtoku movement. The producers' co-operatives were a clever amalgam that subsumed the Hōto-kusha spirit and that of other private credit societies, both at home and abroad, into an institutionally and fiscally modern organization for the dual purposes of enhancing farm output and protecting a traditional landowning elite.

As organizations like the agricultural associations and producers' cooperatives spread after 1900, the rural leader-ship class upon which Yamagata Aritomo's political follow-ers depended for electoral support was gradually strength-ened.[56] Hirata spent many years building both Nōkai and Sangyō Kumiai in the countryside. Beginning with twenty-one producers' cooperatives founded in 1900 under the new law, the movement expanded so rapidly that 1,671 coopera-tives had been started by 1905, when Hirata formed the Central Union of Cooperative Societies (Dai Nihon Sangyō Kumiai Chūōkai).[57] This semiofficial agency gave the Nō-shōmushō somewhat greater control over the cooperative organizations, whereby it urged local units to increase their credit services starting in 1906. In 1909 the government officially recognized the Central Union, and by 1914 there were 11,160 cooperatives, representing 90.4 percent of the nation's 12,342 cities, towns, and villages. In the same year 82.2 percent of cooperative members were farmers.[58] The Meiji emperor added his blessing with a gift of 20,000 yen on June 18, 1911, at Hirata's urging.

---

identifies few differences between the Hōtokusha and the Sangyō Kumiai.

[56] Tetsuo Najita, *Hara Kei in the Politics of Compromise 1905-1915* (Cambridge, Mass.: Harvard University Press, 1967), p. 48.

[57] Katō, p. 190; Wikawa, p. 434; Fisher, pp. 480-481.

[58] Tsunazawa, p. 27; Morita, pp. 7-8; Hugh Borton, *Japan Since 1931, Its Political and Social Development* (New York: Institute of Pacific Relations, 1940), pp. 22-23.

83

By World War I, most of the cooperatives (9,274 of 11,160) were primarily or exclusively concerned with credit,[59] although amendments to the original law now permitted multipurpose associations. The impact of the cooperatives on farm debt in the early twentieth century should not be exaggerated. In 1912 there were nearly 10,000 Sangyō Kumiai with more than 650,000 members throughout the country, but only three percent of total farm debt was represented by loans from these organizations. By contrast, banks and insurance companies were creditors for 28 percent of farm debt, mostly with large borrowers, and 69 percent of the total rural debt was owed to pawnshops, merchants, friends, and similar sources.[60] The cooperative movement expanded after World War I, so that by 1925 there were 14,517 Sangyō Kumiai with deposits of 230,-377,645 yen.[61] After 1919 the cooperatives were permitted to engage in warehousing, and in 1923 they obtained added capital from the National Federation of Purchase Societies, a cooperative banking scheme. Nevertheless fragmented leadership and a lack of money prevented the cooperatives from funding a significant share of rural debt during the 1920s and 1930s, and when the Sangyō Kumiai and Nōkai were merged under wartime mobilization into the Nōgyōkai (Farm Society) in 1942 it seemed that the cooperative movement had never fulfilled the promise held out for it by Hirata in 1900.

Political, social, and economic currents flowed together in the 1890s to form the first major stream of consciously protective profarm thought in modern Japan. The credit society bill and producers' cooperative law were dim stars in the constellation of government agricultural laws and programs during this decade, but they cast considerable light on the process by which diffuse, often contradictory,

[59] Ogura, p. 22.　　　　　[60] Denda, *Nōsei*, p. 139.
　[61] Katō, p. 185. On the Sangyō Kumiai, see also Morita, pp. 9-20; Fisher, pp. 481-491; Ogura, pp. 21-22, 251-252; Wikawa, p. 434.

sentiments about farming held by landowners, generals, economists, bureaucrats, and politicians were combined into a body of conservative agrarianist thought which affected both official policy and private responses to it for the next forty years. Its most prominent spokesmen, Shinagawa and Hirata, were modern men with modern assumptions, living in an industrializing age, who developed defensive, profarm doctrines that smacked romantically of traditional village life without recapturing the premodern ethos that encompassed it. They were primary catalysts in that strange chemistry of history and nostalgia now known as Nōhon-shugi thought.

Chapter IV

Small Farms and State Policy, 1900-1914

HISTORIANS of Europe have often been titillated by an interpretive puzzle: should the years between 1900 and World War I be regarded more as an extension of the old century or as the beginning of a new one? The same riddle applies a fortiori to the history of Japan during this period. The death of the Meiji emperor in 1912 symbolizes the continuities at work in the early twentieth century, as though the entire Meiji era was of one piece. Until 1912, politics remained under the domination of the old oligarchy; the political party movement had yet to approach its potential impact. Thanks to the new school system, Japan had become a well-educated country during Meiji's reign, but cosmopolitanism and cultural sophistication remained the attributes of a tiny elite until after World War I. Even today a popular stereotype has it that the long Meiji era, from 1868 until 1912, was a cohesive chunk of time. A person born before 1912 is often called *Meiji jidai no hito*, a person of the Meiji period, leaving little doubt that he is identified with a bygone era.

Yet in a sense there were several Meiji periods between 1868 and 1912, the last of which, consisting of the early years of the twentieth century, seems distinctly new in many respects. Japan's diplomatic and military prowess took a quantum leap when she achieved the end of extra-territoriality in 1899, signed the Anglo-Japanese Alliance in 1902, and defeated the Russians in 1904-1905. Accompanying her sudden position of preeminence in East Asia was a rising sense of public self-confidence that soon displaced the defensive nationalism of the preceding century. New too were socialist and anarchist currents, especially within the immature urban labor movement.

The Japanese economy from 1900 to World War I likewise showed signs of great change, but within a recognizable pattern. Wartime industrial expansion was financed through heavy taxes and foreign borrowings. Once the firing stopped in 1905, Japan found herself with a swollen empire and a much greater industrial capacity. Shipbuilding, machinery, mining, transportation, and textiles grew especially fast in the late Meiji years.[1] Total production and real income had virtually doubled by 1914, compared with their 1890 levels.[2] Secondary and tertiary industry expanded enormously in the same period, especially after the Russo-Japanese War; for one of many recent estimates, see Table 4.

Equally remarkable was the ongoing agricultural growth that made such industrial increases possible, continuing a trend set in the early Meiji era. The total value of tertiary industrial output finally overtook that of the primary sector at the beginning of World War I, although primary production itself stood about 75 percent higher than a quarter century before. Both exports and imports doubled in the first decade of the new century.[3] Specialization and commercialization became widespread in rural Japan during the period 1900-1914. By the start of World War I, industry had clearly replaced agriculture as the more productive economic sector, but farming remained both the main source

[1] For a summary of late Meiji economic growth, see William W. Lockwood, *The Economic Development of Japan: Growth and Structural Change 1868-1938* (Princeton: Princeton University Press, 1954), pp. 18-37.

[2] Ibid., pp. 20-21.   [3] Ibid., p. 22.

TABLE 4

REAL NET OUTPUT BY INDUSTRIAL SECTORS, 1890-1915
(1928-1932 Prices, in Million Yen)

Year	Primary Industry		Secondary Industry		Tertiary Industry	
	Amount	Index	Amount	Index	Amount	Index
1888-1892	1,150	100	356	100	664	100
1893-1897	1,467	128	528	148	829	134
1898-1902	1,757	153	793	223	1,177	177
1903-1907	1,791	156	803	226	1,354	204
1908-1912	2,040	177	1,037	291	1,820	274
1913-1917	2,025	176	1,479	415	2,150	324

SOURCE: *Agricultural Development in Modern Japan*, ed. Takekazu Ogura, 2nd ed. (Tokyo: Fuji Publishing Co., 1968), p. 683.

of employment and an important underpinning for the new increases in manufacturing.

Government farm policy in the years from 1900 to World War I was built directly on the foundations laid during the transitional decade of the 1890s. The state unapologetically and consistently favored the interests of landowners, both great and modest, within the framework of small-scale farming. At the same time, the logic which dictated these policies changed as bureaucrats adopted new views about the importance of agriculture itself. After reviewing the main landmarks of government agricultural policy during 1900-1914, I shall take up the agrarianism of the farm educator Yokoi Tokiyoshi (1860-1927), whose ideas provided the most elaborate justification for nurturing small-scale agriculture and village society in the early twentieth century.

Government Farm Programs and the Twentieth-Century Hōtoku Movement

The agricultural associations chartered under the Nōkaihō of 1899 and the producers' cooperatives authorized a year later were two main ways the state supported larger and smaller landholders, respectively, at the beginning of the twentieth century. Government policy in these years paid attention to technical and organizational detail, resulting in added crop output and a reasonable degree of village stability. Given their bias toward private-property owners in a system of small-scale farming, state agricultural programs up to World War I appear to have been quite successful in meeting their goals.

This new hardheaded professionalism can be detected in the decision of the Ministry of Agriculture and Commerce (Nōshōmushō) in 1901 to conduct an exhaustive land survey, to serve as a basis for future farm policy.[4] Three years and 500,000 yen were alloted to examining soil quality, land use and size, tenancy, rural capital resources, educational levels, and the like. One result was a renewed push to spread vocational education beyond the small numbers of persons studying formal agricultural administration in universities. Agricultural continuation schools, at a popular level of understanding, were created with the aid of the Nōkai. From 1,436 such schools in 1904, the number grew to 5,530 in 1912 and a peak of 12,053 in 1925.[5] Another result was a fourteen-point code, issued by the Nōshōmushō in 1903 to the Nōkai, calling for better insect extermination and prevention, improved rice inspection, better management techniques, and above all increased rice productivity.[6] This code was carefully fitted to the possibilities of small farming.

[4] Kokura Kuraichi, "Nōsei oyobi nōkai" [Agricultural Administration and the Agricultural Associations], Nihon nōgyō hattatsushi [History of the Development of Japanese Agriculture], ed. Nōgyō Hattatsushi Chōsakai (Tokyo: Chūō Kōronsha, 1955), v, 314-315.

[5] Agricultural Development in Modern Japan, ed. Takekazu Ogura, 2nd ed. (Tokyo: Fuji Publishing Co., 1968), p. 337 (hereafter cited as Ogura).

[6] Denda Isao, Kindai Nihon nōsei shisō no kenkyū [Studies on Modern Japanese Agricultural Administration Thought] (Tokyo: Miraisha, 1969), p. 137. Nine of the fourteen points concerned improving rice production.

SMALL FARMS AND STATE POLICY

Most of its recommendations required no money, just hard work. Two state programs adopted in this period illustrate the new emphasis: (1) rice inspection and import duties and (2) the rural land improvement movement after 1905.

Farm prices are tricky to predict in even the most tightly controlled economy, and they were mercurial in the highly laissez-faire context of Meiji Japan. By the 1880s landlords found it advantageous to establish voluntary rice inspection programs as a hedge against uncertain prices, since the best rice was presumably the least vulnerable to unexpectedly low prices. At least thirty prefectures had voluntary inspection schemes in the late Meiji era.[7] When prices rose again in the 1890s, quality-conscious landlords profited the most. After the Russo-Japanese War, voluntary measures no longer seemed adequate, and producers persuaded the government to pass two ordinances in 1910 setting national inspection standards. As a rule landlords benefited the most and tenants the least, to the extent that tenants paid rents in low-quality rice, which landlords now had difficulty marketing, causing them to penalize tenants.[8]

Rice prices also touched on the sensitive question of self-sufficiency once Japan became a net rice importer after the Sino-Japanese War. As recently as 1889, rice had accounted for 10 percent of total Japanese exports, but population growth and a higher standard of living in the 1890s led the government to import colonial rice from Taiwan, and later Korea, when demand began to outrun supply. Landowners in Japan proper immediately protested the damage such imports were causing to domestic rice prices, while certain defense-minded officials simultaneously called for greater output at home to maintain self-sufficiency in wartime. The government responded by promoting production (as in the Nōshōmushō code of 1903) and imposing a 5 percent ad valorem emergency duty on rice. In 1906 the duty became a

[7] Ann Waswo, "Landlords and Social Change in Prewar Japan," Ph.D. dissertation in history, Stanford University, 1969, p. 64.

[8] Ogura, p. 165.

protective one on a permanent basis, as a specific duty of 0.64 yen per 60 kg.[9] This duty was a victory for landowners and a defeat for free traders and consumers. When the tariff was extended with only slight revisions in 1910, the state was committed to protecting agriculture artificially against natural market trends, the ultimate price for which was the rice riots of 1918 in Toyama Prefecture and elsewhere.

State policies on rice inspection and import duties worked fairly well before World War I but required many changes thereafter. By contrast, the land improvement movement after 1905 met with uncertain short-term economic results but enjoyed great long-range success. Since 1899 the government had urged landlords to take part in land adjustment and replotment programs that would both raise the national output and increase landowners' incomes. These efforts were intensified after 1905 in the government's rural improvement movement, or Chihō Kairyō Undō. In this complex program, the state capitalized on energies stirred by the recent war with Russia to mobilize the countryside for national service. The Ministry of Internal Affairs tried to bolster the administrative village (*mura*) as the lowest unit of local rule by merging Shinto shrines, tax functions, and other aspects of rural life heretofore centered in the smaller residential hamlets (*buraku*). The state also fostered village youth groups (Seinendan) to muster local enthusiasm for the movement. Current research is defining how effective these measures were,[10] but insofar as agriculture was concerned the program had two main features.

On the one hand, the Nōshōmushō called on landholders

[9] Ibid., p. 169.
[10] See Wilbur M. Fridell, *Japanese Shrine Mergers, 1906-12* (Tokyo: Sophia University Press, 1973). At the University of Washington, Kenneth B. Pyle is studying the Chihō Kairyō Undō and Christopher E. Lewis is investigating its relationship with rural youth groups. See also *Naimushōshi* [History of the Ministry of Internal Affairs], ed. Taikakai (Tokyo: Chihō Zaimu Kyōkai, 1971), I, 477, 490.

to expand their lands further, build new irrigation ditches, dikes, and drainage works, improve roads and bridges, and raise productivity in lands already under cultivation. Although the ministry spoke of increasing the average farm size,[11] the small landowner benefited far less from the land-improvement plan than the large proprietor with the capital to invest in upgrading his operations. More forward-looking landlords welcomed this movement for its economic rewards, even though in the long run it enhanced the depersonalization of landlord-tenant relations by upsetting traditional practices.[12] By 1940 more than one million hectares had been improved and land yields had risen substantially as a direct result.[13]

On the other hand, the Ministry of Internal Affairs used the land-improvement movement to revive a moral emphasis on peasant forbearance and restraint. Hirata Tōsuke, minister of internal affairs in the second Katsura cabinet, issued an edict on October 13, 1908, which set the spirit for the land-improvement campaign. Known as the *Boshin shōsho*, or imperial rescript of 1908, this document counseled national unity, hard work, and loyalty to fulfill the national destiny. Spiritual strengthening, it said, must accompany the material gains which Japan was experiencing.[14]

[11] Nōshōmushō [Ministry of Agriculture and Commerce], *Chūshōnō hogo seisaku* [Policy of Protecting Middle and Small Farmers], 1912, pp. 20, 32, quoted in Sakurai Takeo, *Nihon nōgyō no saihensei* [The Reorganization of Japanese Agriculture] (Tokyo: Chūō Kōronsha, 1940), p. 29.

[12] Waswo, pp. 74-79. It is true that large landlords did not uniformly leave the villages in all areas of Japan. In some cases the moderately wealthy departed for more profitable urban investments, leaving the largest landowners securely in charge of village society. Still the predominant trend was for larger rather than smaller landlords to move out.

[13] Ibid., p. 68.

[14] Miyaji Masato, "Chihō kairyō undō no ronri to tenkai—Nichirosengo no nōson seisaku" [Logic and Development of the Rural Improvement Movement—Farm Policy After the Russo-Japanese

At the instance of Ichiki Kitokurō (1867-1944), vice-minister of internal affairs and son of Okada Ryōichirō, the rescript also emphasized service to the emperor, whom it described as the "nucleus" of the state.[15] Like countless such exhortations in the past, this document received wide circulation, but its practical effects are impossible to determine. At the very least it reveals the ethical component which the government injected into its land-betterment program.

If the state carried out educational, technical, and organizational activities to support its long-standing policy of helping large producers raise output, what was the fate of Shinagawa's and Hirata's concern for small landowners after 1900? The government, to be sure, conscientiously nurtured producers' cooperatives under the Sangyō Kumiaihō. The state also boosted owner-cultivators through the semiofficial Hōtokukai (later Chūō Hōtokukai, or Central Hōtoku Association), founded by the Naimushō and Nōshōmushō in early 1906 to spread economic self-improvement and fortify the village leadership.

Since the late 1880s the Hōtoku societies scattered throughout eastern Japan had developed warm ties with these national ministries and cooperated closely with the movements to establish Shin'yō Kumiai and Sangyō Kumiai. It seemed natural for the leading Naimushō official Tomeoka Kōsuke (1864-1934) to turn to the Hōtoku associations for aid when his ministry began to plan local land improve-

---

War], *Shigaku zasshi* [Historical Journal], LXXIX, 8, August 1970, 20-21; Katō Fusakura, *Hakushaku Hirata Tōsuke den* [Biography of Count Hirata Tōsuke] (Tokyo: Hiratahaku Denki Hensan Jimusho, 1927), pp. 120-125; Emori Itsuo, "Chihō kairyō undō ni okeru sonraku kyōdōtai no saihensei" [Rebirth of Village Communalism in the Rural Improvement Movement], *Nihon kindaika no kenkyū* [Studies of Japanese Modernization], I, January 1972, 371-398.

[15] Miyaji, p. 20. See also Miyaji Masato, "Chihō kairyō undō no ronri to tenkai—Nichirosengo no nōson seisaku," *Shigaku zasshi*, LXXIX, 9, September 1970, 26.

ments in 1903.[16] As soon as it was founded, the Hōtokukai began to issue publications on rural life, including its house organ, *Shimin* (These People), and it sent some of the leading farm officials of the day on lecture tours all over the country to stimulate land improvement. The Hōtokukai also invited local landowners to form their own Hōtoku units—credit banks that also engaged in educational, charitable, and technical work within the villages. Hōtoku leaders declared that only through such societies could farmers achieve the spirit of cooperation, something which was lacking in the producers' cooperatives and other credit facilities.[17] Figures on the size of the late Meiji Hōtoku movement are hard to come by, but something more than six hundred associations, with about twenty-seven thousand members, are believed to have existed in the Shizuoka area by 1912, a plateau which was maintained until World War II.[18]

Rural improvement through self-help, as taught by the Hōtoku societies, was one major government objective in establishing the Hōtokukai. Tomeoka worked through the Hōtoku associations because their stress on hard work and prompt tax payments appealed, as it had since the 1870s, to bureaucrats responsible for agricultural output. The Hōtokusha were also public spirited, cooperating fully with conscription and other programs of state service, and as a rule they supported the government and bureaucracy rather than the political party movement, which they regarded as

[16] Miyaji Masato, "Chihō kairyō undō ni okeru Hōtokusha no kinō" [Function of the Hōtokusha in the Rural Improvement Movement], *Shigaku zasshi*, LXXX, 2, February 1971, 2.

[17] Kiyoshi Ogata, *The Co-operative Movement in Japan* (London: P. S. King & Son, Ltd., 1923), p. 78. See also Miyaji, "Chihō kairyō undō ni okeru Hōtokusha no kinō," p. 3; Ogata, pp. 77-78.

[18] Okutani Matsuji, *Ninomiya Sontoku to Hōtokusha undō* [Ninomiya Sontoku and the Hōtokusha Movement] (Tokyo: Kōyō Shoin, 1936), p. 294.

divisive and selfish.[19] A second aim of the Hōtokukai was "to build communities for the sake of the nation"[20] by urging village leaders to rededicate themselves to self-rule. Nakagawa Nozomu, a founder of the Hōtokukai, wrote that the purpose was not to impose central supervision upon village mayors but "to encourage self-rule while guiding and teaching—in short, leadership."[21] The Hōtoku spirit of cooperation and community decision-making, the government believed, was obviously congenial with restoring local responsibility. But why was self-rule so essential?

For Tomeoka and other champions of rural improvement, self-rule would provide the *mura* leadership to fortify the central government. As Tomeoka wrote in 1915, "if we do not also give rise to local improvement and prosperity we can never expect the state to develop. . . . Thus it is absolutely necessary to develop a self-rule system."[22] Others, such as the Hōtokukai official Shimizu Tōru, saw social advantages: "Like a single family, the comrades of city,

[19] Miyaji, "Chihō kairyō undō ni okeru Hōtokusha no kinō," pp. 4-6.

[20] Ibid., p. 1. On the founding of the Hōtokukai, see also Denda Isao, *Kindai Nihon keizai shisō no kenkyū—Nihon no kindaika to chihō keizai* [Studies on Modern Japanese Economic Thought—Japanese Modernization and Rural Economics] (Tokyo: Miraisha, 1962), pp. 134-142; Okutani, p. 283; Okutani Matsuji, "Nihon ni okeru nōhonshugi shisō no nagare" [Trends in Agrarian Thought in Japan], *Shisō* [Thought], No. 407, May 1958, pp. 6-7; Ishida Takeshi, *Meiji seiji shisōshi kenkyū* [Studies on Meiji Political Thought] (Tokyo: Miraisha, 1954), pp. 182-202.

[21] Nakagawa Nozomu, quoted in Ishida, p. 189.

[22] Tomeoka Kōsuke, "Waga Hōtokukai to jichi no kaihatsu" [Our Hōtokukai and the Development of Self-rule], 1915, *Tomeoka Kōsuke Hōtoku ronshū* [Collection of Tomeoka Kōsuke's Theories on Hōtoku] (Tokyo: Chūō Hōtokukai, 1936), pp. 491-492. On Tomeoka and self-rule, see Thomas R. H. Havens, "Two Popular Views of Rural Self-Rule in Modern Japan," *Studies on Japanese Culture* (Tokyo: The Japan P.E.N. Club, 1973), II, 249-256.

town, or village unite in natural harmony and lay plans for the happiness of the whole community—this is the essence of self-rule."[23] Clearly the Hōtokukai wanted to revitalize the rural ruling classes—but who were they?

Until recently it was assumed that the state used the Hōtokukai to restore large landlords to the prominence they held before the commercial economy expanded. In reviving Ninomiya's teachings, for example, it was thought that the state intended to harmonize class relations (especially between landlords and tenants), reviving the solidarity of the nineteenth-century villages in which large landowners predominated.[24] As Nakagawa put it, "landlords are not called landlords but landfathers; tenants are called son-cultivators. Thus they preserve parent-child relations."[25] The Hōtokukai often made contacts with local landlords' associations in order to seek out "eminent persons" and "top-grade men" to lead village rehabilitation.[26] From this it has been inferred that the main purpose of the Hōtokukai was to bring large landlords back into village leadership roles, as a part of a larger national policy of social harmony.

Although the late Meiji state was undoubtedly interested in both social and economic stability in the countryside, it now seems that the small proprietor, rather than the big landlord, may have been uppermost in the Hōtokukai's activities. Sasaki Ryūji's investigations of the Hōtokukai in Shizuoka Prefecture have established that *jisakunō* and even tenants were often prominent and that the Hōtokukai was usually strongest in areas where there were few large land-

---

[23] Shimizu Tōru, "Jichi gyōsei no hongi" [Basic Principles of Self-Rule], *Shimin* [These People], II, 5, 1907, 10, quoted in Ishida, p. 190.

[24] See Okutani, "Nagare," p. 7.

[25] Nakagawa Nozomu, "Jichi no kassei" [Trend Toward Self-Rule], quoted in Ishida, p. 191.

[26] Ishida, pp. 190-194. See also Okutani, "Nagare," p. 7.

lords.[27] A relatively broad-based following for the Hōtokukai existed precisely where small owner-farmers comprised the village elite. This view, in short, rejects the
contention that large landlords were the main beneficiaries,
or even the chief targets, of the Hōtokukai.

At the same time, there is no reason to deny that the
state's motives included a strong measure of social control.
Indeed, the conservative *jisakunō* class, firmly rooted in the
soil for many generations, was especially well suited to the
government's views of hierarchy and order. Owner-cultivators had less to gain from the spread of capitalism than
larger landowners with surplus funds to invest in the cities,
and they could be counted on to take over local rule as the
large landlord class gradually disintegrated.[28] Small owner-
farmers, anxious to add a hectare or two to their holdings,
seemed particularly enthusiastic about land-improvement
measures in Shizuoka Prefecture. Although the evidence is
ambiguous, it seems prudent to conclude that the state used
the Hōtokukai to foster rural stability in cooperation with
large landlords in some cases and small ones in others. The
net effect was to reinforce the economic aid accruing to
jisakunō through the producers' cooperatives with a strong
dose of political support, with the avowed intention of restoring the village self-rule, cooperation, and stability which
had eroded since the previous century. The state did not
cater exclusively to big property owners. Instead its farm
policies simultaneously pressed for further technical progress and a conservative, almost reactionary, shoring up of
village life by supporting owner-cultivators. This is a sign
of how the government, having created a thriving farm
economy based on private land ownership in the nineteenth
century, devoted more and more effort in the twentieth century to keeping the system from wobbling.

[27] Sasaki Ryūji, "Hōtokusha undō no kairyūteki seikaku" [Class
Character of the Hōtokusha Movement], *Hōkei kenkyū* [Studies in
Law and Economics], XVII, 3, 1969, 31-69; XVIII, 1, 1969, 31-60.
[28] Ibid., XVIII, 1, p. 54.

Yokoi Tokiyoshi and Small Farming

The most widely known exponent of the bureaucratic Nōhonshugi which guided state farm policy during the period 1900-1914 was Yokoi Tokiyoshi (Jikei; 1860-1927), who was not a bureaucrat at all but a professor of agricultural administration at Tokyo Agricultural College (Tokyo Nōka Daigaku). Yokoi was the ideologue who completed the shift in direction and meaning of Nōhonshugi thought begun by Shinagawa Yajirō and Hirata Tōsuke. Whereas Japanese agrarianism before 1900 was generally forward looking and oriented toward growth, the mature Nōhonshugi expressed by Yokoi was now primarily retrogressive and clearly defensive against capitalism. The earlier agrarianism rationalized farming as a vital contributor to national wealth and insisted that it be promoted equally with trade and industry. From Yokoi's time onward, Nōhonshugi could no longer claim that agriculture was the main source of national wealth. As a result a new justification appeared, stressing farming as the social, military, and ethical foundation of the country. Above all it was the small cultivator, living in the classical farm village, who represented the ideal social type to twentieth century Nōhonshugisha such as Yokoi Tokiyoshi.

The development of Yokoi's farm thought bears witness to these changes in the basic character of Japanese agrarianism. He was born in 1860 as the fourth son of a samurai in Kumamoto and joined the first class to enter the Komaba Agricultural School, graduating in June 1880.[29] During the

[29] For Yokoi see Sakurai Takeo, "Yokoi Tokiyoshi hakushi" [Dr. Yokoi Tokiyoshi], *Kyōiku* [Education], II, 7, July 1934, 86-101; Ishikawa Ken and Katayama Seiichi, "Yokoi Tokiyoshi no nōgyō kyōikuron ni okeru bushidōshugi—kindai Nihon no kyōiku ni miru shinpō to dentō" [Bushido Ideology in the Educational Theories of Yokoi Tokiyoshi—Progress and Tradition in Modern Japanese Education], *Gendai kyōiku to dentō* [Modern Education and Tradition], June 30, 1963, 79-83; Sumiya Kazuhiko, "Keiseiki Nihon burujoajī no shisōzō" [Images of the Japanese Bourgeoisie During the Formative

next nine years he held agricultural administration posts in Hyōgo and Fukuoka Prefectures and also taught in both normal and agricultural schools. In 1889 he received an appointment to the Ministry of Agriculture and Commerce, but he soon resigned after a row with Maeda Masana. In 1894 he took up teaching duties at Tokyo Nōka Daigaku, and in 1911 he was elevated to the presidency of Tokyo Nōgyō Daigaku, where he remained to his death in 1927.

As a young man Yokoi supported progressive farm education: "Historically we have not failed to prize agriculture, nor has education failed to prosper. But education has mainly suited persons of the warrior class and city dwellers. When it comes to rural society, it is not easy to get an education appropriate to the people's occupations."[30] The purpose of learning how to farm, he argued in 1891, was profit: "Agriculture is a business enterprise, and the essentials for making money are not numerous."[31] During the mid-1890s Yokoi continually prodded the state to play a more active part in farm progress. His ideas closely resembled those of the conscientious landlord-officials who agitated for new farm laws at the time. But by the end of the decade Yokoi's outlook on farm policy had changed dramatically and irreversibly. His focus shifted from practical, technical education to more abstract questions relating to the spirit and quality of farm life.

Yokoi left no record to explain this reorientation of his attitudes. It is surely no coincidence, however, that his new

---

Period], *Kindai Nihon keizai shisōshi* [History of Modern Japanese Economic Thought], ed. Chō Yukio and Sumiya Kazuhiko (Tokyo: Yūhikaku, 1969), I, 193-221; Denda, *Nōsei*, p. 136f.

[30] Yokoi Tokiyoshi, "Kōnō ronsaku" [Policy for Improving Agriculture], 1891, *Yokoi Hakushi zenshū* [Complete Works of Dr. Yokoi], ed. Dai Nihon Nōkai (Tokyo: Yokoi Zenshū Kankōkai, 1925), III, 676. (Henceforth *Yokoi Hakushi zenshū* will be cited as *YHZS*.)

[31] Yokoi Tokiyoshi, "Nōgyō hanron" [Summary of Agriculture], 1891, *YHZS*, II, 155. See Sumiya, pp. 188-192.

views evolved after the Sino-Japanese War, when it was growing apparent that agriculture was falling behind trade and manufacturing, requiring new measures for which Yokoi began to supply a rationale. In October 1897, for example, he published an article titled simply "Nōhonshugi," apparently the first such use of the term, in which he decried the growing gap between urban and rural life:

If this is allowed to go on as it is, the pitiful farmers will gradually be oppressed by the urban rich, becoming sacrifices to their interests and growing weaker and more impoverished year by year. In reality our independent, healthy farmers will suddenly be destroyed, and they will become mere paupers, squirming without any independence whatever, unable to tell night from day. The vitality of the nation will thus be sapped, our national power will be exhausted, and in the end there will be no way to rescue it.[32]

Henceforth, he maintained, agriculture was something to be defended, not developed. With the rise of capitalism, farming became "powerless in the arena of competition," and Japan must "prevent its falling prey to the urban millionaires by nurturing the vitality of the country among those who love it, the farmers. . . . This is what agrarianism means to me, and this is why in the future we should fear industrialism and prize farming."[33]

Here, in a few sentences, Yokoi redefined the course of Nōhonshugi thought in Japan precisely when farming was slipping from its top position in the economy:

Commerce and industry are the things which enrich the country, while agriculture is the thing that protects it. Commerce and industry are progressive enterprises, while agriculture is conservative. The development and progress

[32] Yokoi Tokiyoshi, "Nōhonshugi" [Agrarianism], October 1897, *YHZS*, viii, 231.
[33] Ibid.

of trade and industry do not wait on encouragement or protection, whereas farming began under special patronage which gives it healthy growth. For this reason, it must be primarily the state's responsibility to aid the weak and help them escape falling prey to the strong.[34]

If farming was now so weak that it could not defend itself economically, why was it worth protecting? Yokoi's answer was a blend of moral, martial, and patriotic reasons:

In my opinion the vitality of a country is fostered by its middle class families; it is particularly well developed among farm families. Such qualities as innocence, sincerity, obedience, vigor, fortitude, trustworthiness, earnestness, and robust health are appropriate for soldiers and for defending the country. Don't farmers excel in these qualities above all? Although you cannot make a country out of land alone, the country must not become separated from the soil. Therefore the farmers, who have the closest connection with the land, love it the most and thus love the country the most. Likewise they are the people who feel the greatest loyalty for the ruler. If you accept the progressive doctrine that all men are brothers, it certainly is not necessary to define boundaries for countries using mountains, rivers, and lofty peaks, nor is it necessary to distinguish among peoples by means of ethnic differences. Therefore, to establish a country is an act of conservatism, and a country created by conservatism must initially be protected by conservative people. The only people who are particularly conservative are the farmers.[35]

Thus in 1897 Yokoi drew together the diverse strands of nineteenth-century agrarianism into a pattern for almost all farm-first thinking down to World War II: the ethical virtues of village life, the military advantages of farm recruits, the ideological soundness of rural ways of thinking, and agriculture as a source of economic and spiritual vitality,

[34] Ibid., p. 232.   [35] Ibid., p. 229.

no matter how much it had been eclipsed by manufacturing and trade. He devoted the rest of his career to working out these new perceptions in detail.

The Meiji conscription system was greatly resented in the countryside, and even once they were called up farmers made notoriously poor soldiers because of generally inferior health and education.[36] These facts did not deter Yokoi from asserting that all soldiers should spend as much time as possible in the rural areas, to purge the corrupting effects of duty in the cities and to keep farm recruits in touch with their home towns. Sons of the soil, he argued, were apt to be more fit for service physically and spiritually: "It isn't enough just to have a splendid body. You must also be a fine person spiritually, or else you won't make a first rate soldier." Where did such persons come from? "Most are the strong people of the countryside, people from local farm families."[37] Yokoi believed that farmers were also crucial for supplying food in wartime:

The reason our country occupies a position as one of the world's five strongest countries today is the meritorious service of plain dirt farmers who have represented such a superior element in our strong army from the Sino- and Russo-Japanese wars to the recent great war in Europe. This is a result of the prosperity of agriculture. Thus we must realize that, as history plainly shows, there has

[36] Okutani, "Nagare," pp. 4-6.
[37] Yokoi Tokiyoshi, "Tsuguri to kuwa" [Sword and Hoe], April 1914, *YHZS*, VI, 557. On this point see Sakurai, "Yokoi," p. 99; Katayama Seiichi, "Meiji zenki nōgyō shidōsha no nōgyō kyōikuron" [The Farm Education Outlook of Early Meiji Farm Leaders], *Nihon Daigaku Seishin Bunka Kenkyūjo-Kyōiku Seido Kenkyūjo kiyō* [Bulletin of the Nihon University Cultural Research Institute and Educational System Research Institute], IV, June 1967, 198; Takeuchi Tetsuo, "Nōhonshugi to nōson chūsansō" [Agrarianism and the Farm Village Middle Class], *Shimane Nōka Daigaku kenkyū hōkoku* [Shimane Agricultural University Research Reports], No. 8, A, March 1960, p. 232.

never yet been a country which could prosper for long if agriculture was decaying.[38]

Such practical questions of self-sufficiency were nevertheless minor compared with the more intangible benefits of farming in building patriotism. In January 1916 Yokoi identified a close relationship between agriculture and the imperial institution:

> Agriculture in our country has always been maintained thanks to the benevolence of the imperial throne. When the fortunes of the throne have risen, agriculture too has prospered; when the throne has declined, agriculture has occupied a very distressing position. In the Meiji era imperial rule was restored, and as a result agriculture flourished and the farmers were able gradually to grow secure in their dwellings. This is unprecedented since ancient times, and we must humbly give deep thanks for the assistance of the throne.[39]

Thus, in Yokoi's hazy, simplistic formulation, farmers served the state and throne both in the fields and in the ranks, a conviction shared by nearly all bureaucratic agrarianists, and a number of generals and politicians as well, from this time right through World War II.

In redefining the ways in which farming was important in Japanese life, Yokoi developed a set of statements between 1901 and 1909 which included a new producer class ethic similar to the feudal way of the warrior, or Bushido. In "Nōgyō kyōikuron" (Theory of Agricultural Education), written in 1901, he asserted that (1) farm villages formed the basis of the nation and were more circumspect and reliable than cities; (2) farmers were superior to city dwellers,

[38] Yokoi Tokiyoshi, "Nōgyō rikkoku no konpongi" [Basic Meaning of Establishing the Country on Agriculture], April 1914, *YHZS*, VIII, 235.

[39] Yokoi Tokiyoshi, "Tsuguri to kuwa," January 1916, *YHZS*, VI, 613.

physically, spiritually, and in their devotion to the state; and (3) farmers were the main source of social value: "Those who continue our country's Bushido are the mainstays of the country. They protect its discipline [*fūki*]. We must seek out such persons to serve as leaders of society."[40] In sum, reliability, patriotism, and discipline were the desirable qualities found above all in the countryside.

Yokoi recast his ideas in 1909 as "Kokumin gokun" (Five Admonitions to the People), reemphasizing national service, hard work, civic virtue, cooperation, and above all that "farmers should be the model class among the people; as the perpetuators of Bushido they should live self-sufficiently and have self-respect."[41] By farm Bushido Yokoi did not mean that cultivators should ape the elaborate code of honor found in feudal lord-follower relations (*shujū kankei*). Instead he hoped to infuse them with a new unyielding spirit, *makeji damashii*, so that they would fulfill their potential. In this way they would escape poverty, revive the village economy, and stem the exodus to the cities. Yokoi's farm Bushido was thus partly a work ethic to counteract commercialism: "Rather than calling farmers' labor cheap, it is better to say that it is priceless. If we promote enterprise based on this priceless labor, there is no fear that it will suffer competition. . . . It is quite beyond the pale of large scale mechanization."[42] His new spirit of rural self-assertiveness was specifically intended to bolster small farming so

[40] Yokoi Tokiyoshi, "Nōgyō kyōikuron" [Farm Education Theories], 1901, *YHZS*, IX, 90.

[41] Yokoi Tokiyoshi, "Kokumin gokun" [Five Admonitions to the People], 1909, quoted in Ishikawa and Katayama, p. 79. This essay was originally known as "Nōgyō gokun" [Five Admonitions Concerning Agriculture].

[42] Yokoi Tokiyoshi, "Nōka no fukugyōron" [Farmers' Subsidiary Enterprises], 1907, quoted in Sakurai Takeo, *Nihon nōhonshugi* [Japanese Agrarianism] (Tokyo: Hakuyōsha, 1935), p. 227. On farm Bushido, see Sumiya, p. 193; Katayama, pp. 211-215; Ishikawa and Katayama, pp. 82-83.

that the village economy could reestablish itself in Japanese life.

Farm Bushido was also useful for preserving the country's moral fiber, Yokoi believed, now that the warrior class no longer set standards of conduct. "City dwellers merely respect things in monetary terms," he wrote, "calculating everything on the basis of money and making profits without regard for their honor. Their conception of morality tends to be to sell land" (which was disruptive to peasant life). The only solution, Yokoi said, was to turn to farmers, "the only class which does not take money as its standard" and a "class with integrity."[43] In brief, the concept of *makeji damashii* would help cultivators resist commercialization on several counts: economically, through renewed productive vigor; socially, by stabilizing village life; and ethically, by eschewing the attitude of private profit.

In addition to martial and moral reasons for enhancing small farming, Yokoi wrote frequently after 1900 about the evils of city life and the inherent virtues of rural society. He rather petulantly attacked the government in 1907 for charging rural telephone and postal customers higher fees and delivering poorer service than in cities.[44] He also lashed out at its tacit favoritism to the urban rich:

Those who monopolize most of the money arbitrarily dominate. There is nothing that cannot be accomplished through the power of money. By contrast, the poor people who lack money suffer agonizing distress under the oppression of the rich. The wealthy capitalists use every

[43] Yokoi Tokiyoshi, *Nōson hattensaku* [Rural Development Policy] (Tokyo: Jitsugyō no Nihonsha, 1915), p. 13. It is curious that a press known for its publications favoring commercialism should have published Yokoi's tract.
[44] Yokoi Tokiyoshi, "Sonraku o hogo seyo" [Let's Protect the Villages], November 1907, *YHZS*, VII, 167-168. At the University of South Carolina Alan Stone is preparing a study of the Ashio mine case in which he treats its relationship to Nōhonshugi.

sort of means to make the poor people suffer while the state stands idly by. . . . Moreover recently certain ambitious city people have violated the interests of the villages, and I deeply regret that the countryside has become a sacrifice to ambitious persons.[45]

In Yokoi's view the government was robbing Peter to pay Paul by exploiting agriculture for the benefit of industry. He cited unfair taxation, corrupt politicians, and the debilitating effects of conscription on rural labor as examples of wrongheaded policies which should be reversed.

City life itself was corrosive, Yokoi held, because it stirred selfish ambitions. It was bad enough that the Meiji call for *risshin shusse* ("getting ahead") had corrupted the cities, he believed, but the real danger was that this spirit would spread: "I fear that the time is not far off when the metropolitan fever overwhelms the whole country, causing agony in the farm villages. When things come to this, the misfortunes of the farm villages will of course spread to the state. Is there any way to prevent this fever from spreading?"[46] Even more dangerous were subversive political ideas from the cities, especially socialism. Like Tani Kanjō ten years earlier, Yokoi deplored radical doctrines and concluded that "our only resort is the farmers. Whereas the cities are always where revolutions are made, the country is always opposed to revolution and protects the social order. The reason is, as Lord Salisbury put it, that without agriculture it is impossible to ward off revolution and defend the social order. A society with only cities, no countryside, is necessarily very dangerous."[47]

[45] Ibid., pp. 168-169.
[46] Yokoi Tokiyoshi, *Tokai to inaka* [City and Country] (Tokyo: Seibidō Shoten, 1913), pp. 141-142, quoted in Sakurai, "Yokoi," p. 94. At the University of Wisconsin Earl Kinmonth is investigating the Meiji concept of *risshin shusse*.
[47] Yokoi Tokiyoshi, *Tokai to inaka*, quoted in Tsunazawa Mitsuaki, *Kindai Nihon no dochaku shisō—nōhonshugi kenkyū* [Modern Jap-

Village life may have been worthwhile as a ballast against revolutionary ideologies, but Yokoi also believed that it had merit both as the foundation of the current state and as the basic autonomous unit of Japanese society:

Thus from every point of view the farmers must be the backbone of the state and the model class for the people. Accordingly, it goes without saying that the self-ruling villages formed by these farmers are the cornerstone of the state. As the country progresses, increasingly village self-rule becomes the central foundation of the country. The day the farmers' character and dignity fall to the earth and village self-rule fails to flourish will be the day the foundation of the state is endangered. The destiny of the farm villages fundamentally controls the fate of the state. The degree of self-rule represents the level of a country's civilization. We must unite our efforts to develop village self-rule.[48]

This statist affirmation of self-rule appears to align Yokoi with Hirata, Tomeoka, and others associated with the Hōtokukai who extolled village autonomy without decrying the concentration of powers in the national government which worried later agrarianists. Indeed, early in his career Yokoi had spoken out against the inefficiency of decentralized rule,[49] and even as late as 1915 he recognized that "the towns and villages are not practicing very much true self-rule today. At its worst, it is bureaucratic autonomy, because the state governs for them. The state, which has given the towns and villages self-rule, oppresses them."[50] Unfor-

---

anese Home Town Thought—Studies on Agrarianism] (Nagoya: Fūbaisha, 1969), p. 29.

[48] Yokoi Tokiyoshi, *Nōson hattensaku*, pp. 15-16.

[49] Kurihara Hyakuju, *Jinbutsu nōgyō dantaishi* [History of Outstanding Agricultural Association Leaders] (Tokyo: Shinhyōronsha, 1956), p. 47.

[50] Yokoi Tokiyoshi, "Nōson no jichi" [Village Self-Rule], June 1915, *YHZS*, VII, 25.

tunately the administrative units were too large for autonomy to prevail, and Yokoi held out little hope that his ideal could be accomplished, noting wistfully that "I don't think we can have self-rule like this."[51]

Small-scale farming was crucial, according to Yokoi Tokiyoshi, for military, ethical, political, social, and spiritual reasons, and government policy should be shaped accordingly. Although his arguments on behalf of small farms were widely respected in the debates on agricultural laws and programs after 1900, it would be inappropriate to conclude that he had so direct a hand in shaping policy as the many officials who by now supported bureaucratic Nōhonshugi. Nevertheless, as a senior specialist at a government agricultural college, Yokoi closely reflected the official cast of mind which upheld the importance of Japan's characteristic form of agriculture. He summarized this outlook in these words: "Agriculture is most honorable, profitable, and wholesome. Without yearning for money, it draws close to the land and takes mother nature as its friend. Being not covetous, it does not take impure persons as its partners. It is as free and independent as heaven. There is pleasure simply in working. It is relaxing."[52]

However welcome this salubrious vision of farming was to the state, even Yokoi's greatest admirers within the bureaucracy recognized that it was tinged with unrealism. To oppose capitalism was easy in theory but no longer a reasonable alternative for a government which for forty years had staked its reputation on building national wealth and power. Nevertheless the lesser option of rescuing agriculture from the predicament thrust upon it by capitalism remained open to the state, and Yokoi's voice was widely heard when measures to aid the villages were presented to the Diet.

[51] Ibid., p. 26.
[52] Yokoi Tokiyoshi, quoted in Fukutake Tadashi, *Nihon no nōson shakai* [Japanese Rural Society] (Tokyo: Tokyo Daigaku Shuppankai, 1953), p. 181.

To what degree was Yokoi a spokesman for the interests of landlords, and which ones? When he wrote as a young man of shaping farm education "appropriate to people's occupations,"[53] he evidently sought different training for tenants, owner-farmers, and large landlords—a sign that he accepted the hierarchy of village society dominated by the big landholders. Somewhat later, in advocating farm Bushido, he specified that "the only way is to nurture it among the higher ranking farmers in the localities."[54] Yokoi was also an ardent believer in agricultural tariffs, which especially benefited large landowners, and he spoke forcefully in support of the rice duty measures in 1904 and thereafter.[55]

But Yokoi's views, like those of many late Meiji policymakers, transcended the landlord classes themselves. As someone concerned with protecting village society, he was obliged to work through whatever local leaders remained— in many cases, the small, more conservative owner-farmers who had replaced large landowners by default. It would be wrong to cast the mature Yokoi as an opponent of better education, land rehabilitation, credit societies, and the like. But he deemphasized these aspects of rural betterment after 1900 in order to stress ethical maxims and an antiprogressive outlook that appealed more to smaller, less imaginative landholders than to those large landlords who took a favorable view of technical development. *Jisakunō* were more apt to agree with his opposition to commercialization than the large landlords who were profiting from it.

In reality Yokoi upheld small farming by petty owner-cultivators with such determination that, as the economist Fukuda Tokuzō (1874-1930) put it, his anticapitalist theories

[53] Yokoi Tokiyoshi, "Kōnō ronsaku," p. 676. See also Sakurai, "Yokoi," p. 101.

[54] Yokoi Tokiyoshi, quoted in Sumiya, "Keiseiki," p. 194.

[55] See Sakai Yoshirō, "Nihon jinushisei to nōhonshugi [The Japanese Landlord System and Agrarianism], *Keizai ronsō* [Collection of Economic Theories], LXXXVIII, 5, 1961, 68; Sakurai, *Nihon nōhonshugi*, pp. 284-289.

failed to take account of "the economic inability of small farmers to subsist."[56] It would have been out of character for Yokoi to be a mouthpiece for large landlords, since they were too citified and profit oriented to suit his tastes. Yokoi's ideal type was the small village landowner who formed the same backbone of rural society that state officials had tried to strengthen in the 1890s. From this point forward the main stream of Nōhonshugi thought was identified not with large landlords but with self-ruling village society as a whole, under the leadership of the small landowners who exemplified the rural virtues so keenly sought by Yokoi and his followers.

[56] Fukuda Tokuzō, quoted in Okutani, "Nagare," p. 8. See also Sakai, p. 70; Sakurai, "Yokoi," pp. 95-96; Tsunazawa, p. 83.

Chapter V

Popular Agrarianism in the Early Twentieth Century

A DYSPEPTIC revolutionary once said that a person need not be able to comprehend Marx in order to be a good Marxist. In a way this was true of popular agrarianism in Japan during the first two decades of the twentieth century, in the sense that attitudes toward farming expressed by the most significant nonofficial agrarianists of the day showed a good deal less consistency and rigor than the bureaucratic Nōhonshugi set forth by Hirata Tōsuke, Shinagawa Yajirō, and especially Yokoi Tokiyoshi. Of course even Yokoi's astute ideas on the subject fell far short of the logical clarity and integrity expected of a formal system of philosophical or social thought. Still there was a certain evenness of temperament and outlook in official agrarianism during the late Meiji and early Taishō (1912-1926) periods, compared with the inchoate, diffuse canons of even the most perceptive Nōhonshugi advocates within Japanese society at large during the period 1900-1920.

Although Yokoi may have had a better understanding of his dogma, many other popular ideologues beat the drums of agrarianism in the early twentieth century. Just as Yokoi had redefined the target of Nōhonshugi ideas to center henceforth on small village farming led by owner-cultivators, so a fresh group of agricultural thinkers not closely associated with state farm policies amplified and extended Nōhonshugi doctrines to all levels of rural society during the period from 1900 to the close of World War I. In the process they hastened the trend begun by the bureaucratic agrarianists in the 1890s whereby Nōhonshugi ideas became clearly identified with resistance to the overall direction of Japanese modernization. From this point forward it is proper to speak of Nōhonshugi thought not merely as a response to national development but also, at many points, as an outright reaction to it. In this respect it became a form of counter-thought, denoting ideas formed in response to the effects of capitalism on the countryside but also connoting a reverse, or reactionary, drift of thought in which men glorified premodern village life.

The early years of the twentieth century were rife with farm thinkers in Japan. Most persons have forgotten that the great social anthropologist Yanagida Kunio (1875-1962) began his career as a minor officeholder in the Nōshōmushō (Ministry of Agriculture and Commerce) and wrote on farming at the end of the Meiji era.[1] Yanagida bluntly criticized government farm policies for their landlord bias and their failure to pour in more funds to help the villages.[2]

---

[1] Tsunazawa Mitsuaki, *Kindai Nihon no dochaku shisō—nōhonshugi kenkyū* [Modern Japanese Home Town Thought—Studies on Agrarianism] (Nagoya: Fūbaisha, 1969), pp. 147-166; Tsunazawa Mitsuaki, *Nōhonshugi no kenkyū* [Studies on Agrarianism] (Nagoya: Fūbaisha, 1968), pp. 37-60; Denda Isao, *Kindai Nihon nōsei shisō no kenkyū* [Studies on Modern Japanese Agricultural Administration Thought], p. 139f. At Princeton University Ronald Morse is preparing a study of Yanagida, and at Columbia University Carol Gluck is investigating the rise of conservative ideology in late Meiji.

[2] Takeuchi Tetsuo, "Nōhonshugi to nōson chūsansō" [Agrarianism and the Farm Village Middle Class], *Shimane Nōka Daigaku kenkyū hōkoku* [Shimane Agricultural University Research Reports], No. 8, A, March 1960, p. 232; Sumiya Kazuhiko, "Keiseiki Nihon burujoajī no shisōzō" [Images of the Japanese Bourgeoisie During the Formative Period], *Kindai Nihon keizai shisōshi* [History of Modern Japanese Economic Thought], ed. Chō Yukio and Sumiya Kazuhiko (Tokyo: Yūhikaku, 1969), I, 218.

Although he had no objection to the Hōtokukai in itself, he opposed its "excessive feudalism and lack of modernity"[3] as inadequate for carrying out a rural improvement campaign that would really help the small producer.

Other famous authors echoed Yanagida's concern for rural culture. During the teens the eminent novelists Natsume Sōseki (1867-1916) and Arishima Takeo (1878-1923) both lamented the decline of the village spirit and the sudden rise of tenancy disputes.[4] Shortly before he died in 1923, Arishima wrote:

> Although I cannot say that I have looked too deeply into the problem of the villages, I think at least we can say that the time is probably coming when landlord-tenant relations will collapse. . . . What should be done about this? So long as the state believes as a matter of principle that the private ownership of land and capital represents the ideal economic condition and provides security for private-property owners, I think that it will not be possible to solve this problem completely. National ownership or ownership by society would be fine. At any rate I think it essential that private ownership disappear.[5]

Acting upon his convictions, Arishima symbolically eradicated the landlord class by distributing his lands to tenants and taking his own life.

Yet another writer to search for the ideal village community was the novelist Mushakōji Saneatsu (1885-), who founded the first of several utopian settlements known as Atarashiki Mura, or new villages, in 1918.[6] Like Yanagida, Natsume, and Arishima, he was especially eager to abolish

---

[3] Tsunazawa, *Kindai*, pp. 31-32.   [4] Tsunazawa, *Nōhonshugi*, p. 20.
[5] Arishima Takeo, "Nōson mondai no kiketsu" [Solution to the Rural Village Problem], 1923, *Arishima Takeo zenshū* [Complete Works of Arishima Takeo] (Tokyo: Sōbunkaku, 1924-1925), VII, 491-492.
[6] See B. D. Tucker, "Mushakōji Saneatsu: His Life and Influence," M.A. thesis in Far Eastern Languages, Harvard University, 1958.

class conflict by improving the quality of rural life. "What we are trying to do," he wrote, "is to create a new society. We will create a society in which, in exchange for a fixed amount of work, we will escape from all worries about food, shelter and clothing, and fulfill our destinies without need of money."[7]

The impress of modern ideologies is apparent in the case of each of these well-known writers who ventured into agrarianism early in the twentieth century. Socialist ideas appealed strongly to both Arishima and Mushakōji, and they as well as Yanagida and Natsume were well versed in liberal individualism from the contemporary West. Their farm writings accounted for mere fragments of their total repertoire, but the very existence of this literature suggests that anxiety about the fate of village Japan had now spread far beyond those officials most directly responsible for farm policy to affect the outlooks of many thoughtful and influential people in society as a whole.

Among the many popular agrarianists of the day, most noteworthy were two very diverse personalities, the famous Marxist theoretician Kawakami Hajime (1879-1946) and the obscure farm labor leader Yokota Hideo (1889-1926). Although he is best known for his brilliant critiques of capitalism prepared during his long teaching career at Kyoto University, as a young man Kawakami spent several years teaching agricultural economics and became a protégé of Yokoi Tokiyoshi. His views of Japanese farming in this period resembled bureaucratic agrarianism in a number of respects, but the young Kawakami broke with the previous interpreters of Nōhonshugi on several points, thus marking himself out as a fresh voice on behalf of aiding farmers. Yokota, one of the few Japanese agrarianists who were also owner-cultivators, confronted the clash between capitalism

[7] Mushakōji Saneatsu, "Tochi" [The Land], *Gendai Nihon bungaku zenshū* [Collection of Modern Japanese Literature], xxvi, *Mushakōji Saneatsushū* (Tokyo: Kaizō, 1928), p. 418, quoted in Tucker, p. 35.

and small-scale farming in a series of essays on the "rural revolution" during the teens. By the close of his career he expanded the scope of his own Nōhonshugi thought to treat not only landlords and owner-farmers but also the tenant masses, whom he believed to be the true victims of of commercialization. After summarizing Kawakami's brief encounter with farm thought, I shall take up Yokota's rural revolution and its position in the Japanese agrarianist tradition.

Kawakami Hajime: Farming Without Capitalism

A native of Yamaguchi Prefecture, Kawakami Hajime graduated from Tokyo University with a degree in law in September 1902. Frustrated in his attempts to find work with either the Mitsui Bank or the *Mainichi*, a major daily newspaper in Tokyo, he finally took a position in 1903 as a lecturer at Tokyo Nōka Daigaku, where he soon became acquainted with Yokoi Tokiyoshi.[8] Within a year he had produced his major essay on agriculture, "Nihon sonnōron" (Respecting Japanese Agriculture), which was published in 1904 in a journal edited by Yokoi. Kawakami began this work on a brash note by challenging those critics who no longer believed farming could be defended on economic grounds:

> In my opinion most people who argue in favor of emphasizing agriculture do so because of its relationship with either the military, public order, or hygiene. Thus, in the end, they do not consider it advantageous for economic reasons. Therefore those who are prone to despise agriculture say that of course the preservation of agriculture has certain benefits, but in the end isn't it economically unprofitable? This is a most regrettable misconception, and I'd like to pay particular attention to clarifying it.[9]

[8] Sumiya Etsuji, *Kawakami Hajime* (Tokyo: Yoshikawa Kōbunkan, 1962), pp. 61-63.

[9] Kawakami Hajime, "Nihon sonnōron" [Respecting Japanese

The Japanese government, he continued, was wrong to mimic England by permitting such massive urbanization while doing nothing to stop the impoverishment of the farms. If the villages were poor, he asked rhetorically, who could buy the industrial goods produced in the cities?[10]

Kawakami feared that Japan would overemphasize manufacturing in the flush of victory in warfare: "Our first reason for attacking the economic policy of favoring commerce is that it is the branch and agriculture the root. Thus we advocate limiting domestic commerce."[11] He attacked trade and industry as unproductive in comparison with farming, echoing physiocratic views from the eighteenth century. Nevertheless Kawakami did not wish to abolish the urban sector; instead he wanted to develop agriculture more fully than the state had previously done. If this were accomplished, he claimed, the whole economy would gain: "A second reason for rejecting the idea of basing the country entirely on industry and for advancing the benefits of preserving agriculture is that the development of agriculture cheapens the production costs of industrial goods [by providing inexpensive raw materials] and thus causes export trade to flourish."[12] To this he added that the villages supplied reliable workers for the factories as well as the food to sustain the population.

Kawakami elaborated on the economic advantages of farming in *Nihon nōseigaku* (Studies on Japanese Agricultural Administration), published in 1906. Here he said that it was not enough to regard agriculture as an activity that was good because it fed the nation or employed the most persons. Instead, he reiterated, farming must be stimulated

---

Agriculture], 1904, *Kawakami Hajime chosakushū* [Collected Writings of Kawakami Hajime] (Tokyo: Chikuma Shobō, 1964), I, 135. This essay first appeared in a journal called *Kyoyūken bunko* in June 1904.

[10] Ibid., pp. 150-152.   [11] Ibid., p. 166.

[12] Ibid., p. 175. See Denda, pp. 145-148; Sumiya, *Kawakami Hajime*, pp. 73-74.

equally with trade and industry, "to plan and promote all the people's prosperity."[13] He also opposed free imports of agricultural goods as harmful to the villages, establishing himself as a protectionist rather than physiocrat on the trade issue.[14] Writing in a tradition set by Ishikawa Rikinosuke and Maeda Masana, he called for enhancing farm output because it would benefit the whole country. Kawakami dismissed Yokoi's view that trade and industry enriched the nation, while farming protected it: "When I think about enriching the country, I believe that agriculture is equally indispensable as trade and industry as an economic element."[15]

Kawakami's valiant but quixotic efforts to rationalize agriculture on its economic merits did not represent much of an advance beyond the ideas of conscientious landlord-officials twenty years before him. However, he also offered a series of noneconomic reasons for promoting farming which placed him in the mainstream of Nōhonshugi thinking in his day. Although personally a pacifist and humanist at this stage of his career, Kawakami adduced several military advantages in having a strong rural economy. One was self-sufficiency in wartime; another was that industry was more susceptible to shocks under wartime conditions than agriculture. A third reason was that farm life produced robustness and close interpersonal relations, characteristics of a sound army.[16]

"In short, agriculture is the wellspring of a strong army and the preservation of agriculture is essential for victory. Nowadays individuals do not resort to struggles of brute force; instead our disputes are all settled by the state" through laws.[17] But since the ideal of world peace was beyond reach and international quarrels were still settled by

[13] Kawakami Hajime, *Nihon nōseigaku* (Tokyo, 1906), p. 143.
[14] Sumiya, "Keiseiki," p. 197.
[15] Kawakami Hajime, *Nihon nōseigaku*, p. 143.
[16] Kawakami Hajime, "Nihon sonnōron," pp. 185-195.
[17] Ibid., p. 198.

117

force, he noted, "it is necessary to maintain brute force. Because brute force is necessary, we must also preserve agriculture."[18] Regardless of this egregious non sequitur, it would be unfair and irrelevant to expect the twenty-five-year-old Kawakami to hold the unbridled antimilitarist opinions which characterized his later Marxist phase. Still his rather ingenuous outlook on the connection between farming and the army was typical of the orthodox nationalist position embraced by most Nōhonshugisha from Tani Kanjō and Yokoi Tokiyoshi onward.

There were other reasons as well why agriculture should be nurtured. Kawakami advocated population growth and contended that "there is an important relationship between the countryside and people's health and fertility."[19] Country living was more hygienic and wholesome, he believed, although he conceded that "I am not so bold as to deplore the flow of population into the cities; I merely regret it when this flow is at an excessively high level." He called the gradual shift of population from country to city a "law of nature," something he said he did not wish to resist. However, he warned, "the cause of our continued suffering is the reduction of the numbers of farmers below the number needed. Indeed the existence of rural people is the foundation of a nation's wealth and strength. Therefore the decline of these basic farmers truly endangers the cornerstone upon which the country is built."[20]

Kawakami's suggestions for correcting the contradictions between the state's industrial and agricultural policies were concentrated on the small farmers who comprised the majority of Japan's cultivators. He recommended land-adjustment programs, improved irrigation and transportation, and better credit facilities. He also supported the protective tariff measures before the Diet in 1904, and he called for a

[18] Ibid. See Sumiya, Kawakami Hajime, pp. 72-73, on Kawakami's pacifism.
[19] Kawakami Hajime, "Nihon sonnōron," p. 207.
[20] Ibid., p. 210.

cut in land taxes.[21] The small owner-cultivators themselves, he asserted, must take the initiative by forming producers' cooperatives under the recent Sangyō Kumiaihō.[22] Such policies closely resembled the programs initiated by bureaucratic agrarianists in the early twentieth century, although Kawakami did not idealize local autonomy or village communalism and took a distinctly forward-looking view of farm growth compared with that of Yokoi Tokiyoshi.

The purpose of protecting agriculture through such producer-oriented programs, Kawakami argued, was to thwart the "collision" between modern commerce and indigenous morality which underlay the rural quandary. He slammed the capitalist lust for profits in uncompromising terms, warning that "farmers must not be dazzled in vain by the prosperity of merchants and workers."[23] The spirit of money-making was the epitome of selfishness, he believed, and it was also contrary to human nature to be greedy for profit.[24] It was the capitalist economy which inculcated such false values, and it behooved farmers not "to abandon their precious occupations or leave the priceless fields of their ancestors."[25] Kawakami insisted that the countryside was the repository of true values, such as frugality, harmony, altruism, and cooperation; farmers could both cut their own costs and thwart the spread of selfish norms of commercialism by working together through Sangyō Kumiai and other joint enterprises.

Unlike the many gloomy agrarian prophets of his age, Kawakami Hajime believed that farming could still be upheld on economic grounds, provided the spirit which guided

[21] Kawakami Hajime, *Nihon nōseigaku*, pp. 152-155. See Sumiya, "Keiseiki," pp. 195-198, 202.

[22] Kawakami Hajime, "Nihon sonnōron," p. 209.

[23] Ibid., p. 213. See Gail Lee Bernstein, "Kawakami Hajime: Portrait of a Reluctant Revolutionary," Ph.D. dissertation in history, Harvard University, 1967, pp. 46-47.

[24] Kawakami Hajime, "Nihon sonnōron," p. 166.

[25] Ibid., p. 213.

it was selfless and optimistic. It is true that he never fully resolved the dilemma posed by his modern and traditional arguments for fostering agriculture.[26] On the one hand, he taught that the villages supplied materials, labor, and markets for the urban sector; on the other, he praised farmers as the bearers of time-honored ethical standards. But it is patent that Kawakami wanted rural development to offset the encroachment of capitalist values. He hoped to find a way for farmers to live within a modern commercial economy without accepting its profit motive. He regarded the Diet as the protector of landlord interests rather than those of all cultivators, and he vehemently denounced its continuing policy of financing industrial growth through heavy land taxes.[27] Hence Kawakami differed from Yokoi Tokiyoshi and most contemporary Nōhonshugisha on two vital points: (1) he spoke for the needs of all rural workers, rather than landlords (large or small), insisting that the nation could be strong only if all village dwellers were prosperous; (2) he took a more progressive view of historical development that permitted him to see beyond commercialism to modern national wealth without the selfish spirit of acquisitiveness.

Although Kawakami never worked out the details of this vision, it is evident that he responded to the clash of commerce and farming not by seeking a revival of premodern village solidarity but by suggesting some guidelines for modern agrarian growth without the evils of capitalism. In this respect his form of counterthought was more a response than a reaction to the rise of commerce. To achieve farm prosperity without capitalism would have been nearly impossible, and it is not surprising that Kawakami soon abandoned the agricultural question to concentrate directly on the problem of capitalism itself. As a partisan of the view that the villages must be protected on economic, military, and spiritual grounds, the young Kawakami wrote from a Nōhonshugi viewpoint, but his rejection of policies favoring

[26] See Bernstein, p. 56.   [27] See Sumiya, "Keiseiki," p. 207.

private landholders and his forward-looking image of rural development made him a progressive agrarianist who cast the net of the farm-first tradition well beyond the assumptions of its previous bureaucratic adherents. It remained for popular agrarianists such as Yokota Hideo to carry these themes forward, from very different perspectives, during the decade of the teens.

Yokota Hideo's Rural Revolution

Since Yokota Hideo (1889-1926) devoted the most important years of his short life to the tenant movement which began during World War I, it was natural that he should confront the problem of rural class conflict in his farm thought more directly than earlier Japanese agrarianists. Yet he accepted the general premises of Nōhonshugi thought, unlike the many subsequent Nōmin Undō (Peasant Movement) leaders who were propelled by a simple animus against landlords. Little is known of Yokota's early years.[28] He was born in Saitama Prefecture in 1889 to an owner-farmer (*jisakunō*) family with about one hectare of farmland. He apparently lived in Fukushima Prefecture as a child, but dropped out of middle school to return to his native village to work on the family farm. He worked in Tokyo as a journalist for the *Yomiuri* from 1909 to 1917, the period in which he wrote nearly all his works on agriculture. He left the city to return to farming and soon became involved with the Hoku Nihon Nōmin Kumiai (Northern Japan Peasants' Association). On April 20, 1924, he was made head of the Central Japan Peasants' Association in Gifu Prefecture, where he remained active in the tenant movement until he died of tuberculosis in February 1926.

Conflict between landlords and tenants was certainly not unknown in Japan before World War I, but the enormous

[28] For Yokota see Tsunazawa, *Kindai*, pp. 135-146; Yamamoto Gyō, "Yokota Hideo no shisō" [The Thought of Yokota Hideo], *Gifu Daigaku Gakugei Gakubu kenkyū hōkoku* [Gifu University Faculty of Arts Research Reports], No. 9, 1960, pp. 64-72.

industrial expansion of the war years intensified old class frictions in the countryside and soon led to the birth of a full-dress tenant movement. The last nine years of Yokota's life coincided with a huge increase in tenancy disputes, leading to the creation of the first tenant union in 1922.[29] The acceleration of rural class conflict in the teens may be traced primarily to the changing relationships between landlords and tenants brought about by capitalism. The economic consequences of the decision of large landlords gradually to abandon land in favor of city living and investments are uncertain, but plainly these big landowners came decreasingly to play the important social roles in village life that had once preserved harmonious relations with their tenants.[30] As landlords left the countryside, they no longer settled local disputes, negotiated marriages, celebrated feasts, or provided relief in lean years. To this increasingly anonymous relationship between renter and tenant must be added the influence of universal education, conscription, and the mass media in dissolving rural paternalism and raising tenants' awareness of national political and economic issues. With landlord-tenant ties thus already weakened in most areas of Japan by the teens, the 1918 rice riots and consequent drop in farm prices caused by fresh rice imports from Korea and Taiwan played havoc with class relations by rendering farm incomes for all rural groups very uncertain.[31] The result was the massive tenant movement of the 1920s and 1930s.

Yokota Hideo was a main figure in the early tenant move-

[29] See *Nihon nōmin undōshi* [History of the Japanese Peasant Movement], ed. Nōmin Undōshi Kenkyūkai (Tokyo: Tōyō Keizai Shinbunsha, 1961); *Nihon nōmin undōshi* [History of the Japanese Peasant Movement], ed. Aoki Keiichirō, 6 vols. (Tokyo: Nihon Hyōron Shinsha, 1959-1962). Statistics must be used with care, since mild petitions and even simple requests for delayed payments were often classified as disputes.

[30] Ann Waswo, "Landlords and Social Change in Prewar Japan," Ph.D. dissertation in history, Stanford University, 1969, pp. 113-117.

[31] See Ronald P. Dore, *Land Reform in Japan* (London: Oxford University Press, 1959), pp. 20-22.

ment who regarded landlord-tenant relations as one aspect of the larger question of agricultural development. In 1914 he turned out his major work, *Nōson kakumeiron* (On Rural Revolution), in which he set forth his farm thought in terms notable both for their indignation and for their occasional opacity. Yokota frankly noted the gap between the ideal condition of Japanese society and its present predicament. In theory, he said, "the relationship between rulers and ruled is like the relationship between lord and minister or father and son."[32] In common with many Japanese social theorists, Yokota thought that "our country is uniquely classless in all the world, an ideal country unique in all history."[33] The farmer was the central prop of this ideal society:

> Isn't it true that the brilliance of our national essence, which all lands should envy, is that it is maintained by the farmers? . . . The most important thing our farm villages produce are the silent apostles of nationalism. . . . Our two-thousand-year-long history is the history of one great family, with the imperial throne at the center. Thus the farmers are truly the creators of this brilliant history.[34]

Such romantic words make it tempting to label Yokota an agricultural determinist insofar as historical causation is concerned.

But in actuality Yokota's very orthodox, tutelary view of society could not be attained so long as rural poverty was widespread:

> If we were to comment without reserve, it would be more appropriate to call the farmer's life today the life of an animal, not a man. At least if we take the middle class city

[32] Yokota Hideo, *Nōson kakumeiron* [On Rural Revolution] (Tokyo: Hakubunkan, 1914), p. 35.

[33] Yokota Hideo, *Nōson kaikakusaku* [Rural Reform Policy] (Tokyo: Hakubunkan, 1916), p. 284.

[34] Yokota Hideo, *Nōson kyūsairon* [On Rescuing the Farm Villages] (Tokyo: Hakubunkan, 1914), pp. 32-33.

dweller's standard of living as average, the farmer's life is really half human, half animal. He lives in an unrepaired, ramshackle home, wears dirty, unmended clothing, sleeps on old, cold straw mats, and eats food that city dwellers have turned their backs on. Who can really imagine what it is to live like a farmer, tyrannized by poverty and exhausted in mind and body? . . . Who can speak of the natural harmony of the farm villages? Who says that the villages are gardens of flowers? Who can talk about the spontaneous happiness of the villages? . . . The starting point for discussing the farm villages is the phrase "among the farmers there is no food to eat."[35]

Symptomatic of this state of affairs, Yokota maintained, were the decline of *jisakunō* and the sharp clash of interests between landlords and tenants caused by the impoverishment of the latter. Ultimately both symptoms could be attributed to the shameless exploitation of agriculture by rich capitalists and government administrators. As Yokota wrote in 1916, the farmers had failed to attain prosperity because of "bureaucratic politicians enmeshed in feudal thought and controversial scholars whose nature it is to act out of self-interest."[36] Although he shared the Nōhonshugi ideal of social harmony under the throne, Yokota was a heretic to bureaucratic agrarianists because he exposed intravillage class conflict, something which Shinagawa, Hirata, and Yokoi had always denied. He also set himself off as an outsider by sharply attacking the Satsuma-Chōshū bureaucratic clique which, he believed, set farm policies for the benefit of landlords alone. Under present practices, he said, all farm profits "end up in the hands of landlords as tenant fees."[37]

[35] Yokota Hideo, *Nōson kakumeiron*, p. 44.
[36] Yokota Hideo, *Nōson kaikakusaku*, pp. 11-12. See Sakai Yoshirō, "Nihon jinushisei to nōhonshugi" [The Japanese Landlord System and Agrarianism], *Keizai ronsō* [Collection of Economic Theories], LXXXVIII, 5, 1961, 72-75; Yamamoto, p. 68.
[37] Yokota Hideo, *Nōson kakumeiron*, p. 120.

Nevertheless Yokota was no mere opponent of centralized government. Instead he spoke as a small farmer who could see the changing nature of village society and feel the economic stresses wrought by commercialization. Like Kawakami Hajime, he said that the root of the problem lay in the declining fertility of the soil. He believed that "the land is the thing closest to nature. The land is the most powerful thing. The land is the source of all life."[38] He knew from personal experience that this visionary outlook was tempered by niggardly land yields in many parts of rural Japan, an evil he ascribed to the effects of the landlord system which the state so carefully promoted (conveniently ignoring the many local improvements instituted by conscientious landlords during the Meiji era).

Yokota's analysis of the rural revolution was more apocalyptic than hopeful. The first phase of this fearsome revolution, he said, was already well under way: the conversion of owner-cultivators into tenants. This led unavoidably, he maintained, to demands that rents be reduced: "I do not hesitate to predict that in the near future our country's farmers will continue to promote movements to reduce rents."[39] Yokota admitted that tenancy conflicts "were class disputes between landlords and tenants over the division of profits"[40] but regarded them as both ineluctable and necessary if the rural revolution were to be halted. It was true, he observed, that Japan used conciliation to settle conflicts of interest more than the West, but with the rise of capitalism this indigenous method would no longer suffice: "Class conflicts in the West are based completely on self-interest and cannot be solved until one side submits, but class conflicts in Japan are settled by exchanges of kindness. To the extent that clashes of interest between landlords and tenants

---

[38] Yokota Hideo, *Yomiuri shinbun* article, August 2, 1917, quoted in Sakai, p. 79. See Tsunazawa, *Kindai*, pp. 139-140.

[39] Yokota Hideo, *Nōson kakumeiron*, p. 128.

[40] Ibid., p. 136.

are increasing, however, it is impossible to prevent class antagonisms in advance merely by anticipating that they will be resolved."[41]

Yokota found the drive to reduce rents "regrettable" in the sense that it would not have been necessary had big financiers and government policy-makers prevented the demise of rural living standards. However, since Japan was deeply immersed in the first revolutionary phase, Yokota argued that "from the point of view of both national interest and the interests of agriculture, is it not essential to limit tenant rents and provide them with minimum national living expenses? Hence the advantages of limiting tenant fees can clearly be recognized: it would prevent the land-lord-tenant disorders which are forecast for the farm world of the future and would cure the social diseases born from class conflict."[42]

If rents were not reduced and small proprietors became completely submerged by large landlords, Yokota warned, Japan would enter a second more serious revolutionary stage in which landlord-tenant relations would give way to capitalist methods of production. He feared that the rural masses would be reduced to the condition of daily wage laborers: "Ever since the impoverishment of the self-culti-vating farmer class, the owner-farmers have fallen, the tenant system has expanded, and they [the former *jisakunō*] have come to lead the lives of tenants. Finally the tenant system will be abolished, and some day the owner-farmers, after any number of changes, will become agricultural laborers."[43] Like their cousins in city factories, they would end up working on ranches and plantations in the hire of huge agricultural businessmen. Here the rural revolution ended, Yokota thought. Henceforth there would be virtually nothing except "large landlords with agricultural laborers

[41] Yokota Hideo, "Nihon nōsonron" [On Japanese Farm Villages], 1915, quoted in Takeuchi, p. 233.
[42] Yokota Hideo, *Nōson kyūsairon*, p. 202.
[43] Yokota Hideo, *Nōson kakumeiron*, p. 145.

clustered around them like ants."[44] This, he grimly commented, was the setting for class war.

Yokota's précis of rural revolution was marked by inconsistencies and contradictions, especially in quantifying the actual disparity in income between landlords and tenants.[45] Surely it was unrealistic to expect that Japan could ever lapse into plantation agriculture, given the environmental, technical, and social objections which had scuttled Ōkubo Toshimichi's large-scale farm plans in the 1870s. Yokota spoke of plantations not as a literal possibility but as a metaphor for the absurd state to which commercialism might reduce all cultivators if steps were not taken at once to rescue both owner-farmers and tenants from their common plight. His deliberate rhetorical use of revolution as a negative process, something to be forestalled rather than confirmed, demonstrated the conservative bent of his social thought and distinguished him unmistakably from later leaders of the Nōmin Undō who felt no such commitment to preserving rural harmony.

Just as the government should encourage rent reductions to help tenants, Yokota asserted, so it should also carry out a land reform program to reestablish owner-cultivators: "The state should establish a fixed system with laws to induce landlords to sell land and give tenants subsidies and protection in purchase negotiations so they can buy it. What is more, the state should buy up specially designated lands itself and apportion them among tenants with low interest, annual installment payments."[46] Once such measures were taken, Yokota confidently asserted, there would be little danger that landlordism would emerge anew, because the *jisakunō* would now be settled permanently on their lands, protected by the state from the penetration of capitalism into the rural economy.[47]

The pressing need to rehabilitate owner-cultivators was

[44] Ibid.   [45] See Yamamoto, p. 65.
[46] Yokota Hideo, *Nōson kyūsairon*, p. 45.
[47] See Sakai, p. 74.

compounded by the recent "demise of patriotism," "advent of extreme individualistic thought," and "growth of socialist thought,"[48] which Yokota believed were connected with the decay of the *jisakunō* class. Later in 1914 he wrote that "severe class conflict is occurring in our agricultural world, and as a result the time has come when socialism has swiftly arisen and spread to shake the very foundation of our two-thousand-year-old state. . . . We are on the verge of a fearful national crisis."[49] It was the independent cultivator, well established in his landholdings, who was the best defense against radicalism and the surest guide toward realizing the "two-thousand-year dream of peace," living in a classless society under the imperial throne.

Yokota's portrait of the ideal rural society, as well as his analysis of current village problems, may appear quaint or precious, and it may well seem amusing that he denounced Yokoi Tokiyoshi as "a revolutionary agrarian theorist who would destroy the owner-farmer system,"[50] in light of Yokoi's spirited defense of precisely that system. But it is worth recalling that Yokota, like many another Japanese thinker in his day, was struggling to reconcile his devotion to nation (but not state) with his commitment to justice for the rural poor. Only very reluctantly did he countenance the tenant rent-reduction movement, and only then as a means of restoring the social harmony that had been disrupted by modern market forces.

Land reforms and rent reductions were radical proposals in the Japan of 1914, but Yokota fitted them to his conservative image of a smoothly functioning rural order, renouncing socialism, faithfully serving the throne, and returning the small cultivator to his rightful place as the pillar of the Japanese state and society. In these respects Yokota's thought was consistent with Nōhonshugi teachings and rather divorced from the oppressive realities of rural

[48] Yokota Hideo, *Nōson kakumeiron*, p. 162.
[49] Yokota Hideo, *Nōson kyūsairon*, p. 171.
[50] Yokota Hideo, *Nōson kakumeiron*, p. 319.

poverty—realities which the tenant movement he soon helped to launch protested so vigorously in the 1920s and 1930s.

Although Yokota's chief ideas about farming were already formed before the rise of a broad tenant movement at the end of World War I, his thinking about farming developed in response to new social and intellectual currents in the late teens and early twenties. In 1916, for example, he made it plain that he considered himself a full-fledged Nōhonshu-gisha, even though its earlier partisans had never directly attacked the landlord system.[51] Yet if he denounced land-lords, Yokota wrote a year later, he did not wish to base his criticisms on theoretical grounds. Although he had earlier opposed it as dangerous, Yokota now contended that "social-ism is a reasonable doctrine and a reasonable movement. But is it possible for a theory and a movement which can only expect to be effective when all men show heroic resolve and simultaneously make diligent efforts to be capable of results? I for one doubt it."[52] By the same token, his objec-tions to capitalism derived not from its ideology but from the ill effects it produced—above all the landlord system. "If the only way to escape from poverty is to reject capital-ism," he concluded, "I would have no scruples about re-jecting capitalism in my own life."[53]

After returning to farming in late 1917, Yokota soon saw that tenants must be organized into mass associations if rents were ever to be reduced. Like the urban workers who had formed the labor union movement, he argued, tenants should band together in self-defense:

The time has already come. How about now? Has not the self-consciousness of the workers, stimulated by the victory of democracy, boldly given rise to the labor movement which today demands economic and spiritual

[51] Yokota Hideo, *Nōson kaikakusaku*, p. 228.
[52] Yokota Hideo, *Yomiuri shinbun* article, August 29, 1917, quoted in Sakai, p. 78.
[53] Ibid.

liberation for the workers? . . . The tenants, who have suppressed their own class consciousness as though it were a bud of treason, have been shaken by the practical results of the labor movement which is now overwhelming the world. Are they not shedding the husk of their slave mentality day by day?[54]

Although he flirted briefly with the idea of starting a farmer-labor alliance (*rōnō dōmei*), Yokota soon rejected help from urban workers: "At the same time that we start a movement against landlords to reduce tenant rents, it would not be contradictory to begin an anti-consumer movement to preserve high farm prices. . . . In their self-help movement, the tenants need to depend on no one's help apart from those who produce rice."[55] Obviously city laborers would ridicule any action to keep food prices high, and Yokota was probably correct when he judged that a farmer-labor tie-up would lead to mutual frustrations and disappointments.[56] He further concluded that the labor movement wanted to make basic changes in the Japanese social system, whereas the tenants merely sought to reform it. For these reasons, he said, the Nōmin Undō should concentrate on economic issues and stay out of political and social activity.

Yokota devoted his final years to impassioned pleading for improved tenant conditions in Japan. He insisted in 1920 that land reform from above was vital if political revolution from below was to be prevented.[57] The objective of the tenant movement, he wrote, was "to prohibit the individual from owning land. . . . I believe that it is utterly impossible for us to expect a fundamental solution to the rice problem in

[54] Yokota Hideo, "Nōson kaizō ka nōson kakumei ka" [Will There Be Rural Reconstruction or Rural Revolution?], 1920, quoted in Sakai, p. 79.

[55] Yokota Hideo, "Nōmin no koe o kike" [Listen to the Peasants' Voices], 1919, quoted in Sakai, p. 80.

[56] See Sakai, pp. 73-74, 80; Takeuchi, p. 233; Tsunazawa, *Kindai*, pp. 136-137, 141.

[57] Yokota Hideo, "Nōson kaizō ka nōson kakumei ka," p. 79f.

our country unless there is a total revolutionary reconstruction of the economic system in the farm villages."[58] Once the present system of private property was overhauled, he continued, the cultivator's lot could be made truly better: "What are the methods? First is the process of reducing tenant payments to landlords. Next is the legal guarantee of tenants' rights. Then comes a revision of the share of profits distributed or a modification of the present system of distributing earnings."[59] But however much he concentrated after World War I on means, Yokota retained the same goals which he had defined in 1914: to offset capitalism and the landlord system, to revitalize independent cultivators, to restore social harmony to the villages, and to create a classless national society with agriculture at its core.

Yokota has been criticized for his weaknesses as a practical leader of the early tenant movement.[60] This must have been an ambivalent role for him to play, in view of the paradoxes found in his farm thought. On the one hand, he supported the emperor system, the idea of the nation as a family, and the agrarian foundations of the country. On the other hand, he was a decidedly antiestablishment figure whose tendentious tracts on the errors of the landlord system and the need for reducing rents earned the antipathy of nearly all bureaucratic Nōhonshugisha. One account has it that in Gifu Prefecture "when landlords heard Yokota's name they shuddered, while tenants trusted him as though he were a god."[61] More than three thousand persons attended funeral services for Yokota in Gifu in February 1926. One wonders whether there were any landlords in the crowd.

[58] Yokota Hideo, "Nōson kaizō ka nōson kakumei ka," quoted in Yamamoto, p. 71.
[59] Ibid.
[60] Yamamoto Gyō, "Nōhonshugi shisōshijō ni okeru Yokota Hideo" [Yokota Hideo in the History of Agrarianist Thought], *Gifu Daigaku Kyōyōbu kenkyū hōkoku* [Gifu University Faculty of General Education Research Reports], No. 4, 1968, pp. 71-80.
[61] Yamamoto, "Yokota Hideo no shisō," p. 63.

Even more than Kawakami Hajime, Yokota Hideo demonstrated that agrarianism in early twentieth-century Japan was a diverse and complicated ideology which was far more than merely "a useful legitimation and rationalization"[62] of the interests of landlords and industrialists, as Barrington Moore, Jr., has claimed. Perhaps in its early bureaucratic phase Nōhonshugi was "in essence an antifarmer ideology . . . with its praise for those who could submit to poverty and endure hard toil,"[63] but in the period 1900-1920 Kawakami and Yokota broadened the agrarianist tradition to permit basic attacks on state policies and the excesses of the commercial economy. Yokota in particular helped to build a new constituency for Nōhonshugi ideas—the tenant masses—even though he never tried to use farm-first doctrines as weapons to attack other rural classes.

Nevertheless, despite the enormous gap between the staid farm development theories of bureaucratic agrarianists in the 1890s and Yokota's fiery challenges to the private landholding system, by 1920 none of the variegated adherents of Nōhonshugi had yet mounted a direct assault on the Japanese political or social systems. In any comparison with the full range of Japanese thought in the early twentieth century, Nōhonshugi remained an antiprogressive, often reactionary ideology with little to offer legitimate revolutionaries. It was during the years between the two world wars that Japanese agrarianism entered a new phase, when it produced full-dress critiques of the domestic political and economic elite and interacted with violent reconstructionist movements in the midst of economic depression.

[62] Barrington Moore, Jr., *Social Origins of Dictatorship and Democracy* (Boston: Beacon Press, 1966), p. 296. For a rebuttal of Moore's comments on Japanese fascism, see Ronald P. Dore and Tsutomu Ōuchi, "Rural Origins of Japanese Fascism," *Dilemmas of Growth in Prewar Japan*, ed. James W. Morley (Princeton: Princeton University Press, 1971), pp. 181-209.

[63] Fukutake Tadashi, *Nihon no nōson shakai* [Japanese Rural Society] (Tokyo: Tokyo Daigaku Shuppankai, 1953), pp. 217-218.

Chapter VI

Farm Thought and State Policy, 1918-1937

THE twenty years from the end of World War I to the invasion of China in 1937 encompassed a very unsettled and disquieting period in the modern history of Japan. No longer did the national unity and direction of the Meiji era prevail, yet new leadership and purpose remained very uncertain. Part of the anxiety of the interwar years resulted from international tensions common to the great powers after the Versailles settlement of 1919. Although the treaty ending World War I recognized Japan as the paramount force in East Asia, world diplomats searched in vain for reasonably stable mechanisms to assure harmony in the Pacific during the 1920s and 1930s. Japan took part in the Washington and London naval conferences (1922 and 1930, respectively) and belonged to the League of Nations until after the Manchurian incident of 1931, but the diplomacy of the day failed to impart a true sense of national security to most Japanese. For some persons, in fact, the international arrangements merely reemphasized Japan's vulnerability, since the naval agreements permitted her fewer vessels than certain other powers and smacked uncomfortably of the unequal treaties of a half century earlier. The uneasy mood of Japan's external relations was magnified after 1931 by armed friction with China and the resulting censure of the major Western countries.

At home the nation underwent political, social, and economic upheavals between 1918 and 1937 which intensified the sense of drift, especially by contrast with the steady national course during the Meiji years. After the oligarchy finally lost control about 1910 through old age, Japanese politics became a four-way scramble for power among the political parties, civil bureaucracy, military services, and economic combines (*zaibatsu*). Although the parties held the upper hand by a narrow margin during the teens and twenties and the military establishment became dominant in the thirties, most of the period between the wars was characterized by weak leadership and indecisive responses to crises, compounded by acts of political violence. Changing social relations were also a main feature of the 1920s and 1930s, resulting from such diverse factors as mass education, the enfranchisement of all adult males in 1925, fresh international influences, and great fluctuations in job opportunities. But the nation's economic situation was the most turbulent aspect of the entire era. After gigantic expansion during World War I, when manufacturing output rose six times its prewar level, Japanese industry underwent a sharp contraction in 1920. The industrial shrinkage, together with low international farm prices, created a lengthy recession in the 1920s. Just when the economy was finally turning upward, the great crash of 1929 plunged Japan into another cycle of depression which did not evaporate until the mid-1930s.

The many diplomatic, political, social, and economic changes of the twenties and thirties were evidence that Japan had entered a new phase of development, one in which she was forced to deal with both the successes and problems bequeathed by her first generation of modernizing leaders. The years after World War I were also a time for reappraising the nationalism which had sustained the Meiji drive for wealth and power. New theories concerning Japan's national distinctiveness and historic destiny sprang up in great numbers during the 1920s and 1930s, ranging from anarchism and communism to doctrines of military expansion and rigid social conformity. Among the important new ideologies dealing with modernization and nationalism was a romantic version of Japanese agrarianism, best represented by the teachings of Gondō Seikyō (1868-1937) and Tachibana Kōzaburō (1893-), the two most widely known Nōhonshugi advocates of the interwar period. Since it was in the specific context of the twenties and thirties that Japanese nationalism intersected with agrarianist images of state and society, it is important first to consider the condition of Japanese farming between 1918 and 1937 and the fate of familiar pre-World War I Nōhonshugi doctrines, both official and non-official, during the years of rural crisis. Then in subsequent chapters I shall concentrate on the farm-centered social thought of Gondō and Tachibana, who refashioned agrarianist ideas in ways which prompted both a nostalgic longing for primitive rural society and militant political violence in search of radical structural reform.

The Rural Crisis of the Twenties and Thirties

Hyperbole may be one of the historian's favorite vices, but it would be difficult to exaggerate the dimensions of the economic collapse which afflicted rural Japan after World War I. The farm depression that began in the spring of 1920 was touched off by the postwar industrial retrenchment, but whereas trade and manufacturing recovered enough to grow modestly by the late 1920s, farming did not really prosper again until fifteen years later.[1] Table 5 contains one of many recent estimates showing that real net output in the primary sector stood still in the 1920s, after uninterrupted growth since the mid-1880s. Farm prices, artificially inflated by the demands of World War I, fell 30 percent from 1919 to

[1] Ōuchi Tsutomu, "Agricultural Depression and Japanese Villages," *The Developing Economies*, v, 4, December 1967, 608; Hugh T. Patrick, "The Economic Muddle of the 1920's," *Dilemmas of Growth in Prewar Japan*, ed. James W. Morley (Princeton: Princeton University Press, 1971), p. 215.

TABLE 5

REAL NET OUTPUT BY INDUSTRIAL SECTORS, 1915-1940
(1928-1932 Prices, in Million Yen)

Year	Primary Industry Amount	Index	Secondary Industry Amount	Index	Tertiary Industry Amount	Index
1913-1917	2,025	100	1,479	100	2,150	100
1918-1922	2,409	119	1,826	123	2,977	138
1923-1927	2,551	126	2,253	152	4,529	211
1928-1932	2,552	126	3,373	228	6,463	300
1933-1937	2,862	141	4,713	318	7,420	345
1938-1942	3,156	156	7,050	477	8,534	397

SOURCE: *Agricultural Development in Modern Japan*, ed. Takekazu Ogura, 2nd ed. (Tokyo: Fuji Publishing Co., 1968), p. 683.

1921, recovered substantially by 1925, and plunged again by 1931 to only two-fifths their 1919 level.[2] Contrary to Kawakami Hajime's belief that in times of crisis farming was less vulnerable than industry, agricultural prices fell further than manufacturing prices and took longer to recover, both because of monopolistic pricing in certain industrial product lines and because of farmers' understandable tendency to produce larger crops to offset low prices.[3] Table 6 displays the relationship between rice prices and other main indicators during the depth of the depression.

Increased rice imports from Korea and Taiwan, in response to the rice riots of 1918, helped to drive farm prices still lower. By 1930 net imports of foodstuffs accounted for about 15 percent of domestic food consumption.[4] The

[2] *Agricultural Development in Modern Japan*, ed. Takekazu Ogura, 2nd ed. (Tokyo: Fuji Publishing Co., 1968), p. 28 (hereafter cited as Ogura).

[3] See ibid.

[4] William W. Lockwood, *The Economic Development of Japan: Growth and Structural Change 1868-1938* (Princeton: Princeton University Press, 1954), p. 44.

TABLE 6

SELECTED INDEXES, 1927-1933

(1926 = 100)

	1927	1928	1929	1930	1931	1932	1933
Wholesale prices	95.1	95.6	92.8	76.5	64.6	68.2	75.9
Rice prices	86.0	82.0	80.6	50.6	50.1	61.9	61.3
Stock prices	110.2	92.4	81.0	55.1	42.7	56.4	80.4
Steel production	111.9	126.6	152.3	152.0	125.0	159.2	212.3
Cotton yarn	88.8	84.6	97.3	96.8	101.5	118.9	122.8
Daily average earnings of factory workers	114.9	119.9	121.2	117.5	109.8	112.0	110.3

SOURCE: Chō Yukio, "From the Shōwa Economic Crisis to Military Economy," *The Developing Economies*, v, 4, December 1967, 576.

deflationary policies of the Japanese government during the 1920s, together with the worldwide slump in agricultural prices, compounded the problem for Japanese cultivators.[5] As a result, many farm families turned to auxiliary enterprises to supplement their incomes, only to find the market for the most popular of these, sericulture, virtually wiped out by the great crash in 1929. Between 1925 and 1929, raw silk prices dropped 32 percent, and by 1931 they fell by another one-third,[6] as world demand for Japanese silk vanished.

What these conditions meant for life in the farm villages is exceedingly hard to measure. Statistics can only crudely estimate the narrow margin by which many families survived. According to figures from the Nōrinshō (Ministry of Agriculture and Forestry, carved out of the former Nōshōmushō in 1925), the average rural household in 1925 had a 308 yen surplus of income over expenses, and 81 percent of all farm families had surpluses. By 1930 the average household had a deficit of 77 yen, and only 35 percent of

[5] See Patrick, pp. 218-219.　　　[6] Ibid., p. 219.

farm families had any surplus at all.[7] Certain farm costs fell during this period, such as seed and fertilizer, but other obligations remained constant: taxes, rents, interest on loans, and the like. It is not hard to believe the report that, of 467 girls aged fifteen to twenty-four in one village in Yamagata Prefecture, 250 had left the village by 1930 to become geisha or prostitutes.[8] Even worse was the extensive crop failure of 1933, which is said to have left five thousand children starving in Aomori Prefecture. One-fourth of all villages lacked a resident physician to treat the malnutrition and disease which ensued from chronic depression. In Akita Prefecture, eleven-year-old girls were bound out to brothel keepers for as little as 100 yen.[9]

With rural output virtually constant, farm prices depressed, and village incomes curtailed, Japanese agriculture was obviously confronted with crisis conditions by 1930. However, the urban economy did not grow quickly enough in the 1920s or early 1930s to permit a major redeployment of the rural work force that would help the village economy. Farming and fishing employed 54.9 percent of Japanese workers in 1920, 50.0 percent in 1930, and 44.3 percent in 1940,[10] a very slow ebb for a generally depressed rural sector in an industrializing nation. In fact, in the worst year of the industrial depression (1932) so many urban workers were forced back to the land to subsist that the total number of farm households temporarily rose over its 1920 level.[11] In

[7] Tsunazawa Mitsuaki, *Kindai Nihon no dochaku shisō—nōhonshugi kenkyū* [Modern Japanese Home Town Thought—Studies on Agrarianism] (Nagoya: Fūbaisha, 1969), p. 40. See also Ogura, p. 42.

[8] Tsunazawa, p. 40.

[9] Harry Emerson Wildes, *Japan in Crisis* (New York: Macmillan, 1934), p. 93.

[10] Lockwood, p. 466. Only British India and Finland are said to have had a higher percentage of employment in agriculture than Japan in 1930. Wakakuwa Seiyei, "The Japanese Farm-Tenancy System," *Japan's Prospect*, ed. Douglas G. Haring (Cambridge, Mass.: Harvard University Press, 1946), p. 115.

[11] Ogura, p. 44.

effect, Japan rode out the farm depression without a significant drop in rural population.

In the end farm prosperity returned by the late 1930s, thanks mainly to the sudden growth of manufacturing after 1936, which was partly a product of mobilization for war. By 1936 farm prices had climbed 50 percent above their nadir in 1931.[12] Also aiding the recovery was the fact that investment in agricultural improvements continued with little disruption throughout the depression, since big landowners found production costs lower in a number of cases and the government offered subsidies to upgrade farming, assisting large landlords the most. Mechanization and new fertilizers also helped to pull Japanese agriculture out of depression in the mid-1930s, and farmers aided themselves by shifting production to more profitable lines such as fruits, vegetables, and livestock.[13] More generally, the government's decision to abandon the gold standard in December 1931 inaugurated successful fiscal, monetary, and trade policies which led to much wider exports during 1932 to 1936, a tonic to the economy as a whole.[14] By spending its way out of depression, the state at least indirectly helped to lift farmers back on their feet.

How is one to account for the demoralizing turnabout which Japanese agriculture underwent after World War I? In the first half of the Meiji period farming had truly served as the economic cornerstone of the nation, and even after 1900—despite fears about its economic irrelevance on the part of agrarianists like Yokoi Tokiyoshi—the role of agriculture in financing industrial growth remained highly important. Once the reliable foundation for expanding the urban economy, farming after World War I was now a depressed area needing aid from outside. What had gone wrong?

[12] Ibid., p. 28.   [13] Ibid., pp. 31-38.
[14] Patrick, p. 256.

Part of the problem had to do with the timing of agricultural development. By World War I, Japanese farming had corrected its earlier lag, caused by the retarding effects of a feudal agricultural system, and had probably reached a natural level of maturity. Only with sizeable migrations to the cities could the land-labor ratio be altered to allow further major increases in productivity, but this avenue was blocked by the incapacity of industry and commerce to absorb large numbers of new workers,[15] even under normal conditions.

But the 1920s and early 1930s were anything but normal, which is why agriculture in Japan not merely slowed down but stopped growing entirely. The worldwide drop in farm prices in the mid-1920s buffeted Japan's farmers, and the Wall Street crash of 1929 knocked them flat—especially cocoon growers who were ruined by the fantastic dive of silk prices between 1929 and 1931. Compounding the problem until late 1931 were the deflationary policies of the Japanese government, which insisted on returning after World War I to the gold standard at its prewar par in the hope of lifting exports and trading its way to prosperity. What happened instead was spotty overall growth, rural depression, and a great deal of social unrest which menaced the stability of the government after 1931.[16]

In more general terms, the plight of the countryside was affected by institutional factors beyond politicians' control. Population itself was not a problem, thanks to reasonably favorable employment opportunities in the cities in all but the worst depression years.[17] But the small scale of Japanese farming now impeded output sufficiently to warrant importing colonial rice regularly after World War I, even at the cost of depressing domestic prices. Despite the efforts of generations of agricultural officials, the average farm size by 1934 was only slightly over one hectare, and fully

[15] See Ogura, p. 627. [16] Patrick, p. 213.

[17] See Hugh Borton, *Japan Since 1931, Its Political and Social Development* (New York: Institute of Pacific Relations, 1940), p. 88.

one-third of all cultivators worked less than one-half hectare.[18] Moreover the rural villagers were now a part of the national and international farm markets, exposed to the fluctuations of costs and revenues which they could not control. They could no longer take refuge in self-sufficiency[19] since they were too dependent on chemical fertilizers, modern transport, and a nationwide clientele for their products. At the same time, thoroughgoing technical and mechanical innovation, which might have restored prosperity quickly, was inhibited by the small scale of operations, the abdication of entrepreneurship by many absentee landlords, and a lack of capital. A final point is that, until the war with China began in 1937, the large landlord class was too powerful to allow any compromise with the institution of private property,[20] such as a land reform program, which might have returned the villages more rapidly to their former thriving condition.

This set of factors not only ripped away the facade of rural harmony after World War I but also established an entirely new context for both Nōhonshugi and nationalist thinking—one in which the two began to merge. As a prelude to considering the rise of agrarian nationalism, it is important to review the government's response to the rural catastrophe during the twenties and thirties, as well as the orthodox Nōhonshugi reaction to the state's policies, in order to gauge the fate of agrarianist ideas developed before World War I now that Japan suffered from acute farm depression.

Government Farm Policies, 1918-1937

Since the state's freedom to deal with the farm depression was severely restricted by the timing of Japanese agricultural development, the worldwide depression, a deflationary overall economic program geared to raising exports, and

[18] Ibid.; Akira Kazami, "Whither the Japanese Peasantry?" *Contemporary Japan*, ii, 4, 1933, 681.

[19] Ōuchi, p. 616.   [20] See Ogura, pp. 626-628.

the structural limitations of the country's existing farm system, it was entirely predictable that the government coped with the rural question in the 1920s and 1930s largely by modifying or extending previous farm policies. Earlier agricultural programs had usually relied on landlords to conduct local improvements, with relatively little direct government involvement. This approach was continued after World War I, and as a rule the state took a hands-off attitude toward farming, at least until the rural rehabilitation movement began in 1932.

Despite massive village debts and poverty too obvious to ignore, farmers were still taxed twice as heavily as businessmen with equivalent incomes as late as 1929[21]—an index of how slowly old policies come unstuck. When the state finally acted, it did so hesitantly and often with rather modest effect, treating merely the worst symptoms of the rural distress and not its causes. Three good examples of the government's reluctance to intervene during the 1920s and 1930s on behalf of the village poor were its rice price and import control measures, its attitude toward the tenancy question, and its rural rehabilitation program of 1932-1935. All were potentially excellent opportunities to relieve some of the farmers' anguish, but in each case large landlords managed to thwart legislation that would help peasants unless the proposals coincided with the landlords' own interests. Only after the outbreak of fighting with China in July 1937 were stiff laws passed to aid the rural masses, and then only as a part of the national muster for war.

Vacillation was the government's principal response to the huge dip in farm prices after 1920. Ever since the first rice tariff in 1904, the bureaucratic Nōhonshugi position on rice prices and imports had been protectionist, to guard farm incomes and encourage national self-sufficiency. When rice production fell seriously below demand after World War I, however, the government had no alternative but to

[21] Lockwood, p. 525.

import rice from Korea and Taiwan. By 1934 rice imports had risen nearly seven times their 1920 level, and approximately one-third of the rice available on the market came from the colonies.[22] The government was apparently willing to tolerate the depressing effect which imports had on domestic rice prices because it wished to reduce the cost of living for urban residents. To exclude Korean and Taiwanese rice would have been unthinkable in any case, since Japan had invested so much in developing her colonial possessions.

In April 1921 the Diet passed a rice law which gave the government the power to control prices by buying, storing, and selling rice as needed, as well as the right to regulate rice imports.[23] Despite a continuous clamor from landlords over low prices, the government used this law sparingly, in line with its general deflationary policies before 1931. When rice prices sank to new depths in 1930 as a result of the world depression and colonial imports continued to rise, the Diet finally passed a series of price control bills, culminating in the rice regulation law of 1933. Colonial rice was henceforth to be taxed; new ceiling and floor prices were established for rice; and the state was given almost unlimited powers to stabilize prices. In the same manner, five separate laws were passed between 1931 and 1936 to control silk prices through government regulation. By and large these new measures were more effective in reducing rice and silk price fluctuations than had been the case in the 1920s.[24] But it was the wartime food-control law, passed in September 1937, that finally forced the government to regulate food prices strictly, in order to meet the national emergency in China.

In summary, rice price controls were ineffective in the 1920s, to the detriment of all farm families, and apparently

---

[22] Ōuchi, pp. 610-611.   [23] Ogura, pp. 113, 189, 664-665.

[24] Borton, p. 74. See also Kazami, p. 682; Ronald P. Dore, *Land Reform in Japan* (London: Oxford University Press, 1959), pp. 98-99; Ogura, pp. 17, 192-194, 212-218.

benefited landlords the most once stabilization was achieved in the early 1930s, since tenants were forced to sell their rice at the most unfavorable time of year when controls were least effective, while landlords could store their grain until prices rose. After 1937, however, landlord interests were badly damaged because farm rents were henceforth paid directly to the government, rent controls were applied, and new production stimulants which slashed landlord incomes were introduced. In other words, insofar as rice prices and import controls were concerned, the government followed a deflationary path in the 1920s which hindered local recovery, but one which was consistent with its normally laissez-faire farm policies before World War I. In the early 1930s it more vigorously supported rural producers' interests, adopting protectionist measures that recalled the official Nōhonshugi of the early twentieth century. Once caught in the web of war, however, the state sacrificed landlord privileges to the requirements of village concord and national mobilization.

More complex and politically sensitive were the harsh rural frictions which produced tenancy conflicts during the 1920s and 1930s, serving notice that the communal harmony of the village was threatened by rising class consciousness. Ever since the civil code enforced in 1898 had defined landlord-tenant relations in terms clearly favorable to the former, the government had stayed aloof from the tenancy question, offering no response to demands from tenant leaders like Yokota Hideo that it promote rent reductions or land redistribution. But in the early 1920s the tenancy problem grew too acute to be overlooked.

By custom, most tenant agreements were oral, and many were indefinite in length. Those with specified tenure often ranged from five years for paddies to twenty years for orchards and tea plantations.[25] With the growing depersonalization of landlord-tenant relations, many tenants after

[25] Wakakuwa, pp. 141-142; Dore, pp. 42-44.

144

World War I demanded more precise, written agreements as a protection against the insecurity of working for an unpredictable absentee owner who no longer cared for village affairs. Ann Waswo's studies of tenant disputes in southwestern Japan suggest that the disruption of traditional landlord-tenant ties was the chief agent of the unrest in the 1920s.[26] Tenants apparently now needed mechanisms for security in the face of unfamiliar situations, much as trade unions have frequently offered the workingman protection against the arbitrariness of new land, labor, capital, and property relations produced by the rise of capitalism. Economic motives also stimulated the tenant movement, in that peasants demanded permanent rent reductions and protection against eviction in the wake of years and years of farm depression. In many cases the rent burden itself was less a factor than the widening gap between urban and rural incomes (compare the rice price and factory wage indexes shown in Table 6). Tenants who knew they could take reasonably well-paying jobs in industry apparently had fewer compunctions about bargaining for rent reductions than those who knew no other way of life.[27]

For their part, the landlords felt equally threatened by depression and social conflict. In the 1920s landholding no longer offered its earlier financial rewards because farm prices had been slashed. Urban investments seemed more attractive, but at the cost of political and social estrangement from the village, where landlords' authority had previously gone unquestioned. After 1925, moreover, tenants

[26] Ann Waswo, "Landlords and Social Change in Prewar Japan," Ph.D. dissertation in history, Stanford University, 1969, pp. 132-142.

[27] Ibid., p. 133; Ogura, p. 37. See also Dore, pp. 19-25, 54-91; Kazami, p. 681; Borton, pp. 88-89; Takeuchi Tetsuo, "Nōhonshugi to nōson chūsansō" [Agrarianism and the Farm Village Middle Class], *Shimane Nōka Daigaku kenkyū hōkoku* [Shimane Agricultural University Research Reports], No. 8, A, March 1960, p. 234; Ogura Takekazu, *Agrarian Problems and Agricultural Policy in Japan* (Tokyo: Institute of Asian Economic Affairs, 1967), p. 9.

could vote and might use party politics to oppose their landlords.[28] Even the government seemed less friendly than before, now that the commercial and industrial elites, newly arisen during World War I, appeared to have the ears of the party politicians who dominated the Diet.

Landlords knew that as early as 1920 the Ministry of Agriculture and Commerce (Nōshōmushō) had tried to win support for a law that would clarify tenant rights. The Nōshōmushō position was not to protect tenants in themselves but to force all rural classes to compose their differences in the interests of harmony and village stability, in line with longstanding bureaucratic Nōhonshugi beliefs. Some officials hated the feudal aspects of landlord-tenant relations and thus wished change;[29] others upheld the traditional village hierarchy. Both groups agreed that landlord interests should not be favored to the exclusion of tenants' needs. Nevertheless, landlord opposition and conservative voices within the privy council[30] blocked all tenant legislation before 1938 except the weak tenancy conciliation law of 1924, which favored large landlords, and the regulations for establishing owner-farmers, passed in 1926.

In reality, the tenant question—despite Yokota Hideo's tireless peasant campaigns—lay outside the scope of both official and popular agrarianism in the 1920s and 1930s. If the Nōshōmushō and Nōrinshō (Ministry of Agriculture and Forestry) were reluctant to let prolandlord policies continue to ignite conflict in the countryside, they were equally unenthusiastic about helping tenants. It would be difficult to sustain the view that the state at any level systematically favored tenants, since the government regularly used the peace preservation law after 1925 to curtail peasant

[28] Ogura, p. 128.
[29] Dore, pp. 86-87. See also Ogura, *Agrarian Problems*, p. 9; Waswo, pp. 160-161; Ogura, pp. 129-130.
[30] Okutani Matsuji, "Nihon ni okeru nōhonshugi shisō no nagare" [Trends in Agrarian Thought in Japan], *Shisō* [Thought], No. 407, May 1958, p. 10.

protests.[31] Instead, the state once again elected a middle course, sanctioned for thirty years by bureaucratic agrarianists: modest efforts to create more small owner-farmers to form the backbone of the village (*jisakunō*).

Under the 1926 regulations for establishing *jisakunō*, tenants could take out twenty-five-year loans at 3.5 percent to purchase the land they worked (provided the landlord wished to sell) at a set price of sixteen times the value of the annual rent paid in kind.[32] Both landlords and tenants thought these provisions were favorable to the former, since the established price was very high for tenants whose incomes were reduced by the depression. The program floundered when land values dropped in 1930 and mortgage subsidy funds from the state evaporated, with the net result that very few tenants were ever aided in becoming owner-cultivators. It is worth repeating Ogura's observation that this policy was not adopted in the late Meiji period, when the number of *jisakunō* was declining and the number of tenants rising, but in the mid-1920s, when pressure from tenants was acute.[33] The figures in Table 7 show that tenancy was quite stable during the twenties and early thirties. Since this table covers only families living on the land, it does not include absentee landlords. Landlords remaining in the village who worked only a portion of their holdings, renting the rest, are included with owner-farmers. Properly speaking, owner-farmers constituted perhaps one quarter of all farm households, while larger landholders accounted for a much more modest proportion.

The state promoted *jisakunō* not to confirm Nōhonshugi ideas about the desirability of owner-farmers but to mollify landlords' fears of tenants by siphoning off some of their unrest, albeit on terms which helped landlords by driving

[31] Takeuchi, p. 233.
[32] Ogura, p. 658; Dore, pp. 79-85. Technically the terms of the loan from the credit cooperative were 4.8 percent, of which the national government paid 1.3 percent.
[33] Ogura, p. 131.

TABLE 7

INDEX OF FARM HOUSEHOLDS BY KIND
OF OPERATION AND FARMLAND UNDER TENANCY, 1922-1936
(1922 = 100)

Year	Total	Owner-Farmer	Type of Household Part Owner-Farmer, Part Tenant	Tenant	Farmland under Tenancy as Percentage of Total Farmland
1922	100.0	100.0	100.0	100.0	46.5%
	(5,525,000)	(1,721,000)	(2,254,000)	(1,550,000)	
1924	100.2	100.3	100.9	98.8	46.0
1926	100.5	100.7	102.7	97.3	45.8
1928	100.8	101.6	104.0	95.6	45.8
1930	101.3	101.3	105.4	95.9	47.8
1932	102.1	102.0	106.0	96.7	47.2
1934	101.7	101.2	105.1	97.3	47.0
1936	101.3	100.6	104.2	97.8	46.5

SOURCE: Ōuchi Tsutomu, "Agricultural Depression and Japanese Villages," *The Developing Economies*, v, 4, December 1967, 623.

land prices higher. Some bureaucratic agrarianists of the day, such as the Nōrinshō official Ishiguro Tadaatsu (1884-1960), actually spoke against the 1926 *jisakunō* regulations, despite a strong faith in small owner-cultivators, because the land-sale arrangements were so blatantly rigged in favor of landlords that rural harmony could only be further disrupted.[34] In any case, sizeable government subsidies to help tenants buy land came only in 1937, under the regulations for assistance in creating and maintaining owner-farmers, which provided 40 million yen per year for loans to buy land. It was hoped that within twenty-five years about 15 percent of the land under tenancy could be converted to ownership by a million new *jisakunō*. The farmland adjust-

[34] Okutani, p. 11.

ment law of 1938 likewise aided tenants by defining lease conditions more precisely, controlling land prices, and improving the terms for mediating tenancy disputes.[35] Again, as in the case of the rice price-stabilization measures, the main motive for these laws was wartime preparedness, not any sudden sympathy for the tenants' predicament.

Although the government was reluctant to act on the farm-price and tenant questions in the 1920s, after the Wall Street crash it took a series of positive steps to help the villages, collectively known as the rural rehabilitation program of 1932-1935. Each year for five years a thousand villages were chosen to receive public money to consolidate debts, extend more loans through producers' cooperatives, assist village handicraft industries, and provide technical aid to farmers.[36] A special Diet session, known as the "farm rescue Diet" of 1932 (*kyūnō gikai*), allocated more than 200 million yen for employment on public works projects in twelve thousand villages, despite objections from some military leaders who feared cuts in their budgets.[37] At the same time the emperor announced a gift of 5 million yen for medical aid in the countryside.

Drawing on a familiar Nōhonshugi cliché, the Saitō cabinet proclaimed the importance of rural "rehabilitation through self-help" (*jiriki kōsei*) in announcing the movement on October 6, 1932:

In order to stabilize the economic lives of farmers, fishermen, and mountaineers, and in order to promote their future welfare . . . we must urge them to sober up and take pains to cut away the causes of their troubles. In order to do this they must make practical use of their spirit of mutual aid with their neighbors, a good custom which has been in existence in the villages for a long time.

---

[35] Ogura, pp. 10, 134-137.
[36] *Ishiguro Tadaatsu den* [Biography of Ishiguro Tadaatsu], ed. Hashimoto Denzaemon *et al.* (Tokyo: Iwanami Shoten, 1969), p. 22.
[37] Wildes, pp. 93-94.

They must thoroughly instill it in their economic life, and they must plan for structural reforms in production and in the overall economy of farming, fishing, and forestry.[38]

Once again it was state policy to encourage village self-sufficiency, after a quarter century during which such agrarianist ideas were rarely expressed in the bureaucracy. Peasants were now urged to weave their own cloth, curdle their own *tōfu*, and improvise through their own ingenuity.[39] To cut production costs, they were told to use liquid manure in place of expensive chemical fertilizers, even though human waste was dirtier, less productive, and not abundant enough to meet farmers' needs.[40]

Despite such pitfalls, this movement was a faithful imitation of the rural improvement program of 1905 in that it tried to bolster the small-scale village cultivator through economic and moral incentives. Kodaira Ken'ichi (1884–), a top Nōrinshō officeholder, reminded farmers that "economic rehabilitation begins with spiritual rehabilitation. . . . we uplift our families by farming, and we rebuild our villages by farming."[41] Kodaira extolled the teachings of Ninomiya Sontoku as worthy goals for Japan's impoverished villagers, especially the virtues of diligence (*kinben*) and yielding to others (*suijō*). As a part of the moral rehabilitation phase of the movement, the state also founded the Tokunō Kyōkai (Conscientious Farmers' Association), which publicized the views of such farm moralists as Ninomiya, Kumazawa Banzan, Ishikawa Rikinosuke, and Maeda Masana.

Ishiguro Tadaatsu, who became vice-minister of agriculture and forestry in 1931, reflected the official agrarianist outlook underlying the rural rehabilitation program when he spoke of restoring the "social equilibrium" of Japanese agriculture after a ravaging capitalist depression. Shortly after the movement had concluded, Ishiguro wrote:

[38] Nōrinshō statement, October 6, 1932, quoted in Tsunazawa, p. 43.
[39] Dore, pp. 99-101.   [40] Kazami, p. 684.
[41] Kodaira Ken'ichi, quoted in Tsunazawa, p. 47.

I believe that properly speaking the essence of agriculture is noncommercial. But commercial is what farm households that are being established under current conditions are becoming. I do not mean that there should be no contact at all with [commercialism]. To live today it is necessary for people to obtain money. But making money means manufacturing and selling things in order to buy other things, and this is not the essence of farmers' livelihood. When you come into contact with a money economy, money gradually becomes more and more necessary, and you become commercial. Finally some people come to believe that making money is the farmer's ideal.[42]

Such sentiments reflected the anticommercialism of such earlier bureaucratic Nōhonshugi partisans as Yokoi Tokiyoshi, and they indicate that farm policies directed toward the small producer, although long held in abeyance, were still vital enough to propel the government's rural antidepression program in the 1930s.

Like the policy of helping tenants buy land after 1926, the rural rehabilitation movement was hampered by a lack of money, and as always it is difficult to assess the impact of ethical pronouncements such as those proffered by Kodaira. The program used the producers' cooperatives as the organizational basis for spreading both loan funds and moral teachings, with the result that 1,108 cooperatives with more than a million members were added between 1932 and 1936.[43] In the absence of regulations to the contrary, landlords soon

[42] Ishiguro Tadaatsu, "Nōmin dōjōchō ni atau" [To the Head of the Agricultural Training Center], *Mura* [Village], v, 5, August 1938, *Ishiguro Tadaatsu den*, p. 16. For studies of Ishiguro, see *Ishiguro Tadaatsu den*; Takemura Tamirō, "Jinushisei no dōyō to nōrin kanryō" [Agitation of the Landlord System and the Agricultural and Forestry Bureaucracy], *Kindai Nihon keizai shisōshi* [History of Modern Japanese Economic Thought], ed. Chō Yukio and Sumiya Kazuhiko (Tokyo: Yūhikaku, 1969), 323-356; Kodaira Ken'ichi, *Ishiguro Tadaatsu* (Tokyo: Jiji Tsūshinsha, 1962).
[43] Borton, p. 23.

dominated the cooperatives and rehabilitation committees[44] in exactly the same way as they had seized direction of the late Meiji rural improvement drive, and it was only with the passage of general mobilization laws after 1937 that the cooperatives really proved to be responsive to the state plans for village aid.[45]

An example of the marriage of ethics and economics in the rehabilitation campaign was the farm debt adjustment association act of 1933, which created units within the cooperatives to mediate village debt settlements and promote local harmony. Total rural debt in 1931 was nearly 5 billion yen, or an average of 830 yen per household (more than four-fifths the average farm family's income in that year).[46] Through debt adjustment, the government hoped to help cultivators recover by drawing on the "spirit of old farmers": mutual aid, diligence, thrift, and deference.[47] Creditors might excuse a portion of the obligations due them, the reasoning went, if debtors exhibited these qualities and returned at once to the fields to increase their yields. Such a scheme was intended to force farmers to take their repayments more seriously by making them collectively responsible for debts through their cooperatives.[48] Such negative methods apparently had little effect on the astounding rural debt in the mid-1930s; what finally brought relief to debtors was wartime inflation after 1937.

Hindered by insufficient money, landlord resistance in the cooperatives, and unrealistic ethical solutions for hard economic problems, the rural rehabilitation program at best met with indifferent success. According to a 1942 Nōrinshō report, a total of 5,990 villages participated in the program,

[44] Ogura, pp. 669-671; Dore, pp. 104-106.

[45] Borton, p. 25. See also Morita Shirō, *The Development of Agricultural Cooperative Associations in Japan* (Tokyo: Japan FAO Organization, 1960), pp. 12-15.

[46] Ogura, pp. 267-268. Lockwood, p. 72, gives the figure 5-6 billion yen for 1930-1931.

[47] Tsunazawa, pp. 49-50.   [48] Dore, pp. 101-104.

but many seemingly took part in name only, to avoid appearing unpatriotic.[49] Surely the thriving condition of the urban economy by 1936 was chiefly responsible for pulling the farms out of the depression. Still it is revealing that the state, confronted by a grave rural crisis for which it developed almost no solutions for a decade, finally chose to build its countermeasures around the familiar idea of bolstering agriculture against commercialism. The remarkable endurance of such teachings is verified in these wartime remarks by Ishiguro Tadaatsu after he had become minister of agriculture and forestry in 1940:

> In our country the words "agriculture is the foundation of the nation" have virtually become the racial faith of the Yamato people. During the era of free enterprise we have been most oblivious of the point that agriculture must be respected, and it has been easy to scorn it. During my nearly thirty years as an agriculture and forestry official, I have always done my best to battle the emphasis on free enterprise capital. . . . To say that "agriculture is the foundation of the nation" is never to stress merely the benefits of agriculture alone. Our ideal, from both the point of view of Nōhonshugi and that of the world at large, is not such a selfish way of thinking. Because it is the foundation of the country, we respect agriculture. Agriculture which is not the foundation of the country has no value whatever.[50]

Popular Agrarianism and the Rural Rehabilitation Movement

Like any important ideology, popular agrarianism in Japan during the depression years included among its enthusiasts both doctrinal innovators and orthodox bearers of accepted teachings. Although writers who improvised on the Nōhon-

[49] Tsunazawa, p. 47.
[50] Ishiguro Tadaatsu, speech at Uchihara, Ibaraki Prefecture, November 1940, *Ishiguro Tadaatsu den*, p. 15.

153

shugi tradition, such as Gondō and Tachibana, have attracted attention because of the bizarre uses found for their ideas, the orthodox stream of popular agrarianism, centering on the small village landowner, continued to receive forceful expression during the 1920s and 1930s. Even big landlords, whom many agrarianists distrusted as cryptocapitalists, sometimes found Nōhonshugi platitudes useful. The Dai Nihon Jinushi Kyōkai (Japan Landlords' Association), for example, declared at its inaugural meeting in October 1925: "Agriculture is the foundation of the state and the source of the people's livelihood. Now, as the result of the exhaustion of the essentials for livelihood and an excessive public tax load, the farm villages have at last lapsed into an economic and spiritual crisis. . . ."[51]

Still it was the man who cultivated most or all of his holdings who felt especially comfortable with popular agrarianism. Unlike the large landowner, he had no urban investments to carry him through the slump, and since he still lived in the village he probably believed that agriculture really was the pillar of society. Unlike the tenant, the small owner-cultivator was not encumbered by debts so steep as to be inescapable, nor did he live in the legal limbo imposed on tenants by the existing civil code. If he thought much about tenants at all, he probably wished that they would cease embroiling the countryside in contentious upheavals. However, most small owners seemed to have eschewed conceptual or theoretical questions, such as the defense of private-property rights or the assertion of tenant class principles, in favor of the practical problems of village life. The activities of the Dai Nihon Kōnōkai (Japan Association for Improving Agriculture), one of many small landowner societies, suggest a concern for reducing tenant disputes, conciliating thorny local issues, repairing public works, and

[51] Dai Nihon Jinushi Kyōkai, "Sengen" [Declaration], October 1925, Nihon nōmin undōshi [History of the Japanese Peasant Movement], ed. Aoki Keiichirō (Tokyo: Nihon Hyōron Shinsha, 1959-1962), III, 206.

boosting village harmony.[52] These are signs that village solidarity was much stronger than class consciousness in rural
Japan and that the basic impulse of the local leadership was
toward communal cohesiveness, not abstract matters of
justice or legal rights. Nōhonshugi appealed strongly to this
impulse.

Okada On was probably the most widely known nonofficial advocate of small-scale family agriculture during the
depression, notwithstanding the large landlord orientation
of the Imperial Agricultural Association, of which he was
secretary. Okada fully supported the idea of "rehabilitation
through self-help," but refused to believe that self-help
could be reconciled with farm policies formulated by the
central government. As a result, he became a leading critic
of the rural rehabilitation movement because he believed
that state subsidies, debt-reduction schemes, and measures
to conciliate tenancy disputes threatened the independence
of family-operated farming. Small-scale agriculture was
closely tied to the national essence (*kokutai*), Okada wrote
in 1929: "Agriculture in our country has the family system
as its base and is a system of agriculture which is well
articulated with the family system. . . . Family-managed
farming, i.e., the small-farm system, promotes and nurtures
the broad spirit of protecting the *kokutai* and is consistent
with the *kokutai*. I believe that this is the true meaning of
'agriculture is the foundation of the country.' "[53] The
difficulty, he continued, was that after World War I the
villages "lost their guiding principles, their leaders, their
equilibrium, and their control."[54] Yet none of the political

[52] Takeuchi, p. 234. See also Waswo, pp. 143-146; Mori Takemaro,
"Nihon fuashizumu no keisei to nōson keizai kōsei undō" [The
Formation of Japanese Fascism and the Rural Economic Rehabilitation Movement], *Rekishigaku kenkyū* [Historical Studies], special
number, October 1971, pp. 135-152.

[53] Okada On, *Nōgyō keiei to nōsei* [Agricultural Administration
and Policy] (Tokyo: Ryūginsha, 1929), p. 88.

[54] Ibid., p. 56. See Fukutake Tadashi, *Nihon no nōson shakai* [Jap-
anese Rural Society] (Tokyo: Tokyo Daigaku Shuppankai, 1953),

factions in the Diet was offering practical solutions: "The existing parties maintain capitalistic policies and the proletarian parties embrace socialistic policies. Each of them is busy trying to extend its influence in the farm villages."[55] A clue to Okada's basic response to the rural crisis emerged from his appraisal of the tenancy movement: "The tenant problem is a grave one for both agriculture and the nation. However, it is not a problem involving the entire agricultural sector. It at least does not involve those who cultivate their own farms. It is a problem of distribution within agriculture itself."[56] The real trouble was thus not conflict between tenants and landlords but the rise of commercialism: landlords, he wrote, "have been chased into the same huge net with the tenant farmers by industrial and commercial capitalism and are wrenched just as much as the tenants."[57] By whitewashing village class conflicts, Okada shifted the focus of his analysis to the opposition of city and country and was thus prepared to attack big city bureaucrats' prescriptions for solving the agricultural dilemma when the rural rehabilitation program was revealed in 1932.

The fundamental flaw in the rehabilitation movement, Okada asserted in 1933, was that it spoke vaguely of spiritual uplift but ignored the fact that "all the problems of agriculture are rooted in farm management."[58] Citing Ishikawa Rikinosuke's mid-Meiji era proposals for "appropriate pro-

---

p. 181; Sakurai Takeo, "Shōwa no nōhonshugi" [Agrarianism in the Showa Period], *Shisō*, No. 407, May 1958, p. 47.

[55] Okada On, *Nōgyō keiei to nōsei*, p. 55.

[56] Ibid., p. 10.

[57] Ibid. See Adachi Ikitsune, "Nōhonshugiron no saikentō" [A Reappraisal of Theories on Agrarianism], *Shisō*, No. 423, September 1959, p. 63; Takeuchi, pp. 234-235.

[58] Okada On, *Nōson kōsei no genri to keikaku* [Basic Principles and Plans for Farm Village Rebirth] (Tokyo: Nihon Hyōronsha, 1933), p. 57.

duction investigation" (*tekisanchō*),[59] he criticized the Nō-rinshō for failing to survey local conditions carefully and ignoring differences between villages in resources and capabilities. Instead, he maintained, villages must be left alone to rescue themselves from the depression imposed by the urban economy. Okada reasoned that landlords and tenants were all part of a single rural brotherhood and that they alone could lay realistic plans to improve themselves, since "the rebirth of the villages means primarily economic rebirth, not spiritual."[60] The greatest obstacle, he concluded, was not a lack of will, to be corrected through diligence and thrift as the government thought, but "the pressure of taxes, the pressure of interest, the pressure of the marketplace, the pressure of ideologies, the pressure of cities, and the like, but probably the source of it all is the pressure of capitalism."[61] In this respect Okada agreed with Ishiguro Tadaatsu that farmers should renounce the capitalist profit motive, a position earlier taken by Kawakami Hajime. But the fact remained, he believed, that Ishiguro's was a lonely voice in a bureaucracy which regularly favored industrial and commercial development, bringing enormous pressures to bear on the countryside.

Rather than succumb to impractical, poorly planned programs imposed by a central government which promoted capitalism, Okada wrote, the villages could shirk the evils of the urban economy by rededicating themselves to small family farming:

> Family farm management does not rely on the power of others, and it does not suffer from others' restrictions and interference. When the sun comes up, we cultivate;

[59] Ibid., p. 163. See Sakurai, p. 46; Tsunazawa, pp. 54-57; Tsunazawa Mitsuaki, *Nōhonshugi no kenkyū* [Studies on Agrarianism] (Nagoya: Fūbaisha, 1968), pp. 13-14.

[60] Okada On, *Nōson kōsei no genri to keikaku*, p. 23. See Takeuchi, p. 235.

[61] Okada On, *Nōson kōsei no genri to keikaku*, p. 81.

when it goes down, we rest. We need neither the eight-hour-day system nor a minimum-wage system, neither unemployment insurance nor a labor movement. Cabinets may topple, Diets may dissolve, parties may disband, corporations may collapse, runs on banks may occur, college graduates may lack jobs—none of this has any relation to the prosperity of our farms. We neither worry about losing our heads nor fret about losing our jobs. Accordingly, there is no spiritual servitude, no threat to our livelihood. If we merely observe the laws of agriculture and work hard at operating our farms, we will have stability of livelihood and we can expect improvement.[62]

How, one may ask, were farmers to go about achieving this splendid state of insulation from the market economy? Okada claimed that, regardless of national or international conditions, "the farm villages possess the essentials for their own rebirth: land, water, fresh air, and sunlight . . . and the labor force and skills to transform these natural elements into foodstuffs and other items necessary for human life."[63] Because Japanese agriculture was based on family operations, in contrast to industrial wage labor, it "cannot be converted to capitalistic management by any means whatever."[64] Urban and rural Japan maintained two mutually antagonistic economies, Okada believed, and only through their own efforts could farmers reestablish local self-sufficiency to fend off the oppression of capitalism: "Thus the basic blueprint for rehabilitation is an enlargement of the self-sufficient economy," together with "an improvement plan based on policies for coping with the marketplace."[65] Unfortunately Okada did not spell out his proposals on this vital point of dealing with the city economy, which was after all the crux of the rural question, and as a result this stands as the fatal lapse in his outlook on rehabilitation.

[62] Ibid., p. 179.   [63] Ibid., p. 80.
[64] Ibid., p. 81.   [65] Ibid., p. 82.

Although he failed to disclose firm suggestions on how to live with capitalism, perhaps Okada's strongest suit was simply making farmers conscious of their own potential and encouraging them to help themselves. "The source of village rebirth," he wrote in 1933, "is the self-awareness of rebirth by each individual farmer. If farmers do not have this perception of rebirth, there can be no rehabilitation leaders."[66] So Okada ended up restating agrarianist positions taken by Yokoi Tokiyoshi and others thirty years earlier: the requirement of village self-sufficiency, the need to counteract the spread of commercialism, and especially the importance of strong local leaders—the owner-cultivators who were the prototype of family-operated farming. Most crucial, Okada said, was a new spirit of leadership based not on the regressive moralizing of Ninomiya Sontoku but upon the economic autonomy of the village:

The rebirth project requires an infusion of life by creating a spirit of leadership. The spiritual leadership of the farm villages is built upon the special characteristics of family-managed agricultural enterprise. It must be forged from the following elements:
1. implanting the great spirit of loyalty and patriotism
2. perfecting the spirit of independence
3. understanding the current national situation
4. appreciating the essence of agriculture
5. understanding present conditions in the villages
6. realizing both self-respect and the charms of village life; and
7. building the ideal village.[67]

Okada's agrarianist response to the rural crisis was based on a vision of farm life that dismissed the tenant movement as a minor ripple in the overall rural harmony which should be protected against urban pressures through local self-help.

66 Ibid.   67 Ibid., p. 215.

Preserving the farm-based family system, he argued, would "increase the prosperity of the imperial throne and permanently protect the *kokutai*": "The small-farm system in our country is a form of agriculture firmly based on the family system. . . . If the family system collapsed, most of the conditions for securing the small farmer's livelihood would be lost. . . . The *kokutai*, the family system, and the small-farm system are inseparable. If any of them perishes, the others will perish too."[68] Hence agriculture must be retained in its characteristically Japanese form, Okada believed, not just to rescue farmers' economic fortunes but also to assure a truly placid society that was faithful to a national essence stemming in great measure from agriculture.

Considering his overarching concern for village economic self-determination, it is surprising that Okada never stressed the mainstream Nōhonshugi goal of local self-rule. Although political autonomy was implicit in his call for new rural leadership, Okada apparently considered self-rule itself too hazy an idea to merit attention amid the economic collapse of the day. Nevertheless other popular agrarianists offered self-rule as a better way out of the rural crisis than the government's rehabilitation plans. For example, Yamazaki Nobukichi (1873-1954), Okada's associate in the Teikoku Nōkai, agreed fully that the family was the basis of Japanese agriculture and that household harmony was crucial for national prosperity—indeed, Yamazaki's ideas were called household thought, or *ie no shisō*.[69] But whereas Okada attributed the rural misery primarily to capitalist pressures, Yamazaki singled out the decline of self-rule as the main factor:

[68] Ibid., p. 11.
[69] Adachi Ikitsune, " 'Ie no hikari' no rekishi" [History of "The Light of the Household"], *Shisō no kagaku* [Science of Thought], No. 18, June 1960, pp. 64-66. For studies of Yamazaki, see Inagaki Kiyoshi, *Waga nōsei Yamazaki Nobukichi den* [Biography of Yamazaki Nobukichi, Our Farm Teacher] (Nagoya: Fūbaisha, 1966); Tsunazawa, *Kindai*, pp. 97-125.

Village character, the objective of self-rule, means the dignity and personality of the village. Some people say that self-rule means acting within the scope of what is permitted by law, turning the expenses of each person into the increased mutual profit of everyone in the community, and promoting the happiness and tranquility of all. In short, they say it means not doing what is bad and doing what each person wants. But I think this is insufficient. . . . For my part, we must make the dignified, self-respecting villages which form the foundation of our Japanese empire the objectives of self-rule.[70]

Elsewhere Yamazaki identified this path of "dignity and self-respect" as the way of the farmer, or *nōmindō*. Writing in the time-honored agrarianist tradition of coupling farming with military service, Yamazaki evoked Yokoi's farm Bushido: "There is no great difference between the way of the farmer and the way of the warrior. He who holds a sword is a warrior and he who holds a plow or a hoe is a farmer."[71] By observing self-rule and taking steps to restore village prosperity in cooperation with his neighbors, Yamazaki believed, the small cultivator could fulfill the *nōmindō* and help rescue farmers from their miseries.

Okada On and Yamazaki Nobukichi championed popular Nōhonshugi views in the late 1920s and early 1930s in their strong insistence on village autonomy, whether economic or political, and their certainty that local leadership must be reinvigorated to lead farmers back to prosperity. Distrustful of bureaucratic solutions drafted by a government which was both ignorant of rural life and partial to big business,

[70] Yamazaki Nobukichi, *Nōson jichi no kenkyū* [Studies on Farm Village Self-Rule], 1908, *Yamazaki Nobukichi zenshū* [Complete Works of Yamazaki Nobukichi] (Tokyo: Yamazaki Nobukichi Zenshū Kankōkai, 1935-1936), I, 436.
[71] Yamazaki Nobukichi, *Nōmindō* [The Way of the Farmer], 1930, *Yamazaki Nobukichi zenshū*, v, 51.

Okada and Yamazaki fancied their approaches to the crisis to be more realistic and likely of success than the state rehabilitation program. Right though they were that Tokyo had previously done little for the countryside and that the rehabilitation scheme offered no real hope of change, Okada and Yamazaki could not deny the government's counter-claim that, left to their own devices in the 1920s, the villages had only decayed under de facto self-rule.

Few bureaucrats rejected the principle affirmed by Yokoi, Hirata, and Okada that happy, healthy farmers were needed to uphold the nation, emperor, and *kokutai*, but most now doubted that laissez-faire was the best policy, given the severe depression after 1929. Orthodox popular agrarianism thus found itself ranged squarely against bureaucratic agrarianism over the critical question of who should have charge of farm relief. However modest the state's efforts on behalf of the cultivators may have been before war broke out with China, the Okada alternative was even less satisfactory. Not only did his proposals ignore very real class tensions, but they also breathed an air of impracticality reminiscent of an earlier age when agriculture could still hope to be immune from market forces and village autonomy under a less centralized state was still possible. By the 1930s Japanese farming and village life were so integrated with the national economy that such Nōhonshugi doctrines were simply no longer realistic options for improving rural life.

Chapter VII

Gondō Seikyō: The Inconspicuous Life of a Popular Nationalist

SUDDEN fame seldom strikes any individual, but rarer still is the person who achieves instant notoriety at the end of a long career that has hitherto escaped public notice. Such was the case with Gondō Seikyō (1868-1937), who sprang into prominence at the age of sixty-three as the supposed ideological inspiration for a series of violent episodes in the winter and spring of 1932 that shocked the Japanese political world and hastened the end of parliamentary dominance. Gondō was most closely linked with the Ketsumeidan incidents of February 9 and March 5, 1932, in which a band of rural terrorists and radical young military officers assassinated two leaders of Japan's financial establishment in a vain effort to solve the crisis brought on by the depression. In February their victim was Inoue Junnosuke, the former minister of finance; in March it was the director general of the Mitsui enterprises, Dan Takuma. Gondō's way of thinking was also cited as a stimulus to the young officers and rural activists who attempted a bloody coup d'etat on May 15, 1932.

When the police picked up Gondō for questioning shortly after Inoue was shot on February 9, few Japanese were familiar with the teachings of this frail ninety-pound scholar whose ideas, the authorities said, had ignited such outrageous

163

attacks. Gondō's basic doctrines seemed innocuous: the Japanese people should restore local self-rule and village self-sufficiency in order to overcome the current farm depression. Unlike most agrarianists, however, he embellished his theories with a complicated view of society and history that defied simple comprehension. Eager to classify his evanescent thinking under some familiar heading, the press variously labeled him a simple agrarianist, a utopian socialist, a scholar of the Chinese and Japanese classics, a reactionary, a fascist, an anarchist, and a nihilist.[1] As facts about his life emerged in the weeks that followed, it became evident that Gondō was not quite any of these but rather a new type of Japanese social theorist, the romantic agrarian nationalist.

Gondō was eminent not only as an advocate of a novel kind of Nōhonshugi in the 1930s but also as a major contributor to Japanese nationalist ideology between the wars. For these reasons, as well as his alleged connections with the political tumult of the early thirties, it is worthwhile considering his outlook in detail. First I shall review his fitful career, to help explain the day-to-day preoccupations of this enigmatic theorist. Then I shall examine some important aspects of Japanese nationalism, in order to help place Gondō's dogmas in the context of the nationalist thinking of his day. Subsequent chapters will take up his social and political thought and the consequences of his ideas for radical political activism in the Ketsumeidan and May 15 incidents of 1932.

Gondō's Early Years

Gondō's life spanned the period from the Meiji restoration in 1868 to the outbreak of war with China in 1937, fitting

[1] Hashikawa Bunzō, "Shōwa chōkokkashugi no shosō" [Various Aspects of Ultranationalism in the Shōwa Period], *Chōkokkashugi* [Ultranationalism], ed. Hashikawa Bunzō, *Gendai Nihon shisō taikei* [Collection on Modern Japanese Thought] (Tokyo: Chikuma Shobō, 1964), XXXI, 48; Arahara Bokusui, *Dai uyokushi* [Full History of the Right Wing] (Tokyo: Nihon Kokumintō, 1966), pp. 124-127.

dates to bracket the career of a person so closely involved with modern Japanese nationalism. It is difficult to describe the first fifty years of Gondō's life, because relatively little is known of his writings before 1919 and few biographical data exist to fill in the details of his erratic career. He was born in Kurume, Fukuoka Prefecture, on April 13, 1868, as the eldest son of the samurai class scholar, physician, and farmer Gondō Nao.[2] His childhood name was Zentarō; he is sometimes also identified as Seikei or Nariaki. By profession the Gondō family had served as doctors to the local fief lord during the Edo period, although by the early nineteenth century they had lapsed into the status of masterless samurai (*rōnin*). During the 1850s Gondō Nao studied European medicine in Kyoto, Edo, and also Nagasaki, where he became a youthful friend of the future minister of agriculture and commerce, Shinagawa Yajirō. Soon after Seikyō was born, Nao gave up his practice to live a self-sufficient life as an owner-farmer (*jisakunō*), now that the Meiji government had made it legal for samurai to choose any occupation. Gondō Nao and his family henceforth worked a single hectare of land at the foot of Mt. Kōra, near Kurume.

Gondō Seikyō thus gained his knowledge of agriculture at first hand by being reared in a *jisakunō* household. Perhaps because of his training in Western medical science, Nao was among the first farmers in his district to use new scientific techniques to grow potatoes, peas, Western watermelons,

---

[2] Biographical details for Gondō's early life are taken from Takizawa Makoto, *Gondō Seikyō oboegaki* [Notes on Gondō Seikyō] (Nagaokashi: privately published, 1968), pp. 3-37; Takizawa Makoto, *Gondō Seikyō* (Tokyo: Kinokuniya Shoten, 1971), pp. 11-28; Ifukube Takahiko, "Gondō Seikyō hyōden nōto" [Critical Biographical Notes on Gondō Seikyō], *Kokuron* [National Theory], part 1, III, 9, September 1955, 16-17, and part 2, III, 10, October 1955, 22-23; *Senjin no omokage Kurume jinbutsu denki* [Biographical Images of Eminent Former Residents of Kurume] (Kurume: Kurumeshi, 1961), pp. 124-125; *Senzen ni okeru uyoku dantai no jōkyō* [Circumstances of Right-Wing Groups Before the War], ed. Kōan Chōsachō (Tokyo: Kōan Chōsachō, 1964), I, 483.

and the like, and the family also ate pork from pigs that they raised. Whatever advantages these progressive methods may have brought were doubtless welcome, since the Gondō landholdings had to support a family of five sons and three daughters, several of whom later became well known in their respective occupations.

From this it is easy to imagine that Seikyō grew up in an environment far more stimulating than that of the usual owner-farmer household which had worked its meager lands for generations. His father Nao considered himself an amateur scholar of institutional history (*seidogaku*), an avocation which the family had pursued for many generations. As a result Seikyō was taught the rudiments of the Confucian classics at an early age. After finishing the village primary school, Seikyō was sent to work in an Osaka trading company at the age of fourteen. Two years later he gave up his job to study briefly at a Confucian academy, after which he declined an offer from Shinagawa Yajirō to become a librarian in the Imperial Household Ministry and instead returned home.

Travel Abroad and Study at Home

In lieu of much formal schooling, Gondō's lifelong interest in Chinese history was apparently stimulated by a lengthy trip he took to China and Korea beginning in February 1886. Gondō went as a traveling companion of Miyazaki Shunji, a family friend from Kurume who had just been appointed to the Japanese legation staff in Peking. Little is known about Gondō's trip except that he spent at least several years abroad before returning to marry Kuzuhara Nobue, a sixteen-year-old Kyoto girl, in 1891. Tomioka Tessai (1836-1924), an accomplished painter and Meiji loyalist, acted as go-between. A few years after the wedding, Gondō lost a sizeable investment he had made in a fishery operated by his close friend Takeda Noriyuki on a Korean offshore island, forcing him to turn to his father for funds. When Nao refused to give him money, Gondō left his pregnant wife at the family home in late 1895 and went to live alone at a temple, Shuntokuji, in Nagasaki.

The six and one-half years in Nagasaki were a period of both personal unhappiness and intellectual excitement for Gondō. He seems to have lived a secluded life at Shunto-kuji,[3] devoting nearly all his hours to the temple's large collection of Dutch and Chinese books and only rarely returning to Kurume to see his family. Shuntokuji was a gathering place for Japanese, Chinese, and Korean poets who wrote in the classical Chinese style, and through them Gondō became friendly with future Chinese revolutionaries and people who were later active in the movement to annex Korea to Japan.[4] He earned a living during this period by ghostwriting reports for public officials and essays for students sent from China on government scholarships. The Nagasaki years, confined to study and reflection rather than political or business activity, came to a close early in 1902 when Gondō's six-year-old son Ichirō died of meningitis. This tragedy led to reconciliation with his family and was followed by a new career in Tokyo beginning in 1902.

Gondō and Contemporary China and Korea

The Amur River Society was formed in January 1901 by Uchida Ryōhei (1874-1937) and two dozen other patriots who were eager to press Japan's continental interests to the Amur, thus sealing off Russian influence in East Asia.[5] Gondō's younger brother Shinji, a founding member, arranged Seikyō's appointment to a staff position with this blatantly propagandistic organization in 1902 as a writer and editor. In the course of his duties as a lobbyist for a more forthright China policy, Gondō soon became acquainted with members of both major groups of Chinese exiles then

[3] Takizawa, *Gondō Seikyō oboegaki*, pp. 33-34.
[4] Ibid., pp. 35-36; *Senjin no omokage*, pp. 124-125; Ifukube, part 2, III, 10, October 1955, 22-23.
[5] See Marius B. Jansen, *The Japanese and Sun Yat-sen* (Cambridge, Mass.: Harvard University Press, 1954), pp. 35-36.

living in the Kantō region: the followers of the frustrated reformer of 1898, K'ang Yu-wei, and the future revolutionaries of the T'ung Meng Hui, a nationalist society led by Sun Yat-sen and Huang Hsing. These contacts presumably made Gondō a knowledgeable observer of Chinese politics, since his advice was solicited from time to time by the Ministry of War and he occasionally lectured military officers on the current situation in China.[6]

Although he was never an outstanding figure in the Amur River Society, Gondō served as editor of its main periodical, *Tōa geppō* (East Asia Monthly), from its beginning in April 1908. Gondō was a faithful contributor, but most of what he drafted for *Tōa geppō* was ghostwritten for Uchida and other top leaders of the society. He prepared a monthly commentary on Chinese affairs in which he displayed a great interest in anarchism and its connections with revolution. Writing in an early issue of *Tōa geppō*, Gondō noted a report that Manchu officials had proscribed a political meeting in Shanghai on March 23, 1908. His own view, he said, was that "self-rule is the origin of people's government. The origin of government always seeks the path of self-rule and is very roundabout. The fact that they feared revolution and banned the people's meeting is no way to calm popular sentiment."[7] The incipient Chinese revolution thus provided Gondō the first of many chances to counsel self-rule as a solution for political disorder. Apart from such theoretical blandishments, nevertheless, he seems to have remained aloof from the practical events leading up to the 1911 revolution, and there is no reason to think that he joined in the intrigue promoted by the Kokuryūkai in China during these years.

Such detachment was not the case, however, in Gondō's approach to the other main question facing the Amur River Society, the annexation of Korea in 1910. As a visitor to

---

[6] Takizawa, *Gondō Seikyō oboegaki*, pp. 40-41.
[7] Gondō Seikyō, column in *Tōa geppō* [East Asia Monthly], 1908, quoted ibid., pp. 55-56.

Korea in the 1880s and unlucky investor in a Korean fishery in the early 1890s, Gondō had long known about the chameleonic status of the Korean empire in international diplomacy. Once he began working for the Amur River Society, Gondō became a specialist on the Korean question and traveled to Seoul in April 1906 to establish secret contacts with leaders of the Ilchinhoe, an annexationist Korean reform group created in the wake of the unsuccessful Tonghak rebellion of 1894.[8] Together with Yi Yong-gu and Song Pyŏng-jun, he helped to form a Japanese counterpart to the Ilchinhoe, called the Jichi Zaidan (Self-Rule Foundation), to advocate Korean-Japanese amalgamation and local self-rule.[9] Gondō and the Korean leaders spoke of an ideal "comradeship of East Asians" who could jointly establish an independent Manchuria and eventually merge it with a unified Japanese-Korean empire. Such designs obviously fitted well with the Amur River Society's anti-Russian objectives, but they also conformed to Yi's and Song's plans for abolishing the decrepit Korean monarchy, reforming currency and taxes, and creating new forms of local administration—in short, modernization without Western colonialism.[10]

Gondō apparently understood that amalgamation, while probably unavoidable, would mean erasing Korean independence and that the Japanese would be regarded as conquerors. His solution, according to Yi Yong-gu's son, was to urge a maximum of local autonomy throughout the empire. Yi and Gondō reportedly "investigated the basic principles of Asian self-rule and coexistence that were com-

[8] On the Tonghaks and the Ilchinhoe, see F. Hilary Conroy, *The Japanese Seizure of Korea: 1868-1910* (Philadelphia: University of Pennsylvania Press, 1960), pp. 229-241, 415-416.

[9] For Yi and Song, see ibid., pp. 415-416; Takizawa, *Gondō Seikyō oboegaki*, pp. 62-63; Takizawa, *Gondō Seikyō*, pp. 35-42, 48-51; Ōhigashi Kunio, *Ri Yōkyū no shōgai* [The Career of Yi Yong-gu] (Tokyo: Jiji Tsūshinsha, 1960), pp. 9-10. Song's Japanese name was Noda Heijirō. Ōhigashi is the Japanese name of Yi's posthumous son.

[10] Conroy, pp. 417-418.

mon to China, Korea, and Japan. They studied earnestly, hoping to establish something appropriate for the condition of Korea. . . ."[11] While there is no reason to doubt the sincerity of Gondō's concern for Korean self-rule within a single empire, he was apparently also very active through the Jichi Zaidan and Amur River Society in supporting specific plans for developing Korea and Manchuria that were clearly colonialist in implication.[12] Still, when annexation came in 1910 it was realized on terms far different from the Ilchinhoe's program. Internal political improvements, self-rule, and Manchurian emigration were all ignored in favor of direct military government and immediate strategic objectives, and the Ilchinhoe, far from leading the reforms, was forcibly dissolved.[13] After this turn of events Gondō abandoned his dreams of a self-ruling brotherhood of East Asians, and when he wrote many years later of Manchurian development his new rationale was based mainly on the needs of Japanese farmers to have a place to practice self-rule.

The year 1911 marked the beginning of a new phase of uncertainty in Gondō's restless life. By then the Ilchinhoe was gone, his close friend Yi Yong-gu was dead, and the Jichi Zaidan's plans for developing Korea and Manchuria were discredited. Most of the Chinese revolutionaries who had regularly visited his Tokyo house were now back in their homeland overthrowing the Manchus. Takeda Noriyuki, Gondō's erstwhile business partner and perhaps his closest friend, also died in 1911. Leaving the Chinese and Korean questions behind him, Gondō turned to mining, an enterprise in which his father had once been interested.[14] He also became a small-time stock breeder on the outskirts of Tokyo. Finally, in 1914, he found a new calling which

[11] Ōhigashi, p. 66.
[12] Takizawa, *Gondō Seikyō oboegaki*, pp 56-65; *Senjin no omokage*, pp. 125-126.
[13] Takizawa, *Gondō Seikyō oboegaki*, p. 68; Conroy, pp. 439-441.
[14] Ifukube, part 4, IV, 1, January 1956, p. 22.

occupied him for the rest of his life: teaching and lecturing on the institutional history of early China, Korea, and Japan.

Lecturing at Nationalist Study Societies

Private study societies have been popular among Japanese intellectuals since the earliest years of the Meiji period, and most have had little effect other than providing periodic amusement for their members. This was certainly true of the Nanki Bunko no Kai (Nanki Library Association), a short-lived circle of writers and advocates of continental expansion who first gathered in October 1914 at the Nanki Library at Iigura Katamachi, near the present St. Alban's Church in Tokyo.[15] Despite its anonymity, the society gave Gondō an opportunity to lecture on early history and meet like-minded persons who put him in touch with some of the best thinking during the teens, a time of great ideological unrest in Japan as elsewhere. In October 1918, through contacts established at the Nanki Bunko no Kai, he became a charter member of the well-known Rōsōkai, an ostensibly nonpartisan forum for debating current domestic and international problems which nevertheless gave rise to a great many nationalistic societies after World War I.[16] Gondō lectured this group on Japanese history and became acquainted with such nationalist ideologues as Kita Ikki (1883-1937), Ōkawa Shūmei (1886-1957), and Shimonaka Yasaburō (1878-1961). At the same time Gondō made his living by tutoring pupils who came to his home in the Mikawadai district of Tokyo, near Roppongi.

[15] Ibid., p. 23. The Nanki Bunko, originally the private collection of the Kishū Tokugawa family, became a public library in November 1908. In July 1932 its holdings were turned over to Tokyo University, whose library collection had been destroyed in the great Kantō earthquake of 1923. Today the 96,000 books in the Nanki Bunko form a special unit within the general university library with greatest strength in Japanese history and literature.

[16] *Uyoku zensho* [Full Book on the Right Wing], ed. Kōan Keibi Kenkyūkai (Tokyo: Kindai Keisatsusha, 1957), pp. 150-151; Takizawa, *Gondō Seikyō*, p. 82.

171

For Gondō the years from 1914 to 1919 were ones of extensive research but also active interchange with some of Japan's brightest critics. After years as a ghost-writer, non-official diplomatic intermediary, and tutor-lecturer, the modest esteem which this fifty-year-old scholar now enjoyed thanks to his appearances at study societies no doubt encouraged him to strike out more independently. Immediately after World War I, Gondō asserted himself in two ways. First, he wrote *Kōmin jichi hongi* (Basic Principles of Imperial People's Self-Rule) during 1919 and published it a year later. This book was reprinted verbatim as the latter half of his masterpiece, *Jichi minpan* (People's Guide to Self-Rule), in 1927.[17] *Kōmin jichi hongi*, a summary of his views of state and society, was Gondō's first important written work, although its impact was slight compared with the full *Jichi minpan* published seven years later. Second, in June 1920 he established the Jichi Gakkai (Self-Rule Study Society), based on the remnants of the former Nanki Library Association, to study and publicize the early institutional history of Japan.[18] Since the Jichi Gakkai brought a steady supply of private pupils to his door, Gondō could henceforth devote himself to reading, writing, and teaching about his first love, the study of Japanese society, without further need for an outside job.

The Jichi Gakkai and Self-Rule

Gondō wrote a "Declaration" for the Jichi Gakkai in 1920 outlining its principles in words similar to *Kōmin jichi*

17 Gondō Seikyō, *Kōmin jichi hongi* [Basic Principles of Imperial People's Self-Rule] (Tokyo: Fuzanbō, 1920); Gondō Seikyō, *Jichi minpan* [People's Guide to Self-Rule] (Tokyo: Heibonsha, 1927). Subsequent references to *Jichi minpan* denote the 2nd ed., published by Heibonsha in 1932. *Jichi minpan* occupies vol. 1 of *Gondō Seikyō chosakushū* [Collected Writings of Gondō Seikyō], published in Tokyo in 1972 jointly by Girochinsha, Nebīsusha, and Kokushoku-sensensha. Eight volumes in all are projected.

18 See Takizawa, *Gondō Seikyō oboegaki*, pp. 86-90; Ifukube, part 5, IV, 2, February 1956, 20; *Chōkokkashugi*, p. 417.

hongi. His view of contemporary society was expressed in the first paragraph of this document:

Self-rule arose gradually and naturally. It developed as food, clothing, and shelter were taken care of. It is harmonized by the true values of coexistence and mutual prosperity. But the institutions of our country throughout the centuries have not yet attained this. The ravages of nature and the biases of the authorities have blocked the progress of self-rule. There is a general trend toward ruin and outbreak of evils, [evident from] the divergence between those who work and those who are idle, the estrangement between the rich and the poor, the fact that those above adhere to conservatism and those below preach reform doctrines, the fact that those on the right embrace capital and those on the left cling to labor, and the fact that we have not stopped opposing each other's arguments.[19]

In light of these antagonisms in postwar society, Gondō's "Declaration" continued, "we are merely advocating the expansion of pure self-rule, and we must lay plans to attain it." Why was this ideal so desirable?

Self-rule is the authority over our lives. It is an article of faith for peace. It is the origin of human progress. It is the foundation for independence and self-strengthening. Thus we intend to set its rules and standards in good order and to examine it carefully in the past. Likewise, in planning for the future, we intend to establish guidelines and procedures for implementing it.[20]

This document was obviously more an affirmation than an explanation of the merits of self-rule, but it shows that Gondō's fundamental concern, as had been true during his years with the *Tōa geppō*, related to the sociopolitical goal

[19] Gondō Seikyō, "Sengen" [Declaration] of the Jichi Gakkai, June 1920, quoted in *Senzen ni okeru uyoku dantai no jōkyō*, I, 484.
[20] Ibid.

of local autonomy, long a staple of Nōhonshugi ideology in Japan. But whereas Shinagawa Yajirō, Tomeoka Kōsuke, Yokoi Tokiyoshi, and other mainstream agrarianists spoke of self-rule as one dimension of a larger farm-first outlook, for Gondō the agricultural village was merely the vehicle for achieving the overall objective of autonomy. Clearly self-rule and farm village society were inseparable, but without tarnishing his credentials as a Nōhonshugisha Gondō reversed the emphasis in such a way that he could argue some years later that self-rule was possible (and very desirable) even for city residents.[21] Hence it is understandable that farming was not mentioned in this "Declaration" (although self-rule implied village self-rule to almost any Japanese in 1920), nor is it surprising that agriculture occupied a relatively minor place in his later writings on Japanese society.

The Nan'ensho *Controversy*

Beginning with thirty-four charter members, the Jichi Gakkai soon fell into the pattern of monthly meetings and occasional publications typical of small intellectual associations at the time.[22] Then, in the spring of 1922, it suddenly drew attention when Gondō and Ozawa Dagyō brought out a three-volume edition of a previously unknown manuscript, titled *Nan'ensho* (Book of Nan'en), which they claimed was the oldest book written in Japan.[23] Nan'en Shōan was a seventh-century Confucianist and tutor of the Tenji emperor (r. 668-671) whose many writings had entirely disappeared by modern times, according to most scholars in Gondō's day. *Nan'ensho*, its editors asserted, was based on a manuscript by Nan'en himself that had belonged to the Gondō family for generations, supplemented by a variant

21 See *Jichi minpan*, pp. 571-572.
22 Takizawa, *Gondō Seikyō oboegaki*, pp. 88-90; Takizawa, *Gondō Seikyō*, pp. 85-87.
23 *Nan'ensho* [Book of Nan'en], ed. Gondō Seikyō and Ozawa Dagyō (Tokyo: Heibonsha, 1922). See *Senjin no omokage*, pp. 126-128; Ōhigashi, p. 63.

text recently discovered in Sendai. The publishers of this cryptic work, composed in classical Chinese, were sufficiently satisfied of its authenticity to advertise that *Nan'ensho* was sixty years older than the *Kojiki* (Record of Ancient Matters), written in 712 and hitherto considered Japan's earliest book.[24]

Nan'ensho purported to be a record of questions and answers between Nan'en and Tenji when the latter was crown prince. It described early invasions of Korea under the mythical Jinmu emperor (r. seventh century B.C., according to legend), ancient Korean-Japanese trade contacts, victories and defeats in battle, and a harmonious rural society in ancient Japan governed by cooperation and mutual aid. Although the book was said to have been written at the height of Chinese cultural influence on Japan in the seventh century, its view of the state appeared to be closer to the utopian self-rule teachings of the Chinese philosophers Mencius and Mo Tzu than to the imperial Confucianism patronized in Japan at the time.[25]

Anytime a manuscript that is thought to be twelve hundred years old is uncovered, scholars and antiquarians take a lively interest. In the case of *Nan'ensho*, the public at large also soon became aware of its publication because Gondō and Ozawa dedicated the edition to Crown Prince Hirohito and arranged for its formal presentation to the throne through the intervention of Prince Ichijō Saneteru.[26] The newspapers immediately debated its authenticity without reaching a consensus, although most academic experts dis-

[24] Ifukube, part 4, IV, 1, January 1956, 23-24; Takizawa, *Gondō Seikyō oboegaki*, pp. 95-98; Takizawa, *Gondō Seikyō*, pp. 104-118. On Nan'en Shōan, see *Nihon jinmei jiten* [Biographical Dictionary of Japan], ed. Haga Yaichi, reprint ed. (Kyoto: Shibunkaku, 1969), p. 420. (The original edition was published in 1914.) Nan'en Shōan is also read Minamibuchi Shōan.

[25] See Ifukube, part 9, IV, 8, August 1956, 12.

[26] Takizawa, *Gondō Seikyō oboegaki*, p. 96; Ifukube, part 4, IV, 1, January 1956, 23.

missed it as a relatively recent forgery.[27] Today the controversy has receded into obscurity, and the two recent writers on the subject cautiously agree that *Nan'ensho* dates from a later era and that Gondō himself could not have forged it; but who was responsible for compiling it, and in what period, remain unknown.[28]

Regardless of the uncertainty, this book had a long-lasting effect on Gondō and his followers. For those who wanted to believe that it was real, *Nan'ensho* became a sacred text to legitimize the doctrine of self-rule. Once this work had been published, the Jichi Gakkai became much more widely known, and *Nan'ensho* continued to serve as the basis for many of its discussion meetings for several years after 1922. Its influence on two of Gondō's later books is undisputed. The first half of *Jichi minpan*, written between 1920 and 1927, drew frequently on *Nan'ensho* in discussing early Japanese history, while *Hachirin tsūheikō*,[29] published in five classical Chinese volumes in 1931, presented a similar account of the ancient period.

The Jichi Gakkai and the Kinkei Gakuin in the 1920s

Gondō continued his activities with the Jichi Gakkai throughout the twenties, as well as lecturing at private academies and preparing *Jichi minpan* for publication in 1927. During the winter of 1924-1925 the Jichi Gakkai caused a stir when Gondō and his followers marched on the Bank of Japan to demand conversion of 16,000 yen in currency to gold. Gondō and a few other leaders were detained by the police after this affair in January 1925, but no

[27] Ifukube, part 6, IV, 3, March 1956, 21; Takizawa, *Gondō Seikyō oboegaki*, p. 100.

[28] See Ifukube, part 8, IV, 6, June 1956, 19-21; Takizawa, *Gondō Seikyō oboegaki*, pp. 100-102.

[29] Gondō Seikyō, *Hachirin tsūheikō* (Tokyo: privately published, 1931). The title defies translation. See Ifukube, part 9, IV, 8, August 1956, 14.

charges were lodged.[30] This incident had no effect on the deflationary monetary policies of the government, but it was a sign of populist resentment over the state's postwar decision to return to the gold standard as well as its policies preventing currency conversion. Gondō returned to this theme of the monopoly power of big capital and centralized government in his later writings, as the depression deepened at the end of the decade.

By the late twenties Gondō began to meet many of the activists who eventually, to a greater or lesser degree, took his ideas as their inspiration for political violence in 1932. Since 1923 he had lectured on Japanese history at the Kokushikan, a prestigious academic society, and starting the next year he regularly addressed the Kōshikai, an organization that was interested in rural relief measures. From 1927 to 1930 Gondō taught both Chinese and Japanese history at the Kinkei Gakuin, a private school whose object was "to specialize in the study of the East Asian sages and to investigate the spirit of the Japanese people, the national essence, and the ways of government."[31] Among his pupils were Inoue Nisshō, subsequently the leader of the radical Blood Brotherhood (Ketsumeidan), and Yotsumoto Yoshitaka, a main figure in the Ketsumeidan incidents of early 1932.[32] Gondō's lectures on early institutional history reportedly roused little excitement in an academy partial to the national socialism of Takabatake Motoyuki (1886-1928),[33] but his three years at the Kinkei Gakuin were the first systematic access to his thought for both future political

[30] *Senjin no omokage*, pp. 128-129; Takizawa, *Gondō Seikyō oboegaki*, pp. 103-107.

[31] Quoted in Hashikawa Bunzō, "Hoi—Ketsumeidan, goichigo jiken o chūshin to shite" [Addendum—With Emphasis on the Ketsumeidan and May 15 Incidents], in Takizawa, *Gondō Seikyō oboegaki*, p. 118. See also *Senzen ni okeru uyoku dantai no jōkyō*, I, 484-485.

[32] Ifukube, part 9, IV, 8, August 1956, 13; Hashikawa, "Hoi," p. 116.

[33] Hashikawa, "Hoi," pp. 118-119.

activists and the generals, admirals, and government officials
who occasionaly listened to his talks.

The Yoyogi Uehara Academy and the Seishō Gakuen

Useful though the study societies and private academies
had been in expanding his circle of acquaintances during the
preceding fifteen years, it would still be an exaggeration to
say that, as of 1930, Gondō Seikyō was a well-known
ideologue in Japan. In February of that year he gave up
his full-time post at the Kinkei Gakuin and dropped from
public view to concentrate on his writings. Not until September 1931 did he return to regular teaching, this time at
a private school at his new residence in the Yoyogi Uehara
section of Tokyo. Many of the young army and navy
officers who later joined in the direct political action of
early 1932 commuted on weekends from their bases in the
Kantō region to hear Gondō's lectures at the Yoyogi Uehara
academy.[34] What they heard was a digest of his views of
Japanese history and his repeated call for a return to a self-
ruling society to cure the ills of contemporary Japan.

Gondō's pupils seem to have respected him as an exemplary scholar, whether or not they shared his outlook on
current affairs. The eccentric Inoue Nisshō, for example,
described him as "thin" and "apparently poor" but said that
he was "an interesting old man with a very prominent
nose." Inoue found Gondō often argumentative and narrow-
minded but admiringly concluded that "he is a rare sort of
man these days."[35] Nagano Akira thought of Gondō as a
revered scholar from another era: "We are not used to his
vocabulary, and his exegesis is of an entirely different sort
from those of persons now being educated. . . ."[36] Tanaka

[34] *Senzen ni okeru uyoku dantai no jōkyō*, I, 484-485; Takizawa,
Gondō Seikyō oboegaki, pp. 107-110; Takizawa, *Gondō Seikyō*, pp.
133-144.
[35] Inoue Nisshō, quoted in Hashikawa, "Hoi," p. 135.
[36] Nagano Akira, quoted in Hashikawa, "Shōwa," p. 48. On Nagano's outlook on self-rule, see Thomas R. H. Havens, "Two Popular

Kunio preferred Gondō's personality to that of Tachibana Kōzaburō, whose lectures he had also attended:

> When [Gondō] came to lecture, I lost attention after the lecture started, but most of the others would listen. At this time I was not too fond of listening to lectures, so I went no more than once and instead played chess. . . . I did not hear his lectures, but since I was in daily contact with him, I thought he was a person of unusually fine character, a rare scholar, and suitably dauntless. He contrasted favorably with Professor Tachibana Kōzaburō, who was solemn and cowardly.[37]

As important as his school was for bringing together young radicals in the fall and winter of 1931-1932, Gondō's uncertain personal role in plotting assassinations and coups must have been constricted by the time-consuming outpouring of publications which he prepared during the year he lived at Yoyogi Uehara. He brought out five books and at least four articles during 1931 and 1932, the peak of his career as a social critic and spokesman for agrarian nationalism. Although these works essentially restated ideas first expressed in *Jichi minpan*, his reputation as a theorist of terror and insurrection doubtless created a fresh audience for his writings. Still Gondō was never formally charged by the police, and thus he escaped the fanfare of a lengthy political trial. He seems to have faded from public attention almost as quickly as he once captured it, and by late 1932 he had resumed his quiet life as a teacher and author.

The final phase of Gondō's life began in August 1932 when he moved to Nakanechō in the Meguro area of Tokyo. He reestablished the Jichi Gakkai in a modest building known as the Seishō Gakuen, which housed approxi-

---

Views of Rural Self-Rule in Modern Japan," *Studies on Japanese Culture* (Tokyo: The Japan P.E.N. Club, 1973), II, 249-256.

[37] Tanaka Kunio, quoted in Hashikawa, "Hoi," pp. 139-140.

mately a dozen students. In 1934 he renamed his study society the Seidogaku Gakkai (Society for the Study of Institutions) and the next year began issuing a journal on self-rule that was circulated to farm leaders throughout the country, until it ceased publication in early 1937.[38] Gondō was asked to visit China in 1936 as an adviser to the Nationalist government on local administration, but declined because of poor health. Despite chronic asthma, he continued to teach at the Seishō Gakuen until July 9, 1937, when he died of a lung tumor while eating a piece of fish. After Shinto ceremonies, his remains were buried in the family grave near Kurume. Amid the hubbub of Japan's conflict in north China two days earlier, few persons heeded the death of this inconspicuous scholar whose agrarian theories had helped to shape the nationalism that led the country to war.

The State and Japanese Nationalism

When Gondō Seikyō set forth his theories of agrarian nationalism in the 1920s and 1930s, he joined a long line of Japanese writers who have been fascinated by the peculiarities of their country's past. Since early times the Japanese have been conscious of their own distinctiveness in relation to their East Asian neighbors, whose influence they never entirely escaped after the introduction of Buddhism in A.D. 552. Until very recently the main ingredients of their sense of separateness have included geographical isolation, the same language, a high degree of ethnic homogeneity, a shared awareness of the past, strong ties to the land, common beliefs in the gods of Shinto, and the politico-religious continuity of the throne, whose occupant theoretically served as both temporal ruler and chief priest of Shinto.

[38] Hashikawa, "Hoi," p. 150; *Senjin no omokage*, p. 129; Ifukube, part 12, IV, 11, November 1956, 13-14. *Seido no kenkyū* [Studies of Institutions] began appearing in October 1935. Rare copies in the author's possession show that Gondō wrote nearly all the articles in each issue.

This combination of attributes, developed early in their history, provided the Japanese with a degree of cohesiveness perhaps unmatched by any other premodern people, serving at the very least as a foundation for nationality consciousness when Japan entered the modern period.

Whether these factors comprised true Japanese nationalism depends on how precisely we can cut through the many semantic and conceptual ambiguities associated with the term "nationalism" itself. Like any idea, nationalism is easier to describe than define, but it seems useful to start by calling it, in Shafer's words, "that sentiment unifying a group of people who have a real or imagined common historical experience and a common aspiration to live together as a separate group in the future."[39] In order to become aware of this sentiment, the group must be sufficiently interdependent (through such means as language, religious practices, common political institutions, or economic interaction) to constitute a people distinct from other peoples.[40] Most writers agree, moreover, that nationalism involves loyalty to a state; no state, no nationalism. Thus they argue that there was no true nationalism until the French Revolution yoked the self-awareness of Frenchmen as a separate community of people to a newly created state employing modern institutions. The aspirations of central and eastern European peoples to live by themselves are usually called prenational culturalism, but not yet nationalism itself.

Two difficulties arise from the requirement that nationalism be tied to the existence of a state. First, there is confusion between the ideas of nation and state. A good example is Karl W. Deutsch's statement that "a nation is a people who have hold of a state or who have developed quasi-governmental capabilities for forming, supporting, and enforcing a common will. And a nation-state is a state that

[39] Boyd C. Shafer, *Nationalism: Myth and Reality* (New York: Harcourt, Brace & World, Inc., 1955), p. 10.

[40] See Karl W. Deutsch, *Nationalism and Its Alternatives* (New York: Alfred A. Knopf, 1969), p. 14.

has become largely identical with one people."[41] This fuzzy convergence of the two concepts no doubt results from the common tendency to use the hybrid term nation-state for cases in which state is usually intended. Such ambiguity can be avoided by using state to mean "a legal concept describing a social group that occupies a defined territory and is organized under common political institutions and an effective government."[42] A nation, on the other hand, is "a social group which shares a common ideology, common institutions and customs, and a sense of homogeneity. . . . A nation may comprise part of a state, be coterminous with a state, or extend beyond the borders of a single state."[43] Without this distinction, nationalism as a body of loyalties to the social unit (the nation) may become confused with allegiance to the legal entity which governs it (the state). To say that nationalism must be focused on the state is unfortunately to equate it with statism, that is, support for the sovereignty of the state.

The second difficulty with linking nationalism to the state, implicit from the foregoing, is that most states govern more than one nationality group.[44] The nationalisms felt by citizens of such governments are nearly always loyalties to their ethnic nationality groups, not to the state, unless any particular citizen's group happens to control it. When emotional ties to one's nationality group and one's state overlap, the assumption that the nationalistic individual vests his ultimate allegiance in the state may be accurate. Nevertheless, to stress the statist orientation of nationalism invites the twin dangers of underemphasizing those communal bonds which permit a people to feel separate from other peoples

[41] Ibid., p. 19.
[42] Jack C. Plano and Roy Olton, *The International Relations Dictionary* (New York: Holt, Rinehart and Winston, 1969), quoted in Walker Connor, "Nation-building or Nation-destroying?" *World Politics*, xxiv, 3, April 1972, 333.
[43] Ibid.
[44] For statistics, see Connor, p. 320.

and overemphasizing the omnipotence of the state in sub-
suming other loyalties within the society.

Japan is a fascinating example of nationalism because
state and nation have been so closely identified with each
other throughout her history. During most periods since
about A.D. 550 the imperial clan has acted as the link between the two, since the emperor was considered to be both
political sovereign and symbolic patriarch of the Japanese
race. To speak of nationalism in premodern Japan is risky,
however, because before the nineteenth century communications were too sporadic, the economy too localized, and
patterns of social interdependence too fragmented to permit the degree of integration needed for a people to feel
nationalism as it is understood today. Thus there is no particular reason to depart from the convention that nationalism
is a modern phenomenon, confined to the past two centuries, so long as we acknowledge the diffuse but strong
self-awareness by most premodern Japanese of their own
uniqueness.

The forces which activated nationalism in mid-nineteenth
century Japan included strong military, diplomatic, and
economic pressures from Europe and America, discontent
with the Tokugawa government's shabby treatment of the
imperial institution, and a recrudescence of anti-Chinese
nativist ideas in the early nineteenth century. The ambitious
development program after 1868 was spurred on by intense
nationalistic feelings on the part of Japan's modernizing
oligarchs. And one of the first things they did was to erect
a strong, efficient state. In short, just as traditional Japanese
perceptions of their own distinctiveness were always fastened to the existence of imperial rule, so too recent Japanese nationalism coincided with the rise of powerful and
effective institutions of central government.

But the close convergence of state and nation in Japan
should not deceive us into overestimating the effect of
loyalty to the state as a propellant of Japanese nationalism.
If Hasegawa Nyozekan has spoken of the seeming "intel-

183

lectual vacuity"[45] of nationalist thought in the 1920s and 1930s, the reason is almost surely that the essence of Japanese nationalism cannot be reduced to the tidy logic of support for the state. Instead it must be sought in the complex, often conflicting, web of emotions which have bound the Japanese people to one another as a nation.

From the great flood of nationalist writing since Meiji have come two ideological streams: ethnic or cultural nationalism (*kokuminshugi*), stressing primary affinities for the Japanese as a people, and nationalism focused on the state (*kokkashugi*), sometimes known as statism.[46] Once the 1868 restoration had integrated the people sufficiently to become aware of their common aspirations, National Learning (Kokugaku) was quickly discarded in favor of a utilitarian drive for wealth and power as the basis of state-oriented nationalism. For a decade or more this trend created little friction with popular nationalist thinking. Then in the 1880s Itō Hirobumi (1841-1909) and others institutionalized state power, notably in the constitution of 1889. At the same time Motoda Eifu (1818-1891), coauthor of the education rescript of 1890, defined Meiji *kokkashugi*—a doctrine emphasizing allegiance to the state as the citizen's highest duty. The legal scholars Hozumi Yatsuka (1860-1912) and Uesugi Shinkichi (1878-1923) and the philosopher Inoue Tetsujirō (1855-1944) soon echoed Motoda's defense of state power and urged the people to respect the authorities.

Just as strong were popular nationalist sentiments after the first Meiji decade. The antigovernment freedom and

[45] Hasegawa Nyozekan, *Hasegawa Nyozekan shū* [Hasegawa Nyozekan Collection] (Tokyo, 1960), p. 129, quoted in Kenneth B. Pyle, "Some Recent Approaches to Japanese Nationalism," *Journal of Asian Studies*, xxxi, 1, November 1971, 16.

[46] The remarks in the next paragraphs are developed more fully from a different perspective in Thomas R. H. Havens, "Frontiers of Japanese Social History During World War II," *Shakai kagaku tōkyū* [Social Science Review], xviii, 3, 1, No. 52, March 1973, pp. 1-45. I am indebted to Penelope Brown, Kazue Kyōichi, and Kent C. Smith for helping to clarify my ideas about Japanese nationalism.

184

popular rights movement of the late 1870s was followed in 1886 by the *Nihon dōtokuron* (Theory of Japanese Morality) of Nishimura Shigeki (1828-1902), who wrote not to praise subservience to the state but to build character among the people. Even less ambiguously, men such as Kuga Katsunan (1857-1907), Miyake Setsurei (1860-1945), Okakura Tenshin (1862-1913), and Shiga Shigetaka (1863-1927) debated what it meant to be a Japanese in a modernizing, internationalist milieu. Other *kokumin*-oriented nationalists included the early socialist Abe Isoo (1865-1949) and the Christian spokesman Uchimura Kanzō (1861-1930), both of whom struggled to align their beliefs with their nationality, and somewhat later the folklore specialist Yanagida Kunio (1875-1962).

By the 1920s the social harmony of Meiji had obviously vanished. Pluralism and diversity, products of the modernizing process, now gave Japan a much wider range of ideological choices. Both labor and capital, tenant and landlord clashed openly while various partisans trumpeted class, occupational, regional, and other subnational loyalties. Under such circumstances, it is understandable that political and social theorists, both in government and outside it, began to question previous assumptions about Japanese nationalism. New formulations, stressing myths of social harmony and Japanese uniqueness, appeared precisely when the early Meiji consensus on what it meant to be a Japanese had broken down and the country was growing more like other modern nations. All governments routinely spin out myths of national separateness to build more unity where little exists, and the Japanese state was no exception, especially in the 1930s.[47] Hence politicians and generals joined the statist clamor. Vigorous leaders such as Tanaka Giichi (1863-1929) and patriot-scholars such as Ōkawa Shūmei

---

[47] For an interesting study of government propaganda techniques, see Penelope Brown, "The Thought Control Program of Japan's Military Leaders, 1931-1941," B.A. thesis in history, Connecticut College, 1972.

(1886-1957) broadcast doctrines of state loyalty that appealed strongly to the armed forces.

Kokumin nationalism, now expressed by such liberal activists as Yoshino Sakuzō (1878-1933) and Saionji Kinmochi (1849-1940), resisted absolute allegiance to the state but usually accepted the institutions of government (if not the men and policies guiding them). Such acquiescence was not the case, however, for the national reconstructionists of the day. Kita Ikki (1883-1937), who was statist only in his willingness to use a reformed national government to achieve his goals of public welfare, attacked both personnel, programs, and institutions. Even more quixotic were the popular nationalists like Gondō and Tachibana Kōzaburō, who rebuked centralized rule and touted premodern rural communalism in order to protect the nation-as-people from bureaucratism and monopoly capitalism. In effect they created myths about early village life, based on farming and local autonomy, to serve as the new shared sentiment binding the Japanese people as one nation.

In short, Japanese nationalist thought by the early twentieth century was cleft into *kokkashugi* and *kokuminshugi*, an irreparable erosion of the earlier agreement on national loyalties. Statist thinking was subdivided into emperor-oriented beliefs, often stressing the inviolable national essence (*kokutai*), and government-centered dogmas which regarded the imperial institution as ornamentation. Either way, *kokkashugi* partisans spoke of national uniqueness to create more public unity beneath the state. Hence the bureaucratic agrarianist Hirata Tōsuke drew on a time-honored communalist tradition when he spoke of the emperor as the father of society and the state as a family (*kazoku kokka*), thus attempting to harness popular loyalties to the interests of the state.[48]

[48] Hirata Tōsuke, phonograph recording, June 11, 1923, quoted in Katō Fusakura, *Hakushaku Hirata Tōsuke den* [Biography of Count Hirata Tōsuke] (Tokyo: Hiratahaku Denki Hensan Jimusho, 1927), p. 184.

Ideology focused on the *kokumin*, in turn, was split between doctrines which accepted the established governmental structure (while directing primary loyalties to the people) and those which demanded its removal. Measured against the full span of nationality sentiments expressed during these years, the concept of *kokutai* was frequently irrelevant—to many writers a harmless vestige, worthy of obeisance but not veneration. Most treatises on *kokutai* were linked with statist ideas, whereas nation-centered thinking generally dealt with the happiness and welfare of the people, based on the spiritual core of the country's nationality consciousness.

If *kokumin* and *kokka* ideas were never entirely distinct, neither were they functionally equivalent. On the one hand, nearly all modern Japanese political thinkers (except for anarchists and certain communists) have been nationalists in that they have felt elemental attachments to their fellow countrymen. The advocates of *kokuminshugi* therefore greatly outnumbered the statist ideologues. But since the latter claimed to embrace the people's sentiments within the net of state authority, the handful of *kokumin*-oriented writers who resisted state power provide the most interesting analytical contrast, at least in the twentieth century. On the other hand, as the ideology of the ruled, not the rulers, *kokumin* theories were usually more idealistic and less specific than the statist doctrines of the authorities. The force and direction of these two forms of nationalism were thus very different: statism was aggressive and centripetal, *kokuminshugi* defensive and politically centrifugal.

For most popular nationalists the emperor symbolically unified the people, in his role as chief priest of Shinto and intercessor with the gods on behalf of all Japanese—making them unique among all peoples. Naturally modern Japanese nationalism has also included more secular, noncommunal elements, especially as a result of diplomatic pressures from the West and the ensuing race to big-power status. The emperor also played an important political role, legally

187

recognized in the 1889 constitution which formally made him sovereign. Nevertheless nationalist thought associated with intense convictions about the uniqueness of the ethnic group flooded Japan after World War I. It seems very possible that the country's capacity for national mobilization in the late 1930s and early 1940s was enhanced precisely because the state fitted itself to the "ethno-psychological inclinations"[49] of citizens to identify with one another as a people, rather than because the state extracted unyielding popular devotion to itself as sovereign.

Agrarian nationalists like Gondō and Tachibana are usually labeled political "rightists," and they are routinely glossed in reference works on the right-wing movement in prewar Japan.[50] This emphasis somewhat misses the mark, if "right" and "left" may be taken as relative concepts within a commonly accepted political system. Most agrarian nationalists after World War I rejected not merely the recent dominance of parliamentary parties but the entire political system itself. Hence their loyalties were to the Japanese as an ethno-nationality group rather than to the state. As a result, an inconspicuous scholar such as Gondō, who hardly enjoyed conventional popularity, was nevertheless a popular nationalist in the sense that he wrote as a people's ideologue and bitterly attacked the state from below.

Although it was the doctrine of a subnational interest group (the largest one, farmers), rural nationalism offered a comprehensive view of state and society which was intended to be a common basis of loyalty for everyone in the country.

---

[49] Connor, p. 335.

[50] See, e.g., *Sources of Japanese Tradition*, comp. Ryusaku Tsunoda, ed. William T. deBary (New York: Columbia University Press, 1958), p. 770; *Uyoku undō* [The Right-Wing Movement], ed. Keibi Keisatsu Kenkyūkai, rev. ed. (Tokyo: Tachibana Shobō, 1957), p. 73; *Uyoku undō jiten* [Dictionary of the Right-Wing Movement], ed. Shakai Undō Kenkyūkai (Tokyo: Kōbundō, 1961). The standard survey of Japanese nationalism in English is Delmer M. Brown, *Nationalism in Japan, an Introductory Historical Analysis* (Berkeley: University of California Press, 1955).

The tensions and frustrations resulting from the great changes in public life during the 1920s and 1930s led agrarianists to refashion Japanese nationalism by yoking farm and nation in terms which touched on the emotional and spiritual roots of the people as an ethno-nationality group.

However necessary it is to understand the economic ills of Japan during the twenties and thirties, Nōhonshugi during these years cannot be approached exclusively, or even primarily, in economic terms. Without prolonged rural depression in the 1920s and 1930s, agrarian nationalism would probably never have enjoyed more than scant acceptance, but its widespread appeal—extending to the officer corps of the army and navy in the early 1930s—traces in large measure to the many points of contact it established with the vital core of psycho-cultural beliefs that comprised the essence of Japanese nationality consciousness. Among the most important of these beliefs was a faith in the economic, social, and spiritual benefits of farming.

Chapter VIII

Gondō Seikyō's Ideal Self-Ruling Society

PERHAPS the most vexing dilemma facing the politically knowledgeable citizen of a modern country is how to oppose the programs of his government without seeming unpatriotic. Even in societies with institutionalized channels for expressing nonviolent dissent, it is hard to appear loyal to either state or nation when attacking official policies, especially where nationalism is virtually monopolized by the state.

The political culture of modern Japan has been slow to nurture the idea of loyal opposition, and before 1945 few means existed to protest government decisions that were ultimately sanctioned as the imperial will under the 1889 constitution. It is of course true that between World War I and World War II the Japanese state neither retained the tacit public consensus of the Meiji period on national goals nor imperiously gathered all lesser popular loyalties into monolithic allegiance to its policies of expansion in Asia. Nevertheless the government's legal, institutional, and ceremonial advantages in utilizing nationalism made it extremely difficult to oppose the state and still appear to be a patriot.

This difficulty was fatal to the Japan Communist Party in the 1920s and 1930s, since few Japanese thought it possible to reconcile one's identity as a subject of the throne with membership in an international revolutionary movement. It was also a major flaw of the noncommunist left, since the government usually had no trouble portraying socialist reform schemes as the work of men concerned only with self-interest, not the country as a whole. Even the nationalistic reconstructionist Kita Ikki, whose patriotism is scarcely questioned today, took great pains to assert his devotion to the Japanese nation in the face of Western imperialism,[1] only to have his major works banned by the state because they attacked its policies. Despite the risks of voicing unpopular opinions and the government's enormous powers of suppression under the 1900 police peace law and 1925 peace preservation act, a number of Japanese patriots like Kita flaunted their own antistate brand of nationalism by denouncing the financial cliques (*zaibatsu*), bureaucracy, military services, and political parties—the establishment that had permitted the country to drift into crisis. It even became stylish, at least on the fringes of what the police called the radical right, to revive the spirit of the mid-nineteenth century *shishi*, or "men of high purpose,"[2] who likewise had discarded their allegiances to a depraved state in favor of higher loyalties to the throne. In short, the ideological ferment of the interwar era yielded the clearest division of state and nation in Japanese political thought since the 1860s and forced most Japanese to rethink familiar assumptions about what constituted the basis of the Japanese polity and society.

Gondō Seikyō and the Historical Process

Gondō Seikyō contributed to this reexamination of nationalism by constantly affirming his deep devotion to Japanese society while simultaneously renouncing practically

[1] See George M. Wilson, *Radical Nationalist in Japan: Kita Ikki, 1883-1937* (Cambridge, Mass.: Harvard University Press, 1969), pp. 44, 55, 67.

[2] Marius B. Jansen's phrase, in *Sakamoto Ryōma and the Meiji Restoration* (Princeton: Princeton University Press, 1961).

every aspect of the modern state which governed it. To some this disavowal has made Gondō a prenationalist "reactionary romantic"[3] (technically possible, if loyalty to the current state be a condition of nationalism). To others, Gondō was an "impractical anarchist"[4] whose opposition to Japan's governing institutions was simply too sweeping to provide a useful basis for reform. Before accepting such blanket judgments, it is important to examine Gondō's ideas about Japanese life and politics by way of background for understanding the criticisms he voiced about current affairs during the depression years. This chapter deals with Gondō's views of Japanese history from antiquity through the Meiji era; the next will treat his suggestions for relieving the plight of his own times.

Of the many agrarianist writers in modern Japan whom scholars group as partisans of Nōhonshugi, Gondō was certainly the most knowledgeable about East Asian history and offered the most elaborate views of Japanese society in support of his demands for a return to village self-rule. Estimates of his skill as a historian are properly clouded by the *Nan'ensho* controversy, but my concern is with how, not how well, he understood the past, since the most useful historical myths are rarely created by the best historians. *Jichi minpan* (People's Guide to Self-Rule), written between 1919 and 1927 with *Nan'ensho* as one of its guides, is the earliest detailed source for analyzing Gondō's nationalism. The many works published in 1931 and 1932 which amplified and rephrased earlier themes are also helpful. Another major source is his final book, *Jichi minseiri* (Principles of People's Self-Rule), which appeared in 1936 to summarize arguments developed in his previous writings.[5]

---

[3] *Kindai Nihon shisōshi* [History of Modern Japanese Thought], ed. Tōyama Shigeki, Yamazaki Seiichi, and Ōi Sei (Tokyo: Aoki Shoten, 1956), III, 665.

[4] Arahara Bokusui, *Dai uyokushi* [Full History of the Right Wing] (Tokyo: Nihon Kokumintō, 1966), pp. 124-126.

[5] Gondō Seikyō, *Jichi minseiri* [Principles of People's Self-Rule]

Most thinkers change their minds across time more fully than historians of ideas are usually willing to admit, but in Gondō's case there is an uncommon consistency from first book to last, because his writing career was brief and because *Jichi minpan* laid the foundations for almost all his later publications. It therefore seems reasonable to treat his work as a unit, written during the rural depression to attack evils that remained just as fearsome on the eve of war with China as they had seemed when Gondō started *Jichi minpan* in 1919.

Gondō professed to admire the enduring monuments of the past but also to recognize the inevitability of historical change. He began *Jichi minpan* by noting that "providing for food, clothing, shelter, and harmony between the sexes has been the norm for social stability from antiquity to the present, without change."[6] The goal of society was constant throughout history, namely the utilitarian desire "to live in safety and also to live as much as possible in happiness and full satisfaction."[7] But if human needs were changeless, Gondō continued, history was full of examples of new attempts to satisfy them, sometimes with adverse results. Nevertheless, "regeneration and change are universal laws. Therefore when the time for change comes, the order must change too. . . . 'to advance through change' is truly a constant principle of nature."[8]

(Tokyo, Gakugeisha, 1936). Major portions are excerpted in *Chōkokkashugi* [Ultranationalism], ed. Hashikawa Bunzō, *Gendai Nihon shisō taikei* [Collection on Modern Japanese Thought] (Tokyo: Chikuma Shobō, 1964), XXXI, 239-282, to which version subsequent references are made. On p. 3 of the original edition of *Jichi minseiri*, Gondō noted that because "*Jichi minpan* is not suitable for beginners to study, I have cleared away the overgrowth and extracted the gist."

[6] Gondō Seikyō, *Jichi minpan* [People's Guide to Self-Rule] (Tokyo: Heibonsha, 1927), p. 1. Subsequent references to *Jichi minpan* denote the 2nd ed., published by Heibonsha in 1932. See Sharon H. Nolte, "Gondō Seikyō and the Agrarianist Critique of Modern Japan," seminar paper in history, Yale University, 1973, p. 10.

[7] *Jichi minpan*, p. 1.   [8] Ibid., pp. 3-4.

Like most scholars in early twentieth-century Japan,[9] Gondō was profoundly influenced by evolutionary thought, and he believed in the "gradual development of the good customs" of the past.[10] He often cited Darwinian biology as evidence that change was both natural and proper,[11] and he said that the way to solve Japan's current problems was not to cling to frozen practices from the past but to sweep away the "artificial schemes" and "false paths"[12] which now blocked the ongoing development of good customs observed since early times. Hence Gondō announced the purpose of *Jichi minpan* in standard evolutionist terms: "When I discuss the past I hope to provide a guide to the future, since the future is born of the present and the present is born of the past. . . . I simply intend to cite the past in order to awaken the present."[13] Since he revered the village society of early Japan, it is doubtful whether Gondō managed to avoid the reactionary trap of holding fast to unchanging institutions, but at least he imagined that his historical outlook was a fluid one that rolled with the times.

"Shashoku" and Self-Rule

What were the good customs (*seizoku*) which should resume their natural development if Japanese society were to transform itself? One, Gondō believed, was society itself —the Japanese people as a nation—known as *shashoku*. The other was the practice of self-rule, or *jichi*, which permitted society at large to continue functioning. Since these interdependent concepts lay at the heart of Gondō's historical

[9] See Wilson, pp. 22-23, on Kita Ikki's views of social development.

[10] Gondō Seikyō, "Nisshin minsei idō" [Similarities and Differences in the National Character of the Chinese and the Japanese], ghostwritten for Uchida Ryōhei, ca. 1908 or 1909, quoted in Takizawa Makoto, *Gondō Seikyō oboegaki* [Notes on Gondō Seikyō] (Nagaokashi: privately published, 1968), p. 54; Gondō Seikyō, *Nōson jikyūron* [Theory of Farm Village Self-Help] (Tokyo: Bungei Shunjūsha, 1932), p. 45.

[11] *Jichi minpan*, p. 194f; *Jichi minseiri*, p. 240f.

[12] *Jichi minpan*, p. 4.   [13] Ibid., pp. 3, 6.

outlook and formed the center of his prescriptions for modern Japan, I shall take them up in turn.

To Gondō *shashoku* meant the Japanese people collectively organized into self-governing units beneath a single ruling institution, the imperial throne. In early East Asian lands, he stated, the rise of human society (*sha*) depended on the produce of the land: "If there is no land, there is no place for men to live; if there is no millet [*shoku*], there is nothing for the people to eat. Therefore the basis of politics in Japan and China has been the *shashoku*."[14] The development of society required cooperation among heaven, man, and earth: "The three great keystones in the formulation of our *shashoku* have been (1) obey the laws of heaven, (2) depend on the goodness of the earth, and (3) promote harmony among men."[15] Lest this formula for pastoral living seem to be a mere copy of Confucian agrarianism, Gondō boldly asserted that Japan's farm-based *shashoku* had been decreed by the sun goddess herself[16] and implemented by the Sujin emperor, who announced that "agriculture is the foundation of the world and is how the people seek their livelihood."[17] From the very start, therefore, Japanese society based on farming enjoyed the favor of the Shinto gods and their descendants, the imperial family.

The goal of life in society, Gondō believed, was not merely to assure survival but also "to live in the utmost

[14] *Jichi minseiri*, p. 248. In ancient China *shashoku* (Ch. *she-chi*) denoted the gods of earth and grain. The *Shu ching* [Book of History] refers to rites propitiating these deities. Gondō applied the term to early Japanese society under Shinto agricultural deities. See Nolte, p. 15. Katherine Maxim prefers the term "society-state" as a translation for *shashoku*: "the less complex socio-political structure of premodern Japan. The use of the word 'state' in this sense connotes an unsophisticated political organization, not to be confused with 'state' as it refers to modern nation states." Katherine M. Maxim, "Agrarian Response to Industrialization: Populism and Nohon-shugi," B.A. thesis in history, Connecticut College, 1970, p. 42.

[15] *Jichi minpan*, p. 4.

[16] Ibid., p. 195; *Jichi minseiri*, p. 241.

[17] *Jichi minseiri*, p. 249.

happiness," something which resulted from laboring to grow agricultural products.[18] This had been achieved in early Japan, he asserted, by building the overall *shashoku* from the bottom up: "In ancient times there was a single individual will, then the group, the community, the village. These natural groupings formed, within which the principles of mutual aid and coexistence were established. Through the operation of mutual aid and coexistence all noxious individuals were curbed and finally the society was formed."[19] At the apex of this harmonious, self-regulating society sat the emperor, whose duties were primarily ceremonial and required almost no secular activity.

Self-rule was the practice which permitted society to develop, Gondō believed, and to attain it men merely had to follow the laws of nature. In 1932 he put it this way:

This idea of "natural rule," or governing through nature, is also called "primitive self-rule" [*genshi jichi*] and forms the basis of autonomy. This basis for self-rule gives rise to the natural intentions of the general public, makes harmony and concord the rule, establishes the norm of mutual aid, and thus by linking hamlets and villages entire counties and provinces are governed. Finally this can be expanded to the whole world. . . . "natural rule is the unselfish unity of the general public."[20]

[18] *Jichi minpan*, p. 198.   [19] Ibid., p. 200.

[20] Gondō Seikyō, "Seizoku no zenka to rissei no kigen" [The Gradual Development of Customs and the Origin of Institutions], *Chūō kōron* [Central Review], June 1932, quoted in Hijikata Kazuo, "Nihonkei fuashizumu no taitō to teikō" [The Rise and Resistance of Japanese Fascism], *Kindai Nihon shakai shisōshi* [History of Modern Japanese Social Thought], II, ed. Furuta Hikaru, Sakuta Keiichi, and Ikimatsu Keizō (Tokyo: Yūhikaku, 1971), p. 155. See also Kinoshita Hanji, *Nihon no uyoku* [The Japanese Right Wing] (Tokyo: Kaname Shobō, 1953), pp. 23-36; Kada Tetsuji, *Nihon kokkashugi no hatten* [The Development of Japanese Nationalism] (Tokyo: Keio Shobō, 1938), pp. 69-71.

Like nature's laws themselves, he wrote, self-rule never changed: "No matter how much you threaten it, no matter how much you oppress it, no matter how much . . . you weaken it, it is able to endure."[21] Gondō thus ascribed to self-rule the same indestructibility enjoyed by society at large, regardless of the vicissitudes of Japanese history. He concluded that the two enduring institutions, the society and self-rule, would benefit more and more people as time went on, provided "our people endeavor not to lose sight of their own interests, strengthen village self-rule and people's livelihoods, equalize prosperity through mutual aid and coexistence, and continually utilize the advantages of civilization to attain the first rank of progress."[22]

Gondō admitted no theoretical contradiction between his evolutionary view of history and his commitment to preserving the *shashoku* and self-rule as indispensable features of Japanese life, but it is difficult to believe that either ever existed in the pure form described in his writings. The summaries in *Jichi minseiri* of military campaigns and political power in the second century A.D., for example, were full of erroneous information and grave distortions, taken mainly from *Nan'ensho*.[23] Gondō's use of myth and legend in lieu of historical evidence to describe the rise of Japanese society made his accounts interesting but unconvincing, especially when he maintained that agriculture was the sole basis of

[21] Gondō Seikyō, *Kunmin kyōjiron* [Theory of Joint Rule by Emperor and People] (Tokyo: Bungei Shunjūsha, 1932), p. 26. See also Okutani Matsuji, "Nihon ni okeru nōhonshugi shisō no nagare" [Trends in Agrarian Thought in Japan], *Shisō* [Thought], No. 407, May 1958, p. 11; Takeuchi Tetsuo, "Nōhonshugi to nōson chūsansō" [Agrarianism and the Farm Village Middle Class], *Shimane Nōka Daigaku kenkyū hōkoku* [Shimane Agricultural University Research Reports], No. 8, A, March 1960, p. 236.

[22] *Jichi minpan*, p. 203.

[23] *Jichi minseiri*, p. 249, for example, greatly exaggerates the effectiveness of the military campaigns of the Keikō Emperor (r. A.D. 71-130).

197

nation and government in early Japan.[24] Fragmented though Japanese politics may have been before the imperial clan arose in the fifth century A.D., strong tribal leaders are thought to have exercised regional hegemony in Japan since the beginning of the Christian era, and once the Japanese state emerged in the sixth century such an idyllic habit of self-rule could scarcely have prevailed in Japanese society.

Surely Gondō's romantic latter-day perceptions of life in old Japan ignored its inequities and hardships, a natural but misguided impulse common to all frustrated modern men and women who forget that early communal life was narrow, intolerant, disease ridden, and poverty stricken almost everywhere in the world. To dwell on such criticisms is fruitless, however, because I am concerned with Gondō the social critic, not Gondō the historian. What mattered in twentieth-century Japan was not whether his view of the past was jaded but how he utilized these plausible, but probably imaginary, good customs culled from the past as a basis for social policy in the midst of the political and economic crises of the interwar years.

Self-Ruling Society and the National Essence

In holding up the self-ruling society of early Japan as a paradigm for people in his own day, Gondō felt obliged to deal with the prevailing *kokutai* ideology that characterized a good deal of Japanese nationalist thinking in the early twentieth century. By then many persons thought that the

[24] On this point see Tsukui Tatsuo, *Nihonshugi undō no riron to jissen* [Theory and Practice of the Japanism Movement] (Tokyo: Kensetsusha, 1935), p. 124; Tsuchida Kyōson, "Gondō Seikyōshi no shoron" [Views of Mr. Gondō Seikyō], *Serupan*, July 1932, *Tsuchida Kyōson zenshū* [Complete Works of Tsuchida Kyōson] (Tokyo: Daiichi Shobō, 1935), III, 389-400; Sakisaka Itsurō, "Gondō Seikyōshi no shoron o hyōsu" [Appraising Mr. Gondō Seikyō's Views], *Kaizō* [Reconstruction], July 1932, pp. 65-75. Tsuchida criticizes Gondō's poor use of fact, his failure to explain the ancient passages which he quotes, and his failure to consult disciplines other than *seidogaku* to explain classical Japanese civilization.

national essence meant allegiance to both state and nation, but Gondō claimed that "historically in Japan there has been no concept whatever of state; since antiquity the national essence of our country has been the system of people's self-rule based on farmers."[25] He rejected the familiar official contention that *kokutai* should be directed toward service to the state, arguing instead that "the Japanese national essence consists simply of ruler and subject cooperating on behalf of the *shashoku*."[26]

By tying his conception of *kokutai* to the Japanese people rather than the government that ruled them, Gondō deliberately challenged the prevailing state-oriented interpretation so evident in official Nōhonshugi before World War I. Those like himself who sought to upset the ideological "status quo," he wrote, were trying "to overturn the definition of *kokutai* advanced by the bureaucratic scholars and turn careful consideration to the true essence of the ancient Japanese system."[27] Once this was done, he confidently predicted, not only would the difference between state (*kokka*) and society (*shashoku*) become clear, but also the enduring importance of the latter would be apparent:

No matter how much you reform institutions, you cannot change society. Mankind cannot go on living if it fails to provide adequate food, clothing, and shelter. If the whole world became a part of the Japanese empire, the concept of the Japanese state would become unnecessary. But it is impossible to discard the concept of society. State is a term

[25] Gondō Seikyō, *Nihon nōseishidan* [Talks on the History of the Japanese Agricultural System], ed. Okamoto Rikichi (Tokyo: Junshinsha, 1931), p. 188. Okamoto was a pupil of Gondō's who recorded his informal talks on Japanese farming at the Kinkei Gakuin in the late 1920s, resulting in this volume.

[26] *Jichi minpan*, p. 530.

[27] Ibid., p. 538. See Ozeki Hiroshi, "Chōkokkashugi no taitō" [The Rise of Ultranationalism], *Kindai Nihon no kangaekata* [Ways of Thinking in Modern Japan], ed. Yamaguchi Kōsaku and Koyama Hitoshi (Kyoto: Hōritsu Bunkasha, 1971), p. 171.

used when countries vie with one another; it is a classification on a world map. Society means, in substance, a country composed of groups of villages, districts, and cities, based on the need for individuals to coexist. Even if each state withdrew from its territory, the concept of society would bar any damage to human existence.[28]

Here is the core of Gondō's approach to the issue of national essence: the *kokutai* was firmly welded to the Japanese people as a nationality group—to their farm economy, their custom of self-government, their society, and the emperor who jointly ruled in cooperation with the people themselves. Because society took precedence over state, both as value and as historical fact, his conception of nationalism focused directly on that irreducible nucleus of indigenous civilization, the Japanese people as an ethnonationality group.

Gondō was no less a nationalist for emphasizing the flexible communalism of the *shashoku* than were his fellow ideologues who made the rigid, institutionalized state the center of their thought. Crucial to both was the imperial throne, which had been ossified by bureaucratic theorists into an organ of government in the 1889 constitution (exactly as Minobe Tatsukichi had pointed out, no matter how virulently his critics attacked the organ theory).[29] To Gondō and others who stressed the familial and tribal aspects of Japanese nationalism, the emperor was at once more personal as an ideal and less tangible as a practical part of governance, since his social role was confined to that of benevolent patriarch, rather than source of political authority and national will as in state nationalism. The variable position of the throne in Japanese nationalism may seem to be an emblem of its functional powerlessness (so weak that no one can define its duties), but more likely this mutability is a

[28] *Jichi minpan*, pp. 261-262. See also *Jichi minseiri*, p. 249.
[29] See Frank O. Miller, *Minobe Tatsukichi: Interpreter of Constitutionalism in Japan* (Berkeley: University of California Press, 1965).

sign of its multifaceted symbolic magnetism to nearly all prewar Japanese political thinkers (so strong that no definition can encompass all its prerogatives).

Gondō's Account of Premodern Japanese History

Once he had established that protecting the *shashoku* and enhancing self-rule were crucial for fulfilling the national essence, Gondō used these as criteria to evaluate Japan's past. In the prehistoric period, he maintained, these practices were observed not merely out of sociological necessity but also as a means of propitiating the Shinto gods. "The provincial governors and land managers at that time were all guardians of the gods," he wrote, and as a result they scrupulously passed on self-rule and a sound society to their descendants.[30] The most serious offense in early Japan was to undermine the agrarian foundations of life:

> "At that time the emperor and gods were not far apart, and the property of the gods was not yet distinct from the property of the government." From this we can imagine the general shape of things.
>
> Moreover Shinto festivals were conducted at slack times in farming, and when the people gathered together the provincial governor purged both heavenly and provincial sins. . . . Eight kinds of heavenly sins—obstructions to agriculture—were recognized throughout the country, as established by the imperial court. Provincial sins were special sins found in the various regions.[31]

Gondō did not elaborate on what he meant by sin, a concept which many authorities regard as very weak in early Shinto. But he patently believed that early Japanese civilization handed on its essential customs to succeeding generations in partnership with the deities of Shinto, whose blessings affected farm fertility and the well-being of society at large.

[30] *Jichi minseiri*, p. 247.   [31] Ibid., p. 248.

In Gondō's opinion, the Taika reforms of the mid-seventh century perfected these desirable customs of *shashoku* and self-rule. He probably idealized these efforts to centralize politics in the Chinese fashion because he was fascinated with Nan'en Shōan, whose pupil, the Tenji emperor (r. 668-671), supposedly brought self-rule to its zenith.[32] Gondō reasoned that "the Taika reforms, although they nominally consolidated powers, in reality did not interfere with the good practices which had developed in the local areas." Instead, he continued, "they utilized the town, village, and county headmen who were well versed in local conditions and adopted policies which did not disturb the local system."[33] Not only did the Taika innovations "permit self-rule in each region, in response to its nature and customs,"[34] but they also provided agricultural marketing laws that "protected farm production as an occupation." By regulating "the exchange of commodities, the standardization of utensils, the accuracy of measurements, and prices,"[35] the reforms guarded the foundation of society.

Although he was suspicious of concentrated political power, Gondō accepted Taika style centralization because he thought that it respected local autonomy and enhanced agricultural prosperity, the basis of the *shashoku*. Another advantage was that the reforms made the imperial throne preeminent and reinforced the principle of joint rule by emperor and people (*kunmin kyōji*), the ideal condition of a self-governed society.[36] Gondō wrote: "At the same time the Tenji emperor's regent said, 'Between heaven and earth is the ruler. He who rules all men must not govern autocratically but must by all means engage the assistance of others. Thus Jinmu ruled jointly with our ancestors. . . .' We must never think that this system of joint rule by emperor

[32] On Gondō and the Tenji court, see Kinoshita, p. 23.
[33] *Jichi minpan*, p. 523.
[34] Ibid., p. 526. See also Hijikata, p. 155.
[35] *Jichi minpan*, p. 479.
[36] See *Kunmin kyōjiron*, esp. pp. 64-72, 111-113.

and people started only as a result of the Taika reforms."[37] Nevertheless, now that imperial prestige had been enhanced by administrative adaptations from the T'ang empire, the benefits of self-rule accrued to society: "When you make this principle of joint rule by emperor and people your basis, the officials' authority no longer rests on autocracy, power, coercion, and arbitrariness but instead establishes mutual understanding and harmony."[38]

The difficulty, Gondō believed, was that self-rule and the welfare of society were threatened by the selfish interests of great feudal clans, powerful religious institutions, the warrior class, and scheming samurai bent on seizing political control.[39] In the Edo period, for example, the money system of the *bakufu* was usually "in confusion, stimulating devious merchants and causing commodity prices to be unstable each time currency was issued."[40] To Gondō this was a token of the malevolent effects of the partially centralized Tokugawa regime, but he was equally convinced that self-rule, despite the considerable concentration of power in Edo, had functioned far more effectively during the Tokugawa era than after 1868. He denounced his contemporaries who criticized the Tokugawa agricultural system and claimed that farmers then were better off than in the 1920s because taxes never exceeded four-tenths of the crop. He admitted that in certain years "both the *bushi* and the lower classes lived very destitute lives," but he concluded that farmers in the larger fiefs lived happier lives than did the tenants during the twenties.[41] Only after the Meiji restora-

---

[37] Gondō Seikyō, "Minkun gōdōron" [Theory of the Identity of People and Emperor], 1932, quoted in Kinoshita, p. 24.

[38] Ibid.

[39] For Gondō's appraisal of feudal Japan, see *Jichi minpan*, pp. 109-180.

[40] Ibid., p. 488. See also Tsukui, pp. 119-120.

[41] *Nihon nōseishidan*, p. 183. See Sakurai Takeo, "Nōhonshugi—sono rekishi, riron, jiban" [Agrarianism—Its History, Theory, and Foundation], *Rekishi kagaku* [Science of History], IV, 3, March 1935, 121.

tion, in short, were the traditions of self-rule and the *shashoku* seriously undermined.

Attack on the Meiji Government's Policies

Few Japanese social critics have been able to remain dispassionate about the early Meiji years, probably as much because of the startling abruptness of the reforms as because of their nature. Like many dissenters in modern Japan, Gondō attacked the policies of the Meiji state as too foreign and too high-handed, and like nearly all historical evolutionists he believed that the new government had eventually adopted arbitrary measures that artificially blocked social development. Where Gondō differed most sharply from other observers was in his conviction that the most truly desirable future social condition for Japan could be discovered in her own past.

Much of what was wrong with the Meiji reforms, Gondō believed, lay in their excessive emulation of the West. However, despite his ardent nationalism and proclivity for glorifying the native tradition, Gondō was no xenophobe. He denounced European influences on Meiji Japan for their corrosive effects on self-rule and society at large, not just because they were foreign. He criticized undesirable Meiji policies that had no overseas precedents just as sharply as those modeled after European counterparts. The sheer weight of Western style reforms was so great, nevertheless, that external ideas and institutions naturally comprised an inviting target for his attacks.

One distasteful result of importing European patterns, Gondō observed, was that "we have permitted extremely competitive activity."[42] This he denounced because if "we allow competitive behavior to spring up unchecked, the individual will harm others' livelihoods in trying to live himself. The strong will eclipse the weak, and finally people

42 *Jichi minpan*, p. 3.

will chew each other up."[43] A related evil recently introduced from abroad was the spirit of selfishness:

The fact that the imported Meiji institutions discarded the model of self-control and instead adopted the norm of selfishness really changed the basis of our politics. By this, of course, I mean that what is now totally confirmed at the apex of this selfish system is private property rights. . . . The most urgent need is to carry out a great reform by reviving self-rule based on self-control. The revival of self-rule based on self-control requires the total abolition of the norms of selfishness. . . .[44]

Competition and selfishness, Gondō continued, were not merely odious because they rotted Japan's self-ruling society but also because they led to the monopolization of property and capital. "In the Meiji period," he noted, "our country converted to a European style private property system. The entire property of society at large was arbitrarily monopolized by a small number of persons."[45] Banks seized control of currency, capital became omnipotent, and noncultivators bought up farmlands: "Although our ancient customs were based on society's traditional path of mutual aid and coexistence, which deeply abhorred monopolistic practices relating to the people's goods, today the farmlands have been united, residences have been combined, and there are hardly any surplus timberlands or swamplands. Finally the entire country has been standardized."[46] These criticisms of the Meiji capitalist ethos show that Gondō rejected the utilitarian outlook which dominated early Meiji social and economic policy. They also suggest that his belief in historical evolution did not extend to social Darwinist teachings about unbridled competition.

Nevertheless, the most outrageous and discordant policy of all, Gondō charged, was the new land tax of 1873:

[43] Ibid., p. 2.
[45] Ibid., p. 491.
[44] Ibid., pp. 534-536.
[46] Ibid.

The main point of this land tax revision was that we avoid "the evil custom of favoritism in tax payments and the inclination of the people toward idleness." But the officials at this time were distracted by their own lust for power and their connections in all directions, and they did not work to achieve equality but instead fostered more evils, losing sight of the main point of the imperial decree. Thus they nurtured the root causes of the present day land amalgamation and oppression of the farm villages.[47]

Gondō did not resist the principle of taxing agriculture, but he believed that the Meiji levy, which was a fixed money payment, hurt farmers (and benefited monopolists) more than the feudal custom of "four parts to the state, six parts to the people" (shikō, rokumin). Corrupt bureaucrats who administered tax collections unfairly merely compounded the problem. Thus, he concluded, "the legal system established by the Meiji government cut the people off from the land, firmly solidified the leaders' positions through the power of wealth, [and] swelled the income of the state,"[48] to the detriment of social harmony and people's well-being.

Still, Gondō believed, in the end these very serious complaints were symptoms of a more fundamental cancer that afflicted modern Japanese civilization: centralized bureaucratic government. Gondō regarded bureaucratic government as the antithesis of self-rule:

In general, in the governance of countries, there have historically been two kinds of policies. The first leaves it to the people to rule themselves, with the officials merely indicating precedent and serving as a good influence. The second is to have the officials seize control of all matters and to rule the people. The former may be called a

---

[47] Ibid., p. 183. See also *Jichi minseiri*, p. 277; *Nihon nōseishidan*, pp. 191-192; Maxim, p. 45.
[48] *Nihon nōseishidan*, p. 191.

system of self-rule, while the latter may be called a system of bureaucratic rule.[49]

Whereas the Taika reforms had actually aided self-rule through partial centralization, Gondō reasoned, the Meiji government modeled itself after the vastly more unified administrative systems of France and Prussia, supplemented by utilitarian doctrines from England.[50] This proved so damaging to traditional village autonomy that the state finally felt obliged to announce a new local government system on April 7, 1888, piously promising that "we will gradually develop the advantages of local cooperation and extend respect for the old custom of neighborhood unity."[51]

Gondō unleashed an attack on this step as a transparent ruse, upbraiding the oligarchs for "inverting the basic principle that self-rule should be the basis of the state and establishing a local government system because it suited the convenience of the national administration."[52] By 1936, he observed, nearly fifty years under the new local government structure had produced poor results: "The development of cooperative advantages has been hindered by respect for individual energies. There has been no way to extend respect for the old custom of neighborhood unity. No powers of food management, mediation in personal affairs, or protection of peace and order can be detected in the self-rule system. All these things are managed by [the state]."[53] Instead of advancing self-rule, Gondō pointed out, Japan had saddled herself with a bureaucratic government so powerful that it had destroyed the harmony of the former self-ruling *shashoku*:

When we look at the changes of the past forty years, we see an increase in government expenses unparalleled in the

[49] *Jichi minseiri*, p. 247. See also *Jichi minpan*, p. 258.
[50] *Jichi minpan*, p. 526.
[51] *Jichi minseiri*, p. 253. At Yale University Richard L. Staubitz is preparing a study of the theoretical origins of self-rule in Meiji Japan.
[52] *Jichi minpan*, p. 278.   [53] *Jichi minseiri*, p. 253.

whole world. Even though there are various pensions and the land tax has tripled throughout the country, we can still observe huge insufficiencies. . . . since bureaucratic government is a system in which officials rule the people, full supervision by the rulers is impossible, even if you appointed an official for each citizen. Bureaucratic government always comes to this.[54]

Gondō further argued that bureaucratic centralism, in corroding self-rule and the traditional *shashoku*, was grounded upon the most dangerous of modern political ideologies, statism (*kokkashugi*). In the Meiji period, he wrote, "a strange doctrine of emperor loyalty and patriotism was born, and a fanciful morality from the desk tops of government scholars was widely enforced."[55] This state-sponsored nationalism, shaped by men such as Motoda Eifu (1818-1891), constituted an "oppressive doctrine of loyalty and filiality" that was "destructive of the *shashoku*."[56] This ideology Gondō called "Prussian style nationalism, the consuming principle of the Meiji oligarchy . . . in which everything is done with reference to the state."[57]

What was wrongheaded about "Prussian style nationalism" in Gondō's judgment? Among other things, he said, it clouded his earlier distinction between state and society (*kokka* and *shashoku*) by attempting to draw to the new centralized government the communal loyalties which had bound the Japanese to each other for thousands of years. Official nationalists failed to make it plain that "the national character of Japanese society was entirely different from the Prussian form of nationalism."[58] The time-honored sentiments of the nationality group represented true loyalty and patriotism in Japan, he concluded, not the false doctrines

[54] Ibid., p. 281. [55] *Jichi minpan*, p. 3.
[56] *Jichi minseiri*, p. 251.
[57] *Jichi minpan*, p. 188. See also *Jichi minseiri*, p. 280.
[58] *Jichi minpan*, p. 188.

and "fanciful morality" foisted off by officially patronized scholars.

Gondō was certainly right that the Meiji government tried very strenuously to redirect long-standing folk loyalties toward the new state, probably with greater success than he would admit.[59] He was not fooled by the oligarchs' efforts to merge the state with the nation as a focus of political allegiances. He understood very clearly that they had manipulated the throne, a symbol shared by communal nationalists and statists alike, in order to dazzle the people into obeying the modern bureaucratized state for which the emperor was the source of authority. Such machinations, Gondō insisted, were not merely cynical; they were downright harmful: "Blinded by misguided statism, those who destroy the laws of our supremely compassionate sovereign family are the wicked sort who would demolish our Japan. They are the bitter enemies of our fellow countrymen. They are the wreckers of humanity everywhere in the world."[60] Statism, in brief, would erase the good custom of joint self-rule by sovereign and people, the true function of the throne in Gondō's ideal self-governing society.

He also excoriated "Prussian style nationalism" for its authoritarian intolerance of dissent. Whenever centralized bureaucratic rule existed, he asserted, "you will find that when you express a slightly different opinion, you are insulted as antinationalistic, invariably regarded as a traitor, and spurned. Most scholarly theories are likewise buried in darkness." So pervasive was the statist spirit of regimentation, Gondō claimed, that when he had earlier differentiated between state and society "I received every sort of attack and oppression from all sides, even though no one has yet criticized me on scholarly grounds."[61]

[59] On the transfer of political loyalties in mid-nineteenth century Japan, see Albert M. Craig, *Chōshū in the Meiji Restoration* (Cambridge, Mass.: Harvard University Press, 1961).
[60] *Nōson jikyūron*, quoted in Kinoshita, p. 26.
[61] *Jichi minpan*, p. 188.

Finally, Gondō maintained, total devotion to the state was dangerous because it threatened Japan's distinctive *kokutai*. "Being blinded by false nationalism and destroying our supreme national essence," he wrote, "are wicked things that will kill Japan."[62] He believed that statism, with its stress on centralized government and commercialism, was harmful to the *kokutai* because "since antiquity the national essence of our country has been the system of people's self-rule based on farmers."[63] In modern Japan, Gondō said, local rule had been replaced by national administration only at the cost of "the public morality of civil and military officials," and he asserted that "it is the extremely bureaucratic government, based on Prussian-style nationalism, that has caused the estrangement of inferiors and superiors and the current suffering of our people."[64]

However limited Gondō's grasp of early history and exaggerated his estimates of Meiji government expenses may have been, he is an excellent example of protest against the modernizing policies of a new state undergoing political and economic development. His view of the past was obviously vitally affected by his dismay at the present. Working from the premise that the putative traditions of self-rule and the *shashoku* were valuable, he blasted the Meiji regime in blunt language for compromising these ideals by adopting shameful foreign values, promoting socially divisive policies, and creating an overly centralized structure. He believed that the government had eclipsed self-rule, disrupted the harmony of society at large, and touted a false nationalism that damaged the country's genuine national essence based on small village farming.

It is notable that Gondō grounded his arguments almost entirely on political rather than economic considerations. Whereas many modern observers ascribed Japan's troubles to the rise of capitalist production,[65] Gondō considered

[62] *Jichi minseiri*, p. 281. [63] *Nihon nōseishidan*, p. 188.
[64] *Jichi minseiri*, p. 282. [65] Okutani, p. 11.

Meiji economic policy to be merely one important aspect of an overall problem that stemmed from centralized rule. This accounts for his raggedness on whether private property rights should be abolished: Gondō opposed the monopolization of capital and land, but he did not wish to eradicate all private ownership. His ideas on the subject were fuzzy because his ideal was the premodern corporate landholding system of village agriculture in which the legal concept of landownership was immature.

In his zeal to attack bureaucratic government, Gondō no doubt distorted the degree to which it differed from earlier political systems in Japan (none of which, in reality, ever achieved his vision of self-rule).[66] The crucial point is that Gondō used the past to refashion agrarianist teachings by emphasizing above all the political necessity of preserving small village farming. Many Nōhonshugi advocates, from Shinagawa Yajirō and Hirata Tōsuke forward, had listed self-rule as an important virtue of agricultural life, but Gondō was the first agrarianist to affirm farming primarily for its political rather than its economic, social, or military benefits. He put this conviction to service in the 1920s and 1930s by designing remedies, based on his understanding of Japanese history, to counteract the rural crisis of the day.

[66] Tsukui, p. 120.

Chapter IX

Gondō Seikyō and the Depression Crisis

Deprive a man of his memory and he will die a slow death. Destroy his hope for the future and you rob him of a life worth living. For the present first becomes meaningful when it is interpreted in terms of what we remember from the past and the yoke of the present becomes light when there is the promise of a new day.[1]

THESE words, written in 1972 by a Protestant missionary in an entirely separate context, capture quite skillfully the tone of Gondō Seikyō's efforts "to cite the past in order to awaken the present,"[2] as he put it in 1927. Gondō believed in the steady development of social institutions, and despite the grave rural depression of the day he optimistically assumed that a self-governing nation, based on village agriculture, could be created if farmers would only seize the initiative themselves. To Gondō, self-rule and society (*shashoku*) were contemporary concepts, designed for men and women in his own times, which he had "interpreted in terms of what [he could] remember from the past. . . ."

[1] John Timmer, "The Editor's Notes," *Japan Christian Quarterly*, XXXVIII, 2, Spring 1972, 65.

[2] Gondō Seikyō, *Jichi minpan* [People's Guide to Self-rule], 2nd ed. (Tokyo: Heibonsha, 1932), p. 6. (First published in 1927.)

Gondō's continual hope for a better day probably stemmed from the favorable view of life associated with the Shinto tradition and the idealistic natural philosophy of agrarian fundamentalism so prevalent in Tokugawa days.

Attack on the Military Establishment

Given his views of Japan's past, it is no wonder that Gondō's prescriptions for solving current problems hinged on sweeping away the obstacles to a self-ruling society. One such hindrance was the military establishment, newly risen as a result of the Sino-Japanese and Russo-Japanese wars. He chided the government for maintaining swollen forces far beyond the economy's ability to equip and supply them,[3] attributing this "deplorable state of affairs" to the political ambitions of certain military leaders after the Russo-Japanese War: "One faction rashly added to the number of people living on army appropriations in order to add to the prestige of the military clique." Gondō quickly added that he was not "an advocate of disarmament nor am I a pacifist. I have a sincere desire for adequate national defense."[4] What he opposed was the concentration of power in an elitist military bureaucracy:

> The bureaucracy, the *zaibatsu*, and the military became the three supports of the state, the political parties attached themselves to them, and the scholars fawned upon them. These groups allied with each other through marriage and they all combined to form a single group. In a country so ordered, it is quite obvious that no matter how it may be kept up in the future, the nation's military affairs cannot be supported by means of the privileged class of military alone.[5]

[3] Ibid., pp. 184-185.
[4] Gondō Seikyō, *Jichi minpan*, quoted in *Sources of Japanese Tradition*, comp. Ryusaku Tsunoda, ed. William T. deBary (New York: Columbia University Press, 1958), p. 771.
[5] Ibid.

Unlike many fellow agrarianists, Gondō did not stress the farmer-soldier tradition in premodern Japan. He identified rule by generals and admirals with "militaristic, Prussian nationalism"—something so despicable "that not even the dogs would eat it." He held that there was "something more or less frightening in any sort of militaristic administration":[6] the monopolization of economic and political power by a small clique, undermining the people's livelihood. Gondō warned, moreover, that the military establishment was not even able to provide for adequate peacekeeping:

Since the conditions under which the people live are in fact as I have indicated, the foundations of the military regime cannot be secure. . . . the soldiers who dutifully have to shed their blood are all sons and brothers of the common people. The great majority of these soldiers were born in poverty and hardship; they entered the barracks, and then had to submit to the orders of their superior officers. As the sons and brothers of the common people, they will not under any circumstances forget that they are themselves common people. . . . Granted, it is the army's duty to maintain peace and order, but the good and obedient soldiers in the ranks whom you are leading are for the most part the sons and brothers of the impoverished common people. They are certainly not people who are serving to kill the common people. No, they are persons who offer their lives and bodies for the sake of the wider public morality.[7]

Explicit as this warning was, it was virtually the only statement Gondō ever made about the connections between rural poverty and military service. Taken by itself, this

[6] Ibid. See also Gondō Seikyō, *Jichi minseiri* [Principles of People's Self-Rule], 1936, in *Chōkokkashugi* [Ultranationalism], ed. Hashikawa Bunzō, *Gendai Nihon shisō taikei* [Collection on Modern Japanese Thought] (Tokyo: Chikuma Shobō, 1964), xxxi, 278-279.

[7] *Jichi minpan*, quoted in *Sources of Japanese Tradition*, p. 773.

paragraph is hardly conclusive evidence that Gondō intended to rouse the troops against their senior officers. Instead, he cited the morale of soldiers as one of many reasons to oppose centralized military rule: the army would be stronger if it eliminated the elitism so prevalent since the 1890s.

The Evils of Plutocracy

Even more menacing to the good traditions of self-rule and the *shashoku*, Gondō believed, was monopolistic capitalism (partly because it was more pervasive than militarism). Although he explained his objections in lengthy chapters on coinage and mechanization in *Jichi minpan*, Gondō characteristically based his attack mainly on the political ground that capitalism inhibited the growth of a self-ruling rural society. Under the Meiji government's capitalist policies, he noted, a few men suddenly became rich without working, most became impoverished, and labor and tenancy disputes grew rife.[8] This, he continued,

> is why the development of industry must be reformed. What is more, the majority of the people cannot bear the coercion of capital power. Thus on the one hand the security of food, clothing, and shelter is destroyed, and on the other ideological tranquility is demolished. The good custom of self-rule, which is the essence of our *shashoku*, is smashed, and men are so preoccupied with mere profit that there is no time for leisure. In this situation the capitalists, using their money power, gradually increase their wealth tens and hundreds of times. Absorbing resources here and there, they finally menace the majority of the people's food, clothing, and shelter, encouraging conflict between the rich and the poor, and as a result, production becomes endangered—this is a mathematical certainty.[9]

[8] *Jichi minpan*, p. 6.   [9] Ibid., p. 519.

Detestable as these consequences of capitalism were, Gondō spoke only of "reforming the development of industry," not of dismantling it entirely. In *Jichi minpan* he offered a long account of the evolution of technology and attributed the growth of industrialism to "the endeavors of all mankind to live as happily as possible." Just as industry was not always undesirable, so "the wealthy and the noble are not necessarily anathema."[10] The real problem, he asserted, was the excessive concentration of political and economic power which had resulted from the policies of the Meiji state.

A main cause of huge accumulations of wealth, Gondō explained, was mechanization. Although he granted that working in industrial plants was ruinous to laborers' health,[11] he believed that the greatest abuse of mechanization was that it gave a few capitalists control over "most of the goods of the *shashoku* which the people ought equally to receive."[12] Great machines, he believed, were nefarious symbols of the private-property system which "has its basis in selfishness and approves of the so-called struggle for existence."[13] What was needed instead, he stated, was a turnabout in national policy: "There is no resort except for Japan to lead the world in returning to the precedent of the *shashoku*. To return to the precedent of the *shashoku* means to establish a framework for the people to coexist. To establish a framework for the people to coexist means to work together, to play together, to enjoy future prosperity equally, to be secure and equal, and to promote the gradual progress of mankind."[14]

Gondō hence wanted not some wildly unrealistic eradication of capitalism but a diminution and redirection of monetary and industrial power in order to restore the smooth development of self-ruling society. Like the many Marxist social critics of his day, he earnestly hoped that wealth would be much more widely shared in the society, but he

[10] Ibid., p. 196. [11] Ibid., p. 499. [12] Ibid., p. 504.
[13] Ibid., p. 506. [14] Ibid., p. 505.

differed from them in his preference for farming as the main occupation and his unshakable faith in the virtues of self-rule. Even though he denounced only the excesses of capital and industry, Gondō's dreams of reshaping commercialism must be called fanciful, because they ignored the fundamental antagonisms between an integrated modern economy and decentralized political control. By Gondō's day Japan was simply too far along the path to modernization to turn in the direction he pointed.

What mattered most about his economic outlook was its bitterness and resentment at the monopolistic practices of a capitalist elite which, like the military establishment, colluded with the central state. Gondō thus understood what so many fellow agrarianists disregarded: that capitalism could never have caused such rural distress without the active encouragement of bureaucratic government. As he put it in *Jichi minpan*,

> When the plutocrats conspire with those who hold political power, the resources of the people fall under their control almost before one is aware of what is happening. When this happens, the common people fall upon evil days; they are pursued by cold and hunger, and unless they work in the midst of their tears as tools of the plutocrats and those holding political power they cannot stay alive. When people are pursued by hunger and have to work tearfully in the face of death, what sort of human rights do you suppose remain?[15]

To solve the crisis, therefore, it was not sufficient to attack urban economic power; it was also vital to reduce central political authority.

Self-Rule and Landlords

As an opponent of monopolistic capitalism and bureaucratic rule, Gondō is sometimes thought to have been a retrograde

---

[15] *Jichi minpan*, quoted in *Sources of Japanese Tradition*, p. 772.

spokesman for the slowly eroding prerogatives of rural land-lords. One source has even labeled him as an apologist for "a movement of the semi-feudal landlords against finance capital."[16] Indeed, since most orthodox Nōhonshugi teach-ings from 1890 to World War II appealed to landowners more than tenants, it is important to check Gondō's views on the landlord question in order to judge whether his social theories matched in any sense the class interests of Japanese landholders.

Gondō made it very clear in *Jichi minpan* that he con-sidered the large-scale farming plans of the 1870s "a reck-less conspiracy of the Meiji government with wealthy per-sons,"[17] foolishly modeled after American and European agricultural practices. Because of secret understandings be-tween bureaucrats and plutocrats, he charged, land owner-ship was gradually monopolized, "farmers' sense of attach-ment to their home villages was destroyed,"[18] and "small landlords slowly lost their land and turned into serfs. They gradually lost the independence they had come to enjoy and had to be content working for others."[19] It was true, he conceded, that agricultural productivity jumped as a result of Meiji farm policies, but most of the profit went to land-lords and banks, not to the cultivators. What was more, Gondō noted, the rise of the large landlord had led to grave social tensions:

> He spends no time at all farming, nor does he ever inquire about the farmland. He spends his time idly in the cities and is addicted to extravagance and lust. Such men form the group known as "idlers amid farm difficulties." The alienation between rich and poor grows steadily more ter-

[16] O. Tanin and E. Yohan, pseuds., *Militarism and Fascism in Japan* (New York: International Publishers, 1934), p. 99.

[17] *Jichi minpan*, p. 548.

[18] Gondō Seikyō, *Nihon nōseishidan* [Talks on the History of the Japanese Agricultural System], ed. Okamoto Rikichi (Tokyo: Jun-shinsha, 1931), p. 184.

[19] *Jichi minpan*, p. 550.

rible. Landlords regard their farmhands as slaves, while the farmhands, although envious, see the landlords as their bitter enemies. Mutual tolerance and harmony have been entirely eradicated. Moreover the Meiji authorities . . . assisted the phenomenon of large landlords and used this as a tool for maintaining their own power.[20]

Gondō thus shared the resentment of most village residents at the declining social role of the landlord class, one of the main causes of the tenant unrest of the 1920s. Like any monopolist, Gondō thought, the large landlord was loathesome both because he plundered the wherewithal of society and because he cooperated with centralized government. Hence if Gondō was a landlord mouthpiece, he could not have been speaking for the large landlords.

Apart from those landowners who had succumbed to the temptations of commercialism, however, Gondō apparently looked favorably on all rural classes and, much like Okada On, minimized the social tensions within farm villages. Instead of harping on petty grievances, Gondō thought, everyone should rededicate himself to harmony and self-rule:

> If jealousy is the weapon of the weak, contempt is the weapon of the strong. If this is so, can the weak and the strong be isolated from each other? A capitalist who unifies some farmland that has no cultivators cannot obtain a great deal of produce on his own. Hence people are equally interdependent, and so are landlords and cultivators. Capitalists and laborers are interdependent. The pressing need of the moment is to put their hearts in order.[21]

Such moralizing was common among official and nonofficial agrarianists alike in the early twentieth century, and surely few landlords could have objected to Gondō's implicit call for an end to tenant quarrels. The most he could muster by way of condemning tenantry was the token

[20] Ibid., pp. 550-551.   [21] Ibid., p. 552.

observation that "the cultivation of land by tenants is not too good." On the other hand, in concert with nearly all Nōhonshugi partisans in his era, he stated that "the most efficacious reform in farming is that the land be owned by owner-cultivators [*jisakunō*]."[22] "To speak justly about landlords, I have no objection to them when they cultivate their lands themselves. . . . To say that the landlord cultivates his own land is to say that he is a resident of the farm village. At any rate his harvest cannot avoid augmenting the wealth of the village."[23] Landlords were important to rural life not only economically but also socially, Gondō said, inasmuch as they had a responsibility to promote the welfare of the entire village: "To the extent that landlords in the villages and hamlets ignore the common profit of the community and do nothing to deal with such matters, they should respond to the situation by bearing various kinds of responsibilities." Still, he concluded, "farmers cannot blame the landlords alone. They must also exercise self-control, and each person must improve his own position. And they must also pay attention to preserving harmony in the village. The essence of self-rule is in unstintingly assuring that there is no lack of food, clothing, and shelter, in supporting life, and in mourning death; also in confirming mutual pledges and fixing our determination not to become a straggler amid the progress of the world."[24]

It is apparent from these words that Gondō sided with most other Nōhonshugisha in affirming rural concord and insisting that the real conflicts in contemporary Japan were those between city and country. He echoed Yokoi Toki-yoshi when he wrote that "the expansion of cities in the various regions, starting with Tokyo, has upset the ratio of farm villages to cities. Their large and imposing buildings have gradually become beautiful and glamorous. But most of the cities are currently in a state of twilight, where wickedness and confusion abound. . . ."[25] He reflected the

22 Ibid.   23 Ibid., p. 558.
24 Ibid., pp. 559-560.   25 *Jichi minseiri*, p. 261.

thoughts of Okada On when he said that "the Japanese farmer, who has a lively tradition of self-control, self-rule, autonomy, and self-help, has been the support of his country. Both today and in the future, the country needs supporters. These supporters have put up with enormous burdens under the patronage of a unique society with the means for great punishments. They have approved the expansion of enormous cities that consume great amounts. They have come to the point of endangering the base for the continued existence of posterity."[26]

In view of these sentiments, to suggest that Gondō parroted landlord interests somewhat misses the point. While it is true that there was little in his thought with which landlords (except absentee ones) might have felt uncomfortable,[27] Gondō's main intention was to lionize the premodern communal village, with its very indistinct class lines.

At the same time, he reasoned, political power had become centered in the cities and was now exploiting the farm villages. This attitude was expressed by one of Gondō's leading pupils, Ifukube Takahiko, who paraphrased his mentor by minimizing landlord-tenant hostilities: "It is a larger and more fundamental problem than this. It is the problem of *the village as a whole*. . . . we must reject absolutely today's fashion for cities to be mere organs for the ruling class."[28]

[26] Ibid., p. 262. Sharon H. Nolte suggests interesting parallels between Gondō and Durkheim in "Gondō Seikyō and the Agrarianist Critique of Modern Japan," seminar paper in history, Yale University, 1973, p. 17.

[27] Ronald P. Dore, *Land Reform in Japan* (London: Oxford University Press, 1959), p. 96. Cf. Barrington Moore, Jr., *Social Origins of Dictatorship and Democracy* (Boston: Beacon Press, 1966), pp. 307-313.

[28] Ifukube Takahiko, quoted in Masao Maruyama, *Thought and Behaviour in Modern Japanese Politics*, ed. Ivan Morris (London: Oxford University Press, 1963), p. 40n. Maruyama gives Ifukube's personal name as Takateru. (Emphasis in original.) See also *Uyoku zensho* [Full Book on the Right Wing], ed. Kōan Keibi Kenkyūkai (Tokyo: Kindai Keisatsusha, 1957), p. 104; Tsunazawa Mitsuaki,

To the extent that sizable landlords still dominated rural society by the 1920s and 1930s, Gondō's call for restoring self-ruling villages of course perpetuated their authority, but his chief aim was certainly to undercut centralized political power by making local autonomy the norm. Such doctrines had the most appeal to the same owner-cultivators who admired Okada On, since in many cases the *jisakunō* were by now the main village elite class and thus could expect to profit the most from reviving self-rule.

New Ideologies from Abroad

Gondō Seikyō, however eye-catching or trenchant his criticisms, was only one of many observers in the interwar years to castigate the militarism, bureaucratism, and capitalism which had led to the city-country split. Amid the numerous solutions for the rural crisis put forth by his contemporaries, why did Gondō believe that restoring the self-ruling *shashoku* was the only worthy way out? Since he wrote almost nothing by way of direct response to the government's farm policies during the twenties and thirties, it is hard to tell whether he knew much about the economic realities of Japanese agriculture in the midst of depression. Gondō was evidently more interested in overall ideology than specific policy. Despite his unyielding faith in Nōhonshugi, he did not dismiss such competing doctrines as communism, socialism, and anarchism out of hand. "Naturally when you say communism," he wrote, "some people shudder merely hearing the name. But its meaning is very simple. It would not be inaccurate to say that it means turning the entire society into a single family."[29] Gondō apparently admired this familistic attribute of communism, and he also applauded the cooperative spirit of socialism.[30] But a major

---

Nōhonshugi no kenkyū [Studies on Agrarianism] (Nagoya: Fūbaisha, 1968), p. 25.

[29] *Jichi minpan*, p. 508. See also *Jichi minseiri*, p. 246.

[30] *Jichi minpan*, pp. 509-510.

difficulty with both doctrines, he claimed, was that they were impractical and idealistic. Likewise he praised nihilism (which he equated with anarchism) for its dislike of centralized government, although he allowed that "the regrettable thing about nihilism—quite distinct from its ideals— is that in order to bring about anarchy in contemporary society men dare to use explosive means."[31] Considering his concern for social harmony and the gradual evolution of good practices, it is not at all surprising that Gondō opposed political violence.

Gondō likewise found another ideology from abroad, parliamentary democracy, very inadequate for coping with the rural plight. Election regulations were so lax, he charged, that virtually all high public officials had come to power by buying votes.[32] After forty years' experience with constitutionalism, he asked, was such "corruption and depravity a result of the fact that the old customs of our countrymen do not adjust to constitutional rule? Or is there some great defect in the formation of constitutional government that invited this result?"[33] Gondō's answer was that there were so many serious flaws in constitutionalism that it was positively harmful to the principle of self-rule.

For one thing, he asserted, the lower house of the original Diet in 1890 had been selected by such a narrow electorate —only those who met stiff property qualifications—that "it could be called a peers' assembly or a huge tax assembly."[34] For another, the country soon lapsed into "tyrannical election interference, and members of the Diet were purchased."[35] What is more, Gondō continued, elections were scheduled at inconvenient times or even during wintry weather, disfranchising large numbers of people. By the Taishō period, the political parties openly countenanced vote

[31] Ibid., p. 513.   [32] *Jichi minseiri*, pp. 253-254.
[33] Ibid., p. 254.   [34] Ibid.
[35] Ibid., p. 255. Shinagawa Yajirō was a leading figure in the election interference episode of 1892. See also *Nihon nōseishidan*, pp. 196-200, on the defects of constitutional rule.

buying: "Because vast sums of money were needed for elections, no one had scruples about making overly generous concessions to capitalists who had absolute control."[36] The result, he claimed, was that oligarchs, party leaders, and capitalists conspired almost continually, to the detriment of true constitutionalism. Whether "conspiracy," "collusion," and "absolute control by capitalists" are appropriate terms to describe Japan in the 1920s is uncertain. But there can be no question that Gondō's attitude reflected the thinking of a person cut off from the wealth and power which resulted from modernization. His bitterness, no doubt shared by many fellow countrymen, was truly one of the dilemmas of growth in modern Japan.

Once universal manhood suffrage was adopted in 1925, Gondō observed, all voting barriers were theoretically dropped for adult males, but in practice the government issued "some extremely detailed administrative regulations" which made it hard for certain persons to cast their ballots. "For this reason," he noted plaintively, "there are many things which make me wonder at what point we can recognize the autonomous rights of our self-ruling people in all of this."[37] Universal manhood suffrage was a sham that damaged the custom of self-rule, Gondō concluded: "Selling the people's election rights and taking care of relatives and secret requests are things that of course squander autonomous rights."[38]

Since elections had failed to fulfill the requirements of true constitutionalism and impinged on the tradition of self-rule, could high state officials perhaps guide the public in a tutelary fashion back toward the correct path? "Originally," he wrote, "the way to reform popular sentiment was always for the leading officials to act decisively by making clear their moral responsibilities, after which . . . the people could presume in what direction they should proceed." But this was no longer possible under contemporary conditions,

[36] *Jichi minseiri*, p. 256.   [37] Ibid.
[38] Ibid., p. 258.

Gondō believed, because Japan's leaders now "merely censure the people severely and never question" their own conduct.[39] Instead of respecting self-rule and governing with a light hand, modern leaders used oppression: "For peace and order to be maintained by the power of bureaucratic officials means that we will never be able to expect true self-rule."[40] Hence "the existence of self-rule is merely in respecting autonomous rights. The duty of our administration and police is not to interfere with these autonomous rights but to protect them."[41]

Gondō plainly believed that neither the legislature nor the executive was capable of implementing constitutionalism, and thus he rejected it as incompatible with self-rule in practice, without ever stating whether he thought the two incongruous in theory. Apparently the corrupt electoral and administrative behavior that had come to light since the first Diet met in 1890 was so much a part of constitutionalism in its Japanese setting that Gondō was simply soured on the whole subject. At any rate, he dismissed parliamentarianism along with communism, socialism, and anarchism as inappropriate for his country and concluded instead that "we must make the *shashoku* our ideology and reinstate self-rule."[42]

Seeking a Self-Ruling Society

Like any sincere nationalist, Gondō believed that a political ideology, to be effective, "must conform to public customs and the conditions of the country." He therefore contended that "the only way to cure the present crisis is to work out a master plan to return to the true meaning of the founding of the country." Such a plan must be "based on the *shashoku*, in order to harmonize the people's food, clothing, and shelter and to insure the tranquility of public opinion."[43]

---

[39] Ibid., p. 257.
[41] *Jichi minseiri*, pp. 257-258.
[43] Ibid., p. 518.

[40] *Jichi minpan*, p. 572.
[42] *Jichi minpan*, p. 515.

What desirable qualities did Gondō think would ensue from restoring self-rule? Mutual aid and tranquility were important, he stated, for regaining the equipoise of the *shashoku*.[44] Such attributes as "love, respect, sincerity, and sympathy, which developed from the pure character of ancient persons,"[45] would also be recovered. The means to attaining these values he described in unmistakably Confucian language: "Since antiquity the only political policy for dealing with changes in men's thought has been to lead the people with good government and virtuous deeds and to have them turn back to this basic thought."[46] Like his earlier descriptions of a harmonious pastoral society, these sentiments grouped Gondō with preimperial Confucianists such as Mencius and Mo Tzu.

To attain a self-ruling *shashoku*, Gondō believed, farmers —not politicians—must grasp the initiative by exercising eight "rights" of self-government:

1. The right to supervise the tranquility of the village.
2. The right to regulate the commodities for the villagers' food, clothing, and shelter.
3. The right to manage village defense, sanitation, and population.
4. The right to deal with the assets and liabilities of the village.
5. The right to negotiate with other villages, and the right to negotiate concerning transportation and irrigation.
6. The right to supervise educational facilities.
7. The right to mediate disputes among villagers.
8. The right to sanction or restrict the enterprises of people living in the village.[47]

If each village carried out these functions, he said, the need for central government would virtually evaporate,

[44] Ibid., p. 540. See also pp. 201-203.
[45] Ibid., p. 2.   [46] Ibid., p. 203.
[47] Ibid., pp. 544-545.

except for the ceremonial functions of the imperial court. Gradually the practice of self-rule would spread from the countryside to each neighborhood and each factory in the big cities[48] until it eventually spilled over to Japan's colonies abroad:

> Needless to say, we must extend the power of self-rule domestically, but it is also imperative for our country to-day to spread and develop it outside the country. The existing farm villages in Japan already seem to have excess population. The general condition of the country today is that the development of colonial enterprises is being planned by capitalists, but this is accompanied by a number of evils. By force of circumstance, we cannot totally renounce this, but I think that a much more appropriate policy would be for a farm village (if one village lacked the power, then joint action by several villages would be possible) to create a second village in a suitable spot at home or abroad, and for the government to support and assist this. If we did this, the liaison between farm villages and colonies would be improved [i.e., frictions over rice imports would diminish] and it would be easy to develop the force of collective action within the colonies. The fact that we have not developed our agricultural colonies in Korea comes from not paying sufficient attention to this.[49]

This was practically the only important statement Gondō made about overseas expansion after World War I, and it is noteworthy that he justified colonial settlement (in line with his support for developing Korea and Manchuria at the time of Korean amalgamation in 1910) as a means of promoting people's self-rule rather than enhancing state power. Through this process of encouraging autonomy in each village in the empire, the entire population could once again enjoy a secure, harmonious society: "I earnestly bid

[48] Ibid., pp. 571-576.   [49] Ibid., p. 547.

227

my fellow countrymen: self-control means discretion and self-cultivation. This is the real origin of self-rule. This is the foundation for reforming everything from the villages and towns to the districts, prefectures, and entire country. The invincible model of our eternal *shashoku* is found in this."[50]

Gondō's Thought in Review

Gondō Seikyō nationalism stood on the twin pillars of village communalism and local self-rule, both of which were venerable themes in Japanese popular thought. From these images of a harmonious *shashoku* and an autonomous system of local government, supposedly found in Japan's ancient past, he constructed a critique of modern centralized rule, capitalist production, and urban life which both rejected the main trends of modernization and reaffirmed the Japanese nation and *kokutai*.

Although he spoke of society at large, or *shashoku*, Gondō wrote in the tradition of ideologues who glorified a form of village communalism known as *kyōdoshugi*.[51] This slippery term connotes both village and land, as distinct from the sociological term *kyōdōtai* (community or collectivity). The ideal village, according to *kyōdoshugi*, was close to nature and the agricultural deities of Shinto.[52] Gondō, for example, warned repeatedly against harming nature and farming. In his fuzzy formulation of village society, what counted was the spirit of cooperation and emotional identification with other members of the community, qualities which prevailed naturally (*mui shizen*) unless blocked from outside. In such a system, landlords and tenants were not

[50] Ibid., p. 521.
[51] See Sakurai Takeo, "Shōwa no nōhonshugi" [Agrarianism in the Shōwa Period], *Shisō* [Thought], No. 407, May 1958, p. 50; Tsunazawa, p. 15; Katherine M. Maxim, "Agrarian Response to Industrialization: Populism and Nohon-shugi," B.A. thesis in history, Connecticut College, 1970, p. 49.
[52] Tsunazawa, p. 26.

antagonists but customary members of a historic hierarchy that permitted village solidarity.[53] The way to solve the rural crisis, Gondō believed, was to restore the virtues of true communalism rather than overthrow landlord-tenant relations, as Nōhonshugi advocates like Yokota Hideo claimed.

Two observations about Gondō's ideal *shashoku* are in order. First, although there is no evidence that he consciously favored the specific class interests of landlords in his social thought, a byproduct of reverting to premodern village unity was that the landlord's place in the village structure was perpetuated. Second, although he had been reared in an owner-farmer household in Kurume, Gondō's personal knowledge of village Japan was confined to his childhood, and like most bearers of the *kyōdoshugi* tradition[54] he idealized the virtues and minimized the woes of peasant life.

Self-rule to Gondō meant a form of local autonomy quite unlike the democracy of city-states or independent villages in European history. He praised the rigid hierarchy of local politics and allowed no place for individualism in his conception of self-rule.[55] Gondō believed that society antedated the state and that the state itself should be weak, because the people governed themselves spontaneously under the monarch. Gondō proffered what was surely an impractical image of self-rule, grounded on a rosy view of human nature;[56] he can certainly be faulted for failing to provide sufficiently for defense, international trade, communications,

[53] Adachi Ikitsune, "Nōhonshugi no saikentō" [A Reappraisal of Theories on Agrarianism], *Shisō*, No. 423, September 1959, p. 65.

[54] See Fujita Shōzō, "Tennōsei to fuashizumu" [The Emperor System and Fascism], *Iwanami kōza gendai shisō*, v, *Handō no shisō* [Iwanami Colloquium on Modern Thought, v, Reactionary Thought] (Tokyo: Iwanami Shoten, 1959), p. 156.

[55] Adachi, p. 66.

[56] Tsukui Tatsuo, *Nihonshugi undō no riron to jissen* [Theory and Practice of the Japanism Movement] (Tokyo: Kensetsusha, 1935), p. 128.

and the like in his eight-point list of self-governing rights.[57] Moreover, it seems apt to criticize him for giving no specific guidelines for how to go about switching from bureaucratic centralism to self-ruling localism.

Gondō was anticapitalist as a result of his political and social misgivings about modern Japanese civilization, not because he opposed industry or money in theory. He attacked their abuses, especially the collusion between plutocrats and bureaucrats, but he wanted merely to reduce, not destroy, the power of capitalism, rechanneling it to the advantage of *shashoku* and self-rule. By contrast, he would have been quite happy to abolish centralized bureaucratic government altogether[58] and revert to local autonomy under a ceremonial emperor.

From this many observers have inferred that Gondō was a variety of political anarchist.[59] If dismantling the elaborate institutions of state created under "Prussian-style nationalism" constituted anarchism, the inference holds true, although Gondō probably would have preferred simply to let the state atrophy. Unlike the reconstructionist Kita Ikki, Gondō offered no concrete plan for setting in motion the reforms he sought. Whereas Kita advocated a military coup to institute his detailed program of change, Gondō merely hoped to stimulate the farmers spontaneously to reassert the village

[57] See Maxim, p. 51.

[58] Tsukui, p. 117, demurs on this point, claiming that Kita Ikki's followers mistook Gondō as an anarchist whereas in fact he wanted merely a reduction of bureaucratic power.

[59] See, e.g., Hijikata Kazuo, "Nihonkei fuashizumu no taitō to teikō" [The Rise and Resistance of Japanese Fascism], *Kindai Nihon shakai shisōshi* [History of Modern Japanese Social Thought], ed. Furuta Hikaru, Sakuta Keiichi, and Ikimatsu Keizō (Tokyo, Yūhikaku, 1971), II, 156; Yamazaki Masakazu, *Kindai Nihon shisō tsūshi* [General History of Modern Japanese Thought] (Tokyo: Aoki Shoten, 1957), p. 263; Maruyama, p. 41; Tsuchida Kyōson, "Gondō Seikyōshi no shoron" [Views of Mr. Gondō Seikyō], *Serupan*, July 1932, *Tsuchida Kyōson zenshū* [Complete Works of Tsuchida Kyōson] (Tokyo: Daiichi Shobō, 1935), III, 394-397.

"rights of self-rule." But there is no evidence that he gloried in destruction like his close friend, the anarchist Ōsugi Sakae (1885-1923), nor of course did he countenance the political violence of nihilists. Unlike true anarchists, he retained the emperor in his system of self-rule as a national focus, speaking frequently of joint rule by emperor and people. Most importantly, Gondō's concept of local autonomy was far from anarchistic: he specified duties for village leaders and assumed a high degree of rural peace and order that was quite inconsistent with unfettered anarchism. Decentralization thus seems to be a more appropriate word for his view of politics.

In light of his outlook on state and society, is it proper to speak of Gondō as a nationalist at all? Some observers have concluded that he was an antinationalist in that he opposed the existing government,[60] a judgment which assumes that nationalism must center on a state. Writing on the eve of war, one of his right-wing critics, Tsukui Tatsuo, even attacked Gondō for being insufficiently nationalist, or Japanist, because he believed that human nature was the same in all countries and ignored the special characteristics of the Japanese.[61]

Such cant aside, Gondō was unquestionably a nationalist in his loyalty to the Japanese people as an ethnonationality group which possessed the distinctive customs of self-rule and the *shashoku*, based on village agriculture and a deep faith in the gods of Shinto. Surely Gondō was more a romantic than a practical critic of Japanese life. Surely, too, his ultimate goals of self-rule and the *shashoku* were reactionary objectives in the context of the 1920s and 1930s, despite his talk of social evolution and conviction that these goals were up to date. Yet his critiques of contemporary society were also radical in the sense that they cut to the

---

[60] Yamazaki, p. 263; Richard Storry, *The Double Patriots: A Study of Japanese Nationalism* (Boston: Houghton Mifflin, 1957), p. 96.
[61] Tsukui, pp. 122-123.

root of Japan's quandary. In sum, the thought of this romantic agrarian nationalist expressed the resentment of millions of peasants, landlords, owner-cultivators, and newly arrived city residents against foreign ideas, material culture, authoritarian rule, and the vexing complications of modern life, typified in the antagonisms between city and country that remained unresolved until long after World War II.

Chapter x

Tachibana Kōzaburō's Farm Communalism

A CONSTANT problem in reconstructing the past is to sort out the age differences among persons who shared a common historical experience. For example, it would be tempting, but erroneous, to assume that the Meiji restoration embodied the same aspirations and significance for men and women in their sixties as it did for the youthful enthusiasts who formed the new oligarchy after 1868. Likewise, since Tachibana Kōzaburō is routinely bracketed with Gondō Seikyō as a foremost agrarian nationalist in Japan during the 1920s and 1930s, it is easy to forget that he was twenty-five years younger than Gondō and necessarily perceived the rural depression in somewhat different ways.

Although they published their major agranianist works almost simultaneously, Gondō wrote at the apex of a checkered life spent primarily in the cities, whereas Tachibana was a village farmer-educator in his mid-thirties when he suddenly appeared as a spokesman for rural nationalism. Gondō, the more senior, reflective, and erudite of the two, had no personal experience with political violence, in contrast with Tachibana, who spent more than eight years in jail for his part in the May 15, 1932 incident. Although their careers, and particularly their ideas, had much in common, Gondō and Tachibana were separated by a generation and deserve to be considered as distinct ideologues. This chapter sketches Tachibana's career as a rural idealist and political activist and outlines the farm communalism that underlay his thought and conduct. The next chapter deals with his criticisms of contemporary society and his proposals for what he called "patriotic reform."

Tachibana's Early Years

As a child Tachibana Kōzaburō enjoyed considerable material comfort but also frequent personal turmoil.[1] He was born on March 18, 1893, as the third and youngest son of a prosperous former samurai turned dyed goods merchant in Mito, a city long known for its ardent patriots. As one of seven children in a busy townsman household, Tachibana apparently spent a lonely childhood in which he regarded his parents with more respect than affection. He later idealized his family situation in rather unusual terms: "My father was a totally unselfish person, without worldly ambitions, and my mother was a woman of unique sagacity, and I felt a sacred love for her resembling one's faith in the Madonna. My brother was a truly distinguished person.

[1] Biographical details for Tachibana's early life are taken from Matsuzawa Tetsunari, " 'Shōwa ishin' no shisō to kōdō—Tachibana Kōzaburō no baai" [Thought and Behavior in the "Shōwa Restoration"—The Case of Tachibana Kōzaburō], *Shakai kagaku kenkyū* [Social Science Studies], XIX, 3, January 1968, 10-25, 50-52; Matsuzawa Tetsunari, *Tachibana Kōzaburō* (Tokyo: San'ichi Shobō, 1972), pp. 25-47; Kinoshita Hanji, *Nihon no uyoku* [The Japanese Right Wing] (Tokyo: Kaname Shobō, 1953), p. 33; Hashikawa Bunzō, "Shōwa chōkokkashugi no shosō" [Various Aspects of Ultranationalism in the Shōwa Period], *Chōkokkashugi* [Ultranationalism], ed. Hashikawa Bunzō, *Gendai Nihon shisōshi taikei* [Collection on Modern Japanese Thought] (Tokyo: Chikuma Shobō, 1964), XXXI, 46; Tachibana Kōzaburō and Takeuchi Yoshi, "Aru nōhonshugisha no kaisō to iken" [Recollections and Opinions of a Certain Agrarianist], *Shisō no kagaku* [Science of Thought], No. 18, June 1960, pp. 15-16. See also Hugh Byas, *Government by Assassination* (New York: Alfred A. Knopf, 1942), pp. 63-65.

Hence when I set about building a utopian village, I had my own family as a model."[2]

Although he was a wayward student in his early teens, Tachibana managed to pass the entrance examinations for the Daiichi Kōtō Gakkō (Number One High School) in Tokyo, widely considered to be Japan's best secondary school at the time. He entered in September 1912 and soon concentrated on European literature and social thought—above all the works of Tolstoy. He also wrote essays and poems for various school journals. Then he suddenly fell ill from nervous exhaustion in November 1914, just a few months before graduation, and returned to Mito to begin his career in agriculture.

It is unclear why Tachibana never completed his education, but it is apparent that the years in Tokyo were ones of continual self-reflection during which he thought a great deal about his country's fate. As he wrote in a student journal in November 1914, "It is impossible to separate thinking about the future of Japan and the Japanese race from thinking about myself. . . . This is because we are thinking most earnestly about the new Japan. But we no longer think about the content of patriotism or loyalism. And I am opposed to the sort of chauvinism that says that anything Japanese is good. At the same time, this is never to say that I reject patriotism."[3] This immature statement was the earliest expression of a concern for nation that came to dominate Tachibana's thinking in the early thirties. He later called the decision to drop his studies for farming a "conversion" (kaishin) experience,[4] a sign that Tachibana himself regarded this new phase of his life as a major turning point in his intellectual development.

2 Tachibana and Takeuchi, p. 15.
3 Tachibana Kōzaburō, "Seishinteki kojinshugi" [Spiritual Individualism], *Yūkai zasshi* [Friendship Society Journal], Daiichi Kōtō Gakkō, No. 242, Nov. 23, 1914, pp. 16-17, quoted in Matsuzawa, "Shōwa ishin," p. 59.
4 See Matsuzawa, "Shōwa ishin," pp. 53-60.

The Kyōdai Mura

Tachibana's farm consisted of two hectares inherited from his father in Tokiwa village, Ibaraki Prefecture, where he began operations in late 1915. Eventually his lands grew to five hectares, where both of his brothers and one sister joined him to form a community known as Kyōdai Mura (Fraternal Village). The choice of name, Tachibana recalled many years later, was not merely descriptive of the blood relationships within the family. It also represented the ideal purpose of farming: working "in the warmth of nature and the good earth and in the fraternal love of one's neighbors and kindred souls, guided by the spirit of the gods."[5] This goal of fraternalism foreshadowed Tachibana's later emphasis on brotherhood in the books he wrote in the early 1930s.

Like many Japanese idealists in the early twentieth century, Tachibana acknowledged his intellectual debt to both Tolstoy and Robert Owen, especially in trying to build a utopian farm that would blend spiritualism and materialism.[6] At Kyōdai Mura, he later stated, he was trying "to realize an ideal society by uniting and fusing personal advantage and the interests of others through collaboration in all spiritual and material relationships." Thus he wanted "to build a utopia on earth" based on the integration of "earth and devotion"[7] (tsuchi to magokoro)—in other words, agriculture and worship.

Aside from these recollections, little is known of Tachibana's life as a farmer, except that he suffered almost continuously from a kidney disease, complicated by nervous difficulties, between 1920 and 1925. During his long convalescence, he became interested in contemporary social questions, especially through reading works by Marx, Spengler, and Henry George. By the mid-1920s Kyōdai

---

[5] Tachibana Kōzaburō, quoted in Hashikawa, p. 47.
[6] Tachibana and Takeuchi, pp. 16-17.
[7] Tachibana Kōzaburō, quoted in Matsuzawa, "Shōwa ishin," p. 60.

Mura had grown famous in Ibaraki, attracting the support of local politicians as well as students who came to hear Tachibana lecture on how to improve farmers' livelihoods.[8] The combined effects of reading Western social theory, living in a period of village poverty, and observing the low educational level of the young farmers he taught finally led Tachibana, on November 23, 1929, to found a producers' cooperative association, called the Aikyōkai (Community Loving Society), that could deal more effectively than pure utopianism with depression in his district.

Tachibana's Credit Society and the Aikyōjuku

Like the Kyōdai Mura a decade earlier, the Aikyōkai was established to fulfill both the spiritual and the material needs of farmers. In the "Declaration" announcing the new society, Tachibana detected specifically patriotic reasons for returning to the soil in order to overcome the current crisis:

> Back to the land! Back to the land! After you've returned to the land, begin a new gait! This alone will rescue us all —ourselves and others, individuals and society—and it is the one and only way open to us. This alone will show us a unique way to reconstruct our beloved Japan by establishing unparalleled unity among our 60 million fellow countrymen in city and countryside alike.
>
> Oh, this rescue and reconstruction! For the sake of this rescue and reconstruction, friends, arise! Standing here we have already taken the first step. The time for us to start has come. Our historic mission for Japanese national reconstruction is coming.
> The season for us to rise and risk our fate fighting for the fatherland has come.
> To the fore! For the earth of Japan!

[8] Matsuzawa, "Shōwa ishin," pp. 62-65; Richard Storry, *The Double Patriots: A Study of Japanese Nationalism* (Boston: Houghton Mifflin, 1957), p. 98.

Advance! To the farmers' era!
Who are the privileged warriors to be?
Those who love their communities and lift up
their pure hearts for their home villages!
The Aikyōkai is the organization of those
who love their communities.[9]

Stirring as these words were, Tachibana's manifesto was not all bombast. Equally important, he believed, was that the Aikyōkai develop "a realistic economic movement" to "rescue the devastated farm villages."[10] He asserted that mutual help, hard work, and love for the community could best be attained through careful organization, "promoting the teaching of farm management to farmers," and "protecting rural society by creating Aikyō cooperatives."[11] Although obviously similar in style to the Meiji Hōtoku movement, Tachibana's Aikyōkai confined its activities to Ibaraki and never approached the scale of either the Hōtokusha or the state-sponsored producers' cooperatives (Sangyō Kumiai). At its height the Aikyō association had approximately thirty branches, most of them lecture clubs which stressed self-help.[12] The main Aikyōkai cooperative lasted barely a year, hardly long enough to put Tachibana's ideas into effect. It purchased such necessities as seed and fertilizer, marketed farm produce, served as a clearinghouse for shared implements, machinery, and tools, and arranged for cooperative tilling and grain processing. This society also began insurance and medical care programs[13] before its

[9] Tachibana Kōzaburō, "Sengen" [Declaration] of the Aikyōkai, Nov. 23, 1929, quoted in *Senzen ni okeru uyoku dantai no jōkyō* [Circumstances of Right-Wing Groups Before the War], ed. Kōan Chōsachō (Tokyo: Kōan Chōsachō, 1964), I, 491.

[10] Matsuzawa, "Shōwa ishin," p. 27.

[11] Tachibana, "Sengen," p. 488.

[12] *Chōkokkashugi*, p. 417; *Senzen ni okeru uyoku dantai no jōkyō*, I, 488.

[13] See Tachibana and Takeuchi, pp. 17-18; Matsuzawa, *Tachibana Kōzaburō*, pp. 97-126; Matsuzawa, "Shōwa ishin," pp. 74-75; Hanzawa

activities ceased in the wake of the May 15, 1932 incident, an attempted coup in which Prime Minister Inukai Tsuyoshi was assassinated by a group of radical military officers and civilians, including eleven members of the Aikyōkai.

Meanwhile, because he believed that rural improvement required better education, Tachibana started a school in April 1931, called the Aikyōjuku (Community Loving Academy), to "educate proper Japanese workers of the earth" and teach "methods of rational small farm management."[14] He divided the students into an elementary group (*shōnenbu*), with a two and one-half year course for primary school graduates, and a youth group (*seinenbu*), consisting of persons aged eighteen or more who pledged "to sacrifice themselves to the movement for the principles of love for the soil and, if necessary, to leave their families and renounce their personal existence to this end."[15] Other students over eighteen who could not leave their families were also permitted to join the youth group to hear lectures and take part in its activities.

Subsequent accounts of the Aikyōjuku usually described it as a seedbed for radical political ideas, since half the civilians who participated in the May 15 incident were connected with it. It is difficult to confirm or deny this judgment, not merely because the content of the Aikyōjuku's curriculum is obscure but also because its active phase lasted for only a year, during which the student body at its

---

Hiroshi, *Dochaku no shisō* [Home Town Thought] (Tokyo: Kinokuniya Shoten, 1967).

[14] Matsuzawa, "Shōwa ishin," p. 35. See also Storry, p. 98; Byas, pp. 63-65; Kinoshita, p. 33; Hashikawa Bunzō, "Shōwa ishin no ronri to shinri" [Logic and Psychology of the Shōwa Restoration], *Kindai Nihon seiji shisōshi* [History of Modern Japanese Political Thought], ed. Hashikawa Bunzō and Matsumoto Sannosuke (Tokyo: Yūhikaku, 1970), II, 227.

[15] O. Tanin and E. Yohan, pseuds., *Militarism and Fascism in Japan* (New York: International Publishers, 1934), p. 221. See also *Senzen ni okeru uyoku dantai no jōkyō*, I, 492-493.

height reached only twenty-three persons.[16] The school apparently taught mathematics, bookkeeping, natural history, farm management, and other relatively nonideological subjects, but it also included lectures on village rebirth and social reform as well as a good deal of practical work in the fields. Fraternalism, hard work, and self-sufficiency were highly prized, and students were forbidden to smoke, drink, or squander their money.[17] It seems likely that the tenor of the school was more idealistic than revolutionary, drawing on the fusion of spiritual and material aims which characterized the overall Aikyōkai movement. But it was precisely such idealism which propelled the youthful farm activists on May 15.

Tachibana and Political Organizations

In addition to its credit and educational activities, Tachibana led the Aikyōkai into political activity after the summer of 1931. The Aikyōkai helped to organize the Japan Village Rule League (Nihon Sonjiha Dōmei) in November 1931. This short lived assembly of intellectuals, publishers, utopians, and farmers included many of the leading Nōhonshugi advocates of the day. Tachibana supported the league less for its vague pronouncements about reforming the national economy than because it focused on wiping away

[16] *Senzen ni okeru uyoku dantai no jōkyō*, I, 492; Storry, pp. 98-99. For views stressing the Aikyōjuku's role in forming activist ideology, see Tanin and Yohan, p. 222; Mito Saburō, "Aikyōjuku?!" *Bungei shunjū*, x, 7, July 1932, 237-240; and, to a lesser degree, Storry, p. 99.

[17] *Uyoku zensho* [Full Book on the Right Wing], ed. Kōan Keibi Kenkyūkai (Tokyo: Kindai Keisatsusha, 1957), p. 109; Matsuzawa, "Shōwa ishin," p. 35; Byas, pp. 63-65. Having suspended operations after May 15, the Aikyōjuku reopened on June 28, 1932, with Tachibana's elder brother Tokujirō as acting headmaster. But on Jan. 8, 1933, one of its students, Yamada Chuichi, was arrested for trying to present a petition for Tachibana Kōzaburō's release directly to the emperor, first at Tokyo station and then on Omote Sandō, near the Meiji shrine in Tokyo. The school closed permanently in March 1933. See *Uyoku zensho*, p. 109; *Senzen ni okeru uyoku dantai no jōkyō*, I, 480, 493-496.

corruption in local government, a main objective of the Aikyōkai in Ibaraki.[18] Gondō Seikyō's influence was evident in the league's pledge to "overthrow materialistic civilization, establish agrarian culture, and realize a self-ruling society,"[19] and even though the group soon dissolved after bickering over methods it was significant as the first concerted political activity by Nōhonshugi ideologues during the depression— activity which shortly divided into rural party organizing on the one hand and illegal direct action on the other.

The Aikyōkai leaders, dissatisfied with how quickly the aloof intellectuals had dominated the Nihon Sonjiha Dōmei, decided in January 1932 to found a farmers' party, the Nōhon Shakaitō (Agrarian Socialist Party), and helped to form a parent body of farm ideologues to sponsor it. The parent body, known as the Nōhon Renmei (Agrarian Federation), was created in March 1932 but collapsed in bitter debate over the merits of organizing a farmers' party within the constitutional process.[20]

Out of the rubble of these fruitless efforts to provide political structure grew the Jichi Nōmin Kyōgikai (Self-ruling Farmers' Council), the greatest achievement of which was the impressive feat of collecting hundreds of thousands of signatures on petitions to the Diet for rural relief measures in 1932 and early 1933.[21] Nagano Akira, a disciple of

[18] See *Senzen ni okeru uyoku dantai no jōkyō*, I, 497-498; Matsuzawa, "Shōwa ishin," pp. 76-77; Hashikawa, "Shōwa ishin," p. 228.

[19] *Senzen ni okeru uyoku dantai no jōkyō*, I, 498. See also Tsunazawa Mitsuaki, "Tachibana Kōzaburō shiron" [Sketch of Tachibana Kōzaburō], *Shisō no kagaku*, No. 142, October 1970, p. 79.

[20] *Senzen ni okeru uyoku dantai no jōkyō*, I, 502-503.

[21] Adachi Ikitsune, "Nōhonshugi no saikentō" [A Reappraisal of Theories on Agrarianism], *Shisō* [Thought], No. 423, September 1959, pp. 63-64; Okutani Matsuji, "Nihon ni okeru nōhonshugi shisō no nagare" [Trends in Agrarian Thought in Japan], *Shisō*, No. 407, May 1958, p. 12. Tanin and Yohan, pp. 218-219, note that the petitions were mild in tone and claim that they served reactionary interests by siphoning off rural unrest. Their impact is hard to gauge, but there can be little doubt that the Diet session convened to consider farm

Gondō's, was the main figure in this federation, but Tachibana supported both its emphasis on action and its general objectives:

1. Politically, to establish a system of mutual self-rule in society;
2. Economically, to make agriculture our basis and to endeavor to satisfy our material needs, such as food, clothing, and shelter, by means of our principles of coexistence and mutual aid;
3. Educationally, to enhance people's performances; and
4. Diplomatically, to prize international harmony with mutual aid as our aim.[22]

It was hard for any agrarianist in the early 1930s to question the rather nonspecific goals of the Jichi Nōmin Kyōgikai, although they conformed only in a general way to the fraternalism and communalism which Tachibana had practiced in Ibaraki since 1915. Indeed, none of the formal political organizations with which he was involved in late 1931 and early 1932 precisely mirrored his own outlook, nor did any of them accomplish enough to nourish his erstwhile belief that legal political action was a promising way to confront the depression. Although it was small consolation to Tachibana at the time, no other agrarianists managed to found political groups that came any closer to realizing Nōhonshugi objectives in the 1930s.

Insurrection, Exile, and Imprisonment

During the three busy years 1929-1932, Tachibana not only led the Aikyōkai in its unproductive economic, educational, and political efforts and developed most of the social and political criticism which established him as a major

---

measures in the summer of 1932 met in a climate of confusion and intense pressure for relief.

22 Jichi Nōmin Kyōgikai, general rules, quoted in *Senzen ni okeru uyoku dantai no jōkyō*, 1, 505.

agrarianist, but he also became acquainted with many of the young terrorists who eventually led the Ketsumeidan and May 15 uprisings in 1932. Like Gondō Seikyō, he first met would-be revolutionaries at lecture societies in the late 1920s. Inoue Nisshō, the radical priest who founded the Ketsumeidan, is known to have visited Tachibana occasionally in Mito starting in December 1929, and Tachibana gradually expanded his circle of right-wing acquaintances until young officers from the Ibaraki air base began attending lectures at the Aikyōjuku regularly in August 1931.[23] He also met a number of impatient patriots at study societies in Tokyo in the summer and autumn of 1931, among them some of the young military officers who later joined in the May 15 upheaval.

Tachibana did not take part in the Ketsumeidan incidents of February and March 1932, although he was probably present when plans were laid for these events.[24] In March Lieut. (j.g.) Koga Kiyoshi invited him to join a conspiracy, eventually consisting of approximately twenty civilians and twenty military officers, to kill the prime minister and party leaders, remove objectionable courtiers, and topple the political parties and the *zaibatsu*.[25] Tachibana eventually agreed, bringing with him almost two dozen students and instructors from the Aikyōjuku to Tokyo in mid-May. Of this group, styled the Nōmin Kesshitai or Death-Defying Farmers' Band, eleven—although not Tachibana himself— actually participated in the various assassination attempts, attacks on the Tokyo police headquarters, and electrical power blockages that comprised the unsuccessful coup of May 15.[26]

[23] Hashikawa, "Shōwa ishin," p. 228; Kenneth W. Colegrove, *Militarism in Japan* (Boston: World Peace Foundation, 1936), pp. 37-38; Matsuzawa, "Shōwa ishin," p. 38; James B. Crowley, *Japan's Quest for Autonomy* (Princeton: Princeton University Press, 1966), p. 174.
[24] Byas, p. 67.   [25] Tsunazawa, p. 71.
[26] See *Senzen ni okeru uyoku dantai no jōkyō*, I, 492-493; Storry, pp. 119-120.

To what degree Tachibana's agrarianism stimulated others to political violence is a question better taken up after considering his social and political thought. Why Tachibana himself joined in this desperate insurrection can perhaps be partly explained by the close liaisons he had built with radical young officers and partly by his perception of an impending national crisis. Since August 1931 he had been close to Ensign Mikami Taku's Kokutai Genriha, or National Principle Group, a clique of violent young officers who indiscriminately vilified the parties, *zaibatsu*, and imperial courtiers as obstacles to a true family state with the emperor at the head.[27] These and many other contacts at the very least predisposed Tachibana to the possibility of direct action if his simultaneous efforts at legal political organization proved to be unavailing, although they alone do not fully account for his conduct, since others, such as Gondō Seikyō, were just as close to militant activists without joining in the violence.

Equally important was Tachibana's self-admitted penchant for headlong, monistic involvement in causes which preoccupied him. He wrote in 1932: "Seeing the crisis of the fatherland closing in hour by hour, as a single human, indeed as a single Japanese, I had to rise up and fling everything aside, just as I had stood up and thrown everything aside twenty years ago when I entered the path of reviving self-rescue. If you call this folly, I grew more and more foolish. If you call it lunacy, I grew more and more lunatic."[28] Unlike Gondō and most other scholarly Nōhonshugisha, Tachibana was motivated toward action as much as reflection and was willing to accept the risks involved.

Without slighting his importance as an agrarian thinker, it seems appropriate to cite Tachibana's own pretrial inter-

[27] See Crowley, pp. 175-176.
[28] Tachibana Kōzaburō, "Kokumin kyōdōtai ōdō kokka nōhon kensetsuron" [Theory of Establishing the Agricultural Foundations for People's Communities and the Imperial State], 1932, quoted in Tsunazawa, p. 71.

rogation record by way of understanding both his personal behavior and his outlook on farmers' joining an attempted coup planned by military men:

Had the young officers who were at the center of the revolutionary activity on May 15 acted independently, without participation by the farmers, their conduct would have been misunderstood as intended to bring about government by military dictatorship. . . . In particular, I read Kita Ikki's *Nihon kaizō hōan taikō* [Outline Plan for the Reconstruction of Japan], which had been given me around March 1931 by Furuuchi Eiji. A military dictatorship was the gist of this book. I came to understand how the most ardent young army officers, in accordance with the concepts of fatherland, fellow countrymen, and national essence set forth in this book, were planning for national reform by extraordinary means. I had to pay special attention to this situation. I thought that if it [the book] caused the sincere young officers to plot a revolution based on a military dictatorship that lost objective recognition of the conditions of society, they would not only be misleading themselves but also seriously threaten the plans laid by the state for the past hundred years. In the end I too threw myself into the midst of this movement and acted in unison with it. Because it was necessary to give it proper guidance, I ended up participating in the right-wing revolutionary movement.[29]

These words contain an air of feigned contrition, as though written by a man determined to intellectualize actions which were prompted by strongly felt emotions. One might question the sincerity of his sudden concern for state policies which the Aikyōkai had long resisted. Nevertheless it may well be true that Kita's ideas appealed strongly

[29] Tachibana Kōzaburō, "Jinmon chōsho" [Interrogation Record], 1932, *Gendaishi shiryō* [Materials on Modern History], ed. Imai Seiichi and Takahashi Masae (Tokyo: Misuzu Shobō, 1963), IV, 112-113.

to the military component of the May 15 conspiracy and that Tachibana chose direct action less out of frustration or friendship than because he was resolved to head off a potentially undesirable turn—the subversion of farm reform objectives—in what might have become a Japanese revolution.

The revolution, of course, never occurred, and at age thirty-nine Tachibana's career as an activist came to an abrupt end. He fled to Manchuria and wrote in outline form the book which best summarized his farm thought, *Kōdō kokka nōhon kenkokuron* (Theory of Building an Imperial State on Agriculture), published by Kensetsusha in 1935. He either surrendered to or was seized by the Kenpeitai (Japanese secret police) in Harbin on July 24, 1932,[30] and was returned to Tokyo to be tried along with the other leaders of the May 15 incident.

"I was told," Tachibana recalled, "that Gondō said, 'if Tachibana follows in Inoue's footsteps, he'll be executed.' Naturally when I heard the word 'executed,' I trembled. I was determined to be anything but a coward, yet when I was thrown in prison, I was suddenly seized with the fear of death."[31] When his trial finally began on September 26, 1933, Tachibana scarcely revealed his fears. He was permitted to make an opening address, taking up nearly three weeks of the trial, in which he attacked the luxury of city life and the misery of the farm villages.[32] He used this sensational trial to

[30] Tachibana claimed that he fled to Harbin not to escape prosecution but to have time to write down the ideas which prompted his actions. Once the manuscript was finished, he said, he voluntarily surrendered. Tachibana and Takeuchi, p. 20. See also *Chōkokkashugi*, p. 417; Matsuzawa, "Shōwa ishin," p. 43; Rōyama Masamichi, *Nihon ni okeru kindai seijigaku no hattatsu* [The Development of Modern Political Science in Japan] (Tokyo: Jitsugyō no Nihonsha, 1949), p. 302.

[31] Tachibana and Takeuchi, p. 20.

[32] For an interesting account of the trial, see A. Morgan Young, *Imperial Japan 1926-1938* (London: George Allen and Unwin, 1938), pp. 190-198.

246

justify the May 15 affair and undeniably aroused great public support for the defendants. As one observer puts it, the remarkable deference paid Tachibana by the court showed "a good deal of toleration if not acceptance of right-wing philosophies by society in general."[33] The proceedings dragged on until February 3, 1934, when Tachibana was convicted and sentenced to an indefinite prison term. He was freed, together with Inoue (who had escaped the fate predicted by Gondō), as a part of a general amnesty in November 1940.

The second half of Tachibana's long life has been mainly devoted to studies of early Japanese history, particularly the emperor system. After World War II he resumed teaching in Mito and published several volumes on the history of the imperial family. In 1960 he described the postwar land reform instituted by the U.S. occupation as "splendid" but said that it was "a disgrace that we did not do it ourselves but had to have others do it for us."[34] In early 1965, according to a former American foreign service officer, Tachibana sent an emissary to the U.S. embassy in Tokyo at the time of increased American military intervention in Vietnam to suggest rural reconstruction programs and village communalism as solutions for the political turmoil in Southeast Asia. Today he leads a quiet life in Ibaraki, continuing to write about early Japanese emperors and ancient rural society.

Land and Community in Tachibana's Thought

Thought and action are so closely joined in the writings of Tachibana Kōzaburō that it would be misleading to regard him as an agrarian theorist in quite the same sense as Gondō or most other Nōhonshugisha. The works he published in the early thirties offered many concrete (although often impractical) plans for action and rather few general

[33] Katherine M. Maxim, "Agrarian Response to Industrialization: Populism and Nohon-shugi," B.A. thesis in history, Connecticut College, 1970, p. 55.
[34] Tachibana and Takeuchi, p. 22.

247

discussions of Japan's dilemma, but his ideas still resembled Gondō's sufficiently to warrant classifying him as a romantic agrarian nationalist. In order to help understand both the basic outlook that underlay Tachibana's patriotic activism and the ground on which he constructed proposals for national reconstruction, it is important first to take up his view of the past and his glorification of land and communalism. The next chapter will then treat his social and political criticism and his program for nationwide reform, based on agriculture as the most desirable form of economic and spiritual activity.

Tachibana's farm thought was most clearly expressed in his first and his last major works dealing with the farm crisis, *Nōsongaku* (Farm Village Studies), published in 1931, and *Kōdō kokka nōhon kenkokuron*, written in exile and published in 1935. His vision of national reconstruction appeared in a lecture series he gave to military officers in January 1932, entitled *Nihon aikoku kakushin hongi* (Basic Principles of Japanese Patriotic Reform), distributed in mimeographed form by his followers on May 20, 1932.[35]

Like both Gondō Seikyō and Kita Ikki, Tachibana consciously accepted an evolutionary view of history, explaining in matter of fact terms the rise of urban civilization based on capitalism.[36] But if the growth of capitalism was unavoidable, he reasoned, so was its displacement by some newer form of social organization. "When a civilization reaches its historical maturity, bequeaths its crystallized culture, and disappears into the past," he wrote, "history necessarily undergoes a great transformation."[37] A new

[35] Tachibana Kōzaburō, *Nōsongaku* [Farm Village Studies] (Tokyo: Kensetsusha, 1931). Subsequent references denote the 2nd ed., dated 1933. Tachibana Kōzaburō, *Nihon aikoku kakushin hongi* [Basic Principles of Japanese Patriotic Reform], mimeographed, 1932, in *Chōkokkashugi*, pp. 213-238. This work comprises lectures Tachibana gave in January 1932 to young officers at a naval air station at Tsuchiura, in southern Ibaraki Prefecture.

[36] *Kōdō kokka nōhon kenkokuron*, p. 184.

[37] Ibid., p. 185.

civilization appears, but it selects certain traditions from previous ones as it constitutes itself. Since Japan in the 1930s was confronting the final crisis of capitalism, Tachibana argued, it was imperative to build anew by drawing upon the best features of her past: "We must sweep clean the dominance of modern Western materialistic civilization and return to the surviving essence of the founding of the country."[38] That essence, he concluded, was to be found only among the cultivators: "Ever since the beginning of the historical period the farmers have been destined to an essential historical position in the organization of society. Without them there is nothing."[39]

Just as Gondō Seikyō emphasized the indestructibility of self-rule and society (shashoku) amid unceasing historical change, Tachibana believed that land and community were permanent ingredients of Japanese civilization. Land, or tsuchi, he regarded as "the origin and foundation of all human existence . . . at this great turning point in human history, the path to rescuing and liberating human society lies in returning to the unique origin and foundation of human existence which has long been discarded: the land."[40] By land Tachibana did not mean agriculture in a technological or economic sense so much as a romantic, pastoral view of farming as the basis of human society. Like Gondō, he believed that "if you ruin the land, you ruin everything."[41] Tachibana explained that "what is meant by the doctrine of the land, or Nōhonshugi, is basically the life of the people who hold land. The reason we call this Nōhonshugi is that people, in order to perpetuate their social livelihood, must construct their communal social system with the land as the foundation. If you become separated from the land, you'll have no foundation for prolonging people's

[38] Ibid., p. 187.   [39] Nōsongaku, pp. 297-298.
[40] Kōdō kokka nōhon kenkokuron, p. 35.
[41] Ibid., p. 203. For Gondō's views on the inviolability of the land, see Jichi minseiri [Principles of People's Self-Rule], 1936, in Chō-kokkashugi, p. 248.

social livelihood. Therefore we can say that agriculture is the foundation."[42] These doctrines were quite consistent with Tachibana's objectives at Kyōdai Mura and, later, in the Aikyōkai, and they indicate a remarkable overlap between action and conviction when contrasted with most other Japanese social theorists at the time.

What were the benefits of rebuilding Japanese society on the land? Tachibana listed the public virtues it engendered—qualities that would blunt the impact of Western materialism, individualism, selfishness, liberty, and the "burgher spirit."[43] Rural Japan was characterized by mutual love, cooperation, and hard work, each of which derived from living close to the land. Tachibana made it plain that he did not wish to denounce the cities "theoretically or to ignore mechanized industry,"[44] so long as the entire society, both urban and rural, rededicated itself to these good values stemming from farming:

Thus we must first return to our true human character and divine nature. The only path of rescue we should discuss is mutual love and cooperation. That is, the sole foundation which should be cultivated is agriculture. Japan's destiny is the capacity for united action of the Japanese race that is unparalleled in the world. This is precisely the path to Japan's rebirth, and this is precisely our allotted destiny in world history. In short, the path is at hand. First we must mark out a spiritual transformation and return to our true nature. We must conquer the spirit of modern Western materialistic civilization and return to the East Asian spirit. This is the spirit of mutual love and cooperation which I have advocated. Now although Westerners speak of the same cooperation, they advocate it within the spirit of materialism, and we must say that

---

[42] Kōdō kokka nōhon kenkokuron, p. 202. See also p. 197. Tachibana believed that Mussolini's policy of rebuilding the farm villages was his greatest accomplishment. See Kinoshita, p. 33.
[43] Kōdō kokka nōhon kenkokuron, pp. 192-193.
[44] Ibid., p. 202.

they mean something entirely different in nature from true cooperation. . . . What I mean here is not a matter of form but of spiritual essence. Thus the spirit of mutual love and cooperation of which I am speaking seeks to fulfill men's lot in life and achieve their true nature: the life of hard work.[45]

Another reason for reviving rural communalism was that it was an essential protection for the state. By upholding the family system, Tachibana wrote, men could build solid villages that would buttress the emperor's realm: "The village community is based on the family structure, and the state is based on both. As far as the state is concerned, nothing will suffice to protect the people's true mutual livelihood except village communalism and the family system. In other words, this is our imperial state."[46] Land and *kyōdōtai* likewise were the main pillars of Japanese nationality consciousness, Tachibana believed, and only by returning to them "will it be possible for the first time truly to have the spirit of patriotism and brotherhood."[47] He thought that the power of the land gave the Japanese their "unique capacity for united action"[48] that was vital for building patriotism.

Tachibana's communalism, cast in the *kyōdoshugi* tradition typical of early twentieth-century agrarianism, securely fastened Japanese awareness of nationality to the earth: "The place where the blessings of the land and nature are, the place which permits people's mutual spiritual union, is the home village. That which protects the home village is none other than the state, which is built on the land. Therefore, if you love the land, you love the country. . . . isn't the spirit of patriotism protected and nourished by farmers?"[49] This spirit of patriotism was an integral part of Tachibana's vague but impassioned understanding of the national essence, or *kokutai*:

45 Ibid., p. 208.
47 Ibid., p. 204.
49 Ibid., p. 261.

46 Ibid., pp. 196-197.
48 Ibid., p. 217.

Without the land, there are no people in Japan; without the people, there is no national society; without national society, there is no humanity. For this reason, he who does not love the country is not human.

Japan has a cohesion unparalleled in the rest of the world, centering on the majestic, eternal imperial line. Japan cannot be found wanting because of the patriotism and brotherhood of our fellow countrymen. Indeed, Japan exists because of patriotism and brotherhood, and patriotism and brotherhood exist because of the national essence.[50]

Patriotism and brotherhood were strongest in rural Japan, and for this reason the farms were the most crucial supports for the national essence.

By emphasizing the village origins of Japanese nationality sentiments, Tachibana joined Gondō and many other contemporary nationalists in affirming primary loyalties to his fellow countrymen, with village society the locus of their common feelings. Although he never attacked the statism of the existing government so directly as Gondō, Tachibana linked affection for the state with its role as protector of the village and reminded his audience that the state was built upon the soil. His concept of state and nation, although less forcefully put than Gondō's, left no doubt that Tachibana made the Japanese people, not the state that ruled them, the principal object of his agrarian nationalism.

After the inevitable collapse of capitalist society, Tachibana thought, Japan must build anew on the long-standing tradition of rural communalism. To do so would not only bring happiness because it was consistent with Japan's customs but also draw out those desirable virtues of mutual love, cooperation, and hard work which he had practiced at Kyōdai Mura. Moreover, the land and *kyōdōtai* would help to protect the imperial state and, most importantly, build the

[50] *Nihon aikoku kakushin hongi*, p. 213.

patriotism and sense of brotherhood that were central to the national essence. Tachibana utilized these beliefs in the early 1930s to scan contemporary society for the major roadblocks to farm communalism and also to propose concrete programs to achieve a true "patriotic reform."

Chapter XI

Tachibana Kōzaburō's Patriotic Reform

ALTHOUGH happiness is a frame of mind and emotion that is difficult to measure, few of Japan's thirty million rural residents thought the countryside was a very pleasant place to live during the depression. Historically, to be sure, Japanese farmers have taken a generally optimistic view of their livelihood, in line with the benevolent natural philosophy that for many centuries has stressed divine favor and agricultural bounty. This was not true of Japanese cultivators during the period between the world wars, however, partly for reasons such as high taxes and low rice prices, but primarily because of new anxieties which nearly all farmers sensed but few understood.

Bad times in themselves were nothing new to the peasants, even though the period from the early 1890s to 1920 had been quite prosperous overall. Indeed, even the worst depression years after World War I were probably less severe for farmers than had been the case for their ancestors during long stretches of the Tokugawa period. What was new, and only dimly understood, was the constellation of modern institutions and ideas which now dominated life in Japan. Almost all village residents were genuinely perplexed by the unseen forces which had cast them into such poverty.

Of the many agrarianists who decried the depression, Tachibana Kōzaburō most forcefully gave expression to the worries that numbed so many farmers during the twenties and early thirties. While Okada On attacked governmental relief measures on economic grounds and Gondō Seikyō developed an elaborate theory of opposition to the establishment, Tachibana voiced some of the deeply felt emotions of the countryside. He was a man of wide learning and great intelligence, and he was also a practicing farmer who understood village moods more fully than most other Nōhonshugisha. At the same time Tachibana transcended purely local concerns to focus his thought on the Japanese nation as a whole. To realize this nationalism meant restructuring Japan's city-based economic and political systems and instituting a program of patriotic reform.

Attack on Capitalism and Cities

"The time has come," Tachibana asserted in 1932, "to urge the defeat of the materialistic civilization of modern capitalism."[1] Patriotic reform meant "a destiny which instructs us that our duty, ordained by the decree of world history, is to sweep the earth clean of capitalist domination."[2] What was so odious about this form of economic organization to Tachibana was its oppression of the poor, especially farmers, and its damaging effects on rural society.

Tachibana believed that capitalism was responsible for upsetting the ancient harmony between city and country in Japan, just as three centuries earlier it had ruined the English countryside, turning Britain into a net importer of foodstuffs.[3] The advent of European capitalism in the nineteenth century profoundly disturbed farming throughout Asia, he noted, and even Japan succumbed to the power of money in

[1] Tachibana Kōzaburō, *Nihon aikoku kakushin hongi* [Basic Principles of Japanese Patriotic Reform], mimeographed, 1932, in *Chōkokkashugi* [Ultranationalism], ed. Hashikawa Bunzō, *Gendai Nihon shisōshi taikei* [Collection on Modern Japanese Thought] (Tokyo: Chikuma Shobō, 1964), xxxi, 222.

[2] Ibid., p. 228.

[3] Tachibana Kōzaburō, *Tsuchi no Nihon* [A Japan Based on Land] (Tokyo: Kensetsusha, 1934), pp. 37-39.

the Meiji restoration: "After leadership by financial power replaced military power, it caused the ripening of the national state based on the modern townsman. Up to now mankind has long defied, or at least turned its back on, the earth. At its most extreme, this completes the process whereby capitalism thoroughly crushes agriculture and ruins the farm villages."[4]

Two malevolent effects of capitalism, Tachibana claimed, were the rise of cities and the corrupting power of money. In the past, he observed, city and country had been interdependent, but now urban areas were swallowing up the countryside:

I am not speaking just about Tokyo, Japan. London and New York are naturally included too. The great cities of the world did not sprout from the land. These world cities exist for themselves. They know nothing about the nation's land. They know nothing about the farm villages. And it is not just that they know nothing. Today they have come to swell up fat by regarding the national land and farm villages as sacrifices on behalf of their own existence. Any mutually developing organic relations between cities and villages are entirely absent. Finally by today the world's great cities have turned into parasites which will not stop until they destroy the farm villages of the world. They are causing the ruin of the national land system that is a basic requirement for the existence of national society. They are trying to bury national society itself.[5]

Big city capitalism had also led to an unconscionable preoccupation with money, Tachibana continued, to the point where greed had supplanted other values:

[4] Tachibana Kōzaburō, *Nōsongaku* [Farm Village Studies], 2nd ed. (Tokyo: Kensetsusha, 1933), p. 169. The 1st ed., almost identical with the 2nd, was published in 1931.

[5] Tachibana Kōzaburō, *Kōdō kokka nōhon kenkokuron* [Theory of Building an Imperial State on Agriculture] (Tokyo: Kensetsusha, 1935), p. 9.

Needless to say, when you have money you can buy and sell things more easily than anyone else. This buying and selling does not stop with trade, of course. They sell off absolutely everything they can, and everyone expends all his might doing this. Stock certificates and commercial goods may of course be properly sold with the objective of making money. But before our very eyes people are selling their positions, their dignity, and their integrity with equanimity. Indeed, they are even selling their colleagues and their families. Finally they even sell the nation. . . . The shame and misery of domestic conditions is unbelievable. Everything is monopolized by the power of wealth. We allow ourselves to overlook the present situation in which the depravity of our leaders has reached its apex and thousands of people are allowed to wither away.[6]

Capitalism was thus responsible for the selfish values it inculcated, the damage it caused rural society, and the urban habit of greed which menaced the very essence of the nation. Whereas Gondō denounced capitalism primarily for its adverse political effects on self-rule, Tachibana was chiefly concerned with the social and ideological damage to rural communalism and Japanese patriotism. Only if the land, the *kyōdōtai*, patriotism, and the spirit of brotherhood were not compromised, he believed, was it possible to tolerate capitalism in Japan.

The Dangers of Authoritarianism

Like many social critics, Tachibana assumed correctly but unanalytically that an interlocking establishment of political,

[6] *Nihon aikoku kakushin hongi*, p. 217. See Tsunazawa Mitsuaki, "Tachibana Kōzaburō shiron" [Sketch of Tachibana Kōzaburō], *Shisō no kagaku* [Science of Thought], No. 142, October 1970, p. 72; Okutani Matsuji, "Nihon ni okeru nōhonshugi shisō no nagare" [Trends in Agrarian Thought in Japan], *Shisō* [Thought], No. 407, May 1958, p. 12; Matsuzawa Tetsunari, " 'Shōwa ishin' no shisō to kōdō—Tachibana Kōzaburō no baai" [Thought and Behavior in the "Shōwa Restoration"—The Case of Tachibana Kōzaburō], *Shakai kagaku kenkyū* [Social Science Studies], XIX, 3, January 1968, 65.

military, big business, and government bureaucracy leaders held most of the power in Japan between the wars. But while Gondō identified the growth of a centralized bureaucratic state as the root of the problem, Tachibana attributed the rise of a privileged class mainly to the power of money. For one thing, he believed that the Meiji restoration represented the victory of financial strength over military prestige. For another, he argued that capitalism had ruined politics at all levels: "The world of national politics is being poisoned by mammon and the gang of corrupt industrialists who sit in the top seats. The corrosion of local politics by dissolute landlords and the sons of liquor dealers must not be overlooked. . . . it is entirely regrettable that a country's budget must be discussed behind fixed bayonets. . . ."[7] Capitalism, he believed, had produced such discord that the Diet could no longer meet without police protection.

To resist the authoritarian clique was difficult, Tachibana realized, but it was vital if people wanted to avoid being exploited. "Because of leadership based on the financial power of the bureaucracy, *zaibatsu*, and political parties," he maintained, "we have arrived at the worst possible leadership situation, in which men are simply being used."[8] Not even rural residents were immune from the trend toward elitism, he thought. Like every respectable Nōhonshugisha, Tachibana vilified absentee landlords for leaving the soil to join the urban monied classes,[9] often shamelessly taking advantage of their tenants back on the farm. Whether absentee or not, he wrote,

The money which lines landlords' pockets is eventually used to send the landlords' children to the great city universities. Naturally this is a very good use for it. But what effect will persons of profound knowledge and high

[7] *Kōdō kokka nōhon kenkokuron*, quoted in Kinoshita Hanji, *Nihon no uyoku* [The Japanese Right Wing] (Tokyo: Kaname Shobō, 1953), p. 35.

[8] *Nihon aikoku kakushin hongi*, p. 230.

[9] See, e.g., *Kōdō kokka nōhon kenkokuron*, pp. 257-258.

accomplishment have upon the villages? Moreover, another way it is used is for banking. For example, the money that ends up in village landlords' purses is converted into loans to tenants, and couldn't you say that this begets profits while the tenants become more impoverished?[10]

This was Tachibana's only important statement on the tenancy question. Like most other agrarianists, he considered absentee landlords a part of the urban establishment and regarded the city-village chasm as the basic social division in the country.

By minimizing rural frictions and positing a harmonious, united nation of common people (mainly farmers) as his goal, Tachibana reduced the leadership question to a simple case of right versus wrong: "Food, clothing, and shelter are the bases of human life. Somehow out of this people become saints or sinners. The privileged classes, party politicians, *zaibatsu*, and all who belong to the leadership stratum continually dare to act traitorously, and when they end up ruling a country, why should the laboring masses, who have become their doormats under their command, think of the country which they rule as their own country?"[11] By calling the establishment "traitorous," he tipped his hand on the central issue of what constituted Japanese nationalism. Its essence was not loyalty to the state, since the elite had certainly not been behaving traitorously toward the state which it controlled. Instead, by exploiting the public the privileged class was being disloyal to the people as a whole— for Tachibana the true basis of nationality sentiments.

Neither Tachibana's appraisal of capitalism nor his critique of contemporary politics was as carefully constructed as Gondō's. Instead he was satisfied to express his contempt for both, based on strong emotions as well as logic. Gondō took great pains to show what was wrong with Japan; Tachibana

10 *Nōsongaku*, p. 218.
11 *Nihon aikoku kakushin hongi*, p. 218.

somewhat impatiently affirmed that things were wrong and moved on to suggest remedies that were much more detailed, if hardly more practical, than Gondō's vague call for returning to a self-ruling *shashoku*.

Tachibana's Program for Economic Change

Since patriotic reform meant "sweeping the earth clean of capitalist domination"[12] and establishing the spirit of patriotic brotherhood (*aikoku dōhōshugi*), Tachibana made it plain that the most important areas for change were "land and money. I think it is safe to say that the question of what to do about these two things will be at the center of the economic system of the new society."[13] His objective, he said, was to build an economy which was man centered, not product centered as under capitalism (or Marxism, he added). It was the *kyōdōtai* alone, he decided, that was based on "the way of man" (*jindō*),[14] and it should form the foundation of the new production system: "The ancient East Asian land system provides the best precedent" for land policy.[15]

Although he once suggested a state land reform program,[16] Tachibana apparently believed that the main point was simply "to fix things so that monopolistic land relations will not be permitted." On the whole he thought that the state was too cumbersome to deal effectively with land reform. He advocated a progressive tax on landlords specifically modeled after the single tax first proposed in 1879 by Henry George in *Progress and Poverty*. "The way to acquire the maximum wealth," he concluded, "is to put farmland under the direct control of the village *kyōdōtai* and city land under the urban *kyōdōtai*."[17] There is understand-

---

[12] Ibid., p. 228. [13] Ibid., p. 233.

[14] *Kōdō kokka nōhon kenkokuron*, p. 239.

[15] *Nihon aikoku kakushin hongi*, p. 234.

[16] Ibid., p. 226. On Tachibana's land program, see Kenneth W. Colegrove, *Militarism in Japan* (Boston: World Peace Foundation, 1936), p. 37; Matsuzawa, "Shōwa ishin," pp. 83–84.

[17] *Kōdō kokka nōhon kenkokuron*, p. 257.

ably no reason to believe that any of Tachibana's proposals received a sympathetic hearing within the government, although measures accomplishing the same general aims were eventually enacted under the press of wartime preparedness after 1937. But it is worth noting that, in common with nearly all agrarianists, Tachibana never challenged the institution of private property, only its monopolization by an urban elite.

To fight monopoly, Tachibana asked for emergency debt and price stabilization[18]—measures supported by almost all agrarianists as well as tenant movement leaders. He favored laws "to ban the monopolization, and investment for private profit, of the resources, means of production, and financial institutions that are vital for the public. . . ."[19] On the crucial question of the money system, which Tachibana ranked with land as a pressing economic problem, he contended that "the method for fundamentally reforming it is of course for rural and urban communities to organize financial institutions on their own and for the single national people's community to create central regulatory institutions based upon them."[20] Likewise, he maintained, credit, production, and consumption should be regulated as much as possible by cooperative societies within each village or city.[21]

Even more erratic than these random suggestions was Tachibana's view of the objectives of economic reform. His goals, he said,

> are the protection, development, and prosperity of the people's cooperative self-rule system, which continues to exist because of the spirit of patriotism and brotherhood. I need hardly say that the entire economic system must be organized and regulated by the national society. From the point of view of individual livelihood, this means a complete welfare economic system. Thus each individual,

[18] *Nihon aikoku kakushin hongi*, p. 227.
[19] Ibid., p. 233.
[20] *Kōdō kokka nōhon kenkokuron*, p. 258.
[21] Ibid., pp. 247-248.

by pursuing his own vocation on behalf of society, is able to maintain himself, protect his family, and fulfill the meaning of human life. On the other hand, both society and the individual cause the economic system to develop, and at the same time it means that the economy must be planned so that it will develop its own functions organizationally. According to this principle, the economy must be planned socially, and at the same time all necessary means must be utilized to rescue individual economic livelihood from money making, as well as price oriented economic activity, and to usher in a welfare economic system.[22]

When Tachibana spoke of a "welfare economy," he apparently meant a system with far more local autonomy than the term usually connotes. Only in the case of the munitions industry did he specifically advocate control by the state, probably because arms manufacturing was so closely connected with national defense. Otherwise he wanted priorities to be set and economic progress to be supervised by society, by which he did not mean the public as represented by the state but rather the national aggregate of Japanese people, organized by communities. In this manner alone, he thought, such humane values as cooperation, mutual aid, and brotherhood could be attained. To leave regulation to the state was foolish, because for sixty years the Japanese government had systematically favored monopolists and forfeited all opportunities to achieve a welfare economy[23]—that is, one in which the people's welfare was uppermost.

Although some scholars say that Tachibana took a more conciliatory attitude toward industrialism than did Gondō, the difference is hard to detect. Neither was in any sense a friend of capitalist enterprise. Those who cast Tachibana as the more moderate critic usually cite his concluding remarks

[22] *Nihon aikoku kakushin hongi*, p. 233.
[23] *Kōdō kokka nōhon kenkokuron*, p. 251.

about the economy in the Tsuchiura lecture series: "I am not attempting to defy big industry and commerce. The point is simply that while we control and regulate mechanized heavy industry for the sake of building a new, cooperative, self-ruling Japanese society, based on the principles of welfare economics, we must not make the dangerous mistake of mechanically extending and expanding heavy industry. . . ."[24] In reality these sentiments, coupled with the foregoing economic proposals, amounted to thoroughgoing opposition to every form of capitalism then known in Japan. It seems safer to conclude that neither Gondō nor Tachibana wanted to dissolve big business, but each wanted to place it under an unprecedented degree of local control.

Political Change and the "National People"

Since Tachibana advocated great economic decentralization and even referred approvingly to "the people's cooperative self-rule system," what sort of new political order did he expect would result from his patriotic reform? In general, he believed, cooperation and consensus were the most desirable political values, and self-rule was an important means to achieve them. "A central government which is not based on a consensus of the people," he declared, "will not be able to accomplish the heavy responsibilities of politics."[25] Tachibana thus accepted the time-honored consensual style of Japanese government, with its emphasis on harmony, reconciliation, and conformity once a decision was reached—a motif which persisted in the 1970s.

[24] *Nihon aikoku kakushin hongi*, p. 235. For views stressing Tachibana's moderation on industry and commerce, see Takeuchi Tetsuo, "Nōhonshugi to nōson chūsansō" [Agrarianism and the Farm Village Middle Class], *Shimane nōka daigaku kenkyū hōkoku* [Shimane Agricultural University Research Reports], No. 8, A, March 1960, p. 237; Matsuzawa, "Shōwa ishin," pp. 2-5; Masao Maruyama, *Thought and Behaviour in Modern Japanese Politics*, ed. Ivan Morris (London: Oxford University Press, 1963), p. 43; Tsunazawa, p. 74.

[25] *Nihon aikoku kakushin hongi*, p. 222.

But whereas Gondō made self-rule the main goal of his political hopes, Tachibana was willing to accept parliamentarianism coequally with local autonomy as a means for finding a consensus. He shared both Gondō's theoretical approval of constitutionalism and his dismay at how party politics worked in practice: "Although the skin is beautiful, the rotten fruit inside is exceedingly dreadful food. Interpreting the constitutional, parliamentary form of government is the same."[26] Still, in criticizing the way money power monopolized the Diet, Tachibana claimed that "I am merely trying to reform it,"[27] not renounce parliamentarianism altogether. As a consequence, he concluded,

Our political system, an imperial people's cooperative self-rule system based on patriotism and brotherhood, at the same time as it is organized with the interests of all the people as its main point, must act only with the consensus of the nation as its foundation. Thus the first thing we must do is advance the interests of all the people. We cannot fail to have voting mechanisms for expressing the national consensus. For that reason, of course we must insure that politics will function by having both a stable central government and local organizations. At the same time we must have a parliament as a national decision-making body. Only in this way will we be able to remove the existing leadership and have cooperative self-rule by the people. . . . our future governmental system must be rebuilt from the foundation, based to the utmost on local communal cooperative self-rule. The concentration of political powers as at present, based on supreme centralism, will be fundamentally reformed and will become decentralized.[28]

Once again Tachibana equated the interests of the nation with those of its people, whose consensus was best achieved

[26] Ibid.
[27] *Nihon aikoku kakushin hongi*, p. 222.
[28] Ibid., p. 231.

through both nationwide and local institutions. For Gondō, the most famous advocate of local autonomy, self-rule under a "stable central government" with "a parliament as a national decision-making body" would have been impossible. Tachibana conceived of this elusive ideal in less absolute or atavistic terms than Gondō, placing himself closer to the main stream of agrarianist thought on the self-rule question.

Like most Japanese social critics in the interwar period, Tachibana was very conscious of Marxist thought, and in important respects his criticism of capitalism and centralized power resembled Marxian economic theory. Since Marxism was probably the most influential school of reconstructionist thinking in the 1920s, Tachibana made certain to explain why he believed it was an inadequate guide for the patriotic reform he advocated. For one thing, he contended, the Marxist program of historical development had not "really occurred anywhere" and was only "an insignificant academic theory." For another, an industrial proletarian revolution was irrelevant in Asia, where the masses who needed liberation were peasants. Moreover, Tachibana claimed, the Marxist emphasis on dialectical interaction between two classes, the exploiters and the exploited, was a great oversimplification of how reform really took place.[29] In Russia, he said, Marxism had led to emulation of industrialism and bureaucratism, the very evils which he hoped to minimize in Japan. This had been accomplished "by sacrificing the farmers, who constitute 85 percent of her population, in order to develop American-style heavy industry."[30]

Although he thought Marxism was the most worthless ideological option open to Japan, Tachibana was hardly less critical of fascism. After blasting the Russian secret police system, he observed that both communism and fascism "coerced the people severely under autocratic control."[31] As bad as Japanese party politics had become in the early thirties, he warned, "it is totally impermissible to replace this

[29] Ibid., pp. 223-224.   [30] Ibid., p. 234.
[31] Kōdō kokka nōhon kenkokuron, p. 259.

with fascism or the dictatorship of the proletariat."[32] A fundamental conflict existed, he believed, between either of these foreign doctrines and the needs of Japan:

In particular Japan is always Japan and is neither England nor Russia nor Germany. Of course Marx did not understand Japan at all; we did not take orders from Lenin, nor are we able to imitate Hitler. However much the revolution brokers say did Marx not put it this way, or did the central communist party of the Russian fatherland not issue instructions, or did Hitler not do thus and such, no matter how much they pretend the naive and ignorant masses are fools, I believe that our masses are growing less foolish.[33]

By choosing the good sense of the Japanese farmers over these ideologies from abroad, Tachibana reaffirmed his belief in a characteristic national essence which he thought could be gained only through patriotism and brotherhood within the communal structure of Japanese society.

"Thus we conclude that the political reform of Japan must use agriculture as the foundation for the doctrine of one ruler for all the people."[34] With these words Tachibana assigned the emperor virtually the same place in his ideal cooperative political system that Gondō had granted him in the self-ruling *shashoku*. Very much like Gondō, Tachibana spoke of establishing communalism "with fundamental self-rule at the base. We must build like a pyramid from the bottom up,"[35] placing the emperor at the apex. Apart from this rather conventional formulation, however, Tachibana seems to have been unconcerned with the institutional functions of the throne. Instead he dwelled on the symbolic importance of the emperor as a patron of agriculture, identi-

[32] *Nihon aikoku kakushin hongi*, p. 231.
[33] Ibid., p. 224. See Tsunazawa Mitsuaki, *Nihon no nōhonshugi* [Japanese Agrarianism] (Tokyo: Kinokuniya Shoten, 1971), p. 138.
[34] *Kōdō kokka nōhon kenkokuron*, p. 261.
[35] Ibid., p. 263.

fying the origins of Japanese monarchy in the worship of Shinto deities in connection with rice planting and harvesting.[36] Although he worked out this emphasis much more fully in his postwar works, Tachibana encapsulated the emotional, nonscientific character of his outlook on communalism and imperial politics in this passage from *Kōdō kokka nōhon kenkokuron*:

> The spirit of sovereign rule possessed by the Japanese imperial throne since the beginning has persisted without change. We must say that this is what created the unity of ruler and people and a national essence unparalleled in the world.... To the extent that the sovereignty possessed by the Japanese imperial throne was retained throughout the ages by the emperor himself, a tranquil livelihood was maintained upon the foundation of the village *kyōdōtai*.[37]

Tachibana believed that eventually all citizens—even city dwellers—could become part of a single, countrywide brotherhood under the throne. "The cities must form urban *kyōdōtai*," he insisted, to act in concert with village communities in building a united national people, or *kokumin*: "I use the words 'complete, entire national people' to indicate the harmonious national society that is produced by the combination of rural and urban society. It is necessarily created by the capacity of farmers and city residents to act as a national people."[39] Hence the national people, the citizens of the country, comprised the nation itself, and they alone—not the state—could execute a true patriotic reform.

The Politics of Patriotic Reform

Tachibana Kōzaburō's most flamboyant distinction as a Nōhonshugisha was his fusion of thought and action, especially in the May 15 incident. If his critiques of capitalism

[36] See Tsunazawa's discussion of this point in "Tachibana Kōzaburō shiron," pp. 68-75.
[37] *Kōdō kokka nōhon kenkokuron*, quoted ibid., pp. 74-75.
[38] Ibid., p. 240.   [39] *Nōsongaku*, p. 177.

and authoritarianism were somewhat sketchy, especially by contrast with Gondō's, Tachibana correspondingly offered more suggestions about what should be done and how to do it. His plan for implementing a patriotic reform is interesting not only because it was presented in January 1932 to young officers at Tsuchiura who later joined the May 15 movement but also because he believed that the means for reconstructing society were closely related to its goals. In the same fashion as the ideal samurai of the past, Tachibana thought that both content and process mattered: not just what one did but also how one did it. Patriotism and brotherhood, he believed, should be learned not only from books and lectures but also from the experience of working with others. In this respect, the Kyōdai Mura blend of classwork and labor in the fields reappeared in Tachibana's stress on both the objectives and the tone of carrying out reform. This near-aesthetic preoccupation with style reflected a long tradition of Japanese political conduct which insisted on a purity of motives and a self-conscious rigor of execution.

By way of proper procedure, Tachibana said, it was crucial to emphasize the human values inherent in reform: "Without relying on politicians, bureaucrats, soldiers, educators, farmers, merchants, workers, or artisans, we should fulfill our vocations with our hearts and attain our destiny as people for the sake of Japan."[40] Only these two counted—people and Japan—and everything else that stood in the way must be swept away boldly and decisively. "When we set out to walk the true path of the patriotic reform of Japan," he exhorted the military officers, "we must cut down with a single stroke, in their very shoes, all who betray this path, no matter what important positions they may occupy or how capable they may be."[41] Although all citizens must join the reform, Tachibana observed, they would be led by "a group of loyalists following the divine will." The sincerity

[40] *Kōdō kokka nōhon kenkokuron*, p. 228.
[41] *Nihon aikoku kakushin hongi*, p. 225.

and dedication of these enthusiasts, he believed, were evident in their willingness to die: "A loyalist has only one death to give to this great undertaking . . . crowds, indeed multitudes, will be led by a few loyalists"[42] who act as exemplars of proper conduct.

Boldness, sincerity, action, sacrifice, death—these were the qualities which loyalists had cherished, thanks in part to the Wang Yang-ming tradition in Japanese moral thought, from the Meiji restoration movement of the 1860s to the putative "restoration" of the Shōwa emperor in the 1930s.[43] Although Tachibana rarely if ever referred to either a Shōwa restoration or Wang Yang-ming, his behavior and ideas were very compatible with Wang's doctrine of uniting thought and action.

In a much more clearcut way than Yokoi Tokiyoshi, who had advocated a confused form of Bushido for farmers, Tachibana idealized farmers equally with soldiers as the new bearers of the loyalist tradition:

Accordingly, when we review the current situation, there is no better place to start looking for patriots than in the military system. And no one is better for acting in concert with them than the farmers. Japan has historically been able to be herself only because of the unity of agriculture and the military. In this unprecedented emergency the first things we must have are a sense of patriotism and a spirit of brotherhood. Needless to say it is you soldiers and we farmers who embrace these most strongly. The thing that will extricate Japan from this unprecedented crisis and cause the world revolution to open fire abso-

[42] Ibid., p. 223.
[43] On the Shōwa restoration, see Hashikawa Bunzō, "Shōwa ishin no ronri to shinri" [Logic and Psychology of the Shōwa Restoration], *Kindai Nihon seiji shisōshi* [History of Modern Japanese Political Thought], ed. Hashikawa Bunzō and Matsumoto Sannosuke (Tokyo: Yūhikaku, 1970), II, 209-231; Ben-Ami Shillony, *Revolt in Japan* (Princeton: Princeton University Press, 1973).

lutely must be sought in the union of agriculture and the military which exists in the great patriotic reform movement of the Japanese people.[44]

Hence he affirmed one of Nōhonshugi's most basic beliefs, the compatibility of farming and military service (*heinō itchi*). In a later lecture he added that it was important to remember "that more than 70 percent of the men in the Japanese army are sons of the rural villages" and "that the actual conditions of farm villages always affect the essence of a strong army."[45] Whether or not the percentage Tachibana cited was accurate, his main point was that peasant armies were indomitable, as the recent Kiangsi uprising in China had demonstrated:

When we ask why the present Chinese communist army defeated the Chiang Kai-shek army, you know better than I that the reason is that it is a farmers' army. I believe we must think very carefully about the separate, specialized problem of organizing a large people's army for national strength and defense, forming this large army around the principle of the soldier-farmer in order to serve as a central pillar of world peace.[46]

Tachibana's pretrial statement that he feared a military coup without participation by farmers was not necessarily inconsistent with his enthusiasm for joint action by soldiers and peasants to carry out patriotic reform. Since the reconstructed society he visualized was far more agrarian than militarist, he presumably expected the armed services to play a modest role once it was established. At the same time he doubtless welcomed soldiers in the reform movement for the selfless spirit they ideally embodied, not the institution they represented. Thus he had every reason to be suspicious of a unilateral military putsch, as he recalled in 1964: "Al-

[44] *Nihon aikoku kakushin hongi*, p. 224.
[45] Ibid., p. 237.   [46] Ibid., p. 238.

though revolution could not be avoided, it was not clear how things would end up if there was a military dictatorship."[47] Probably—although this cannot be proved—Tachibana realized the simple truth that without help from soldiers a patriotic reform led by a band of zealous farmers from Ibaraki was doomed to fail.

Once loyalists arose to lead the movement, Tachibana declared, it was imperative to constitute "an emergency government, composed of talented men from every quarter,"[48] to begin making economic and political changes. Beyond this he was deliberately imprecise, leaving to the reformers themselves such questions as the size, functions, and duration of this body. Still it is certainly safe to infer that he favored moving toward more local autonomy by creating village cooperative bodies as quickly as possible.

Since it was Japan's "destiny, ordained by the decree of world history, to sweep the earth clean of capitalist domination," Tachibana maintained that domestic reform must be followed by "defeating modern capitalist Western materialism"[49] in the West itself. Like the French people who overthrew the *ancien régime* and achieved massive national power, he concluded,

> ... we will have the strength to mobilize our peerless army and navy for the world revolution. Can I now say that it is impossible for us to dream of the historic greater Japan, which at one stroke will be able to pulverize American power in the Pacific, sweep away the influence of the Chinese military clique from 400 million Chinese farmers, liberate India from England, make Russia realize her mistakes and force her to carry out a revolution based on the

[47] Tachibana Kōzaburō, 1964, quoted in Matsuzawa, "Shōwa ishin," p. 84.
[48] *Nihon aikoku kakushin hongi*, p. 227.
[49] Ibid., p. 228. On Tachibana's ideas about world revolution, see *Uyoku undō* [The Right-Wing Movement], ed. Keibi Keisatsu Kenkyūkai, rev. ed. (Tokyo: Tachibana Shobō, 1957), p. 74.

85 percent of her population who are farmers, and rouse the Germans?[50]

Empires were once made of dreams like these, even if they required the centralized state and economy that Tachibana feared. No doubt many of those who heard him agreed with his dreams without sharing his fears.

Tachibana and Agrarian Nationalism

Although Tachibana Kōzaburō spoke only for himself and a few spirited followers from Ibaraki, he touched on rural grievances which were widely felt in the 1920s and early 1930s. He made capitalism his principal bête noire without succumbing to a monocausal interpretation of social development. It is just as tempting to fault Tachibana for his sentimentalism and analytical naiveté as it is to dismiss Gondō Seikyō's outlook as hopelessly unrealistic. In a complementary fashion, nevertheless, the two of them verbalized a great deal of the anxiety and frustration of village Japan during the depression.

To speak of Tachibana simply as a right winger[51] obscures the fact that his mixture of anachronistic village communalism and progressive opposition to capitalism sliced to the root of Japan's prewar crisis. His program of action, elliptical as it may have been, was rare for a social critic in modern Japan, but it should not be mistaken as mere pandering to an audience of enthusiastic, violent young officers. Theory and practice were inseparable for Tachibana, making it somewhat easier to understand why he moved successively from utopian farming to organizing cooperatives, starting a school, forming political groups, and finally indulging in terror.[52]

At the same time Tachibana was a steadfast agrarianist in his opposition to social revolution. He wanted to restore, not erode, the village hierarchy and upheld both private

[50] *Nihon aikoku kakushin hongi*, p. 229.
[51] E.g., *Uyoku undō*, p. 65.
[52] See Matsuzawa's comments on this point in "Shōwa ishin," p. 83.

property in general and land ownership in particular. His ideal political, social, and economic order was less consciously reactionary, and probably correspondingly more utopian, than that of Gondō. His notions of land and community hovered ambivalently between history and illusion, drawing on vague references to early Japanese customs and hazy descriptions of a future world of mutual aid and brotherhood.

Despite the remarkable similarity between Gondō's and Tachibana's outlooks, neither directly influenced the other's thinking. Gondō wrote *Jichi minpan*, the basis of all his future works, at least four years before Tachibana's first book appeared and thus could not have known much, if anything, about his views. Tachibana, on the other hand, met Gondō for the first time shortly before the Ketsumeidan incident of February 1932 but "never had read any of his writings"[53] before the May 15 uprising. By this time, of course, Tachibana's own farm thought was fully developed. Tachibana later expressed great respect for Gondō's learning but deplored his reluctance to act upon his beliefs.[54] Although they differed in age, temperament, and emphasis,

[53] Tachibana Kōzaburō, 1969, quoted in Murakami Ichirō, "Tachibana Kōzaburōshi tokubetsu intabyū—kokka kenryoku to minshū" [Special Interview with Mr. Tachibana Kōzaburō—State Power and the People], *Shihaisha to sono kage* [Leaders and Their Influence], ed. Tanigawa Ken'ichi et al. (Tokyo: Gakugei Shorin, 1969), p. 15.

[54] On July 15, 1964, Tachibana said that "Gondō was quite a scholar for those times. He had much more knowledge of Chinese learning than I. This was because all I knew about was Western learning." Quoted in Matsuzawa Tetsunari, *Tachibana Kōzaburō* (Tokyo: San'-ichi Shobō, 1972), p. 150. In 1960 Tachibana expressed great respect for Gondō but continued: "But he is said to have exclaimed, 'What kind of strange thing is Tachibana doing? What about these pistols he is brandishing?'" Tachibana thought Gondō was an admirable social analyst but noted that "although the things he said were very remarkable, he did no preparatory work himself" to correct the situation. Quoted in Tachibana Kōzaburō and Takeuchi Yoshi, "Aru nōhonshugisha no kaisō to iken" [Recollections and Opinions of a Certain Agrarianist], *Shisō no kagaku*, No. 18, June 1960, p. 19.

273

both men shared the Nōhonshugi concern for the farm village in an age of industrialization together with a strong consciousness of nationality that made agriculture the common denominator of the Japanese as a people.

In Tachibana's case this awareness of nation was grounded on romantic perceptions reaching far beyond logical analysis to glorify a pure earth and *kyōdōtai*, much as literary romanticism tried to return to a pure literature.[55] This same alternation of reason and passion affected his attitude toward European civilization and world history. On the whole he did not wish to destroy the West but merely reform it by purging capitalism, but he also spoke of "pulverizing American power in the Pacific" and carrying out a worldwide farm revolution. By this twisted reasoning, Japan would become "the central pillar of world peace," presumably on terms she alone defined. In any event, Tachibana probably seemed too irrational to inspire, let alone organize, anyone except that small band which responded in May 1932 to words like these:

Japan's crisis must truly be called unprecedented. What is going to relieve it?

Only decisive, patriotic reform.

The only worthwhile thing in life is to use one's life. Japan's patriotic reformers will play a leading part by dying, and only by dying, on behalf of the great principles of patriotic reform. . . .

Aren't we Japanese all brothers? Isn't it precisely because we're all brothers that we've been able to exist? So let's continue to live. We must restore everything to the right path. The time has finally come when we Japanese fellow countrymen must stand up as brothers and embrace Japan.[56]

[55] Tsunazawa, "Tachibana Kōzaburō shiron," p. 74. See Hashikawa Bunzō, *Nihon rōmanha hihan josetsu* [Introductory Criticism of Japanese Romanticists], expanded ed. (Tokyo: Miraisha, 1965).
[56] *Nihon aikoku kakushin hongi*, pp. 213-214.

Chapter XII

Katō Kanji and Agricultural Expansionism

IT IS axiomatic that domestic factors are normally just as decisive as international considerations in determining a country's foreign policy. Despite the political tumult and economic uncertainty of the interwar period, Japanese diplomacy during the 1920s and 1930s leaned heavily on a policy of expansion—first by peaceful means, later by armed aggression against China and other nations.[1] Since it was proportionately still a highly productive sector as well as the largest source of employment, agriculture was naturally an important force affecting Japan's external relations. In the twenties its influence was mainly negative, since most cultivators opposed the low farm tariffs which accompanied the government's internationalist trade policies. Farmers were especially bitter about rice imports from Japan's overseas colonies because they lowered market prices for rice grown at home. Hence from an economic point of view it is understandable that there was scant enthusiasm among rural residents for overseas expansion throughout the 1920s.

As the depression wore on, however, a persuasive counter-

[1] Akira Iriye, "The Failure of Military Expansion," *Dilemmas of Growth in Prewar Japan*, ed. James W. Morley (Princeton: Princeton University Press, 1971), pp. 107-109. For a different appraisal of the period, see Nobuya Bamba, *Japanese Diplomacy in a Dilemma* (Kyoto: Minerva Press, Ltd., 1972).

argument took root in the countryside—the *Lebensraum* doctrine of emigration by Japanese farmers to relieve population pressure on the land. For reasons contrary to those of American growers in the 1890s, who supported foreign expansion to gain markets for their excess output,[2] many Japanese villagers ended up endorsing colonization because it might provide a means for exporting the surplus rural labor that clogged the countryside. Few adherents of this dogma tarried for long over the antecedent question of whether the country was truly overpopulated and, if so, judged by what standard. They simply assumed it was and accordingly favored emigration. Unlike the American farmers who accepted military cooperation in their search for markets (e.g., the Spanish-American War), rural expansionists in Japan had little direct connection with the armed forces, and neither the Manchurian incident of 1931 nor aggression in northern China six years later was motivated by agrarian desires for rural colonies on the continent.

Overseas expansion, usually based on the *Lebensraum* rationale, had been a persistent subtheme in Nōhonshugi discourse since the 1890s. In 1894 Enomoto Takeaki (1836-1908), the minister of agriculture and commerce, vigorously promoted the idea of sending Japanese farmers abroad to relieve the land problem.[3] In a similar vein, leaders of the late Meiji Hōtoku movement endorsed developing new areas overseas as one way of improving the land to labor ratio in Japan proper.[4] Gondō Seikyō, long a partisan of farm ex-

[2] See William A. Williams, *The Roots of the Modern American Empire* (New York: Random House, 1969). In his introduction to *Dilemmas of Growth in Prewar Japan*, p. 19, Morley sets forth the Kōzaha Marxist interpretation that Japan was driven to imperialism by rich landlords and manufacturers seeking markets.

[3] Enomoto Takeaki, 1894 speech to the Dai Nihon Nōkai, quoted in Sakurai Takeo, *Nihon nōgyō no saihensei* [The Reorganization of Japanese Agriculture] (Tokyo: Chūō Kōronsha, 1940), p. 28.

[4] Sasaki Ryūji, "Hōtokusha undō no kairyūteki seikaku" [Class Character of the Hōtokusha Movement], *Shizuoka Daigaku Jinbun-*

pansion in Korea, attacked the government's current colonial policies in 1927 because they were "being planned by capitalists" and called instead for development programs that would promote the ideal of self-rule.[5] Tachibana Kōzaburō also opposed the way Japanese expansion in Manchuria was being carried out and suggested that cooperative associations form the basis for colonial policy.[6] Although hopes for cheap land motivated most persons who were interested in colonial settlement in the 1930s, Japanese agrarianists found political, moral, and social reasons for endorsing foreign expansion by farmers. Still nearly all important Nōhonshugisha believed that, however evil the market and ideological forces from abroad, the rural crisis must be solved primarily at home.

The first major agrarianist who made overseas colonization the core of his proposals for rescuing Japanese agriculture was Katō Kanji (1884-1965), a writer and farm educator who became a leading advocate of emigration in the 1930s. After three decades of combat with official farm policies, popular Nōhonshugi reached its climactic phase in Katō's militant expansionism, joining with bureaucratic agrarianism in support of his Manchurian settlement schemes. Katō used his farm-centered doctrines to support the overall imperial foreign policy, even though he did not welcome the principal means employed during the 1930s to carry it out—military adventurism.

Kato was much more than a simple rural colonialist. His intellectual development included successive experiences with Christianity, socialism, Shinto, and (after 1945) democracy, but from 1913 onward his thought was consistently

---

gakubu hōkoku [Bulletin of the Faculty of Humanities of Shizuoka University], XVII, 4, 1970, 55.

[5] Gondō Seikyō, *Jichi minpan* [People's Guide to Self-Rule, 2nd ed. (Tokyo: Heibonsha, 1932), p. 547. (First published in 1927.)

[6] Tachibana Kōzaburō and Takeuchi Yoshi, "Aru nōhonshugisha no kaisō to iken" [Recollections and Opinions of a Certain Agrarianist], *Shisō no kagaku* [Science of Thought], No. 18, June 1960, p. 21.

based on an intuitive faith in the soul of the Japanese farmer, which he equated with the spirit of Japan. He was neither a landlord nor a spokesman for landlords as a group, and indeed his thinking often seems to have been shaped less by objective analysis of his milieu than by inner inspiration. Katō's ideas deserve examination because they reemphasized Shinto's ties with modern day farming and because they represent the closest approach agrarianism ever made to supporting Japan's drive for overseas empire in Asia.

Katō as a Farm Educator

Katō Kanji bears out the familiar dictum that city people are often the loudest, if not the most sensitive, spokesmen for farmers. Born in 1884 in the former Honjo district of Tokyo, Katō was the son of a peer who died a month before his birth.[7] He attended Kanazawa Fourth High School, where one of his teachers was the philosopher Nishida Kitarō. As was true for so many of his contemporaries, a high point in Katō's intellectual development occurred when he encountered Christianity as a high school student, but he left no record detailing his youthful conversion and it is impossible to know the scope or depth of his convictions. Nevertheless, his principal publication, *Nihon nōson kyōiku* (Japanese Farm Education), which appeared in 1934, reveals that he retained a deep respect for Christian ideas long after he had formally become an adherent of Shinto.[8]

[7] Biographical details are taken from Okada Kōsaku, "Katō Kanji no nōmin kyōiku shisō" [Katō Kanji's Farm Education Thought], *Shisō no kagaku*, No. 18, June 1960, pp. 33-42; Takeda Kiyoko, *Dochaku to haikyō—dentōteki etosu to purotesutanto* [Home Town and Apostasy—The Traditional Ethos and Protestantism] (Tokyo: Shinkyō Shuppansha, 1967), pp. 280-313.

[8] *Nihon nōson kyōiku* [Japanese Farm Education] (Tokyo: Tōyō Tosho, 1934), pp. 129-131. Katō's spiritual outlook is treated more fully in Thomas R. H. Havens, "Katō Kanji (1884-1965) and the Spirit of Agriculture in Modern Japan," *Monumenta Nipponica*, xxv, 3-4, Autumn 1970, 249-266.

278

Katō's years at Tokyo Imperial University, from 1908 to 1912, were ones of ill-health and intellectual disarray. Somewhere in the jarring interaction of his studies of farm administration, experiences with Christianity and socialism, readings in Tolstoy, and realization that many of his Tokyo neighbors were "urban trash who ought not to be sent out from the farm villages,"[9] Katō decided to renounce the government post he received at graduation and devote his life to stabilizing the farm villages. In late 1913 he took a position as a teacher at the Aichi Prefecture Anjō Agricultural and Forestry School (Anjō Nōrin Gakkō) thanks to his friendship with the headmaster, Yamazaki Nobukichi (1873-1954), who later advocated the way of the farmer (*nōmindō*) and became a major agrarianist. Thus, at age twenty-nine, Katō set out on a half-century long career in farm education that would lead him both to important duties for the state in the 1930s and, ultimately, to the depths of quiet ignominy in the postwar era.

What did agriculture mean to the novice instructor? "When I began to affirm my own life, I was able truly to understand the meaning of agriculture. . . . To determine what it is 'to live' is to understand agriculture. When agriculture is understood, you decide to live by being diligent at it. Thus, to exert one's self in the production of food, clothing, and shelter is good."[10] Farming was much more than an economic activity to Katō: it related directly to the purpose of existence, and there was virtue in the act of production. From this grew his firm resistance to the commercialization of farming and his affirmation of the premodern farm economy. Each village, he wrote, must realize the value of cooperation: "Not only can agriculture not be isolated, but also, if you think about it in practical terms, it is important to have cooperative unity for agriculture."[11] He approved of producers' cooperatives and thought that

[9] Quoted in Takeda, p. 283.   [10] *Nihon nōson kyōiku*, p. 4.
[11] Ibid., p. 108.

their most commendable function was as a gathering place where members could share their farm experience. But since Katō was less concerned with such practical questions as land tenure, grain prices, and interest rates than with his abstract vision of the natural economy, he believed that rural resuscitation finally depended on ethical and spiritual qualities.

Possibly acting under the influence of Tolstoy's primitive Christianity, Katō began to idealize the patriarchal, communal small-farm system which had been the bulwark of the economy, the society, and the national spirit since antiquity. "I think that the farmers must clearly understand the farm villages where they live from the viewpoint of the Japanese spirit . . . and they must understand clearly what sort of place the farm village is."[12] What was this national spirit? Its essence, he found, was loyalty to the family, nation, and monarch all at once:

> To put it simply and clearly, the Japanese spirit is to devote one's self to something. This is no lie. This is different from that selfishness which tramples everything before it. To devote one's body and spirit to something, to devote one's self in the case of the family to the family head and in the case of the nation to the current monarch of the unbroken imperial succession, and thus to expend all one's efforts, steadily and evermore, to prospering the great destiny of Japan—this is the essence of the Japanese spirit.[13]

How was it that Katō had managed, in the space of a few years, to link his youthful concern for agricultural poverty with the virtues of production, village cooperation, and spiritual devotion? By all accounts, the crucial influence was his introduction to the Kannagara no Michi doctrines of the Shinto scholar, Kakehi Katsuhiko, during the years 1913-1914. Kakehi labeled ancient Shinto a form of "expressive

[12] Ibid., p. 101. [13] Ibid., p. 100.

pantheism," in which all men, natural objects, gods, and forms of worship were manifestations of the single spirit of the Ame-no-minakanushi-no-kami, or gods in the world.[14] Katō began to support a spiritual tradition which was closely linked to crop production and fully compatible with that inviolable modern ideology, *kokutai* or national essence.

Now he could see the importance of the familial orientation of early Japanese society (as opposed to the individualism of the West), since the family was a basic unit of the Japanese nation.[15] It was through the power of the gods that rice and wheat could be grown, and hard work on the rough land was the basis of the farmer's soul, which Katō made equivalent to the spirit of Japan. This farm soul, based on rural communalism, received its ultimate expression in emperor loyalty:

> In this country the emperor, from the unbroken imperial succession, is pleased to stand at the head of the entire state. He has been pleased to cause the great life force known as the Japanese empire to prosper steadily. In nurturing this great life force and all the people, to borrow the words of Professor Kakehi, his superintendence has been manifested. . . . The people, obeying the imperial will and fulfilling their respective callings, likewise make strenuous efforts to increase the great life force known as the Japanese empire.[16]

Even more strictly than Tachibana, Katō thus upheld the hierarchical order of village society and the imperial state with strong local communities as its foundation. In this way he merged his visions of nation and state under the throne, through the process of expressive unity. Yet his conception

---

[14] Okada, pp. 37-38; Takeda, pp. 285-286. See also D. C. Holtom, *Modern Japan and Shinto Nationalism* (Chicago: University of Chicago Press, 1943), p. 64; Shōzō Kono, "Kannagara no Michi: The Meaning of Kannagara," *Monumenta Nipponica*, III, 2, 1940, 9-31.

[15] *Nihon nōson kyōiku*, pp. 101-103.

[16] Ibid., pp. 103-104.

of state was strongly tinged with the primitive tribalism of early Shinto, based on a spiritual devotion to the nation best expressed in agricultural labor.

When the farm crisis of the 1920s brought attention to the problem of rural decay, one result was the National Higher Level School (Kokumin Kōtō Gakkō) scheme, of which Katō became a principal leader. At heart this moralistic movement tried to revive a self-sufficient farm economy that had been mortally wounded by commercialization and urbanization. It sought to instruct owner-farmer (*jisakunō*) families in household management, community administration, cooperative association management, group living, and village self-sufficiency through farm school communities throughout Japan.[17] Sponsored in part by the Ministry of Agriculture and Forestry and the Ministry of Education, the schools were nominally self-supporting but in reality heavily financed by public and private contributions.[18] The first of these schools, under the imposing title of Japan National Higher Level School (Nihon Kokumin Kōtō Gakkō), was founded in May 1926 in Tomobe, Ibaraki Prefecture, with Katō as headmaster.[19]

Katō took pains to remind his pupils that agriculture demanded a unity of theory and practice,[20] as the school's routine showed. But his prescription for practical experience (*jisshū*) involved a blend of religious, military, and agricultural functions. Foremost were *misogi*, or ritual purification, and *sanpai*, or worship at shrines. The local shrine should be the unifying institution in the village, he believed, and training the young people in Shinto beliefs would

---

[17] Tsunazawa Mitsuaki, *Nihon no nōhonshugi* [Japanese Agrarianism] (Tokyo: Kinokuniya Shoten, 1971, pp. 103-104; Takeda, pp. 293-294.

[18] Sakurai Takeo, *Nihon nōhonshugi* [Japanese Agrarianism] (Tokyo: Hakuyōsha, 1935), p. 112; Takeda, p. 293.

[19] Kodaira Ken'ichi, *Ishiguro Tadaatsu* (Tokyo: Jiji Tsūshinsha, 1962), pp. 89-96.

[20] *Nihon nōson kyōiku*, pp. 95-97.

assure the prosperity of the farms.[21] Also important for practical experience was military training, through wrestling, fencing, and drill. Individual rivalry through competition in the martial arts was an excellent way to harden the Yamato spirit,[22] which was synonymous with the farm soul: whether wielding a hoe or a sword, the farmer would strengthen his spirit through bodily discipline.

The remaining aspects of *jisshū*, book learning and knowledge of scientific matters, related more directly to agriculture, but even here Katō stressed the value of devotion and the discipline of repetition, rather than the scientific techniques of modern farming.[23] Just as he preferred the armor, weapons, and spirit of feudal warfare to modern military technology, Katō emphasized experience and the age-old methods of peasant farming with sickle and hoe. He did not blindly reject modern agricultural science; he fancied himself a "progressive" because he preached the importance of protein and therefore encouraged soybean production. But Katō's method, which he dubbed "single hoe-ism," dismissed mechanical methods in favor of human labor wherever possible. Even capital, he believed, should only be used to cover production costs, and any notion of profit was a modern, Western poison which must be purged through hard work.[24]

In its stress on *kami* beliefs, Katō's approach to farm education bore a resemblance to the National Learning (Kokugaku) school of the later Tokugawa era, but its true precursor in the native tradition was probably the warrior ideology of the Ancient Learning scholar Yamaga Sokō (1622-1685). Yamaga's *Shidō* (Way of the Samurai) had provided elaborate ethical underpinnings for the feudal warrior code, emphasizing the twin disciplines of the civil and military arts as methods to attain Bushidō.[25] In choosing

[21] Ibid., pp. 125-126.   [22] Ibid., p. 138.   [23] Ibid., pp. 127-128.
[24] Tsukuba Hisaharu, *Nihonjin no shisō—nōhonshugi no sekai* [Japanese Thought—The World of Agrarianism] (Tokyo: San'ichi Shobō, 1961), pp. 183-184.
[25] See *Sources of Japanese Tradition*, comp. Ryusaku Tsunoda,

to promote the military arts at Tomobe, Katō consciously followed the teachings of Yamaga: "The military arts are the basis of Bushido; after all, the persons who created Bushido were samurai. The thing that disciplined the souls of the samurai was the military arts. . . . The thought of someone like Yamaga Sokō was splendid, but I thoroughly admire and respect Yamaga's life in itself. In Yamaga's day Neo-Confucianism was very effective and powerful, but in Sokō the spirit of Japanism, i.e., respect for the emperor, burned fiercely."[26] Some would have it that Katō felt comfortable with Yamaga because both sought to confirm the feudal order in Japanese land relations.[27] It is probably safer to say that neither Yamaga nor the National Learning school shared Katō's pressing concern for village rebirth; at the same time, it is easy to imagine that a country schoolmaster of Katō's persuasions would feel more at home with Yamaga's talk of spiritual discipline than with the bookish studies of ancient mythology by the Kokugaku scholars.

This concern for hardening the Japanese character led to Katō's implacable antiforeignism, especially in the realm of ideas. As he put it,

Japan has just recently managed to create Manchukuo between Russia and China, but there is America on the other side of the Pacific. Of these, China is a truly mysterious country, from which has come an ideology of extreme individualism. From Russia have come communist doctrines, and from America have come teachings of freedom and equality. In short, all these ideologies are swirling around the Japanese archipelago, and the people's

ed. William T. deBary (New York: Columbia University Press, 1958), pp. 394-400.

[26] "Robata zatsuwa" [Fireside Chat], *Iyasaka*, No. 106, March 1931, quoted in Okada, p. 41. At Waseda University Matsumura Ken'ichi is preparing a study of Katō's farm education theories.

[27] Okada, p. 41.

mood is very confused. It is in this sense that the problem of ideology is the most pressing question in Japan.[28]

His remedy was the predictable premodern one of rekindling the farm spirit: "I believe that, rather than studying these various kinds of thought, it is most important for us to discipline and cultivate the Japanese spirit—in other words, to be alert and diligent about disciplining and cultivating the spirit of the Japanese farmer. Accordingly, I believe that the only way is to build up a firm faith, stand up erect amid the eddies, and tide over the great waves."[29] Katō went on to excuse Japanese imperialism and militarism on the ground that Japan was only mirroring the West on these counts, and he dismissed foreign ideologies in these anti-intellectual terms:

[The] Japanese have assiduously studied all sorts of ideologies. It is perfectly reasonable for one or two scholars to do this sort of thing; there is absolutely no need for every Tom, Dick, or Harry to study philosophy or to learn who Kant and Fichte were. Whatever becomes of theory, I am a Japanese, I love Japan, and whenever I die is fine if it is for Japan. I don't understand theories, but for the sake of my ancestors and my descendants, I absolutely cannot accept the enslavement of Japan by foreign countries. If this outlook becomes clearly established, no theory can destroy it.[30]

He concluded with a strong affirmation of the countryside and its cleansing qualities which left no doubt that Katō stood emotionally and intellectually in the nativistic tradition of the Tokugawa era:

If this is the case, when we ask where the best place is for cultivating and training the ideal faith of the Yamato race, the answer is the farm villages. The city people have all

[28] *Nihon nōson kyōiku*, p. 162.   [29] Ibid., p. 163.
[30] Ibid., p. 165.

come from the countryside, i.e., the people who have come from the countryside have gathered in the cities. When they get there they immediately come into contact with various ideologies and become confused. But if we clearly inculcate the Japanese spirit while they are still in the countryside, they will be quite unmoved no matter how many kinds of doctrines they confront when they get to the city. . . . I believe that it is most important for everyone to appreciate the meaning of the farm villages, to put the spirit of the Japanese empire into the hearts of the farmers, to protect the villages, and finally to cultivate and train the spirit that protects the country. When this is accomplished in the farm villages, I really believe that we hardly need be worried about the problem of ideology.[31]

From this outlook flowed the substance of Katō's work as an educator, and it was this that shaped his approach to foreign affairs, especially during the 1930s. The depression formed the backdrop for Katō's entrance into the political arena, first in connection with government farm education policy and later concerning overseas colonization, and it was the depression which redirected the emphasis of his agrarianism toward aggressive, xenophobic expansion abroad.

Katō and Manchurian Colonization

Among the measures adopted by the government to help the countryside in the 1930s was a Ministry of Agriculture and Forestry plan to "nourish the backbone village leadership class" and "enrich the farmers' spirits" by creating agricultural training centers (*nōmin dōjō*) throughout the country. The first training center was officially instituted in 1934 when Katō Kanji moved his farm school from Tomobe to a 275 hectare tract of national forest land in Uchihara, Ibaraki Prefecture, and named it the Uchihara Kokumin Kōtō Gakkō. The Uchihara school was lionized by the Nōrinshō as the model of what an agricultural training

[31] Ibid., pp. 166-167.

center should be. It acted as a forum for Katō's plunge into foreign affairs in the mid-1930s by serving as a training ground for Japanese emigrant farmers before being sent abroad to Manchuria.

As a result of Japan's twenty-one demands in 1915, the Chinese had permitted Japanese citizens to lease lands throughout Manchuria, but a lack of farmers willing to leave Japan, plus harassment by local officials in Manchuria, had kept immigration to a minimum. As late as 1931, only 308 of the 64,662 farm families in the Kwantung Peninsula and the Southern Manchuria Railway zone were Japanese.[32] When Japan seized Manchuria in September 1931 and established the puppet state known as Manchukuo, she decided to cut off Chinese immigration and encourage Japanese settlement, in order to increase overall agricultural output in the empire. The Kwantung army pressed the government for subsidies to carry out emigration on a large scale, as a means of securing its newly won territory. Since such a policy would also be regarded as a positive solution to the domestic land problem, Prime Minister Hirota Kōki won approval from his cabinet in August 1936 for a twenty-year plan to resettle one million farm families in central and northern Manchuria, each to receive twenty hectares of farmland.[33] Many of the first settlers were sent to Uchihara for training before departing for the continent.

Why did Katō, who sought to restore the village autonomy that prevailed during Japan's centuries of feudal isola-

[32] Kungtu C. Sun, *The Economic Development of Manchuria in the First Half of the Twentieth Century* (Cambridge, Mass.: East Asian Research Center, Harvard University, 1969), p. 52.

[33] Ibid., p. 53; Sakurai, *Nihon nōgyō no saihensei*, p. 30. Ishiguro Tadaatsu, vice-minister of agriculture and forestry at the time of the Manchurian Incident, supported colonization abroad—both on the continent and in South America—as a means of reducing population pressure. He became Katō's chief bureaucratic patron during the mid-1930s. See *Ishiguro Tadaatsu den* [Biography of Ishiguro Tadaatsu], ed. Hashimoto Denzaemon *et al.* (Tokyo: Iwanami Shoten, 1969), pp. 22-23.

tion, become an advocate of colonization? One factor was his long-standing belief, derived from Kakehi Katsuhiko, that Shinto was a supreme religion that knew no national boundaries. His oft-stated concern with the Japanese spirit, which he had defined as devotion to the Shinto legitimized emperor, had led him to exhort the farmers to "make strenuous efforts to increase the great life force known as the Japanese empire."[34] There were no scruples in his world view to confine his focus to Japan proper, and as a practical matter Japan's activities on the continent, he had made plain, were fully as justified as those of the Western powers.

A more important reason was Katō's insistence that colonization in Manchuria was only a tactic, not an end in itself:

> People are clamoring for the construction of Manchukuo, but I believe that rather than constructing Manchukuo we should merely concentrate on making our own country splendid. I believe that this is the destiny of the Japanese people. . . . If the spirit of making the Japanese nation splendid truly enters people's hearts, everyone, whether Manchus, Germans, or Arabs, will come to show true human respect for us Japanese. Thus I never want emigration in order to construct Manchukuo but in order to fulfill the destiny of the Japanese people.[35]

Katō clearly equated the country's interest with those of the people and rejected any Manchurian development program that would further the ambitions of the state or its politicians, generals, or investors. The chief ground on which colonization had to be justified was spiritual.

While the spiritual problem was the most important question facing Japan, Katō also acknowledged that as a result of the depression there was a critical shortage of land and jobs. Just as the Kokumin Kōtō Gakkō movement (and the plan for farm training centers) would help to solve the spiritual crisis, emigration to Manchuria would not only

---

[34] *Nihon nōson kyōiku*, p. 104.   [35] Ibid., p. 109.

promote the national destiny but also mitigate the rural unemployment problem. What Katō had in mind was sending to the continent the same cultivators who were the objects of so much official attention in the rural rehabilitation campaign. He specifically excluded from his scheme the scruffy drifters and urban unemployed: "In conducting such an emigration movement, we should assemble the sons of the farm villages, have worthy persons train them as settlers, and send them abroad. Gathering city people for the emigration movement would be exceptional."[36]

As might be expected from one who was so opposed to mechanization and the corrupting efforts of Western-style commercialized agriculture, Katō stressed the human factor in colonization: "They must be people with the ability to colonize. What I'd call most appropriate for agricultural colonization would be people who understand the true meaning of agriculture. If they have any ability at producing the food, clothing, and shelter necessary for human life, they should be able to like farming. . . . In short, the reform of the farm villages lies in the people. The success of colonization likewise lies in the people. In the last analysis, I believe that the people themselves form the center of everything."[37] Here is the kernel of Katō's interest in colonization: it would benefit precisely those rural people who stood at the center of his vision of society and nation, the same people who tilled the soil with the gods' assistance and, in the Kakehi formulation, manifested the unity of man, gods, and nature. It was these persons, not the urban industrialists, politicians, or generals, who should be both the leaders and the beneficiaries of colonization. It was typical of his nonanalytical, spiritualistic outlook that Katō reacted to the depression with colonization schemes that were justified only secondarily on grounds of supplying new lands and new jobs. Like the exclusionists of the late Tokugawa period, Katō believed that the basic problem was the internal, moral one,

[36] Ibid., p. 180.　　　　　　[37] Ibid., pp. 197-199.

and hence his expansionist Nōhonshugi teachings often developed more according to inner perceptions than external realities.

Soon after Katō's Nihon Kokumin Kōtō Gakkō moved to Uchihara in 1934, it began to serve the twin purposes of showcase for the agricultural training-center movement and orientation ground for prospective emigrants to Manchuria. Both functions were actively encouraged by the Ministry of War and the Ministry of Agriculture and Forestry. Later the facility became known as the Uchihara Kunrenjo (Uchihara Training Institute), signifying that preparation for settlement had become its main activity. The Kunrenjo, in line with Katō's convictions, devoted much attention to Kakehi's Kannagara no Michi and paid special obeisance to the Yasaka Shrine, after which an early settlement in Manchuria was named. Each village created in Manchuria was centered architecturally around a shrine. By the eve of Pearl Harbor Katō had managed to convert a number of the agricultural training centers into sites for preparing "continental soldiers of the Yamato race acting under a vast ideal,"[38] and even Prime Minister Konoe Fumimaro felt obliged to praise Katō's endeavors in public.

For reasons of national destiny, spiritual fulfillment, and population pressure on the land, Katō maintained, it was imperative that the frontier settlements consist exclusively of Japanese. No Chinese or Manchus should be employed, he believed, the more so because they were not trustworthy. Even in Korea, he observed, "The Chinese respect the right to use [the land] and ignore ownership. For this reason Chinese have moved into the wastelands of Korea and are farming them without permission. When we voice protests against this, they think that there is nothing wrong with entering empty lands and farming them, and they believe that absolute rights belong to the users of the land."[39] Else-

[38] See Sakurai Takeo, "Shōwa no nōhonshugi" [Agrarianism in the Shōwa Period] Shisō [Thought], No. 407, May 1958, p. 48.
[39] Nihon nōson kyōiku, pp. 210-211.

where he reproached the Chinese habit of sending settlers to the borderlands when conditions were bad at home,[40] although this was precisely what he was advocating for Japan.

The hostile environment for settlement led Katō to propose the standard Nōhonshugi suggestion (ironically of Chinese derivation)—the farmer-soldier: "Now when we ask what sort of person is best for colonization in Manchuria and Mongolia, not only should he be thoroughly devoted to agriculture but he must also be ready to draw his gun and risk his life fighting for his country should bandits invade. That is, while being a person who takes quiet pleasure in farming, he must also enthusiastically draw his gun in a pinch."[41] In short, the settlers must always grasp the hoe in one hand and the rifle in the other. But it is important to note that Katō did not call for the militarization of Manchuria. There was no suggestion in his writings of collaboration between the Kwantung army and his frontiersmen. Indeed, he asserted that weapons were not a paramount concern: "Small arms and machine guns will suffice. . . . The Japanese understand the Chinese mentality very well," Katō fancied, "and the only defense is vigilance."[42]

It is true that Katō's colonizers were armed and that ideally they would produce surpluses which the Kwantung army among others would consume, but it is an exaggeration to compare them to "colonial troops" and to dismiss their freedom of action as inconsequential.[43] When Katō spoke of arms-bearing and farming as harmonious, he did so in the premodern setting of self-sufficient agriculture that characterized his educational thought:

Nothing is more important than hardening the spirit of Japan, the spirit of Yamato. Accordingly, precisely by taking charge of agriculture as Japanese and devoting themselves to increasing the prosperity of the country, the

---

[40] Ibid., p. 205.   [41] Ibid., p. 199.   [42] Ibid., p. 214.
[43] Takeda, p. 307, overemphasizes their military role, especially since most pioneers everywhere bore arms of the sort Katō advocated.

true farmers living in this faith will for the first time be able to become imperial farmers. For this reason the farmers must for a time spring up, lay aside their sickles, and take up swords. The unity of agriculture and the military is a natural thing. The true farm spirit is precisely the spirit of Yamato.[44]

It was in this primitive sense of the farmer-soldier that Katō's outlook on the military was grounded, not in support for the modern mechanized forces typified by the Kwantung army.

Katō and his supporters were disappointed when the settlers in Manchuria turned out to be more land hungry than altruistic and to prefer modern farm methods. Instead of enhancing the national destiny, they were looking for security and a comfortable life. This reality led Katō to stop recruiting adult immigrants and instead to take teenagers who would presumably be young men of high purpose. He persuaded the Ministry of Development (Takumushō) to announce a Youth Volunteer Corps for Manchurian development on December 30, 1937, and he trained them personally at Uchihara for "Yamatobataraki" ("work for Yamato"). Their fate abroad was tied to the vicissitudes of the larger stream of Japanese emigrants to Manchuria during the war years: cold, hunger, illness, enforced military service, and for many slaughter by Russian troops when the Soviet army rolled into Manchuria in August 1945.[45] Although the Japanese government spent large sums of money on its emigration program, land acquisition proved wearisome, frictions with Chinese and Manchu residents were severe, and agricultural output in Manchuria never regained the level it had reached in the mid-1920s before the Wall Street crash. By 1942, only 57,401 Japanese families had

[44] "Kōkoku nōmin no jikaku to shimei" [Consciousness and Destiny of Imperial Farmers], *Iyasaka*, No. 161, February 1936, quoted in Takeda, pp. 305-306.
[45] See Takeda, pp. 309-312.

resettled in Manchuria, far fewer than either Katō or the state had hoped.[46] According to Foreign Ministry figures,[47] only 150,000 of the 270,000 Japanese citizens present in Manchuria when the war ended escaped with their lives and were repatriated.

By the time Japan was mobilizing for a wider war on the eve of Pearl Harbor, Katō's colonization schemes had already lost much of their vigor. He averted his attention briefly in 1940 to the problem of landlordism at home, calling on the state to encourage more farmers to work their own lands.[48] After the war, by all accounts, Katō's convictions remained the same: Ronald Dore found his school at Uchihara little changed in 1956 from its prewar regimen.[49] In 1960, five years before his death, Katō had 110 boys and 90 girls studying at Uchihara, despite a relatively high tuition fee, and Kakehi's Kannagara no Michi remained the cornerstone of his teachings. He reportedly still held to his belief in self-sufficiency for Japanese farmers, and, despite Japan's defeat in wartime, he took a measure of consolation from the fact that the occupation land reform program had at last made owner-farmers the norm.[50]

Initially attracted to the plight of the farmer by his youthful encounters with Christianity, socialism, and the urban poor newly arrived from the villages, Katō Kanji glorified agriculture because of his devotion from 1913 onward to Shinto beliefs, themselves products of a premodern village com-

---

[46] Sun, pp. 53-60. See Yoda Yoshiie, "Dai niji taisenka no Manshū imin no jittai—imindan kankei no hanzai o chūshin ni" [Actual Conditions of Japanese Settlers in Manchuria During World War II— With Special Reference to Crimes Involving Colonizing Groups], *Shakai kagaku tōkyū* [Social Science Review], XVIII, 1, July 1972, 41-78.

[47] *Ishiguro Tadaatsu den*, p. 25.   [48] Okada, p. 42.

[49] Ronald P. Dore, *Land Reform in Japan* (London: Oxford University Press, 1959), p. 393.

[50] Okada, pp. 33-34.

munalism that was grounded in farming. This inspiration, rather than any profound understanding of economic forces, guided his form of agrarianism. Katō's importance lies not in the following he attracted or the colonies he promoted but in showing how rural energies and anxieties were shaped to justify expansion in search of a long lost national soul.

Throughout his career Katō undeniably groped in the dark, both on domestic village reform and colonization abroad. Just as his emphasis on traditional village virtues flew in the face of the hard facts of farm life in an industrializing society, his unrealistic plans for Manchurian settlement by self-sufficient farmers proved illusory without more political, economic, and military help from the top. But Katō was dealing with the spirit of agriculture, not its substance. His thought represents that process whereby farmfirst ideas were gradually transformed during the depression years into expansionist doctrines based on the equivalence of the farm soul and the Japanese spirit. Still, no matter what he contributed to Japanese imperialism by cooperating with a government policy of colonial development, Katō's thought was not basically statist: he resisted politicians, capitalists, bureaucrats, generals, and the privileged classes which had displaced his beloved self-sufficient farmer as the backbone of the country. Since the establishment responsible for extending Japan's empire consisted of precisely those persons whose modernizing activities he opposed, not even Katō proved able to bring about a firm union of popular agrarianism and state programs during the brief interval in the mid-1930s before total national mobilization erased serious public debate on farm policy.

Chapter XIII

Agrarianism and Modern Japan

THE agrarianist response to Japanese modernization was fully as diffuse as the remarkable array of profarm ideologues who extolled village life during the period from the Meiji restoration to World War II. The most prominent defenders of agriculture ranged from aristocrats, statesmen, and generals to scholars, landlord-officials, peasant movement leaders, and rural educators. The doctrines they advocated were equally diverse: they variously called for large farms and small ones, progressive techniques and traditional methods, cooperation with commercialism and opposition to it, support for state programs and resistance to them, expansion abroad and reform at home.

The complicated nature of Japanese agrarianism resulted primarily from the uneven course of modernization in the late nineteenth and early twentieth centuries. For this reason, it is difficult to say either that Nōhonshugi smoothed the path for Japan's modernizers or that it created major obstacles for them. If it is unreasonable to conclude that agrarianists served as apologists for big landlords and investors by mollifying discontented peasants, neither can it be said that they were powerful enough to raise much opposition to those aspects of national development which they deplored. Instead, agrarian ideologues on the whole simply reacted to modernizing forces that lay beyond their control.

295

Most Nōhonshugi partisans confronted urbanization and industrialization by reaffirming that agriculture was an indispensable economic activity. They agreed that village communities formed an ideal model for society at large, that farmers made excellent soldiers, and that rural life inculcated the most appropriate ethical virtues. Many agrarianists, especially in the twentieth century, agreed further that farming was essential to the unique spiritual qualities of the Japanese people. Village communalism, they thought, should be the cornerstone of national society under the emperor. They also believed that the depression crisis could be solved by shoring up the rural economy, village society, local political autonomy, and the spiritual and moral qualities associated with the countryside. Whatever else may have divided them, all agrarianists sincerely thought that farming was the foundation of the nation, although what constituted the nation eventually became a ground of controversy for almost all Japanese social critics after World War I.

The consequences of this inchoate bundle of dogmas extended far beyond the laws and subsidies designed to protect small-scale farming that were periodically approved by the central government beginning in the 1890s. As Nōhonshugi grew more and more dissociated from state agricultural policies, it became involved with larger ideological currents such as anticapitalism, plans for national reform, expansionism, and the nature of Japanese nationalism. Out of the tangle of ideas and emotions which comprised agrarianism after World War I came not only spirited theoretical attacks on the prevailing ideology of capitalism and centralized rule but also violent acts of political terror directed against established institutions in search of domestic reconstruction. By way of assessing the main implications of Nōhonshugi thought, it will be useful to consider the attraction it held for Japan's armed forces, its distinctiveness in comparison with American populism, and its relationship to modern Japanese nationalism.

Gondō, Tachibana, and Political Violence

The most notorious moment for agrarianism came when it interacted with dissent and restlessness within the officer corps of the Japanese armed services on the eve of the Ketsumeidan (Blood Brotherhood) and May 15 incidents of 1932. Contact with the teachings of Gondō Seikyō and Tachibana Kōzaburō obviously complicated the outlook of the young officers who participated in these events, but to what extent did Nōhonshugi ideas decisively motivate their conduct? Thanks primarily to the painstaking research of Hashikawa Bunzō,[1] it has been established that few of the terrorists themselves attributed much direct influence to Gondō or Tachibana—a judgment which complements the general nonviolent drift of Gondō's and Tachibana's writings. Based on what is known of his thought, Gondō's capacity to inspire political radicalism seems weak indeed; Tachibana's was somewhat greater by virtue of his preference for merging thought and action, but apparently his appeal reached only a limited circle of followers.

Both Gondō and Tachibana, of course, were well known to the men who plotted the Ketsumeidan assassinations, although Tachibana was only casually involved with the planning. Many of the Ketsumeidan members used Gondō's home as a gathering place during 1930 and 1931, although Inoue Nisshō was the undisputed leader of the group. Gondō's closest link with the Ketsumeidan was Lieut. (j.g.) Fujii Hitoshi, a naval pilot stationed at Kasumigaura who was Inoue's most active recruiter. Fujii and his half brother, Yotsumoto Yoshitaka, brought other members of the Blood Brotherhood to hear Gondō's lectures and apparently wanted him to advise them on statecraft after the revolution occurred—a hope dashed first by Fujii's death in combat

---

[1] Especially in "Hoi—Ketsumeidan, goichigo jiken o chūshin to shite" [Addendum—With Emphasis on the Ketsumeidan and May 15 incidents], in Takizawa Makoto, *Gondō Seikyō oboegaki* [Notes on Gondō Seikyō] (Nagaokashi, privately published, 1968), pp. 116-163.

over Shanghai on February 5, 1932, and then by the collapse of the Ketsumeidan later in the year.[2]

Although less directly involved with the conspirators, Tachibana was an avowed admirer of Inoue Nisshō. Inoue was a professional troublemaker who had served variously as a boxing instructor in police academies, a spy in southern Manchuria for the army general staff, and an agent in Shantung for Gen. Banzai, the Japanese military adviser to President Yüan Shih-k'ai of China during 1914-1915. He became a Nichiren sect priest, built a "Temple for the Defense of the Fatherland" near Mito in 1928, and two years later formed the Blood Brotherhood, a group of patriots who "mixed their blood and drank it as an accompaniment to their initiation oath."[3] Their purpose was to use terror against "the corrupt political parties connected with the plutocracy."[4] When Tachibana first met Inoue in December 1929, he was apparently well impressed with Inoue's readiness to act, and he claimed later that Inoue's example had helped him decide to plunge headlong into the May 15 movement.[5]

What Inoue thought of Tachibana is unclear, but he presumably felt comfortable enough with Gondō not only to send his followers to study under him but also to borrow a vacant house from Gondō near Gondō's Yoyogi Uehara

[2] Ibid., pp. 120-127; Ifukube Takahiko, "Gondō Seikyō hyōden nōto" [Critical Biographical Notes on Gondō Seikyō], *Kokuron* [National Theory], part 9, IV, 8, August 1956, 13.

[3] A. Morgan Young, *Imperial Japan 1926-1938* (London: George Allen and Unwin, 1938), p. 190.

[4] O. Tanin and E. Yohan, pseuds., *Militarism and Fascism in Japan* (New York: International Publishers, 1934), p. 221.

[5] Tachibana Kōzaburō, "Kokumin kyōdōtai ōdō kokka nōhon kensetsuron" [Theory of Establishing the Agricultural Foundations for People's Communities and the Imperial State], 1932, quoted in Tsunazawa Mitsuaki, "Tachibana Kōzaburō shiron" [Sketch of Tachibana Kōzaburō], *Shisō no kagaku* [Science of Thought], No. 142, October 1970, p. 71.

home, to which he had moved in September 1931.[6] Here the Inoue clique, consisting mostly of naval officers, met on January 9 and January 31, 1932, to map out plans for the Ketsumeidan assassinations.[7] At the latter meeting, according to Ifukube Takahiko, Gondō showed the group how to stab someone to death with a dagger:

He also asked those present if they knew whether to stab a man to death with the dagger in the right hand or in the left. When no one answered, he said, "It is not the right hand, it's the left." When he said this, we all looked dubious, so he continued, "the dagger should be held on the hip ready for use with the left hand. Ordinarily people do not do this, trying instead to stab them with the right hand, and hence end up letting their victims escape."[8]

Ifukube discreetly failed to mention whether this method was ever used by any of the assassins. Gondō's final gesture toward the Blood Brotherhood was providing sanctuary to Furuuchi Eiji, one of the conspirators in the murder of Dan Takuma on March 5. Inoue, meanwhile, took refuge for several weeks with the right-wing organizer Tōyama Mitsuru before surrendering ostentatiously to the police, who had reportedly been too timid to seize him at the home of so influential a patron.[9]

Although he supplied a modest degree of material aid and comfort to the Ketsumeidan, Gondō did not rank as a prophet among the brotherhood itself. Inoue later acknowl-

---

[6] Hashikawa, pp. 128-129, 135-136; *Chōkokkashugi* [Ultranationalism], ed. Hashikawa Bunzō, *Gendai Nihon shisōshi taikei* [Collection on Modern Japanese Thought] (Tokyo: Chikuma Shobō, 1964), XXXI, p. 417.

[7] Royal J. Wald, "The Young Officers Movement in Japan, ca. 1925-1937; Ideology and Actions," Ph.D. dissertation in history, University of California, Berkeley, 1949, pp. 116-117.

[8] Ifukube, part 10, IV, 9, September 1956, 16.

[9] Wald, p. 118.

edged that *Jichi minpan* was well known among his group: "Starting with me, all my comrades read it. . . . Fujii called this book a work unparalleled in the whole world and apparently made all his comrades in the navy read it."[10] Inoue insisted, however, that Gondō had no direct connection with the Ketsumeidan's decision to act:

The young officers read Gondō's *Jichi minpan* and praised it. All those who were aspiring at revolution in Japan at the time read it. I too read it, but it was difficult and I did not understand it. However, none of us comrades thought of studying it exhaustively. Since we were resigned to being killed after we undertook destruction, we had no interest in studying blueprints. It is not true that we comrades read Gondō's books and listened to his lectures and decided to leap forth. Our decision had already been taken before reading him. . . .[11]

Tanaka Kunio, a member of the Blood Brotherhood, corroborated Inoue's account: "The last thing I want to emphasize is that we all at this time relied on Inoue Nisshō's thought and never based our actions on Gondō's theories. Needless to say, Gondō's theories had no direct or indirect relevance to this incident; I think it is just that everyone respected Professor Gondō's character."[12]

These statements cannot be accepted by themselves as conclusive evidence of Gondō's insignificance to the terrorists, since a variety of motives may have prompted their denials, ranging from jealousy or contempt to a desire to shield Gondō from prosecution. But there are ideological grounds as well for doubting Inoue's affinities with Gondō.

[10] Inoue Nisshō, "Ume no mi" [The Fruit of Plum Trees], quoted in Hashikawa, p. 143.

[11] Inoue Nisshō, *Nisshō jiden* [Autobiography of Inoue Nisshō], pp. 265-266, quoted in Hashikawa Bunzō, "Shōwa chōkokkashugi no shosō" [Various Aspects of Ultranationalism in the Shōwa Period], *Chōkokkashugi*, p. 50.

[12] Tanaka Kunio, quoted in Hashikawa, "Hoi," p. 140.

In his prison diary, Inoue attacked not only the state but also the values of loyalty and patriotism as absolutes, claiming that the "ruling classes" were "deceiving the public for their private convenience."[13] What was needed, he believed, was not political or institutional reform, as Gondō thought, but an undefined philosophical and spiritual reconstruction that would occur spontaneously as the ruling classes were eliminated. Consequently, the Ketsumeidan offered no sketch whatsoever of the postrevolutionary world; as Inoue said, "before we can build we must first destroy."[14]

Regardless of his advice about techniques for murder, Gondō was a well-known foe of anarchism who hardly shared Inoue's fondness for destruction. He was both more institutionally conservative and personally reticent than the brusque and impetuous leader of the Ketsumeidan. Most importantly, Inoue made no special provision for either agriculture or a self-ruling society, since he believed that removing the elite was all that mattered.

If Gondō clashed with Inoue on such issues, his ideas nevertheless had some effect on other members of the Blood Brotherhood. Suda Tarō, for example, expressed respect for Gondō's learning but confessed that "I find many mysterious points in his thought."[15] Konuma Shō, the murderer of Inoue Junnosuke, characterized Gondō's ideas as "solid" once he managed to grasp them.[16] Yotsumoto Yoshi-

[13] Inoue Nisshō, "Ume no mi," quoted in Ozeki Hiroshi, "Chōkokkashugi no taitō" [The Rise of Ultranationalism], *Kindai Nihon no kangaekata* [Ways of Thinking in Modern Japan], ed. Yamaguchi Kōsaku and Koyama Hitoshi (Kyoto: Hōritsu Bunkasha, 1971), p. 164.

[14] Ibid., p. 166.

[15] Suda Tarō, quoted in Hashikawa, "Hoi," p. 141.

[16] Konuma Shō, quoted ibid., p. 142. See Konuma and Takahashi Masae, "Aru kokkashugisha no hansei" [Half-Life of a Certain Nationalist], *Shōwa shisōshi e no shōgen* [Evidence toward a History of Shōwa Thought], ed. Mainichi Shinbunsha, rev. ed. (Tokyo: Mainichi Shinbunsha, 1972), pp. 183-270. See p. 270 for materials relating to Konuma's experiences in the Ketsumeidan incident.

taka, who together with Fujii Hitoshi was closest to Gondō of any of the members of the Ketsumeidan, summarized his impressions in ambivalent terms: "While Professor Gondō's theories and ideas had an effect on the fermentation of our revolutionary thought, we understood only a portion of them. What we understood we used in our own enlightenment movement. Needless to say, our revolutionary thought did not stem from Gondō."[17]

In short, it is difficult to imagine that Gondō played more than a peripheral role in provoking the assassinations of February and March 1932. Not only was his thought ill suited for such violent measures, but also both Inoue and his followers deemphasized Gondō's influence on their bold actions. The Ketsumeidan was dominated by Inoue's personal charisma and penchant for individual killings,[18] not by Gondō's quasi-scholarly treatises on social and political ills. Indeed, ideology seems to have been less important to the Blood Brotherhood than the reckless style exemplified by Inoue himself. Probably Gondō directly stimulated none of the conspirators to act violently, but still his ideas clearly had secondary effects on the terrorists in that they frequently borrowed his terms and analytical categories in their subsequent court testimony.[19]

Gondō's connection with the other infamous conspiracy of 1932, the alliance of young officers and Ibaraki farmers which perpetrated the May 15 uprising, was inconsequential compared with Tachibana's celebrated involvement. Gondō had grown cool toward the remnants of the Blood Brotherhood after Dan's murder in March 1932. Relatively few of the army and navy officers who joined the May 15 plot had attended his lectures,[20] whereas many of them had

[17] Yotsumoto Yoshitaka, "Gondō Seikyō sensei no gakusetsu to watakushi nado to no shisō no kankei ni tsuite" [Regarding Professor Gondō Seikyō's Academic Theories and Their Relationship with Our Thought], quoted ibid., p. 136.
[18] See Ozeki, p. 162.   [19] Hashikawa, "Shōwa," p. 50.
[20] Tanin and Yohan, p. 223; Hashikawa, "Hoi," pp. 147-148. See

heard Tachibana speak. Nevertheless Gondō was present when general plans were laid for the May 15 episode, and he later helped Tachibana with his escape to Manchuria. After the attempted coup turned into a fiasco and the police rounded up the participants, Lieut. (j.g.) Koga Kiyoshi acknowledged the cogency of Tachibana's and Gondō's theories but disagreed with the idea of pure self-rule:

Tachibana illustrated the distress of the farm villages to us concretely, using tabular data. He made us see that the cause was exploitation by the capitalist clique. Hence we who had up to then regarded Nōhonshugi thought such as *Jichi minpan* as something abstract now for the first time were able to recognize the farm village problem concretely. . . . At present the essential structure of the Japanese state is the nation as a family, something which has been handed down from the time the country was founded. In this nation as a family, purely bureaucratic or purely people's government should not be allowed. This is the error in their theories.[21]

At the court-martial for army defendants, a cadet named Sakamoto reiterated this scorn for Gondō's remedies: "He was sometimes mentioned as the brains of the movement, but when he was asked his opinion as to how the agrarian crisis might be alleviated, all he could recommend for the farmers was self-help."[22] Other conspirators generally admitted that they had read his works without attributing a decisive impact to them.[23] Surprisingly, even though Tachibana had a direct hand in the events of May 15, he was mentioned far less often than Gondō in the defendants' statements, and

---

also Wald, pp. 119-129, for a vivid account of the planning and execution of the May 15 incident.

[21] Koga Kiyoshi, quoted in Hashikawa, "Hoi," pp. 143-144.
[22] Quoted in Young, p. 193.
[23] For statements, see Hashikawa, "Hoi," pp. 144-146; Hashikawa, "Shōwa," p. 49.

only Koga Kiyoshi seems to have found his thought especially praiseworthy.

Meanwhile Gondō himself claimed shortly after May 15 that he had not only not encouraged the plotters but had actually warned against direct action:

> I gave various talks on revolution and other subjects in the history of institutions to the army and navy officers who visited my place. But the only ones who really seemed to understand my talks were Fujii and Murayama Kiwayuki of the navy. The others misunderstood somewhat and rushed into practical action on behalf of national reconstruction. Since I cautioned them against such rash conduct whenever I saw them, I believe I must have advised Koga Kiyoshi against it too.[24]

Yamagishi Hiroshi, a naval officer, confirmed that Gondō had misgivings about the uprising, testifying that Gondō told him in early May that "the objectives of the Ketsumeidan were too sweeping and thus repugnant. Koga and Nakamura seem to have some sort of plan, but how would it be if we made them stop for the moment?"[25]

At the trial of civilians accused of complicity in the May 15 plot, even the prosecution admitted that Gondō's and Tachibana's ideas were not responsible for the terrorism. After noting the indirect impact of Kita Ikki's and Ōkawa Shūmei's reconstructionist ideologies, the government attorneys exonerated the agrarian nationalists:

> Gondō Seikyō (Zentarō)—This man emphasized one ruler for all the people, agrarianism, and self-rule. Among the defendants, Yotsumoto Yoshitaka and others in his group of students received Gondō's teachings. Thus Yotsumoto and others received Gondō's intellectual influences, but it is recognized that his direct influence was

24 Gondō Seikyō, quoted in Hashikawa, "Hoi," p. 147.
25 Yamagishi Hiroshi, quoted ibid., p. 148.

not to be found in the resolute action involved in this criminal case.

Tachibana Kōzaburō—This person participated in the May 15 incident by leading his followers, the students from the Aikyōjuku, at the instance of Lieut. Koga. . . . He stressed as his pet theory what he called constructing people's communities and an imperial state. He embraced the idea that the people, under Nōhonshugi, would cooperate with brotherly love and that each person should fulfill his appointed occupation. Since he did not essentially cherish destructive thought, his ideas, it is recognized, did not influence this criminal case.[26]

In short, Gondō's involvement with the May 15 clique was minimized by prosecution, defendants, and Gondō himself—making him even more subordinate a figure than in the Ketsumeidan incidents.

Tachibana, on the other hand, had renounced his earlier role as a bystander during the Blood Brotherhood assassinations to join directly in the violence of May 15. Nevertheless, neither the government prosecutors nor very many of the military participants acknowledged his guidance, either organizationally or ideologically. There is no reason to think that the members of his small band from Ibaraki managed to persuade their military comrades to support the rural cause. Indeed, the Aikyōjuku pupils were probably

[26] Ibid., pp. 149-150. See also Hata Ikuhiko, *Gun fuashizumu undōshi —sangatsu jiken kara ninirokugo made* [History of the Military Fascist Movement—From the March Incident until after the February 26 Incident] (Tokyo: Kawade Shobō Shinsha, 1962), pp. 50, 57; Kinoshita Hanji, *Uyoku tero* [Right-Wing Terror] (Kyoto: Hōritsu Bunkasha, 1960). On Kita and Ōkawa, see Takizawa Makoto, "Kita Ikki to Ōkawa Shūmei no ketsuretsu" [Fissure Between Kita Ikki and Ōkawa Shūmei], *Rekishi to jinbutsu* [History and Personality], III, 7, July 1973, 260-272; and for Ketsumeidan materials, *Ketsumeidan jiken jōshinsho gokuchū shuki* [Ketsumeidan Incident Report and Prison Notes], ed. and pub. Ketsumeidan Jiken Kōhan Sokkiroku Kankōkai (Tokyo, 1971).

willing to join the conspiracy, even in a secondary capacity, because they held hopes that somehow things would get better in the countryside if they were part of a successful revolution from the beginning. Thus Tachibana's major contribution to the May 15 incident was doubtless as a spirited, loyal, and decisive example for his sparse circle of farm followers from the impoverished northeast.

Although Gondō broke with Tachibana on terrorism, both opposed violent social change and favored reform based on the village, not long-range programs imposed by a central government.[27] Neither wanted fascist or militarist rule for Japan. Ensign Mikami Taku, one of Tachibana's closest links with the young officers, echoed his teacher's outlook when he stated, "If the nation were to shun the 'true national principle' and dance to the flute of fascism, it will be a critical day for Imperial Japan."[28] Tachibana cooperated with military officers on May 15 because of his eagerness for "patriotic reform," not because he was fond of centralized military rule—something obviously inimical to village communalism. Although he had taken pains in his lecture series in January 1932 to emphasize the similarities between farming and military service, Tachibana remained an agrarianist whose diagnosis of the ills of contemporary Japan made far more sense to military men than did his romantic remedies.

Gondō likewise had more stature as a critic than as a reconstructionist among the young officers. Intimate though he may have been with certain activists, Gondō was a long-standing opponent of "Prussian style militarism" who could never have tolerated military rule. As he wrote in 1932,

[27] See Nagano Akira, "Hijōji haigo no hito—Gondō Seikyōshi to sono gakusetsu" [A Background Figure during a Time of Emergency—Mr. Gondō Seikyō and His Academic Theories], *Kaizō* [Reconstruction], October 1933, p. 190.

[28] Mikami Taku, quoted in James B. Crowley, *Japan's Quest for Autonomy* (Princeton: Princeton University Press, 1966), p. 177.

militarism and fascism were contrary to the principle of self-rule:

I do not agree that transferring politics from the existing parties to the hands of the military will make a splendid social revolution. The thing to which we should entrust the lives of our people is not fascism. There is another, finer basic force, the people. If the people would only restore a single concept and put it directly into practice, revolution would come about without any difficulty at all. That is, the people should all rise up together and unite in self-rule.[29]

Thus it seems fair to conclude that liaisons with young army and navy officers who themselves chafed under the weight of Japan's cumbersome military establishment in no way compromised the civilian, rural character of Gondō's and Tachibana's overall outlook on politics.

Just as these ideologues had little use for military government, so the young officers were wary of agrarian fundamentalism. The army defendants cited farm poverty as one of their grievances when the Ketsumeidan and May 15 trials began, but none showed much enthusiasm for a new social order based on local communities. Instead, Gondō's and Tachibana's main impact on political terrorism in 1932 was confined to showing the young officers the flaws of modern society and the basic contradictions of capitalism. Important as these analytical functions were, agrarian nationalism was far less crucial for inspiring political murder than the web of personalities, emotions, and perceptions of crisis that enveloped the would-be revolutionaries.

[29] Gondō Seikyō, *Kunmin kyōjiron* [Theory of Joint Rule by Emperor and People] (Tokyo: Bungei Shunjūsha, 1932), p. 171. See Tsukui Tatsuo, *Nihonshugi undō no riron to jissen* [Theory and Practice of the Japanism Movement] (Tokyo: Kensetsusha, 1935), p. 240.

Agrarianism and the Military

If the teachings of Japan's two most famous agrarianists played an indecisive part in the political violence of early 1932, what of the more general affinities between Nōhonshugi and the military services during the 1930s? At this time the army, for example, began to take an active interest in some of the same rural problems that had long disturbed farm ideologues. In October 1934 the Ministry of War, apparently dissatisfied with the government's rural rehabilitation program that had started in 1932, published its own plan for "the rebirth of farm, mountain, and fishing villages."[30] The scheme provided for direct procurement of food, clothing, and rural handicrafts from the poorer districts, job placement for the unemployed, and public works projects as well as community health programs in the villages. In return for rural support for larger military budgets, the army also endorsed proposals for farm debt relief in 1934.[31] Hence although the radical officers preferred general critiques of society to specific agricultural proposals, others in the armed forces were willing to give detailed attention to improving village life.

A common explanation for why the army became interested in farm relief in general and why its activist officers liked Nōhonshugi teachings in particular is that a disproportionately high number of both officers and enlisted men came from the countryside and presumably favored plans for its resuscitation. Writing a generation ago about the complicity of military men in the Ketsumeidan and May 15 plots, Kenneth W. Colegrove stated that "the attraction of Young Officers to these terrorist societies is easily explained. Most of the privates and many of the officers in the army

[30] Sakurai Takeo, *Nihon nōhonshugi* [Japanese Agrarianism] (Tokyo: Hakuyōsha, 1935), p. 133.
[31] Ronald P. Dore and Tsutomu Ōuchi, "Rural Origins of Japanese Fascism," *Dilemmas of Growth in Prewar Japan*, ed. James W. Morley (Princeton: Princeton University Press, 1971), p. 198.

came from poor peasants and workingmen, and naturally their sympathies are with these overburdened classes. They also resent the ease with which young men of the upper strata are able to evade military service by simply continuing in school. They read with abiding interest the books of Gondō, Kita, and Tachibana."[32] More recently Masao Maruyama has observed that, as far as the army was concerned, "among domestic problems the exhaustion of the villages is given first place. That this was the direct motive which specifically turned the young officers to radicalism is easily understandable in light of the fact that many of these officers were the sons of lesser landowners or small independent cultivators."[33]

The sketchy statistics available to test these assertions are difficult to evaluate. One estimate in 1927 placed the number of army officer candidates from "the lower middle classes" —i.e., small landholders and shopkeepers—at 30 percent.[34] Army figures in 1930 showed that 40 percent of the cadets at the Tokyo Shikan Gakkō (Military Academy) were sons of farmers.[35] (Comparable data for the backgrounds of

[32] Kenneth W. Colegrove, *Militarism in Japan* (Boston: World Peace Foundation, 1936), p. 38.

[33] Masao Maruyama, *Thought and Behaviour in Modern Japanese Politics*, ed. Ivan Morris (London: Oxford University Press, 1963), p. 45. Tamagawa Haruzō, *Kindai Nihon no nōson to nōmin* [Farmers and Farm Villages in Modern Japan] (Tokyo: Seiji Kōronsha, 1969), p. 170, and Tsukuba Hisaharu, *Nihonjin no shisō—nōhonshugi no sekai* [Japanese Thought—The World of Agrarianism] (Tokyo: San'ichi Shobō, 1961), p. 198, make similar claims about rural overrepresentation.

[34] Horace Williston, Jr., "General Araki's Contribution to Japanese Militarism and Ultra-Nationalism in the 1930's," M.A. thesis in history, University of California, Berkeley, 1951, p. 10. Barrington Moore, Jr., *Social Origins of Dictatorship and Democracy* (Boston: Beacon Press, 1966), p. 303, repeats this figure.

[35] Ben-Ami Shillony, "The Young Officers and the February 26, 1936, Army Rebellion in Japan," Ph.D. dissertation in history, Princeton University, 1970, p. 27.

young naval officers are not available.) Among enlisted men in the army, 46 percent in 1937 came from village families.[36] Without placing too much weight on these fragmentary figures, it seems fair to say that rural Japan was in no sense overrepresented, either among officers or in the ranks, since a majority of the population as a whole lived in villages under ten thousand population throughout the 1930s. Therefore it is unlikely that the concern of either the young officers or the Ministry of War for farm problems can be explained on the basis of numbers alone—even if one assumed that a peasant army would necessarily support village-oriented ideas and policies.

Another reason why military men might patronize agriculture was its potential for promoting expansion abroad. To the extent that Nōhonshugisha like Katō Kanji encouraged emigration, the extensive rural interest in acquiring new lands was theoretically compatible with plans for enlarging the empire. Such goals were cherished mainly by high-ranking commanders rather than the activist junior officers, who focused instead on domestic reform. Accordingly, the Ministry of War helped to finance farm training centers for overseas settlers in the mid-1930s. Nevertheless, Katō himself feared the military establishment, and peasant demands for more land were an insignificant factor in the military expansion that plunged Japan into World War II.

In reality, the army as a whole had little cause to back Nōhonshugi doctrines. Instead its farm policy during the depression was prompted mainly by a concern among its top leaders for the poor health of rural recruits and by a desire to shore up Japan's self-sufficiency in foodstuffs in case of war—a likely prospect in the 1930s.[37] The Ministry

[36] Hugh Borton, *Japan since 1931, Its Political and Social Development* (New York: Institute of Pacific Relations, 1940), p. 93.

[37] See Ōuchi Tsutomu, "Agricultural Depression and Japanese Villages," *The Developing Economies*, v, 4, December 1967, 619-620; Tamagawa, p. 170. Many inductees from farm regions had tuberculosis and other chronic diseases.

of War was also well aware that the farms continued to pay a large share of the taxes that financed steadily growing military budgets. As a result of its professed interest in the farmers' plight, the army received a good deal of rural backing in the mid-1930s, even though the Ministry of War ended up doing relatively little for the villages and, indeed, finally aided the expansion of big business and centralized control after 1937 because of the industrial and organizational requirements of modern warfare.[38]

Even if Japan's forces were not overwhelmingly rural in composition and the army's motives for helping village residents were primarily self-interested, certain young officers nevertheless shared some of the anxieties of the Nōhonshugi ideologues. One of the May 15 defendants, for example, said at his court-martial that "the impoverishment of the rural villages is a cause of worry to men who have hearts. . . . While soldiers at the front stand between life and death, their families are groaning from hunger. This distress and anxiety are very dangerous."[39] Statements such as this have strengthened the belief that the rural origins of Japan's troops made them especially conscious of farm poverty, but on the whole the young officers were worried less about the villages than about Japan as a whole. Only insofar as rural decay threatened the country, it seems, did most of them remain upset about the farm dilemma.[40] In

[38] Nakamura Yūjirō, *Kindai Nihon ni okeru seido to shisō* [Thought and Institutions in Modern Japan] (Tokyo: Miraisha, 1967), p. 292; Borton, pp. 21, 93-97. See also Dore and Ōuchi, p. 198; Maruyama, p. 46; Chō Yukio, "From the Shōwa Economic Crisis to Military Economy," *The Developing Economies*, v, 4, December 1967, 585. At Yale University Miles Fletcher is preparing a study of the Shōwa Kenkyūkai, with particular emphasis on Ryū Shintarō. On village organization and the armed forces, see Richard J. Smethurst, *A Social Basis for Prewar Japanese Militarism: The Army and the Rural Community* (Berkeley: University of California Press, 1974).

[39] Sakurai Takeo, "Shōwa no nōhonshugi" [Agrarianism in the Shōwa Period], *Shisō* [Thought], No. 407, May 1958, p. 50.

[40] Ronald P. Dore, *Land Reform in Japan* (London: Oxford Uni-

this sense they too, like Gondō and Tachibana, turned the village question into an abstraction, further reducing the possibility that the military insurgents could have done anything concrete to help the countryside.

There is little doubt that many of the radical officers of the 1930s shared Gondō's and Tachibana's intense patriotism and general opposition to the elite which dominated Japanese society, although most resisted above all the privileged senior officers who controlled the military command.[41] But conservative Nōhonshugi doctrines had far less appeal to them than the more resolute reconstructionist dogmas of men like Ōkawa Shūmei and Kita Ikki, because few young officers sympathized with the agrarianist zeal for restoring decentralization, pastoralism, and the premodern hierarchical social relationships characteristic of the top military leadership which they hated. Indeed, by the time of the February 26, 1936 incident, most of the rebel officers were young but successful career men from urban backgrounds, not occupationally frustrated persons from impoverished or culturally narrow homes. In one way or another most of the activist officers in the 1930s were modernizing in intent, if not in style, posing a basic and unresolved contradiction with the romantic agrarian communalism of Nōhonshugi.[42] Only insofar as the agrarianist emphasis on social solidarity and emperor loyalty encouraged national harmony did it accord well with military reconstructionism—although it is doubtful whether such autonomous communal concord could ever be reconciled with central military leadership of politics.

Against these fundamental divergences between Nōhon-

---

versity Press, 1959), pp. 94-95. On pp. 120-122 Dore refutes the contention that the young officers sought a mass rural base for revolution.

[41] See Richard J. Smethurst, "The Military Reserve Association and the Minobe Crisis of 1935," *Crisis Politics in Prewar Japan*, ed. George M. Wilson (Tokyo: Sophia University Press, 1970), p. 22.

[42] Ben-Ami Shillony, "The February 26 Affair: Politics of a Military Insurrection," *Crisis Politics in Prewar Japan*, p. 26.

shugisha and military activists must be set the two groups' affinities in terms of value. Although the young officers had little enthusiasm for primitive agrarianism, they shared Gondō's and Tachibana's alienation from the urban, capitalist values of the political and economic elite. Both farm ideologues and military men could agree that the most desirable qualities for the Japanese people were hard work, devotion, loyalty, thrift, forbearance, and obedience to the throne. Where they differed was in the uses to which these virtues would be put: antimodernizing communalism for the agrarianists, radical reconstructionism for the young officers. In short, it was its vision of a united Japanese nation, forming an ideal society without greed, individualism, or other evils associated with capitalism, that gave Nōhonshugi its greatest appeal to the young enthusiasts in the army and navy officer corps.

The Distinctiveness of Japanese Agrarianism

Since some form of rural ideological reaction has occurred in nearly every industrializing society, a brief comparison of Japanese agrarianism with the American populist tradition in the late nineteenth century may offer perspective on the degree to which Nōhonshugi was a predictable reaction to the modernization process and the extent to which it developed as a peculiarly Japanese phenomenon. Anything more than a surface resemblance between populism and Nōhonshugi would at first appear unlikely, given the enormous differences between Japan and the United States in history, culture, and especially the setting for agricultural production. The land to labor ratios in the two countries were reversed, and America was usually a net exporter of foodstuffs whereas Japan was an importer after 1895. In addition, American farming was highly mechanized while Japan's was not, and American farmers lived alone as miniature businessmen on their lands whereas their Japanese counterparts lived together in small village communities. In light of these major disparities, plus the great differences in sociopolitical culture between the two nations, can a case be made for the similarity of populism and Nōhonshugi? The best evidence for an affirmative answer comes from the economic goals of each movement. In general, both populism and Japanese agrarianism resisted capitalist monopolization and wanted wealth to be much more equally shared.[43] To accomplish this, however, the American farmer was somewhat more willing to have the state intervene on his behalf,[44] probably because American government in the 1880s and 1890s was far less centralized, and thus less suspect to agrarianists, than was the Japanese state when Nōhonshugi flourished. Just as Gondō attacked the gold policies of the Bank of Japan, the populists were dazzled by the prospect of free silver. Moreover both populism and Nōhonshugi affirmed private property while pressing for strong rural cooperative associations, and each held a producer class outlook based partly on the eighteenth-century physiocratic idea that the farmers were the main source of national wealth.[45] In a moral sense, both the American and the Japanese movements argued that capitalist values alienated men from one another, and accordingly they opposed doctrines of unbridled competition—although Gondō and Tachibana both believed in evolutionary social development. Yet the American farmer probably needed big industry to produce his implements and transport his grain to market more than did the Japanese peasant, a factor which may have curbed anti-industrialism in the populist movement.[46]

[43] For populism, see Chester M. Destler, *American Radicalism 1865-1901* (New London: Connecticut College, 1946), pp. 15-17, 23; Norman Pollock, *The Populist Response to Industrial America* (Cambridge, Mass.: Harvard University Press, 1962), pp. 3-12.

[44] Destler, p. 18; Eric F. Goldman, *Rendezvous With Destiny*, rev. ed. (New York: Vintage Books, 1956), p. 41.

[45] For the populists, see Destler, p. 26. Pollock, p. 29, denies the affinity with physiocratic thinking, but the similarity is too obvious to overlook.

[46] Katherine M. Maxim, "Agrarian Response to Industrialization:

Since the corporate economies were more analogous than the systems of government in the two countries, it is understandable that populism made substantially different political demands from Nōhonshugi. The American movement emphasized individual liberties within a democratic tradition that was alien to Japanese farm ideologues: referendums, initiatives, direct election of U.S. senators, and the like.[47] Nōhonshugi, of course, never sponsored a true political movement within the prevailing system of rule, whereas the Populist party became a major national organization whose leader, William Jennings Bryan, was nearly elected president in 1896 on the Democratic ticket. Both movements also opposed institutionalized military power as inimical to the spirit of their respective peoples.[48] In a more general sense, American populists assumed a close connection between farming and democracy,[49] just as Japanese agrarianists believed that rural life was basic to the emperor system. Both movements thus regarded agriculture as essential to their respective political cultures at precisely the time it was growing less so.

Because it used political organizations to seek major changes in the American economy and polity, populism was

---

Populism and Nohon-shugi," B.A. thesis in history, Connecticut College, 1970, p. 64.

[47] For the 1892 Omaha platform of the Populist party, see Goldman, pp. 41-42; Destler, p. 24. See also John D. Hicks, *The Populist Revolt* (Minneapolis: University of Minnesota Press, 1931). For a comparison of political trends in the 1970s with those in late nineteenth-century America, see C. Vann Woodward, "The Ghost of Populism Walks Again," *New York Times Magazine*, June 4, 1972, pp. 16-17, 60, 63-64, 66-69.

[48] For the populists, see Richard Hofstadter, *The Age of Reform* (New York: Random House, 1955), p. 85. The populists were jingoists in the Spanish-American War, but like Gondō and Tachibana they opposed the elitism of the military, political, and economic leadership.

[49] See Grant McConnell, *The Decline of Agrarian Democracy* (Berkeley: University of California Press, 1953), p. 8; A. Whitney Griswold, *Farming and Democracy* (New York: Harcourt Brace, 1948).

315

certainly more multifaceted and probably more progressive in overall tenor than Nōhonshugi. Important to each, however, was an idealized, retrogressive view of farming as a bastion of social virtue. In the American case, the agrarian myth emphasized the bounty of nature, the value of farm output, and the simple honesty of the precommercial cultivator. As Richard Hofstadter put it, this romantic vision represented "a kind of homage that Americans have paid to the fancied innocence of their origins."[50]

Nōhonshugi too glorified premodern agriculture, but its ideal social type was not usually the individual yeoman, as in America, but the village community. This nostalgic concern for the *kyōdōtai* was heightened by the Shinto heritage, whereas America had neither a comparable premodern rural culture nor appropriate religious teachings to reinforce it. The Japanese also lionized farm communalism, especially in the 1930s, in order to mask social conflicts in the countryside. In America, by contrast, there were fewer tenant problems in the late nineteenth-century system of farm enterprise and hence less reason to invent doctrines of collective rural harmony. Because Japanese agrarianism remained primarily a body of social thought and did not develop institutional mechanisms to implement its teachings, the agrarian myth was correspondingly more integral to Nōhonshugi than to its more diverse American counterpart.

Each of these movements arose when farmers still constituted a majority of their respective societies; each tried to retrieve for agriculture a position of influence that was rapidly eroding because of industrialization and urbanization. To implement their ideas, they suggested measures which sometimes seemed radical and sometimes anachronistic.[51] On the whole, populism offered more concrete

[50] Hofstadter, p. 24. For a detailed exposition of the agrarian myth in American history, see pp. 24-42.

[51] Although he is a leading proponent of the view, first expressed by Chester M. Destler, that populism was essentially radical, Norman Pollock carefully distinguishes its economic criticism from that of

proposals for improving farm life than did Japanese agrarianism, although it is true that Nōhonshugi had many partisans in the government bureaucracy who were in a good position to design specific plans. However, most of the official agrarianists in Japan accepted the need for national industrialization and deliberately emphasized the regressive, moral features of Nōhonshugi, not its constructive, programmatic aspects. For Gondō and many other nonofficial farm ideologues, the conservatism of Nōhonshugi, when compared with populism, was compounded by the existence in Japan of a rich and distinctive rural tradition without counterpart in America—a tradition which they believed demanded preservation because of its critical relationship with the essence of the Japanese nation.

Agrarianism and Japanese Nationalism

Japanese agrarianism was a natural product of the transition from an economy based on farming to one dominated by commerce and industry. It was also an important ideological current in the nation's struggle to clarify its self-image during the years from the Meiji restoration to World War II. All societies periodically question their collective identity, but in the case of modern Japan her people have been especially fascinated with the question of what it means to be a Japanese. Most responses have tried to define the nature of Japanese nationalism, or *kokuminshugi*—the common sentiments joining the public together as a unit. But certain theories of Japanese nationalism, above all in the 1930s and early 1940s, held that loyalty to the state was the essence of being a Japanese.

Nōhonshugi contributed to nationalist thinking in modern Japan mainly by insisting that agriculture was the com-

---

Marxism on pp. 68-84. Tsukuba, pp. 18, 215-217, compares Nōhonshugi with Marxism, emphasizing that Japanese agrarianists had little conception of the division of labor and upheld a premodern, hierarchical society characteristic of preindustrial stages in Marxist historiography.

mon denominator of the Japanese as a people. Unlike most statist forms of nationalism,[52] Nōhonshugi was a nondialectical ideology which upheld social harmony and (at least in the twentieth century) rejected the jarring competitiveness of industrial capitalism. In the Meiji period Nōhonshugi as a theory of popular nationality consciousness did not conflict with state-oriented nationalism because the interests of state and nation were sufficiently congruous to permit both bureaucrats and private citizens to agree on agrarianist ideas. Once this congruity dissipated, nonofficial Nōhonshugi became the main stream of Japanese agrarianism, firmly rejecting the statist proclivities of contemporary nationalist thinking in favor of farm-centered theories focused on the people themselves.

Nōhonshugi offered the Japanese public a moral community for collective self-identification to replace the village social entities that were being dissolved by commercialization. In this respect, agrarianists supplied ideological security against socioeconomic changes similar to that provided by the corporate structure of Japanese enterprise (*kigyōsei*).[53] However abstract the Nōhonshugi visions of the new order, they were no more so than the utopias suggested by socialists, urban reconstructionists, or the military establishment itself once it came to power in the late 1930s.

Since Nōhonshugi ideas were primarily centered on the Japanese people rather than the state, it is uncertain how much they reinforced the ultranationalism prevalent during World War II. The ideology of the highly centralized military government which ruled Japan during wartime represented practically everything that was anathema to men such as Gondō Seikyō, Tachibana Kōzaburō, and Katō Kanji. It was grounded on bureaucratic rule, heavy industry, ever greater urbanization, and the monopolization of

[52] Kenneth E. Boulding, *A Primer on Social Dynamics* (New York: The Free Press, 1970), p. vi.
[53] I am indebted to David Swain for comments on this point.

power and privilege by a narrow elite. In addition, although the Ministry of Education praised agrarianist ideals in the wartime ethics textbooks, the state did little to root out the corrupt materialist values of capitalism that so antagonized Tachibana and most other Nōhonshugisha. The agrarianists even chose different terms from those used by ultranationalists to define the framework of their ideal social order. Gondō, Tachibana, Katō, and their fellow farm ideologues almost always spoke of the Japanese people (*Nihon kokumin*) and only rarely referred to the Japanese empire (*Nihon teikoku*), the standard code phrase used by militarists.[54]

Yet in several respects agrarian nationalism was sufficiently compatible with the prevailing statist outlook to provide at least tacit support for Japan's military rulers. Both the government and Nōhonshugisha developed elaborate myths about the ethnic and religious uniqueness of the nation. Agrarianism was also institutionally conservative, advocating rural stability and overall social solidarity of a sort that would please a regime opposed to domestic change in a time of crisis. In addition, although it was more pro-Japan than actively anti-Western, to some extent Nōhonshugi thought probably predisposed its adherents to accepting war with America and the European powers by systematically attacking capitalism, party politics, colonialism, and the decadent values which had invaded Japan from abroad.

Most importantly, Nōhonshugi chose the imperial throne as its emblem of popular nationality sentiments, just as state ultranationalism made the emperor the focus of its doctrines of public loyalty. Both assigned the throne a major symbolic role, although for the purpose of legitimizing two nearly opposite systems of rule—local autonomy and centralized military government. Nevertheless, when agrarianists stressed the *kyōdoshugi* heritage of affection for the

[54] Cf. the stock in trade *Nihon rettō* [Japanese archipelago], popularized by Prime Minister Tanaka Kakuei in the early 1970s.

home village under a benevolent monarch who performed both sacred and secular functions, they created important points of contact with the state ideology of emperor loyalty that dominated Japanese nationalism during the war. The Shinto tradition gave even greater strength to these contacts by linking Nōhonshugi theories of the unity of farming and *kami* worship with the government's program of state Shinto. To the extent that it encouraged village residents to make the spirit of farming synonymous with respect for the gods, Nōhonshugi abetted the government's drive to register all citizens at shrines, where they could more easily be indoctrinated with emperor-centered teachings.

Despite the intentions of its foremost spokesmen in the 1920s and 1930s, Nōhonshugi thus became something of a silent partner of ultranationalism during World War II. In much the same fashion as low farm prices after 1930 had overshadowed tenant disputes and helped to unite all villagers by driving them into a common quandary, the emergency conditions which affected all Japanese after 1937 no doubt enhanced the government's drive for ideological conformity. But even in wartime Japanese political thought was no monolith, and the agrarianist teachings of Gondō and Tachibana never became fully reconciled with the dogmas of the military government.

Indeed, the lack of consensus on what constituted Japanese nationalism during these years is striking.[55] Although nearly every patriotic society and nationalist ideologue sincerely joined the search for harmony in the face of the divisions in modern society, agreement on how to achieve it remained exceedingly elusive.[56] Nōhonshugi contributed most fundamentally to this search by expressing its moral outrage at the acquisitive, self-interested spirit of modern life, a sentiment with which almost every nationalist could

[55] See Borton, p. 31.

[56] Edwin O. Reischauer, "What Went Wrong?" *Dilemmas of Growth in Prewar Japan*, ed. James W. Morley (Princeton: Princeton University Press, 1971), p. 498.

concur. In the end, however, the dream of harmony never materialized. Just as Nōhonshugi's proposed basis for public unity—self-ruling village communalism—proved to be unacceptable, so too the state, despite the enormous powers of thought control at its command, failed to impose its version of Japanese nationalism very effectively upon the public.[57]

Nōhonshugi answered the question of what it meant to be a Japanese by praising farm production, self-sufficiency, local autonomy, and village concord. The futility of agrarianism in prewar Japan was not that it was too romantic or too reactionary, even though individual agrarianists such as Gondō probably were. Instead, its greatest defect was that it was too rustic an ideology for an industrializing age. It was no more capable than the state propaganda machine of reimposing harmony by reversing the pluralism and diversity of a rapidly urbanizing society. This was the pathos and the irony of Nōhonshugi: the industrialism which produced agrarianism also blocked it from achieving the goals for which it stood. The same industrialism has reduced Nōhonshugi today to a shadowy agrarian nostalgia that sends city people to brightly decorated shops to buy village folk crafts as quaint tokens of a rural world which few remember and fewer will ever know.

[57] See Penelope Brown, "The Thought Control Program of Japan's Military Leaders, 1931-1941." B.A. thesis in history, Connecticut College, 1972, pp. 62-69.

Works Cited

Adachi Ikitsune. "'Ie no hikari' no rekishi" [History of "The Light of the Household"], *Shisō no kagaku* [Science of Thought], No. 18, June 1960, pp. 59-76.

———. "Nōhonshugi no saikentō" [A Reappraisal of Theories on Agrarianism], *Shisō* [Thought], No. 423, September 1959, pp. 56-58.

Agricultural Development in Modern Japan, ed. Takekazu Ogura, 2nd ed. Tokyo: Fuji Publishing Co., 1968.

Agriculture and Economic Growth: Japan's Experience, ed. Kazushi Ohkawa, Bruce F. Johnston, and Hiromitsu Kaneda. Princeton: Princeton University Press, and Tokyo: University of Tokyo Press, 1970.

"Aikyōjukusei to nōson mondai o kataru zadankai" [Roundtable Discussion on Farm Village Problems by Aikyōjuku Students], *Bungei shunjū*, September 1932, pp. 204-220.

Akita, George. *Foundations of Constitutional Government in Modern Japan 1868-1900*. Cambridge, Mass.: Harvard University Press, 1967.

Arahara Bokusui. *Dai uyokushi* [Full History of the Right Wing]. Tokyo: Nihon Kokumintō, 1966.

Arishima Takeo. "Nōson mondai no kiketsu" [Solution to the Rural Village Problem], 1923, *Arishima Takeo zenshū* [Complete Works of Arishima Takeo], VII, 491-493. Tokyo: Sōbunkaku, 1924-1925.

323

Armstrong, Robert C. *Just Before the Dawn: The Life and Work of Ninomiya Sontoku.* New York: Macmillan, 1912.

Aspects of Social Change in Modern Japan, ed. Ronald P. Dore. Princeton: Princeton University Press, 1967.

Bamba, Nobuya. *Japanese Diplomacy in a Dilemma.* Kyoto: Minerva Press, Ltd., 1972.

Beardsley, Richard K., John W. Hall, and Robert E. Ward. *Village Japan.* Chicago: University of Chicago Press, 1959.

Beasley, William G. "Introduction," *Select Documents on Japanese Foreign Policy, 1853-1868*, ed. William G. Beasley, pp. 3-93. London: Oxford University Press, 1955.

Bellah, Robert N. *Tokugawa Religion: The Values of Preindustrial Japan.* Glencoe, Ill.: The Free Press, 1957.

Bernstein, Gail Lee. "Kawakami Hajime: Portrait of a Reluctant Revolutionary." Ph.D. dissertation in history, Harvard University, 1967.

Blacker, Carmen. *The Japanese Enlightenment: A Study of the Writings of Fukuzawa Yukichi.* Cambridge: Cambridge University Press, 1964.

Borton, Hugh. *Japan Since 1931, Its Political and Social Development.* New York: Institute of Pacific Relations, 1940.

———. *Japan's Modern Century*, 2nd ed. New York: Ronald Press, 1970.

Boulding, Kenneth E. *A Primer on Social Dynamics.* New York: The Free Press, 1970.

Brown, Delmer M. *Nationalism in Japan, An Introductory Historical Analysis.* Berkeley: University of California Press, 1955.

Brown, Penelope. "The Thought Control Program of Japan's Military Leaders, 1931-1941." B.A. thesis in history, Connecticut College, 1972.

Byas, Hugh. *Government by Assassination.* New York: Alfred A. Knopf, 1942.

Casal, U. A. *The Five Sacred Festivals of Ancient Japan: Their Symbolism and Historical Development.* Tokyo: Sophia University Press, 1967.

Changing Japanese Attitudes Toward Modernization, ed. Marius B. Jansen. Princeton: Princeton University Press, 1965.

Chō Yukio. "From the Shōwa Economic Crisis to Military Economy," *The Developing Economies,* v, 4, December 1967, 568-596.

————. "Nashonarizumu to 'sangyō' undō—Maeda Masana no shisō to katsudō" [Nationalism and the "Production" Movement—The Career and Thought of Maeda Masana], *Kindai Nihon keizai shisōshi* [History of Modern Japanese Economic Thought], ed. Chō Yukio and Sumiya Kazuhiko, I, 85-133. Tokyo: Yūhikaku, 1969.

Chōki keizai tōkei, suikei to bunseki [English title: *Estimates of Long-Term Economic Statistics of Japan Since 1868*], ed. Ohkawa Kazushi, Shinohara Miyohei, and Umemura Mataji, 13 vols. Tokyo: Tōyō Keizai Shinbunsha, 1966–.

Chōkokkashugi [Ultranationalism], ed. Hashikawa Bunzō, *Gendai Nihon shisō taikei* [Collection on Modern Japanese Thought], xxxi. Tokyo: Chikuma Shobō, 1964.

Colegrove, Kenneth W. *Militarism in Japan.* Boston: World Peace Foundation, 1936.

Connor, Walker. "Nation-Building or Nation-Destroying?" *World Politics,* xxiv, 3, April 1972, 319-355.

Conroy, F. Hilary. *The Japanese Seizure of Korea: 1868-1910.* Philadelphia: University of Pennsylvania Press, 1960.

Craig, Albert M. *Chōshū in the Meiji Restoration.* Cambridge, Mass.: Harvard University Press, 1961.

————. "Fukuzawa Yukichi: The Philosophical Foundations of Meiji Nationalism," *Political Development in Modern Japan,* ed. Robert E. Ward, pp. 99-148. Princeton: Princeton University Press, 1968.

Crowley, James B. *Japan's Quest for Autonomy.* Princeton: Princeton University Press, 1966.

Dakin, Douglas. *Turgot and the* Ancien Régime *in France.* London: Methuen & Co., 1939.

Denda Isao. *Kindai Nihon keizai shisō no kenkyū—Nihon no kindaika to chihō keizai* [Studies on Modern Japanese Economic Thought—Japanese Modernization and Rural Economics]. Tokyo: Miraisha, 1962.

————. *Kindai Nihon nōsei shisō no kenkyū* [Studies on Modern Japanese Agricultural Administration Thought]. Tokyo: Miraisha, 1969.

Destler, Chester M. *American Radicalism 1865-1901.* New London: Connecticut College, 1946.

Deutsch, Karl W. *Nationalism and Its Alternatives.* New York: Alfred A. Knopf, 1969.

Dilemmas of Growth in Prewar Japan, ed. James W. Morley. Princeton: Princeton University Press, 1971.

Dore, Ronald P. *Land Reform in Japan.* London: Oxford University Press, 1959.

———— and Tsutomu Ōuchi. "Rural Origins of Japanese Fascism," *Dilemmas of Growth in Prewar Japan,* ed. James W. Morley, pp. 181-209. Princeton: Princeton University Press, 1971.

Droppers, Garrett. "Some Economic Theories of Old Japan," *Transactions of the Asiatic Society of Japan,* series I, XXIV, 1893, v-xx.

Economic Growth: The Japanese Experience Since the Meiji Era, ed. Lawrence Klein and Kazushi Ohkawa. Homewood, Ill.: Richard D. Irwin, Inc., 1968.

Einaudi, Mario. *The Physiocratic Doctrine of Judicial Control.* Cambridge, Mass.: Harvard University Press, 1938.

Emori Itsuo. "Chihō kairyō undō ni okeru sonraku kyōdōtai no saihensei" [Rebirth of Village Communalism in the Rural Improvement Movement], *Nihon kindaika no kenkyū* [Studies of Japanese Modernization], I, January 1972, 371-398.

————. "Meijiki no Hōtokusha undō no shiteki shakaiteki haikei" [Historical and Social Background of the Meiji Period Hōtokusha Movement], *Hōritsu ronsō* [Collection of Legal Theories], Meiji University, part 1, XL, 1, October 1966, 83-124; part 2, XL, 2-3, November 1966, 47-82.

Estimates of Long-term Economic Statistics of Japan Since 1868, see *Chōki keizai tōkei, suikei to bunseki.*

Fisher, Galen M. "The Cooperative Movement in Japan," *Pacific Affairs*, XI, 4, December 1938, 478-491.

Fridell, Wilbur M. *Japanese Shrine Mergers, 1906-12.* Tokyo: Sophia University Press, 1973.

Fujita Shōzō. "Tennōsei to fuashizumu" [The Emperor System and Fascism], *Iwanami kōza gendai shisō*, v, *Handō no shisō* [Iwanami Colloquium on Modern Thought, v, Reactionary Thought], pp. 153-186. Tokyo: Iwanami Shoten, 1959.

Fukutake Tadashi. *Nihon no nōson shakai* [Japanese Rural Society] Tokyo: Tokyo Daigaku Shuppankai, 1953.

Fukuzawa Yukichi. *The Autobiography of Fukuzawa Yukichi*, trans. Eiichi Kiyooka, new translation. Tokyo: Hokuseido Press, 1960.

———. *An Encouragement of Learning*, trans. David A. Dilworth and Umeyo Hirano. Tokyo: Sophia University Press, 1969.

———. *Fukuō jiden* [Autobiography of Fukuzawa Yukichi]. Tokyo, 1899.

———. *Gakumon no susume* [Encouragement of Learning]. Tokyo, 1872.

Furushima Toshio. *Nihon nōgakushi* [History of Japanese Agriculture], 1 vol. Tokyo: Nihon Hyōronsha, 1946.

Gilbert, Felix. "Intellectual History: Its Aims and Methods," *Historical Study Today*, ed. Felix Gilbert and Stephen R. Graubard, pp. 141-158. New York: W. W. Norton & Co., Inc., 1972.

Goldman, Eric F. *Rendezvous with Destiny*, rev. ed. New York: Vintage Books, 1956.

Gondō Seikyō. *Gondō Seikyō chosakushū* [Collected Writings of Gondō Seikyō], vol. 1-. Tokyo: Girochinsha, Nebīsusha, Kokushokusensensha, 1972-.

———. *Hachirin tsūheikō.* Tokyo: privately published, 1931.

Gondō Seikyō. *Jichi minpan* [People's Guide to Self-Rule], 2nd ed. Tokyo: Heibonsha, 1932. (Originally published in 1927.)

———. *Jichi minseiri* [Principles of People's Self-Rule]. Tokyo: Gakugeisha, 1936.

———. *Kōmin jichi hongi* [Basic Principles of Imperial People's Self-Rule]. Tokyo: Fuzanbō, 1920.

———. *Kunmin kyōjiron* [Theory of Joint Rule by Emperor and People]. Tokyo: Bungei Shunjūsha, 1932.

———. *Nihon nōseishidan* [Talks on the History of the Japanese Agricultural System], ed. Okamoto Rikichi. Tokyo: Junshinsha, 1931.

———. *Nōson jikyūron* [Theory of Farm Village Self-Help]. Tokyo: Bungei Shunjūsha, 1932.

Griswold, A. Whitney. *Farming and Democracy*. New York: Harcourt Brace, 1948.

Hackett, Roger F. *Yamagata Aritomo in the Rise of Modern Japan, 1838-1922*. Cambridge, Mass.: Harvard University Press, 1971.

Hall, John W. *Tanuma Okitsugu (1719-1788): Forerunner of Modern Japan*. Cambridge, Mass.: Harvard University Press, 1955.

Hall, Robert K. *Shūshin: The Ethics of a Defeated Nation*. New York: Columbia University Teachers College, 1949.

Hane, Mikiso. *Japan: A Historical Survey*. New York: Charles Scribner's Sons, 1972.

Hanzawa Hiroshi. *Dochaku no shisō* [Home Town Thought]. Tokyo: Kinokuniya Shoten, 1967.

Haraguchi Kiyoshi. "Hōtokusha no hitobito" [Hōtokusha Members], *Nihon jinbutsushi taikei* [Outline History of Talented Persons in Japan], ed. Konishi Shirō, v, 252-283. Tokyo: Asakura Shoten, 1960.

Hashikawa Bunzō. "Hoi—Ketsumeidan, goichigo jiken o chūshin to shite" [Addendum—With Emphasis on the Ketsumeidan and May 15 Incidents], in Takizawa Makoto, *Gondō Seikyō oboegaki* [Notes on Gondō Seikyō], 116-163. Nagaokashi: privately published, 1968.

————. *Nihon rōmanha hihan josetsu* [Introductory Criticism of Japanese Romanticists], expanded ed. Tokyo: Miraisha, 1965.

————. "Shōwa chōkokkashugi no shosō" [Various Aspects of Ultranationalism in the Shōwa Period], *Chōkokkashugi* [Ultranationalism], ed. Hashikawa Bunzō, *Gendai Nihon shisō taikei* [Collection on Modern Japanese Thought], XXXI, 7-58. Tokyo: Chikuma Shobō, 1964.

————. "Shōwa ishin no ronri to shinri" [Logic and Psychology of the Shōwa Restoration], *Kindai Nihon seiji shisōshi* [History of Modern Japanese Political Thought], ed. Hashikawa Bunzō and Matsumoto Sannosuke, II, 209-231. Tokyo: Yūhikaku, 1970.

Hata Ikuhiko. *Gun fuashizumu undōshi—sangatsu jiken kara ninirokugo made* [History of the Military Fascist Movement—From the March Incident Until After the February 26 Incident]. Tokyo: Kawade Shobō Shinsha, 1962.

Havens, Thomas R. H. "Frontiers of Japanese Social History During World War II," *Shakai kagaku tōkyū* [Social Science Review], XVIII, 3, No. 52, March 1973, 1-45.

————. "Katō Kanji (1884-1965) and the Spirit of Agriculture in Modern Japan," *Monumenta Nipponica*, XXV, 3-4, Autumn 1970, 249-266.

————. "Religion and Agriculture in Nineteenth-Century Japan: Ninomiya Sontoku and the Hōtoku Movement," *Japan Christian Quarterly*, XXXVIII, 2, Spring 1972, 98-105.

————. "Two Popular Views of Rural Self-Rule in Modern Japan," *Studies on Japanese Culture* (Tokyo: The Japan P.E.N. Club, 1973), II, 249-256.

Hicks, John D. *The Populist Revolt*. Minneapolis: University of Minnesota Press, 1931.

Higgs, Henry. *The Physiocrats*. London: Macmillan, 1897.

Hijikata Kazuo. "Nihonkei fuashizumu no taitō to teikō" [The Rise and Resistance of Japanese Fascism], *Kindai Nihon shakai shisōshi* [History of Modern Japanese Social

Thought], ed. Furuta Hikaru, Sakuta Keiichi, and Ikimatsu Keizō, II, 111-175. Tokyo: Yūhikaku, 1971.

Hirata Tōsuke. "Sangyō Kumiai to Hōtokushugi" [Producers' Cooperatives and Hōtoku Thought], *Shimin* [These People], II, 4, part 3, 1907, in *Hōtoku no shinzui* [The Essence of Hōtoku], ed. Tomeoka Kōsuke, pp. 102-106. Tokyo: Keiseisha Shoten, 1908.

Hirose Yutaka and Hirose Toshiko. *Ninomiya Sontoku no kōtei Tomita Takayoshi* [Tomita Takayoshi, Ninomiya Sontoku's Senior Disciple]. Tokyo: Nihon Kōshikai, 1953.

Hofstadter, Richard. *The Age of Reform*. New York: Random House, 1955.

Holtom, D. C. *Modern Japan and Shinto Nationalism*. Chicago: University of Chicago Press, 1943.

————. *The National Faith of Japan*. London: Kegan Paul, 1938.

Ifukube Takahiko. "Gondō Seikyō hyōden nōto" [Critical Biographical Notes on Gondō Seikyō], *Kokuron* [National Theory], part 1, III, 9, September 1955, 15-17; part 2, III, 10, October 1955, 22-24; part 3, III, 12, December 1955, 22-23; part 4, IV, 1, January 1956, 22-24; part 5, IV, 2, February 1956, 19-21; part 6, IV, 3, March 1956, 21-22; part 7, IV, 4, April 1956, 22-24; part 8, IV, 6, June 1956, 19-21; part 9, IV, 8, August 1956, 11-14; part 10, IV, 9, September 1956, 15-16; part 11, IV, 10, October 1956, 13-14; part 12, IV, 11, November 1956, 13-14; part 13, IV, 12, December 1956, 13-16; part 14, V, 1, January 1957, 13-15.

Iinuma Jirō. *Nihon nōgyō gijutsushi* [History of Japanese Agricultural Technology]. Tokyo: Miraisha, 1971.

Inagaki Kiyoshi. *Waga nōsei Yamazaki Nobukichi den* [Biography of Yamazaki Nobukichi, Our Farm Teacher]. Nagoya: Fūbaisha, 1966.

Iriye, Akira. "The Failure of Military Expansion," *Dilemmas of Growth in Prewar Japan*, ed. James W. Morley, pp. 107-138. Princeton: Princeton University Press, 1971.

Ishida Takeshi. *Meiji seiji shisōshi kenkyū* [Studies on Meiji Political Thought]. Tokyo: Miraisha, 1954.

Ishiguro Tadaatsu den [Biography of Ishiguro Tadaatsu], ed. Hashimoto Denzaemon et al. Tokyo: Iwanami Shoten, 1969.

Ishikawa Ken and Katayama Seiichi. "Yokoi Tokiyoshi no nōgyō kyōikuron ni okeru bushidōshugi—kindai Nihon no kyōiku ni miru shinpō to dentō" [Bushido Ideology in the Educational Theories of Yokoi Tokiyoshi—Progress and Tradition in Modern Japanese Education], *Gendai kyōiku to dentō* [Modern Education and Tradition], June 30, 1963, pp. 79-83.

Jansen, Marius B. *The Japanese and Sun Yat-sen*. Cambridge, Mass.: Harvard University Press, 1954.

————. "The Meiji State: 1868-1912," *Modern East Asia: Essays in Interpretation*, ed. James B. Crowley, pp. 95-121. New York: Harcourt, Brace & World, Inc., 1970.

————. *Sakamoto Ryōma and the Meiji Restoration*. Princeton: Princeton University Press, 1961.

Kada Tetsuji. *Nihon kokkashugi no hatten* [The Development of Japanese Nationalism]. Tokyo: Keiō Shobō, 1938.

Kajinishi Mitsuhaya. "Maeda Masana," *Nihon jinbutsushi taikei* [Outline History of Talented Persons in Japan], ed. Konishi Shirō, v, 284-311. Tokyo: Asakura Shoten, 1960.

Katayama Seiichi. "Meiji zenki nōgyō shidōsha no nōgyō kyōikukan" [The Farm Education Outlooks of Early Meiji Farm Leaders], *Nihon Daigaku Seishin Bunka Kenkyūjo-Kyōiku Seido Kenkyūjo kiyō* [Bulletin of the Nihon University Cultural Research Institute and Educational System Research Institute], iv, June 1967, 161-215.

Katō Fusakura. *Hakushaku Hirata Tōsuke den* [Biography of Count Hirata Tōsuke]. Tokyo: Hiratahaku Denki Hensan Jimusho, 1927.

Katō Kanji. *Nihon nōson kyōiku* [Japanese Farm Education]. Tokyo: Tōyō Tosho, 1934.

————. *Taiō shokan* [Impressions of Europe]. Tokyo: Sugiyama Shoten, 1929.

Kawakami Hajime. *Nihon nōseigaku* [Studies on Japanese Agricultural Administration]. Tokyo, 1906.

———. "Nihon sonnōron" [Respecting Japanese Agriculture], 1904, *Kawakami Hajime chosakushū* [Collected Writings of Kawakami Hajime], 1, 131-221. Tokyo: Chikuma Shobō, 1964.

Kawakami Tomizō. *Ishikawa Rikinosuke*. Akitaken: Shōwamachi, Ishikawaō Iseki Hozonkai, 1964.

Kazami, Akira. "Whither the Japanese Peasantry?" *Contemporary Japan*, II, 4, 1933, 681-687.

Keene, Donald. "The Sino-Japanese War of 1894-95 and Its Cultural Effects in Japan," *Tradition and Modernization in Japanese Culture*, ed. Donald H. Shively, pp. 121-175. Princeton: Princeton University Press, 1971.

Ketsumeidan jiken jōshinsho gokuchū shuki [Ketsumeidan Incident Report and Prison Notes], ed. and pub. Ketsumeidan Jiken Kōhan Sokkiroku Kankōkai, Tokyo, 1971.

Kindai Nihon shisōshi [History of Modern Japanese Thought], ed. Tōyama Shigeki, Yamazaki Seiichi, and Ōi Sei, 3 vols. Tokyo: Aoki Shoten, 1956.

Kinoshita Hanji. *Nihon no uyoku* [The Japanese Right Wing]. Tokyo: Kaname Shobō, 1953.

———. *Uyoku tero* [Right-Wing Terror]. Kyoto: Hōritsu Bunkasha, 1960.

Kodaira Ken'ichi. *Ishiguro Tadaatsu*. Tokyo: Jiji Tsūshinsha, 1962.

Kodama Shōtarō. *Ijin Ishikawaō no jigyō to genkō* [Words and Deeds of the Illustrious Ishikawa]. Tokyo: Heibonsha, 1929.

Kōgyō ikenta—Maeda Masana kankei shiryō ["Advice on Promoting Enterprise" *et al.*—Materials Relating to Maeda Masana], ed. Andō Yoshio and Yamamoto Hirobumi. Tokyo: Kōseikan, 1971.

Koide Kōzō. *Kyōdo o okoshita senjin no omokage* [Memories of Forebears Who Revived Their Home Towns]. Tokyo: Nihon Jichi Kensetsu Honbu, 1958.

Kokura Kuraichi. "Nōsei oyobi Nōkai" [Agricultural Administration and the Agricultural Associations], *Nihon nōgyō hattatsushi* [History of the Development of Japanese Agriculture], ed. Nōgyō Hattatsushi Chōsakai, v, 309-415. Tokyo: Chūō Kōronsha, 1955.

Kono, Shōzō. "Kannagara no Michi: The Meaning of Kannagara," *Monumenta Nipponica*, III, 2, 1940, 9-31.

Konuma Shō and Takahashi Masae. "Aru kokkashugisha no hansei" [Half-Life of a Certain Nationalist], *Shōwa shisōshi e no shōgen* [Evidence toward a History of Shōwa Thought], ed. Mainichi Shinbunsha, rev. ed., pp. 183-270. Tokyo: Mainichi Shinbunsha, 1972.

Kurihara Hyakuju. *Jinbutsu nōgyō dantaishi* [History of Outstanding Agricultural Association Leaders]. Tokyo: Shinhyōronsha, 1956.

Lockwood, William W. *The Economic Development of Japan: Growth and Structural Change 1868-1938.* Princeton: Princeton University Press, 1954.

Maruyama, Masao. *Thought and Behaviour in Modern Japanese Politics*, ed. Ivan Morris. London: Oxford University Press, 1963.

Matsuzawa Tetsunari. " 'Shōwa ishin' no shisō to kōdō— Tachibana Kōzaburō no baai" [Thought and Behavior in the "Shōwa Restoration"—The Case of Tachibana Kōzaburō], *Shakai kagaku kenkyū* [Social Science Studies], XIX, 3, January 1968, 1-100.

———. *Tachibana Kōzaburō.* Tokyo: San'ichi Shobō, 1972.

Maxim, Katherine M. "Agrarian Response to Industrialization: Populism and Nohon-shugi." B.A. thesis in history, Connecticut College, 1970.

McConnell, Grant. *The Decline of Agrarian Democracy.* Berkeley: University of California Press, 1953.

McEwan, John R. "The Confucian Ideology and the Modernization of Japan," *The Modernization of Japan*, ed. Tōbata Seiichi, I, 229-241. Tokyo: Institute of Asian Economic Affairs, 1966.

Miller, Frank O. *Minobe Tatsukichi: Interpreter of Constitutionalism in Japan*. Berkeley: University of California Press, 1965.

Mito Saburō. "Aikyōjuku?!" *Bungei shunjū*, x, 7, July 1932, 236-240.

Miyaji Masato. "Chihō kairyō undō ni okeru Hōtokusha no kinō" [Function of the Hōtokusha in the Rural Improvement Movement], *Shigaku zasshi* [Historical Journal], LXXX, 2, February 1971, 1-21.

———. "Chihō kairyō undō no ronri to tenkai—Nichiro-sengo no nōson seisaku" [Logic and Development of the Rural Improvement Movement—Farm Policy After the Russo-Japanese War], *Shigaku zasshi* [Historical Journal], LXXIX, 8, August 1970, 1-45; LXXIX, 9, September 1970, 25-86.

Miyamoto Tsuneichi. *Ise sangū* [Pilgrimage to Ise]. Tokyo: Shakai Shisōsha, 1972.

Moore, Barrington, Jr. *Social Origins of Dictatorship and Democracy*. Boston: Beacon Press, 1966.

Mori Hiroshi. *Kome to Nihon bunka* [Rice and Japanese Culture]. Tokyo: Hyōgensha, 1972.

Mori Takemaro. "Nihon fuashizumu no keisei to nōson keizai kōsei undō" [The Formation of Japanese Fascism and the Rural Economic Rehabilitation Movement], *Rekishigaku kenkyū* [Historical Studies], special number, October 1971, pp. 135-152.

Morita Shirō. *The Development of Agricultural Cooperative Associations in Japan*. Tokyo: Japan FAO Association, 1960.

Morley, James W. "Introduction: Choice and Consequence," *Dilemmas of Growth in Prewar Japan*, ed. James W. Morley, pp. 3-30. Princeton: Princeton University Press, 1971.

Murakami Ichirō. "Tachibana Kōzaburōshi tokubetsu intabyū—kokka kenryoku to minshū" [Special Interview with Mr. Tachibana Kōzaburō—State Power and the People], *Shihaisha to sono kage* [Leaders and Their Influence], ed. Tanigawa Ken'ichi *et al.*, pp. 6-17. Tokyo: Gakugei Shorin, 1969.

Nagano Akira. "Hijōji haigo no hito—Gondō Seikyōshi to sono gakusetsu" [A Background Figure During a Time of Emergency—Mr. Gondō Seikyō and His Academic Theories], *Kaizō* [Reconstruction], October 1933, pp. 190-197.

Naimushōshi [History of the Ministry of Internal Affairs], ed. Taikakai, 4 vols. Tokyo: Chihō Zaimu Kyōkai, 1970-1971.

Najita, Tetsuo. *Hara Kei in the Politics of Compromise 1905-1915.* Cambridge, Mass.: Harvard University Press, 1967.

Nakamura, James I. *Agricultural Production and the Economic Development of Japan, 1873-1922.* Princeton: Princeton University Press, 1966.

Nakamura Yūjirō. *Kindai Nihon ni okeru seido to shisō* [Thought and Institutions in Modern Japan]. Tokyo: Miraisha, 1967.

Nan'ensho [Book of Nan'en], ed. Gondō Seikyō and Ozawa Dagyō. Tokyo: Heibonsha, 1922.

Naramoto Tatsuya. *Ninomiya Sontoku.* Tokyo: Iwanami Shoten, 1959.

Nihon jinmei jiten [Biographical Dictionary of Japan], ed. Haga Yaichi, reprint ed. Kyoto: Shibunkaku, 1969. (Originally published in 1914.)

Nihon nōmin undōshi [History of the Japanese Peasant Movement], ed. Aoki Keiichirō, 6 vols. Tokyo: Nihon Hyōron Shinsha, 1959-1962.

Nihon nōmin undōshi [History of the Japanese Peasant Movement], ed. Nōmin Undōshi Kenkyūkai. Tokyo: Tōyō Keizai Shinbunsha, 1961.

Ninomiya Sontoku. *Ninomiyaō yawa* [Ninomiya's Evening Talks], comp. Fukuzumi Masae, *Fukuzumi Masae senshū* [Selected Work of Fukuzumi Masae], *Ninomiya*

Sontoku zenshū [Complete Works of Ninomiya Sontoku], XXXVI, 666-853. Shizuoka: Ninomiya Sontoku Igyō Sen'yōkai, 1931.

Ninomiya Sontoku: His Life and "Evening Talks," ed. Ishiguro Tadaatsu. Tokyo: Kenkyūsha, 1955.

Niwa Kunio. "The Reform of the Land Tax and the Government Programme for the Encouragement of Industry," *The Developing Economics*, IV, 4, December 1966, 447-471.

Nolte, Sharon H. "Gondō Seikyō and the Agrarianist Critique of Modern Japan." Seminar paper in history, Yale University, 1973.

Norman, E. Herbert. *Andō Shōeki and the Anatomy of Japanese Feudalism, Transactions of the Asiatic Society of Japan*, series 3, II. Tokyo, 1949.

———. *Japan's Emergence as a Modern State.* New York: Institute of Pacific Relations, 1940.

Ogata Kiyoshi. *The Co-operative Movement in Japan.* London: P. S. King & Son, Ltd., 1923.

Ogura. See *Agricultural Development in Modern Japan.*

Ogura Takekazu. *Agrarian Problems and Agricultural Policy in Japan.* Tokyo: Institute of Asian Economic Affairs, 1967.

Ōhigashi Kunio. *Ri Yōkyū no shōgai* [The Career of Yi Yong-gu]. Tokyo: Jiji Tsūshinsha, 1960.

Okada Kōsaku. "Katō Kanji no nōmin kyōiku shisō" [Katō Kanji's Farm Education Thought], *Shisō no kagaku* [Science of Thought], No. 18, June 1960, pp. 33-42.

Okada On. *Nōgyō keiei to nōsei* [Agricultural Administration and Policy]. Tokyo: Ryūginsha, 1929.

———. *Nōson kōsei no genri to keikaku* [Basic Principles and Plans for Farm Village Rebirth]. Tokyo: Nihon Hyōronsha, 1933.

Okutani Matsuji. "Nihon ni okeru nōhonshugi shisō no nagare" [Trends in Agrarian Thought in Japan], *Shisō* [Thought], No. 407, May 1958, pp. 1-15.

————. *Ninomiya Sontoku to Hōtokusha undō* [Ninomiya Sontoku and the Hōtokusha Movement]. Tokyo: Kōyō Shoin, 1936.

————. *Shinagawa Yajirō den* [Biography of Shinagawa Yajirō]. Tokyo: Kōyō Shoin, 1940.

Ōuchi Tsutomu. "Agricultural Depression and Japanese Villages," *The Developing Economies*, v, 4, December 1967, 597-627.

Ozeki Hiroshi. "Chōkokkashugi no taitō" [The Rise of Ultranationalism], *Kindai Nihon no kangaekata* [Ways of Thinking in Modern Japan], ed. Yamaguchi Kōsaku and Koyama Hitoshi, pp. 153-180. Kyoto: Hōritsu Bunkasha, 1971.

Patrick, Hugh T. "The Economic Muddle of the 1920's," *Dilemmas of Growth in Prewar Japan*, ed. James W. Morley, pp. 211-266. Princeton: Princeton University Press, 1971.

"Physiocratic School," *Encyclopaedia Britannica*, Chicago, 1959, XVII, 885-886.

Political Development in Modern Japan, ed. Robert E. Ward. Princeton: Princeton University Press, 1968.

Pollock, Norman. *The Populist Response to Industrial America*. Cambridge, Mass.: Harvard University Press, 1962.

Pyle, Kenneth B. *The New Generation in Meiji Japan*. Stanford: Stanford University Press, 1969.

————. "Some Recent Approaches to Japanese Nationalism," *Journal of Asian Studies*, XXXI, 1, November 1971, 5-16.

Reischauer, Edwin O. "What Went Wrong?" *Dilemmas of Growth in Prewar Japan*, ed. James W. Morley, pp. 489-510. Princeton: Princeton University Press, 1971.

Rosovsky, Henry. *Capital Formation in Japan, 1868-1940*. Glencoe, Ill.: The Free Press, 1961.

————. "Rumbles in the Ricefields: Professor Nakamura vs. the Official Statistics," *Journal of Asian Studies*, XXVII, 2, February 1968, 347-360.

Rōyama Masamichi. *Nihon ni okeru kindai seijigaku no hattatsu* [The Development of Modern Political Science in Japan]. Tokyo: Jitsugyō no Nihonsha, 1949.

Saitō Osamu. "Hōtokusha undō no kuronorojii—19 seiki kōhan ni okeru keizaiteki henka e no nōmin no taiō" [Chronology of the Hōtokusha Movement—The Response of Farmers to Economic Changes in the Latter Half of the Nineteenth Century], *Mita Gakkai zasshi* [Journal of the Mita Gakkai], LXIV, 8, August 1971, 219-234.

Sakai Yoshirō. "Nihon jinushisei to nōhonshugi" [The Japanese Landlord System and Agrarianism], *Keizai ronsō* [Collection of Economic Theories], LXXXVIII, 5, 1961, 67-84.

Sakisaka Itsurō. "Gondō Seikyōshi no shoron o hyōsu" [Appraising Mr. Gondō Seikyō's Views], *Kaizō* [Reconstruction], July 1932, pp. 65-75.

Sakurai Takeo. *Nihon nōgyō no saihensei* [The Reorganization of Japanese Agriculture]. Tokyo: Chūō Kōronsha, 1940.

———. *Nihon nōhonshugi* [Japanese Agrarianism]. Tokyo: Hakuyōsha, 1935.

———. "Nōhonshugi—sono rekishi, riron, jiban" [Agrarianism—Its History, Theory, and Foundation], *Rekishi kagaku* [Science of History], IV, 3, March 1935, 119-138.

———. "Shōwa no nōhonshugi" [Agrarianism in the Shōwa Period], *Shisō* [Thought], No. 407, May 1958, pp. 42-54.

———. "Yokoi Tokiyoshi hakushi" [Dr. Yokoi Tokiyoshi], *Kyōiku* [Education], II, 7, July 1934, 86-101.

Sasaki Ryūji. "Hōtokusha undō no kairyūteki seikaku" [Class Character of the Hōtokusha Movement], *Hōkei kenkyū* [Studies in Law and Economics], XVII, 3, 1969, 31-69; XVIII, 1, 1969, 31-60.

Sawada, Shūjirō. "Innovation in Japanese Agriculture," *The State and Economic Enterprise in Japan*, ed. William W. Lockwood, pp. 325-351. Princeton: Princeton University Press, 1965.

Say, Léon. *Turgot*, trans. Melville B. Anderson. Chicago: A. C. McClurg & Co., 1888.

Scheiner, Irwin. "The Mindful Peasant: Sketches for a Study of Rebellion," *Journal of Asian Studies*, XXXII, 4, August 1973.

Seido no kenkyū [Studies of Institutions]. Tokyo, 1935-1937.

Senjin no omokage Kurume jinbutsu denki [Biographical Images of Eminent Former Residents of Kurume]. Kurume: Kurumeshi, 1961.

Senzen ni okeru uyoku dantai no jōkyō [Circumstances of Right-Wing Groups Before the War], ed. Kōan Chōsachō, 4 vols. Tokyo: Kōan Chōsachō, 1964.

Shafer, Boyd C. *Nationalism: Myth and Reality*. New York: Harcourt, Brace & World, Inc., 1955.

Sheldon, Charles D. *The Rise of the Merchant Class in Tokugawa Japan, 1600-1868*. Locust Valley, N.Y.: J. J. Augustin, Inc., 1958.

Shillony, Ben-Ami. "The February 26 Affair: Politics of a Military Insurrection," *Crisis Politics in Prewar Japan*, ed. George M. Wilson, pp. 25-50. Tokyo: Sophia University Press, 1970.

———. *Revolt in Japan*. Princeton: Princeton University Press, 1973.

———. "The Young Officers and the February 26, 1936, Army Rebellion in Japan." Ph.D. dissertation in history, Princeton University, 1970.

Shively, Donald H. "Nishimura Shigeki: A Confucian View of Modernization," *Changing Japanese Attitudes Toward Modernization*, ed. Marius B. Jansen, pp. 193-241. Princeton: Princeton University Press, 1965.

Smethurst, Richard J. "The Military Reserve Association and the Minobe Crisis of 1935," *Crisis Politics in Prewar Japan*, ed. George M. Wilson, pp. 1-23. Tokyo: Sophia University Press, 1970.

Smethurst, Richard J. *A Social Basis for Prewar Japanese Militarism: The Army and the Rural Community*. Berkeley: University of California Press, 1974.

Smith, Thomas C. *The Agrarian Origins of Modern Japan*. Stanford: Stanford University Press, 1959.

———. "Japan's Aristocratic Revolution," *Yale Review*, L, 3, Spring 1961, 370-383.

———. "Ōkura Nagatsune and the Technologists," *Personality in Japanese History*, ed. Albert M. Craig and Donald H. Shively, pp. 127-154. Berkeley: University of California Press, 1970.

———. *Political Change and Industrial Development in Japan: Government Enterprise, 1868-1880*. Stanford: Stanford University Press, 1955.

Soda Osamu. *Maeda Masana*. Tokyo: Yoshikawa Kōbunkan, 1973.

Sources of Japanese Tradition, comp. Ryusaku Tsunoda, ed. William T. deBary. New York: Columbia University Press, 1958.

The State and Economic Enterprise in Japan, ed. William W. Lockwood. Princeton: Princeton University Press, 1965.

Storry, Richard. *The Double Patriots: A Study of Japanese Nationalism*. Boston: Houghton Mifflin, 1957.

Sumiya Etsuji. *Kawakami Hajime*. Tokyo: Yoshikawa Kōbunkan, 1962.

Sumiya Kazuhiko. "Keiseiki Nihon burujoajī no shisōzō" [Images of the Japanese Bourgeoisie During the Formative Period], *Kindai Nihon keizai shisōshi* [History of Modern Japanese Economic Thought], ed. Chō Yukio and Sumiya Kazuhiko, I, 182-221. Tokyo: Yūhikaku, 1969.

Sun, Kungtu C. *The Economic Development of Manchuria in the First Half of the Twentieth Century*. Cambridge, Mass.: East Asian Research Center, Harvard University, 1969.

Tachibana Kōzaburō. "Jinmon chōsho" [Interrogation Record], 1932, *Gendaishi shiryō* [Materials on Modern History], ed. Imai Seiichi and Takahashi Masae, IV, 112-113. Tokyo: Misuzu Shobō, 1963.

———. *Kōdo kokka nōhon kenkokuron* [Theory of Building an Imperial State on Agriculture]. Tokyo: Kensetsusha, 1935.

———. *Nihon aikoku kakushin hongi* [Basic Principles of Japanese Patriotic Reform], mimeographed, 1932, in *Chōkokkashugi* [Ultranationalism], ed. Hashikawa Bunzō, *Gendai Nihon shisō taikei* [Collection on Modern Japanese Thought], XXXI, 213-238. Tokyo, Chikuma Shobō, 1964.

———. *Nōsongaku* [Farm Village Studies], 2nd ed. Tokyo: Kensetsusha, 1933. (Originally published in 1931.)

———. *Tsuchi no Nihon* [A Japan Based on Land]. Tokyo: Kensetsusha, 1934.

——— and Takeuchi Yoshi. "Aru nōhonshugisha no kaisō to iken" [Recollections and Opinions of a Certain Agrarianist], *Shisō no kagaku* [Science of Thought], No. 18, June 1960, pp. 14-23.

Takeda Kiyoko. *Dochaku to haikyō—dentōteki etosu to purotesutanto* [Home Town and Apostasy—The Traditional Ethos and Protestantism]. Tokyo: Shinkyō Shuppansha, 1967.

Takehana Yūkichi. *Akita no hitobito* [Persons from Akita]. Akitaken: Kōhō Kyōkai, 1964.

Takemura Tamirō. "Jinushisei no dōyō to nōrin kanryō" [Agitation of the Landlord System and the Agricultural and Forestry Bureaucracy], *Kindai Nihon keizai shisōshi* [History of Modern Japanese Economic Thought], ed. Chō Yukio and Sumiya Kazuhiko, I, 323-356. Tokyo: Yūhikaku, 1969.

Takeuchi Tetsuo. "Nōhonshugi bunseki e no zenteiteki shomondai—shu to shite bunseki shikaku ni tsuite" [Preliminary Problems in Analyzing Agrarianism—With Emphasis on Analytical Viewpoints], *Shimane Nōka Daigaku kenkyū hōkoku* [Shimane Agricultural University Research Reports], No. 9, A-3, March 1961, pp. 53-59.

———. "Nōhonshugi to nōson chūsansō" [Agrarianism and the Farm Village Middle Class], *Shimane Nōka Daigaku kenkyū hōkoku* [Shimane Agricultural University Research Reports], No. 8, A, March 1960, pp. 226-240.

Takizawa Makoto. *Gondō Seikyō*. Tokyo: Kinokuniya Shoten, 1971.

———. *Gondō Seikyō oboegaki* [Notes on Gondō Seikyō]. Nagaokashi: privately published, 1968.

———. "Kita Ikki to Ōkawa Shūmei no ketsuretsu" [Fissure Between Kita Ikki and Ōkawa Shūmei], *Rekishi to jinbutsu* [History and Personality], III, 7, July 1973, 260-272.

Tamagawa Haruzō. *Kindai Nihon no nōson to nōmin* [Farmers and Farm Villages in Modern Japan]. Tokyo: Seiji Kōronsha, 1969.

Tanin, O. and E. Yohan, pseuds. *Militarism and Fascism in Japan*. New York: International Publishers, 1934.

Timmer, John. "The Editor's Notes," *Japan Christian Quarterly*, XXXVIII, 2, Spring 1972, 65-66.

Tomeoka Kōsuke. "Waga Hōtokukai to jichi no kaihatsu" [Our Hōtokukai and the Development of Self-Rule], 1915, *Tomeoka Kōsuke Hōtoku ronshū* [Collection of Tomeoka Kōsuke's Theories on Hōtoku], pp. 491-492. Tokyo: Chūō Hōtokukai, 1936.

Tradition and Modernization in Japanese Culture, ed. Donald H. Shively. Princeton: Princeton University Press, 1971.

Tsuchida Kyōson, "Gondō Seikyōshi no shoron" [Views of Mr. Gondō Seikyō], *Serupan*, July 1932, *Tsuchida Kyōson zenshū* [Complete Works of Tsuchida Kyōson], III, 389-400. Tokyo: Daiichi Shobō, 1935.

Tsukuba Hisaharu. *Nihon nōgyō gijutsushi* [History of Japanese Farm Technology]. Tokyo: Chijin Shokan, 1959.

————. "Nihon nōhonshugi josetsu" [Introduction to Japanese Agrarianism], *Shisō no kagaku* [Science of Thought], No. 18, June 1960, pp. 4-12.

————. *Nihonjin no shisō—nōhonshugi no sekai* [Japanese Thought—The World of Agrarianism]. Tokyo: San'ichi Shobō, 1961.

Tsukui Tatsuo. *Nihonshugi undō no riron to jissen* [Theory and Practice of the Japanism Movement]. Tokyo: Kensetsusha, 1935.

Tsunazawa Mitsuaki. *Kindai Nihon no dochaku shisō—nōhonshugi kenkyū* [Modern Japanese Home Town Thought—Studies on Agrarianism]. Nagoya: Fūbaisha, 1969.

————. *Nihon no nōhonshugi* [Japanese Agrarianism]. Tokyo: Kinokuniya Shoten, 1971.

————. *Nōhonshugi no kenkyū* [Studies on Agrarianism]. Nagoya: Fūbaisha, 1968.

————. "Tachibana Kōzaburō shiron" [Sketch of Tachibana Kōzaburō], *Shisō no kagaku* [Science of Thought], No. 142, October 1970, pp. 67-80.

Tucker, B. D. "Mushakōji Saneatsu: His Life and Influence." M.A. thesis in Far Eastern Languages, Harvard University, 1958.

Turner, Henry Ashby, Jr. "Fascism and Modernization," *World Politics*, XXIV, 4, July 1972, 547-564.

Uyoku undō [The Right-Wing Movement], ed. Keibi Keisatsu Kenkyūkai, rev. ed. Tokyo: Tachibana Shobō, 1957.

Uyoku undō jiten [Dictionary of the Right-Wing Movement], ed. Shakai Undō Kenkyūkai. Tokyo: Kōbundō, 1961.

Uyoku zensho [Full Book on the Right Wing], ed. Kōan Keibi Kenkyūkai. Tokyo: Kindai Keisatsusha, 1957.

Wakakuwa Seiyei. "The Japanese Farm-Tenancy System," *Japan's Prospect*, ed. Douglas G. Haring, pp. 115-173. Cambridge, Mass.: Harvard University Press, 1946.

Wald, Royal J. "The Young Officers Movement in Japan, ca. 1925-1937: Ideology and Actions." Ph.D. dissertation in history, University of California, Berkeley, 1949.

Waswo, Ann. "Landlords and Social Change in Prewar Japan." Ph.D. dissertation in history, Stanford University, 1969.

Watsuji Tetsurō. *A Climate—A Philosophical Study*, trans. Geoffrey Bownas. Tokyo: Japanese National Commission for UNESCO, 1961.

——. *Fūdo* [Climate]. Tokyo: Iwanami Shoten, 1935.

Wikawa, Tadao. "Our Co-operative Movement," *Contemporary Japan*, I, 3, December 1932, 431-440.

Wildes, Harry Emerson. *Japan in Crisis*. New York: Macmillan, 1934.

Williams, William A. *The Roots of the Modern American Empire*. New York: Random House, 1969.

Williston, Horace, Jr. "General Araki's Contribution to Japanese Militarism and Ultra-Nationalism in the 1930's." M.A. thesis in history, University of California, Berkeley, 1951.

Wilson, George M. *Radical Nationalist in Japan: Kita Ikki, 1883-1937*. Cambridge, Mass.: Harvard University Press, 1969.

Woodward, C. Vann. "The Ghost of Populism Walks Again," *New York Times Magazine*, June 4, 1972, pp. 16-17, 60, 63-64, 66-69.

Yamamoto Gyō. "Nōhonshugi shisōshijō ni okeru Yokota Hideo" [Yokota Hideo in the History of Agrarianist Thought], *Gifu Daigaku Kyōyōbu kenkyū hōkoku* [Gifu University Faculty of General Education Research Reports], No. 4, 1968, pp. 71-80.

——. "Yokota Hideo no shisō" [The Thought of Yokota Hideo], *Gifu Daigaku Gakugei Gakubu kenkyū hōkoku* [Gifu University Faculty of Arts Research Reports], No. 9, 1960, pp. 63-72.

Yamazaki Masakazu. *Kindai Nihon shisō tsūshi* [General History of Modern Japanese Thought]. Tokyo: Aoki Shoten, 1957.

Yamazaki Nobukichi. *Nōmindō* [The Way of the Farmer], 1930, *Yamazaki Nobukichi zenshū* [Complete Works of Yamazaki Nobukichi], v, 71-158. Tokyo: Yamazaki Nobukichi Zenshū Kankōkai, 1935-1936.

————. *Nōson jichi no kenkyū* [Studies on Farm Village Self-Rule], 1908, *Yamazaki Nobukichi zenshū* [Complete Works of Yamazaki Nobukichi], i, 13-600. Tokyo: Yamazaki Nobukichi Zenshū Kankōkai, 1935-1936.

Yoda Yoshiie. "Dai niji taisenka no Manshū imin no jittai— imindan kankei no hanzai o chūshin ni" [Actual Conditions of Japanese Settlers in Manchuria During World War II—With Special Reference to Crimes Involving Colonizing Groups], *Shakai kagaku tōkyū* [Social Science Review], xviii, 1, July 1972, 41-78.

Yokoi Tokiyoshi. *Nōson hattensaku* [Rural Development Policy]. Tokyo: Jitsugyō no Nihonsha, 1915.

————. *Tokai to inaka* [City and Country]. Tokyo: Seibidō Shoten, 1913.

————. *Yokoi Hakushi zenshū* [Complete Works of Dr. Yokoi], ed. Dai Nihon Nōkai, 10 vols. Tokyo: Yokoi Zenshū Kankōkai, 1925. The following articles are cited:

"Kōnō ronsaku" [Policy for Improving Agriculture], 1891, iii, 663-703.

"Nōgyō hanron" [Summary of Agriculture], 1891, ii, 1-172.

"Nogyō kyōikuron" [Farm Education Theories], 1901, ix, 88-112.

"Nōgyō rikkoku no konpongi" [Basic Meaning of Establishing the Country on Agriculture], April 1914, viii, 232-236.

"Nōhonshugi" [Agrarianism], October 1897, viii, 225-232.

"Nōson no jichi" [Village Self-Rule], June 1915, VII, 13-32.

"Sonraku o hogo seyo" [Let's Protect the Villages], November 1907, VII, 167-170.

"Tsuguri to kuwa" [Sword and Hoe], 1911-1916, VI, 549-696.

Yokota Hideo. *Nōson kaikakusaku* [Rural Reform Policy]. Tokyo: Hakubunkan, 1916.

———. *Nōson kakumeiron* [On Rural Revolution]. Tokyo: Hakubunkan, 1914.

———. *Nōson kyūsairon* [On Rescuing the Farm Villages]. Tokyo: Hakubunkan, 1914.

Yoshimoto Tadasu. *A Peasant Sage of Japan: The Life and Work of Ninomiya Sontoku.* London: Longmans, 1912.

Young, A. Morgan. *Imperial Japan 1926-1938.* London: George Allen and Unwin, 1938.

Index

Library of Congress Cataloging in Publication Data

Havens, Thomas R   H
   Farm and nation in modern Japan.

   Bibliography: p.
      1. Agriculture—Economic aspects—Japan.
   2. Agriculture and state—Japan.   3. Japan—Rural
   conditions.   4. Nationalism—Japan.   I. Title.
   HD2092.H366   338.1'0952   74-3475
   ISBN 0-691-03101-0